Poetic Theory and Practice in Early Modern Verse

Poetic Theory and Practice in Early Modern Verse

Unwritten Arts

Edited by Zenón Luis-Martínez

EDINBURGH
University Press

Edinburgh University Press is one of the leading university presses in the UK. We publish academic books and journals in our selected subject areas across the humanities and social sciences, combining cutting-edge scholarship with high editorial and production values to produce academic works of lasting importance. For more information visit our website: edinburghuniversitypress.com

© editorial matter and organization Zenón Luis-Martínez 2023, 2024, under a Creative Commons Attribution-NonCommercial NoDerivs licence
© the chapters their several authors 2023, 2024

Edinburgh University Press Ltd
13 Infirmary Street, Edinburgh, EH1 1LT

First published in hardback by Edinburgh University Press 2023

Typeset in 11/13 Adobe Sabon by
IDSUK (DataConnection) Ltd

A CIP record for this book is available from the British Library

ISBN 978 1 3995 0782 0 (hardback)
ISBN 978 1 3995 0783 7 (paperback)
ISBN 978 1 3995 0784 4 (webready PDF)
ISBN 978 1 3995 0785 1 (epub)

The right of Zenón Luis-Martínez to be identified as the editor of this work has been asserted in accordance with the Copyright, Designs and Patents Act 1988, and the Copyright and Related Rights Regulations 2003 (SI No. 2498).

Contents

Acknowledgements   vii
Notes on Contributors   ix

    Introduction: Unwritten Arts   1
    Zenón Luis-Martínez

Part I   Origin: Poetic Aetiologies

1. Justified by Whose Grace? Poetic Worth and Transcendent Doubt in Late Elizabethan and Early Jacobean Poetry   27
   Joan Curbet Soler

2. The Logical Cause of an Early Modern Poetics of Action   47
   Emma Annette Wilson

3. Atomies of Love: Material (Mis)interpretations of Cupid's Origin in Elizabethan Poetry   74
   Cassandra Gorman

Part II   Style: Outgrowing the Arts

4. Bloody Poetics: Towards a Physiology of the Epic Poem   101
   Rocío G. Sumillera

5. Figuring Ineloquence in Late Sixteenth-century Poetry   121
   David J. Amelang

6. Eloquent Bodies: Rhetoricising the Symptoms of Love in the English Epyllion   139
   Sonia Hernández-Santano

Part III   Poesis: Art's Prisoners

7. Philip Sidney's Sublime Self-authorship: Authenticity, Ecstasy and Energy in *The Defence of Poesy* and *Astrophil and Stella*   165
   Jonathan P. A. Sell

8. From Favour to Eternal Life: Trajectories of Grace and the Poetic Career in the Sonnets of Henry Constable and Barnabe Barnes 191
   María Jesús Pérez-Jáuregui

9. Thomas Lodge's 'Supple Muse': Imitation, Inspiration and Imagination in *Phillis* 216
   Cinta Zunino-Garrido

10. The Worthy Knots of Fulke Greville 238
    Sarah Knight

11. George Chapman's 'Habit of Poesie' 258
    Zenón Luis-Martínez

    Afterword 286
    Clark Hulse

Bibliography 296
Index 324

Acknowledgements

This book is the result of research developed as part of the Project of Excellence *Towards a New Aesthetics of English Renaissance Poetry: Critical Reassessments and New Editions of Neglected Works*, funded by the Spanish State Research Agency of the Ministry of Science and Innovation, Government of Spain.[1] Support for this project has materialised in multiple forms of funding, but most especially in making possible this volume's publication in Open Access form. In the context of the activities organised under the auspices of this project, this book originated in the international symposium 'Unwritten Arts: Keywords in English Sixteenth-Century Poetry and Poetics', which took place at the Faculty of Humanities, University of Huelva, on 29 and 30 October 2019 (pre-pandemic era). This was the 'II Symposium on English Renaissance Poetics: Speaking Pictures', which aspires to consolidate itself as a quinquennial event. The scholarly conviviality provided by the occasion enabled fruitful discussions of the presentations that became the germ of the finished chapters. All contributors have shown an unflinching commitment to an idea that since then has undergone many metamorphoses. Clark Hulse's contribution of an Afterword when a first draft of the chapters had been finished opened a number of new paths that are traceable in the volume's pages. The editor wants to thank Professor Hulse for his magisterial influence, and for first drawing his attention to the work of Joris Hoefnagel, whose small creatures' liminal habitations between nature and art, and between theory and practice, have made their way on to this volume's cover.

The Department of English at the University of Huelva, the PhD Partnership in Languages and Cultures (Universities of Córdoba, Extremadura, Huelva and Jaén), the Research Group in Comparative Literatures and Cultures (PAIDI HUM-766), and the Centre for Research in Historical, Cultural and Natural Patrimony (CIPHCN, University of Huelva), have been also instrumental in making this project possible.

We are very grateful to the editorial team and the anonymous readers of Edinburgh University Press for their technical guidance and scholarly expertise throughout the completion of a project that the life paradigm shifts experienced in the last three years have made particularly challenging though ultimately most rewarding.

Huelva, November 2022

Note

1. The project has developed under the auspices of the Spanish Agency for Research during the years 2018–22: Agencia Estatal de Investigación – Ministerio de Ciencia e Innovación; research project FFI2017-82269-P. An earlier project, "Preceptivas poéticas y tratados retóricos del periodo Tudor" (FFI2010-19279), started our research on poetic theory and practice.

Notes on Contributors

David J. Amelang is Assistant Professor of English Literature at the Universidad Autónoma of Madrid. He also currently serves on the board of directors of the Madrid Institute for Advanced Study (MIAS). His research focuses on early modern drama, and more specifically on the comparison between the dramatic literature and theatrical cultures of Shakespearean England and Golden Age Spain. His upcoming monograph *Playgrounds: Urban Theatrical Culture in Shakespeare's England and Golden Age Spain* (Routledge, 2023) analyses the dramatic cultures of early modern England and Spain in terms of infrastructures, physical arrangements, and production techniques, and explores the causes and consequences not just of the visible differences, but also of the remarkable similarities between the two theatre systems.

Joan Curbet Soler is Senior Lecturer in the Department of English at the Autonomous University of Barcelona, from which he received his PhD. He has an MA from the University of Leeds. He has translated and edited John Milton's *Paradise Regained* and *Samson Agonistes* (Cátedra, 2007) and *Areopagitica* (Tecnos, 2012), as well as Lord Byron's *Manfred* and *Cain* (AKAL, 2019). He is author of many articles and book chapters published by, among others, Oxford University Press, Longman, Routledge and Manchester University Press. He co-edited the volume *Images of Holy Women: Selections from Isabel de Villena's Vita Christi* (Tamesis/Boydell and Brewer, 2015). He is a member of the editorial board of *Medievalia*, where he has co-edited several special issues, among them *Translatio: Translation, Culture and Mobility in Medieval Europe* (with Alberto Reche, 2015). He is currently vice-president of the Institute for Medieval Studies at the Autonomous University of Barcelona.

Cassandra Gorman is Associate Professor of Early Modern Literature and Philosophy at Anglia Ruskin University. Prior to this she held lecturing posts at Trinity College, Cambridge, and Oriel College, Oxford, after completing her doctorate at the University of Cambridge in 2014. Her research explores ways in which English imaginative literature of the seventeenth century was not only responsive to but a part of scientific progress, with interests in early modern women's writing and the reciprocal influence between corpuscular philosophy and theological thought. She is the author of *The Atom in Seventeenth-Century Poetry* (Boydell and Brewer, 2021). She has published articles and book chapters on Henry More, Lucy Hutchinson and Thomas Traherne, and co-edited a volume of essays on the latter with the theologian Elizabeth Dodd: *Thomas Traherne and Seventeenth Century Thought* (Boydell and Brewer, 2016). From 2018 to 2022, she served on the executive committee for the international research group *Scientiae: Disciplines of Knowing in the Early Modern World*.

Sonia Hernández-Santano is Associate Professor of English at the University of Huelva (Spain), where she teaches English literature. She has edited William Webbe's *A Discourse of English Poetry* (2016) for the MHRA Critical Texts Series. She has also co-edited with Zenón Luis-Martínez the special issue *Poetry, the Arts of Discourse and the Discourse of the Arts: Rethinking Renaissance Poetic Theory and Practice* for *Parergon* (2016), which includes her chapter entitled 'William Webbe's *A Discourse of English Poetry*: Vindicating Spenser as an Act of Self-Fashioning'. She is currently working on an edition of Thomas Lodge's *Scillaes Metamorphosis* for MHRA as part of the research project 'Towards a New Aesthetics of Elizabethan Poetry' (Ministry of Science and Innovation, Government of Spain, FFI2017-82269-P).

Clark Hulse is Professor Emeritus of English and Art History and Dean Emeritus of the Graduate College at the University of Illinois at Chicago. His books include *Elizabeth I: Ruler and Legend* (University of Illinois Press, 2003), *The Rule of Art: Literature and Painting in the Renaissance* (University of Chicago Press, 1993), *Metamorphic Verse* (Princeton University Press, 1983) and, with Peter Erickson, *Early Modern Visual Culture: Representation, Race, Empire* (University of Pennsylvania Press, 2000). His articles on subjects ranging from Spenser and Shakespeare to Titian have appeared in journals in Britain, Germany and the United States. His research has been supported by fellowships from the Guggenheim Foundation and National Endowment for the Humanities, and grants from the College Art Association and the British Academy.

His prize-winning 2003 exhibition 'Elizabeth I: Ruler and Legend' debuted at the Newberry Library, Chicago, and toured 40 cities. The project was named a 'Milestone' by the National Endowment for the Humanities. He has been a member of the Illinois Humanities Council, executive director of Creative Santa Fe, and formerly was chair of the board of directors of the Chicago Humanities Festival. He is currently working on three projects: *Counterfeiting Men*, a book about verbal and visual portraiture in the age of Henry VIII, with a focus on Hans Holbein, Thomas More, Thomas Wyatt and Henry Howard, Earl of Surrey; *Reading Cities*, a book about the cultural experience of modern urban life; and studies in the Ovidian tradition.

Sarah Knight is Professor of Renaissance Literature in the School of Arts at the University of Leicester. Her academic background is in Classics and English, and she is particularly interested in sixteenth- and seventeenth-century English and Latin literature, especially drama, poetry and rhetoric. She has published widely on the association between literary composition and educational experience, and on works written at or about early modern institutions of learning (schools, colleges, universities, Inns of Court). Her first book was a translation and co-edition of Leon Battista Alberti's Latin prose satire *Momus* for the I Tatti Renaissance Library (Harvard University Press, 2003). She has edited and translated the accounts of Elizabeth I's visits to Oxford and several other texts for the new multi-authored critical edition of John Nichols's *The Progresses and Public Processions of Queen Elizabeth I* (5 volumes, Oxford University Press, 2014). She has co-edited three essay collections related to her research and teaching interests: *The Oxford Handbook of Neo-Latin* (Oxford University Press, 2015), *The Cultural and Intellectual World of the Early Modern Inns of Court* (Manchester University Press, 2011) and *The Progresses, Pageants, and Entertainments of Queen Elizabeth I* (Oxford University Press, 2007). She is currently editing and translating John Milton's student speeches (the *Prolusiones*) and his letters (*Epistolae Familiares*), and editing Fulke Greville's two tragedies *Alaham* and *Mustapha*. She is co-editor, with Emma A. Wilson, of *The European Contexts of Ramism* (Brepols, 2019).

Zenón Luis-Martínez is Senior Lecturer in English at the University of Huelva (Spain), where he teaches medieval and early modern literature. He has edited Abraham Fraunce's *The Shepherds' Logic and Other Dialectical Writings* (2016) for the MHRA Critical Texts

Series. He is the author of *In Words and Deeds: The Spectacle of Incest in English Renaissance Tragedy* (Rodopi, 2002). His articles on English Renaissance and Restoration literature have appeared in journals such as *ELH, Cahiers Élisabéthains, Parergon, English Studies, Philological Quarterly* and *Studies in Philology*. He has also co-edited several collections, among them, with Luis Gómez Canseco, *Between Shakespeare and Cervantes: Trails along the Renaissance* (Juan de la Cuesta, 2006), and, with Sonia Hernández-Santano, the special issue *Poetry, the Arts of Discourse and the Discourse of the Arts: Rethinking Renaissance Poetic Theory and Practice* for *Parergon* (2016). His current research includes a critical edition of Chapman's *The Shadow of Night* and *Ovid's Banquet of Sense* for the MHRA and a monograph on Chapman's poetics. He leads the research project 'Towards a New Aesthetics of Elizabethan Poetry' (Ministry of Science and Innovation, Government of Spain, FFI2017-82269-P). Since May 2018 he has been president of SEDERI (Spanish and Portuguese Society for English Renaissance Studies).

María Jesús Pérez-Jáuregui is Lecturer in the Department of English and North-American Literature at the Universidad de Sevilla, Spain, where she teaches a variety of literature courses at the undergraduate and graduate levels. Her research focuses mostly on early modern English poetry. She was a keynote speaker at the 60th Annual Conference of the Catholic Record Society held in Cambridge in 2017, and she has contributed articles to *English Studies* and *Studies in Philology* among others. She is currently finalising her critical edition of the sonnets of Henry Constable for the Pontifical Institute of Mediaeval Studies in Toronto.

Jonathan P. A. Sell is Professor of English Literature at the Universidad de Alcalá, Spain. His publications include *Shakespeare's Sublime Ethos: Matter, Stage and Form* (Routledge, 2022), *Shakespeare's Sublime Pathos: Person, Audience, Language* (Routledge, 2022), *Conocer a Shakespeare* (Laberinto, 2012), *Allusion, Identity and Community in Recent British Writing* (Universidad de Alcalá, 2010) and *Rhetoric and Wonder in English Travel Writing, 1560–1613* (Routledge, 2006). He has also edited and translated into Spanish Eleonora Tennant's *Spanish Journey* (Renacimiento, 2017) and Florence Farmborough's *Life and People in National Spain* (Renacimiento, 2017). He is currently researching the impact of religious controversy on eighteenth-century Shakespeare criticism.

Rocío G. Sumillera is Senior Lecturer in English Literature at the University of Granada. Her most recent publications include the monograph *Invention. The Language of English Renaissance Poetics* (Legenda, MHRA, 2019), and a co-edition of the volume *Translation in Knowledge, Knowledge in Translation* (John Benjamins Translation Library, 2020). She has edited and translated into Spanish John Knox's *The First Blast of the Trumpet against the Monstruous Regiment of Women* (*El primer toque de la trompeta contra el monstruoso gobierno de las mujeres. Tratado contra María Tudor y otras reinas de la edad moderna*, Tirant lo Blanch, 2016), and produced a critical edition of Richard Carew's *The Examination of Mens Wits* (1594), the first translation into English of Juan Huarte de San Juan's *Examen de ingenios para las ciencias* (1575) (Tudor and Stuart Translation Series, MHRA, 2014). She has published articles in, among others, *The Sixteenth Century Journal*, *Parergon*, *Notes and Queries* and *Bulletin of Hispanic Studies*. As a translator, she has rendered into Spanish John Dryden's *All for Love: Todo por amor, o el mundo bien perdido* (Publicaciones de la Asociación de Directores de Escena de España, 2018).

Emma Annette Wilson is Assistant Professor of English at Southern Methodist University. She is co-editor of *Ramus, Pedagogy, and the Liberal Arts* (Routledge, 2011), *The European Contexts of Ramism* (Brepols, 2019) and *Quick Hits for Teaching with Digital Humanities* (Indiana University Press, 2020), and author of the textbook *Digital Humanities for Librarians* (Rowman and Littlefield, 2020). Her current project, *The Internet: A Biography*, traces links between ancient and early modern modes of thought and communication, including the evolution of the book and printing, and the development of the internet in the twentieth century. Her research interests span early modern logic and literature, project management and its history, the history of libraries and book technologies, and digital humanities, and she is co-editor of the digital project *Mill Marginalia Online*, which is digitising and making discoverable John Stuart Mill's extensive handwritten annotations. She recently co-authored an article with Albert Pionke in *Nineteenth-Century Prose* bridging her early modern and digital work by using *Mill Marginalia Online* to examine Mill's annotations on Franco Burgersdijck's *Institutionum Logicarum*.

Cinta Zunino-Garrido is Senior Lecturer at the University of Jaén (Spain), where she teaches English literature. Her research focuses on

Elizabethan drama and poetry. She is the author of *Mimesis and the Representation of Experience: Dramatic Theory and Practice in pre-Shakespearean Comedy 1560–1590* (Peter Lang, 2012), which was awarded the Best Publication in Literary Studies Prize by the Spanish Association for English and American Studies (AEDEAN) and was shortlisted for the Best Publication in English Literature Award by the European Association of Studies in English (ESSE). She edited the first English translation of Benito Arias Montano's *The Practical Rule of Christian Piety* (Bibliotheca Montaniana, 2017) and is currently preparing for the MHRA a critical edition of Thomas Lodge's *Phillis* (1593).

Introduction: Unwritten Arts
Zenón Luis-Martínez

In 1584 the Edinburgh presses of Thomas Vautrollier issued *The Essayes of a Prentise, in the Divine Art of Poesie*, a collection of original poems and translations by the 18-year-old King James VI of Scotland. The author's advertised status as a novice contrasted with the inclusion at the end of the volume of a brief assortment of precepts entitled 'A Treatise of the airt of Scotis Poesie', a succinct *ars poetica* in which the monarch donned the master's robes. James's possible inspiration was George Gascoigne's *Posies* (1575), the volume that 'Corrected, perfected, and augmented' – as its title page announced – Gascoigne's earlier *A Hundreth Sundrie Flowers* (1573) with, among other additions, 'Certayne Notes of Instruction concerning the making of verse or ryme in English'. Exhibiting a less self-assured manner than Gascoigne, James's disclaimer that 'I made noght my treatise of that intention, that eyther I, or any others behoued astricktly to follow it' reads as a modest avowal of his own poetry's failure to 'shew the perfection of poesie' as set out in his treatise.[1] Yet this statement could otherwise suggest that poets should not be perpetually bound ('behoued') by the strictures of precept, nor should the theorist's task be to constrain poets to meticulous observance of doctrine. James's collection furthers a dialectic between, on the one hand, the 'treatise of the airt', or systematic elucidation of its 'reulis' and 'cautelis', and, on the other, the poems and translations as self-reflexive 'essayes in the airt'.[2] These 'essayes' advance literary practice as a flexible space accommodating a body of statements about poetry that cuts across the contents and procedures of normative literary criticism.

James's work inspires a shared assumption of the chapters in this collection, namely that the creative impulse that animates Renaissance writing of and about poetry grew out of Renaissance poetics but also outgrew the scope of what came to be systematised in the form of norms and precepts. This general framework for thinking the interconnections of theory and practice has often been put forward, even if only recently have its deeper implications begun to be considered.³ Our subtitle, *Unwritten Arts*, points to that active thinking about the making, matter, forms and functions of poetry as that thinking is generated in practical writing rather than in normative discourse. It is inspired by Rosalie Colie's phrasing in her half-century-old methodological sketch for the study of Renaissance genres:

> [From the *artes poeticae*] we can recover the ideas consciously held, governing the written criticism and theory of the Renaissance. From 'real' literature as opposed to criticism and theory . . . we recover what is far more important, the *unwritten poetics* by which writers worked and which they themselves created.⁴

In making Colie's emphasis ours, the contributors to this volume explore ways in which texts of various kinds emerge as *unwritten arts* complementing and/or contesting the period's formally written poetics. Three major thematic grids organise its contents: the preoccupation with origin or cause (understood as reflection on both poetry's origins and its own generating potential), considerations of style, and the production of individual, author-based poetics. These themes are explored in light of a common methodology: a focus on words and lexicons, conceived as points of entry into ideas about poetry at a time when systematic criticism was being established in English literature.

This introduction substantiates the volume's central notion of poetry's *unwritten arts* in four sections. It first contextualises the production of poetic concepts and notions in the margins and intersections of the Renaissance *artes poeticae* and poetic praxis. It then places the collection's interests alongside recent scholarly attention to the relations between early modern poetic theory and practice. It further assesses its focus on specific lexicons as modes of access to practical thinking about poetry. Finally, it introduces individual chapters along the volume's thematic axes.

Poetry and Poetics

Accepting Colie's statement as a working principle should lead us to explain why it is, if not 'far more important', at least as necessary to attend to an unformulated set of assumptions informing the writing of Renaissance poetry as to the explicit principles and rules that regulated its composition. Writing about the normative character of Italian sixteenth-century treatises on poetry, Bernard Weinberg has argued that their rule-of-thumb quality often 'tended to replace active thinking about poetics by routine answering of a set of questions'.[5] Weinberg's assertion is partly an incitement to seek for relevant poetic 'thinking' outside the official poetic 'thought' found in the texts of the more conventional treatises – a crucial distinction for the present introduction and the essays in this collection. His work also reminds us that the propensity to regulate the field of poetic composition relied on the consideration of poetry – and of poetics – as an *art*. Conceding the status of art to *both* the system of rules *and* the activity that derived from it is symptomatic of the slippery boundaries between poetic theory and practice. The consideration of art as the *genus* of poetry – that is, the element that identified it as a member of a larger class of disciplines of discourse – guaranteed its dependence on a systematic body of precepts. The Stoic definition of *techné*, or *ars*, transmitted to Renaissance humanism via Lucian of Samosata, found formulations in English such as Abraham Fraunce's in *The Shepherds' Logic* (c. 1585): 'An art, as Lucian doth define it, is nothing else but a collection, or, as it were, a body of certain precepts which are practised and used for some profitable end and purpose in man's life.'[6] Arts were originated in theory, materialised in practice and justified by their pragmatic aims.

The precedence of doctrine over practice was then a condition for the conception of poetics as an art in the likeness of classical logic, rhetoric and grammar. The medieval *artes poetriae*, which flourished in England in the early thirteenth century and which adapted the classical tradition, were conceived as 'system[s] for generating verse' out of the rhetoricians' prescriptions for topical invention, order and ornament, as well as the grammarians' recommendations for style and versification.[7] Yet the prescriptive impulse of the medieval *artes* had no sustained influence in early sixteenth-century England. As Chris Stamatakis has argued recently, early Tudor poetry was 'ostensibly written in a critical vacuum', thus promoting its own self-referential 'critical lexicon' through which 'poetry becomes its own place of criticism'.[8] The last quarter of the century altered the picture, mainly due to the growing influence of Italian theory. Yet, with the relative exceptions of George Puttenham's *The Art of English Poesy* (1589) and William Scott's *The Model of Poesy* (c. 1599), English treatises lacked the systematic character of Italian models such as Francesco Robortello's *In librum Aristotelis de arte poetica explicationes* (1548) or Julius Caesar Scaliger's *Poetices libri septem* (1561). Even if Robortello's ordered outline featuring definition, effect, end, subject matter and means and Scaliger's procedure through the Aristotelian four-cause scheme inspired Puttenham and Scott, English poetic treatises, in the words of Michael Hetherington, 'persistently undo their claims to systematic completeness, reinscribing theory and practice alike in a more personal and contingent world of work, memory, and habit'.[9] It is not infrequent to find in the pages of Sidney, Puttenham or Scott reminders of those corners of poetic practice that remained inaccessible to the strictures of art. Conversely, active thinking about those corners is frequent in poetic practice and in other genres of writing. The production and expansion of the scope of poetics in the margins or between the lines of the official theory remained a reality in late sixteenth-century England.

Discussions of the relations between art and nature in the English treatises of poetry offer an example of those gaps in the theory. The notion of poetics as an art in the sense of a written compendium of rules for the composition and understanding of poetry is actively questioned in the most representative theoretical work of the period, Sidney's *Defence of Poesy* (c. 1580). For Sidney, the poet's faculty is a prerogative that escapes the subordination to nature that binds other arts: the poet is thus 'lifted up with the vigour of his own invention'. The effect of this capacity is the creation of a 'second nature', the only restriction upon his 'erected wit' and the 'golden' quality of his creation being the awareness of his 'infected will' – that is, the fallen nature of his human condition. God is, for Sidney, the ultimate rule that sets limits to his 'freely ranging within the zodiac of his own wit'.[10]

Sidney's somewhat unruly notion of the poet's art, which unwrites the boundaries of the conventional *ars poetica*, is echoed in the more systematic *artes* written after him. Discussing *sprezzatura* in the conclusion to his *Art of English Poesy*, Puttenham adapts Sidney's argument regarding the superiority of the poet over other artificers by claiming poetry's identification with nature's work. Accordingly, poetry's highest excellence is shown when the poet's inventive and imaginative qualities fly from the constraints of art affecting other disciplines:

> But for that in our maker or poet, which rests only in device and issues from an excellent, sharp, and quick invention, helped by a clear and bright fantasy and imagination, he is not as the painter to counterfeit the

natural by the like effects and not the same, nor as the gardener aiding nature to work both the same and the like, nor as the carpenter to work effects utterly unlike, but even as nature herself, working by her own peculiar virtue and proper instinct and not by example or mediation or exercise as all other artificers do, is then most admired when he is most natural and least artificial.[11]

Puttenham's poet has licence to leave aside 'example or mediation or exercise' – the forms adopted by a praxis derived from art's predisposition to precept. His constant winks in this final chapter at Castiglione's notion of *sprezzatura* stress the potential of practice for the undoing of precept: art's concealment of art leads to the adoption of nature's 'proper instinct'.[12] By endorsing proximity to nature, the conclusion of *The Art of English Poesy* seems to promote courtly nonchalance as the foundation for a poetic praxis that subtly unwrites the system that its own pages had so painstakingly designed.

In the last decade, our understanding of English sixteenth-century poetics has been significantly enriched by the addition of William Scott's *The Model of Poesy* (1599) to the canon of early modern literary criticism. Both in structure and content, the *Model* provides, in the words of its editor, 'a sort of complete *ars poetica*'.[13] Completeness and systematicity are made evident in the attempt to umpire the relations between art and nature in unprecedented ways for English poetics. Scott endorses the Stoic tradition in his definition of art as 'an instrument of reason, consisting in the prescribing certain sufficient rules how to work to some good end'.[14] The written rules of art transform 'natural propenseness and supernatural inspiring' into 'the active habit or habitual understanding of poetry'.[15] Art's taming of nature into habit posits the latter as a convenient middle term that advocates a moderate balance between observance of rule and creative freedom. For Scott, art provides 'the furniture of poesy, the rules and laws that the poet must observe in his imitation'. Yet habit also remains a safety valve not only to circumvent the realm of rigid prescription, but also to increase the resources of poetry beyond the boundaries of the written arts. Scott's discussion of poetry's rules is thus prefaced by a significant caveat:

> It is neither possible nor needful to set down so absolute a frame of rules in the institution of our poet as shall be able to direct him to every particular circumstance required and belonging to the setting forth and dressing of every poem, because then we should grow infinite and run through all arts, even more than Quintilian in his Oratory or than

Scaliger in our faculty. Besides there are many things which must, in so infinite variety of device and ornament, be left to the prudence and discretion which is to be an unseparable companion of the poet's.[16]

Habit encourages freedom and discretion in equal measure. It does not necessarily incite poets to eschew the rules expounded in the treatise. Rather, it is an invitation to explore the possibilities offered by 'every particular circumstance' in light of the 'infinite variety of devices' at the poet's disposal. Habit calls for an active poetics to work side by side with the written arts. In view of this suggestion, the idea of an unwritten poetics explored in this volume does not ignore normativity. Instead, it detects in poetic practice a different sort of criticism, which can be at times apologetic, but is most often speculative and creative. This is the effect of its discursive medium, often outside the bounds of the treatise. But it is also the consequence of its content and aim, derived from and intent on attending to situations beyond the repertory of problems formulated in the conventional arts.

Displacing the scope of poetics from its own conventional medium – the 'art' or treatise – calls for an interrogation of the 'places' in which the thinking about poetry is materialised. In a recent collection that understands these 'places of criticism' in their topical, geographical and textual senses, Gavin Alexander, Emma Gilby and Alexander Marr advocate 'the necessity of looking afresh at the scope of criticism and what happens at its margins'.[17] Even if the present collection does not have 'place' as its main focus, its importance necessarily emerges as an effect of research. In a survey article on the theory of the Renaissance lyric, Roland Greene proposes to seek a fuller understanding of the emergence, theory and practice of poetic forms 'in many untoward places, and witnessed alongside other events'. Among these, Greene usefully reminds us that 'the most acute poetics of the early modern lyric is written out in the poems themselves'.[18] The argument should be extended beyond lyric or any other genre. Even at a time when the early Tudor critical void was being extensively filled, poetry continued to offer a privileged space for self-reflection.

Two select instances of poetry's occupying the realm of theory are brought here. The first brings back James VI's *Essayes of a Prentise* as proof that the division of labour between the normative 'treatise' and the practical 'essayes' was often more formal than real. About his own translations, James comments that they are 'replete with innumerable and intolerable faultes: sic as, Ryming in tearmes, and dyvers others, whilkis ar forbidden in my own treatise of the Art of Poësie'.[19] Yet theory's intolerance of licence or fault coexists in the king's writing with suggestive explorations of the foundations, methods and aims of poetic composition. The limited scope of his theoretical programme makes the discussion predictable: sound and prosody (chapters 1 and 2), decorum (3), poetic ornament, more specifically similes, epithets and proverbs (4), figures of repetition (5), poetic invention, strictly understood as originality of subject and conceit (6 and 7), and the correspondence between stanzas and generic forms (8). For other themes, James refers his reader to more comprehensive *artes poeticae*. Yet he also defers his most appealing considerations about the writing process to his poetic 'essayes'. Thus, the first original piece in the collection, 'Twelf Sonnets of Inuocations to the Goddis',[20] does better service as a working poetics than any of the treatise's chapters. In these sonnets, the poet asks the Olympian gods, collectively and individually, to endow him with the necessary tools to make his verse attractive to its audience. Their subject is less divine inspiration than the poet's ability to induce certain operations in the readers' minds. Without naming the terms, these sonnets are a practical handbook on two key notions that are nominally absent in the treatise: *energeia* and *enargeia*, that is, efficacy of style and poetry's capacity to make absent things present. In their discussion of these principles, the sonnets fulfil one minor prescription in the treatise: 'And finally, quhatsumeuer be zour subiect, to vse *vocabula artis*, quhairby ze may the mair viuelie represent that person, quhais pairt ze paint out'.[21] The recommendation that the poet use *terms of art* is materialised in the deployment of a full practical lexicon around the performative efficacy of poetry: verbs such as 'descryue' (1.7, 2.3, 2.9, 3.1, 7.1, 10.4), 'deuyse' (2.6), 'display' (3.13), 'reherse' (4.3), 'declare' (8.2), 'loaue' (i.e., praise, 9.3), 'flyte' (i.e., abuse, 9.6), 'delate' (i.e., enlarge upon, report, 12.12), nouns such as 'Ingyne' (11.4), adverbs such as 'viue[ly]' (2.12, 4.1, 5.13) or noun phrases such as 'description trew' (5.2) account for poetic agency in the pursuit of *energeia*. Simultaneously, an extensive lexical field develops *enargeia* as the intended effects on the readers, who are induced to 'think' (in the sense of believe, 1.6, 3.14, 4.4, 4.9, 5.3, 5.9, 6.1, 6.7, 6.11, 7.3, 7.5, 7.9, 7.11, 9.8, 10.3, 11.5, 11.9), 'esteme' (2.4, 3.5) and 'trow' (5.9) that they 'see', (1.8, 3.5, 3.14, 5.10, 6.7, 9.8, 9.12, 10.4), 'smell' (3.8, 4.11), 'fele' (4.4, 6.1), 'heare' (4.9, 6.5, 6.11, 7.5, 9.9, 9.11) and 'taste' (4.11), as well as to 'conuoy' (5.3), or transport, the sonnets' representations into their referents in nature, thus acquiring the capacity of witnessing to and experiencing the actions that the poems purport to represent.

Rather than pointing to a gulf between theory and practice, James's volume proves that differentiating between their concerns is neither easy nor useful.[22] Ultimately, his practical 'essayes' doubly unwrite the volume's intended theoretical programme. First, because they exceed thematically the scope of the 'treatise'. Second, and more importantly, because in representing *energeia* and *enargeia* they suspend their own role as practical instruments of poetic representation.[23] The rhetorical mechanics of the sequence, of which an instance is shown here, fosters that effect:

> AND when I do descriue the Oceans force,
> Graunt syne, ô Neptune, god of seas profound,
> That readars think on leebord, and on dworce,
> And how the Seas owerflowed this massiue round:
> Yea, let them think, they heare a stormy sound,
> Which threatnis wind, and darknes come at hand:
> And water in their shipps syne to abound,
> By weltring waues, lyke hyest towres on land. (7.1–8)

The apostrophe to the gods involving a request for the fulfilment of the effects of a future poetic action circumscribes *energeia* and *enargeia* to hypothesis rather than actuality, foregrounding the theoretical, metapoetic force of the sonnets.

Explicitly refusing to dedicate his work 'to any particular personis',[24] James imagines his readers as a distant, generic mass from whom homogeneous responses are expected. His poetics is egotistically author-centred. A quarter of a century after the *Essayes*, Aemilia Lanyer's *Salve Deus Rex Judaeorum* (1611) similarly imagined a divine agent – a Christ that nevertheless appears more human than Sidney's God – acting as mediator between her poetry and its audience. Unlike James, Lanyer unapologetically identified her distinguished community of female readers – presided over by James's wife Anne and daughter Elizabeth. In the absence of an explicit *ars poetica*, Lanyer made extensive use of outstandingly artful verse paratexts that paradoxically claim to unwrite – that is, delete, disavow – her poetry's own artfulness. Rejecting a tradition of male poets and audiences, Lanyer vindicates the superiority of feminine 'Nature' over masculine 'Art':

> Not that I Learning to my selfe assume,
> Or that I could compare with any man:
> But as they are Scholers, and by Art do write,
> So Nature yeelds my Soule a sad delight. (147–50)[25]

Insistence on the artlessness of its 'rude unpollisht lines' (35) substantiates poetry's claim to authenticity while it downplays the merits of the poet. Lanyer's favourite conceit for her poem is the 'glasse', or 'mirrour', a recurring trope regulating the relations between art and nature in the English treatises.[26] Yet her glass/poem eschews its traditional meaning as a cunning reflector of nature. The poem's mirror quality is justified by its having made Christ's nature its own content. As Lanyer bids Queen Anne,

> Looke in this Mirrour of a worthy Mind,
> Where some of your faire Virtues will appeare;
> Though all it is impossible to find,
> Unlesse my Glasse were chrystall, or more cleare:
> Which is dym steele, yet full of spotlesse truth,
> And for one looke from your faire eyes it su'th. (37–42)

The unassuming 'Mirrour' of Christ's 'worthy Mind' grants the poem its capacity to reflect the image of the 'spotlesse truth' of its readers' worth. Reciprocally, these ladies' 'faire Virtues' dignify the mirror's own humble status. Imagining Princess Elizabeth, and then her mother Queen Anne of Denmark, reading her poem, Lanyer can exclaim: 'O let my Booke by her faire eies be blest, / In whose pure thoughts all Innocency rests. // Then shall I thinke my Glasse a glorious Skie, / When two such glittering Suns at once appeare' (95–8). Lanyer's complex operation follows the contrary path to James's in its apparent deflation of the artificer and the artefact in favour of its promotion of her poem's eminent readers and divine subject matter. Her mirror/poem unwrites the conceit's conventional uses in the period's official poetics. Yet her vindication of nature over art is not far from theorists such as Puttenham. After all, Lanyer's poetics inhibits art in an operation of seeming that resembles courtly *sprezzatura*. The plethora of styles in which her eight distinguished female readers are addressed include verse forms such as the quatrain, the sixain, rhyme royal or *ottava rima*, thus undoing in practice any claim to artlessness. Lanyer's novel theory and subtle practice are remarkable for simultaneously advertising and disavowing their own complexity.

The poems of James VI and Aemilia Lanyer emerge as samples of sophisticated thinking about poetry produced in the margins of the *artes poeticae*, yet enlightening poetic practice in more lucid ways than the *artes* themselves. As such, both are instances of Scott's endorsement of poets' 'active habit' and their reliance on the reader's 'habitual understanding' of poetry. The present collection aims to offer full-fledged instances of the habit of experiencing poetry and of thinking the conditions of existence of the early modern poem from writerly and readerly perspectives.

Stating the Art

Looking into the margins of the written critical tradition involves excavating an unsystematic and ever-growing body of ideas from the period's inventive forms of literature. This volume's emphasis on these ideas' often *unwritten* character should make us aware of the word's inherent polysemy. In the sixteenth century, the term could appear in legal and religious contexts, mostly in reference to the oral traditions of the English common law and Catholic doctrine. Phrases such as 'unwritten verities' and 'unwritten traditions' traverse the reformist religious literature of the Elizabethan period, repeatedly signalling the distrust towards what is admitted by mere consensus against the authority of the scriptures and underlying the 'new literalism' of Protestant culture.[27] *Unwritten* thus invites exploring unformulated critical assumptions outside official theory. The word also suggests the blank surface that is left unmarked by writing and that admits – palimpsest-like – unexplained, marginalised or novel meanings. In our discipline, the search for ways of historicising critical practice beyond the rigid literalism of theory's official forms has illustrious precedents. A classic example is R. S. Crane's quarrel with the exclusive attention to doctrinal content of early twentieth-century historians of English literary criticism.[28] In Crane's opinion, the practice of positivist histories of the discipline reduced the thought of particular critics to 'a series of discrete assertions or denials' about topics with 'no serious interest in themselves for readers in a later age'.[29] Consequently, a mere classification of statements about imitation, origin, style, genre or prosody could only produce an 'inadequate, and mainly external conception' of literary criticism by presenting 'the material content of doctrine in abstraction'. Alternatively, Crane's recommendation consists of an 'internal' perspective that might regard the critical writings of a period as 'historical events, made meaningful individually in terms of . . . concrete problems', and enabling a focus on 'a more or less common framework of characteristic fundamental terms and distinctions which critics . . . for all their disagreements on points of doctrine or appreciation, found it natural to utilize in the statement of their questions and the justification of their answers'.[30]

Unlike Colie's focus on literature, Crane's object is criticism. Yet both encourage alternative considerations of theory and praxis, among them the possibilities of deriving theory from praxis or reading theory as praxis. The former involves reversing the traditional assumption that theory precedes praxis. S. K. Heninger's *Sidney and Spenser: The Poet as Maker* (1989) provides an example of that procedure. Heninger's compelling monograph begins with preparatory essays on the sources and contexts for Sidney's *Defence*, then derives a systematic poetics out of Sidney's apologetic text, and studies first Spenser's 'poetical praxis' as the result of a Neoplatonic model that seeks truth outside poetry, and finally Sidney's poetry as the illustration of his own inventive, pictorial poetics.[31] In contrast with this methodology, Catherine Bates's recent *On Not Defending Poetry* (2017) reads the interplay between theory and writing practice in Sidney's *Defence* as an unresolved dialectics between an 'official' and an 'unofficial voice', which she calls 'the speaker' and 'Sidney' respectively: while the former registers the arguments of classical and Renaissance theory, the latter suggests 'more of an undertone than a voice, more of a Freudian slip than a full-blown analysis' of the author's disaffection with conventional ideas.[32] Heninger's method allows for reading deviations as exceptions from the norm – for instance, his contention that Spenser's *Muiopotmos* is a self-conscious exercise in the Sidneian ideal of 'right poetry' in which 'the ontological situs lies not outside the poem but immediately in it'.[33] Conversely, Bates promotes attention to a constant interplay of contending voices (the creative poet, the aesthetic thinker and the conventional apologist) and subtexts (moral, aesthetic, political, economic) to reconfigure the Sidneian textual field beyond traditional divisions of theory and praxis. Like Heninger, the essays in the present collection often attend to the interplay of theory and poetry. Like Bates, their conception of the textual field tends to unsettle received discursive boundaries.

Four important arguments for the purposes of the present collection can be drawn from these approaches. The first addresses the originality of the poetic thinking conveyed by our primary texts. In this sense, an unwritten or unofficial poetics could variously relate to officially accepted principles. This issue emerges prominently in the last section of this collection, devoted to individual poets. Writing about energy and the sublime in Sidney in the third section, Sell argues that 'the written art of Sidney's theory is more consistent with his practice than is often thought, while the unwritten art that transpires from that practice partially completes the theoretical model'.

The chapters by Zunino-Garrido and Pérez-Jáuregui also demonstrate how the poetic texts of Thomas Lodge, Henry Constable and Barnabe Barnes actively engage in offering perspectives on well-established questions in poetics such as the scope of originality or the design of the poetic career. Conversely, the chapters by Knight and Luis-Martínez show that poetic practice can explicitly counter established notions in Renaissance criticism and in later critical appreciations of Renaissance poetry, namely the mystifying nature of poetic difficulty when approached from the far-from-mystifying aims of the writings of Fulke Greville or George Chapman.

The second concerns the discursive – or, as Hulse stresses in the 'Afterword' to this collection, genre-oriented – status of the sources: while poetic practice provides a constant forum for dialogue with received critical thought, the difference between an official and an unofficial poetics can also cut across the distinction between the treatises and the poems. The inherent capacity of poetic praxis to generate its own poetics surfaces in some of the essays in this volume: Curbet Soler's focus on 'grace' as a legitimising stimulus of the poet, or Amelang's detection of 'a poetics of the unpoetic' that privileges emotive over aesthetic functions, are examples at hand. However, this capacity does not necessarily sanction the poem as the exclusive site for alternative models to received forms of poetic knowledge. Sumillera's analysis of the key function of 'blood' as a defining term for a formal poetics of genre in the treatises demonstrates that the literary theory of the sixteenth and seventeenth centuries fostered the production of aesthetic *thinking* beyond the bounds of its official *thought* – that is, the explicit repertory of questions and problems invoked by Crane.

The third argument extends the second in claiming that the body of evidence that acquaints us with the relations between an official and unofficial poetics often points to discourses outside what counts strictly as poetic theory or praxis. As Glyn P. Norton puts it, 'nothing distinguished [Renaissance] poetics more . . . than the scope of its prerogatives', particularly as 'poetry came to assume the panoply of political, scientific, philosophical, artistic, and moral achievement'.[34] The reason partly lies in the Renaissance classification of poetry as one of the instrumental disciplines, which enabled the treatment of a wide variety of subjects poetically. But it was also motivated by other disciplines' encouragement to think about poetry, or by the use of poetic examples as illustrations of other arts.[35] In the present collection, Wilson's essay on logical 'cause' as a constitutive force in late sixteenth-century poetic praxis proves that Renaissance logic was 'one of the unwritten arts underpinning sixteenth-century poetics'. In addition to logic, natural science (Gorman), medicine (Sumillera) or religion (Curbet Soler, Pérez-Jáuregui) have been recently proven less and less 'untoward places' for the accommodation of poetic ideas.

The fourth argument concerns the textual and rhetorical strategies that favour Renaissance thinking about poetry. Also nodding at Greene, Heather Dubrow has proposed to trace the 'untoward places' of genre theory in the period's delight in 'the indirections of metaphoric language and of mythological narrative'.[36] The interpretable nature of myth in Renaissance culture explains its functional affinity with rhetorical trope. Clark Hulse's seminal work on the epyllion has drawn attention to the experimental, speculative nature of a late sixteenth-century form that remained 'unanointed by theory'.[37] Hulse has made us aware of the recurrence in these Ovidian poems of the 'metamorphic image', whose focus on the 'resemblance' between two objects 'gradually extinguishes all points of unlikeness' between them.[38] This same logic is invoked in the poetic treatises' discussions of metaphor. Thus Puttenham:

> Or to call the top of a tree or of a hill, the crown of a tree or of a hill: for indeed 'crown' is the highest ornament of a prince's head, made like a close garland, or else the top of a man's head, where the hair winds about, and because such term is not applied naturally to a tree or to a hill, but is transported from a man's head to a hill or tree, therefore it is called by *metaphor*, or the Figure of Transport.[39]

The publication of *The Art of English Poesie* was strictly coetaneous with that of the first English Ovidian epyllion, Thomas Lodge's *Scillaes Metamorphosis* (1589), a poem in which metaphoric/metamorphic 'transport' represents 'discourse' as the 'steersman' and 'conceit' as the 'ship', in an inventive voyage across the 'bay' of the poet's 'fancie'.[40] Metaphor and metamorphosis are analogous strategies, generating a poetics of genre in the poem's linguistic praxis: by extinguishing all unlikeness between the uncertainties of a sea voyage and a theory of poetic invention, Lodge's metaphoric formula advertises the exploratory character of a nascent genre. This view of Lodge's adventurous poetics accords with recent assessments of the epyllion as an educational form, both in its indebtedness to school rhetoric and in its formative role for the young poet's apprenticeship of his – masculine gender intended – art.[41] In line with these studies, Hernández-Santano's chapter on *Scillaes Metamorphosis* and Shakespeare's *Venus and Adonis* (1593) and

The Rape of Lucrece (1594) reads in the poems' allegorising of the body's engagement in rhetorical *actio* a facet of the epyllion's self-generating critical discourse about the disciplining practices of Elizabethan literary education. But the potentials of myth to produce an unwritten poetics are exploited elsewhere in this volume: Gorman's chapter interprets the Renaissance mythography of Cupid as an aetiology of love poetry in authors such as Sidney, Drayton, Marlowe or Chapman; and Luis-Martínez attends to the latter's reinterpretations and reinventions of Ovidian myth as templates for his theories about writing and reading.

Vocabula artis

Attention to figurative language, philological perspectives on relevant words, close readings of literary texts, and a focus on intertextuality are analytical techniques used throughout this book. All its contributions share an interest in the ways in which specific lexicons function as entrance gates into a work or into a web of texts, enlightening specific problems about the nature, origin, making, style or function of poetry. This volume implicitly assigns to certain words the status of *keywords*, thus signalling its debt to a methodology which in the fields of cultural theory and history was inaugurated and popularised by Marxist critic Raymond Williams's groundbreaking *Keywords: A Vocabulary of Culture and Society*. Originally published in 1976, and conceived as an instrumental companion to *Culture and Society* (1958), *Keywords* draws on philology and lexicography to weave an interlocking, comprehensive historical lexicon of Western culture. Williams's outline of his book's function as 'the record of an inquiry into a vocabulary' is of interest to our critical practice: in Williams's own definition, a word qualifies as a keyword when 'the problems of its meanings seemed . . . inextricably bound up with the problems it was being used to discuss'.[42] A word acquires complex meanings because of its capacity to explain a problem, and vice versa: a word's explanatory power complicates the history of its semantic scope. 'Art' is such keyword precisely for that double, paradoxical dimension. Williams stresses the word's potential to establish, but also to blur, the differences between the fields of human knowledge and crafts in terms of intellectual/creative or manual/mechanical skills, selfless or utilitarian aims. Williams points to the sixteenth and seventeenth centuries as the critical moment that activates, and therefore problematises, the previously inexistent division between the manual artisan and the creative artist. Similarly, though perhaps more subtly, the above-quoted passage from Puttenham suggests that explaining the poet's dealings with 'nature' in opposition to the 'art' of the painter, the gardener or the carpenter does not simply stress those emerging divisions; it also renders problematic the very distinction between art and nature that has traditionally justified poetic praxis.[43]

The influence of Williams's book is patent in its subsequent editions (1989, 2015), and in later attempts to complement its content and scope in the form of sequels, mostly in the field of the social sciences.[44] In early modern literary studies, keyword analysis has enjoyed a special position in the last decade. Roland Greene's monograph *Five Words: Critical Semantics in the Age of Shakespeare and Cervantes* (2013) and Ita Mac Carthy's edited collection *Renaissance Keywords* (2013) respectively take five (*invention, language, resistance, blood, world*) and seven (*sense, disegno, allegory, grace, scandal, discretion, modern*) words as their bases for methodologies which, under labels such as 'critical semantics' or 'new philology', pay historical attention to words with a special relevance to early European – or in Greene's case, transatlantic – modernity.[45] The application of philological methods to the analysis of culture relies on Renaissance practices such as dictionary-making, or on humanist procedures such as the Ramist organisation of the specialised vocabularies of the arts by means of comprehensive diagrams and eye-friendly outlines.[46] Yet, for all our indebtedness to these methodologies, our chapters do not aspire to comprehensiveness in the manner of Williams, nor even of Ramus. The refusal to organise the book into keyword-titled chapters conspicuously signals a different working principle here. In this sense, attention to words in this volume resembles Patricia Parker's opening argument in her recent monograph on Shakespeare: Parker's 'critical keywords' are

> meant not as a claim to words that were necessarily (or all) 'key' terms in early modern culture, but as words and phrases *that provide a critical way into interpreting* the language, contexts, and preoccupations of particular Shakespeare plays, together with issues of historical intersections that have been marginalized or have gone unnoticed by editors and critics.[47]

Our version of this method consists of conceiving these words primarily as windows into the critical discourse on poetry in early modern England. While their status as cultural keywords is still crucial for the terms analysed in this volume, their relevance is gauged by their capacity to identify, contextualise or explain a specific question in relation to early modern poetry.

The case of two prominent terms in this volume – *grace* and *blood* – can exemplify our privileging a focus on certain words' accession to the condition of *vocabula artis*, or 'terms of art' of a practical poetics, over their usefulness as culturally loaded terms. The study of grace has a valuable precedent in the work of Ita Mac Carthy, whose cultural history of the word enables her conclusion on sixteenth-century Italian painting: 'grace became key in the contest for supremacy that made Renaissance art as a whole so distinctive'.[48] The polysemy of grace in the public discourses of aesthetics, religion, politics and the law, but also in the private sphere, is a feature in the essays by Curbet Soler and Pérez-Jáuregui in this volume; yet the cultural dynamics of grace-giving and the relevance of grace-as-gift in the origination of poetic discourse (Curbet Soler), or the pious trajectories of grace-seeking as tropes for the Renaissance poetic career (Pérez-Jáuregui), are semantic potentials that early modern English poetic practice employs for self-discerning purposes. Similarly, Sumillera's chapter proves that it is the poetic medium that can put the medical discourse of the double condition of blood as fluid and humour at the service of ideas of stylistic fluidity, balance or excess. In the context of larger theories of texts as fleshly, bony or sinewy structures (Sumillera), or in the textual milieu of the fashionable erotic epyllion, in which the *actio* of corporeal limbs and physiological processes supplants rhetorical *elocutio* (Hernández-Santano), poetic discourse transmutes the meanings of the body in physiology and rhetoric into novel ideas of genre unavailable in the official theory of poetry.

The examples of medicine, physiology and rhetoric evince that our attention to words frequently relies on the communicating vessels between the various disciplines that compounded the all-encompassing and largely undefined field of early modern 'philosophy'. George Chapman's allegory of the ability of 'Poesie' to rescue 'Philosophy retirde from darkest caves' (of which more in Luis-Martínez's chapter) serves here as a working trope for a critical activity that regards poetic practice as a laboratory in which different sorts of knowledge are transformed into self-reflexive thinking. Thus, the confluence of physics and mythography, of *atoms* and *Cupids*, supplies the material for exploring the aetiologies of motion and emotion of 'an ever-evolving, complex erotic poetics' (Gorman). Renaissance logic is the local habitation that gives a name to *cause* and *habit*, which in the present volume respectively foster the enquiry into 'poetry and poetic inspiration as agents of change' (Wilson), or into attitudes and dispositions to the composition and elucidation of complex poetic artefacts (Luis-Martínez). But the originating concepts in other chapters may be terms whose familiarity with received poetic theory is beyond doubt: sometimes inhering in the 'deep structure' of the research question informing each chapter (*sublime, difficulty, [in]eloquence*), other times featuring more prominently in the surface of the poetic texts chosen (*Muse*), these terms provide the matrix for figures, lexicons and tropes that allow novel acts of interpretation of poetic texts and/or alternative grasps on conventional aesthetic doctrines: for example, lyric effusions as aestheticised extensions of poetic theory (Sell), expressions of the edifying power of difficulty (Knight), deliberate rejections of eloquence as enquiries into the nature of poetic artifice (Amelang), or vindications of individual experience as fountains of authentic poetic matter (Zunino-Garrido).

Origin, Style, Poesis

Due to the miscellaneous character of the present collection, its chapters relate to one another and to the volume's main topic in various ways, allowing for independent reading though also engaging in frequent cross-referentiality. The marginal or oblique relation that the topics included here claim to issues dealt with in the period's official poetics justifies the volume's non-exhaustive nature: other topics, other poets and other texts could contribute new perspectives to this proposal for a complementary, *unwritten* poetics, and in that sense the volume invites further research. Among a number of other possibilities suggested by this non-exhaustive character, the volume's ordering principle has been dictated by its *invention* – specifically, the unwritten arts of Renaissance poetry – rather than its methodology – that is, the possible semantic links suggested by the lexicons explored in the chapters, which, as implied in the previous section, could have advanced alternative arrangements. Thus, its three-part structure allocates each chapter on grounds of its primary interest in questions of poetic art that ultimately relate to *origin*, *style* or individual *poesis* – the latter thus differing from the other two in its attention to specific poets. These three divisions do not claim any integral treatment of the scope of Renaissance poetics either. They are nevertheless representative of major concerns found in the pages of the treatises addressed in the present introduction, as well as other theoretical writings about poetry in early modern England – even if the specific question or the orientation of that question remains extraneous or elusive to the received poetics.

The essays in the first part, 'Origin: Poetic Aetiologies', variously investigate ideas of causation and origination. Arguments and narratives about the origins of poetry or about poetry as origin and cause of civilised life abound in poetic theory. Sidney and Puttenham write about the divine origins of poetry and about the poets' status as first politicians, prophets and lawmakers.[49] Sidney's own treatise is motivated by the urge to refute the idea that poetry is the origin of major moral and social evils. And Scott lingers on the causes that impel the poet to write as 'he ruminates on the true loveliness of virtue', of which 'he grows enamoured', as well as on the aid of art as the 'divine instrument' that bridles this passionate impulse into reasonable ends.[50] The three chapters in this part engage in narratives of causation that could be seen as alternative or complementary to those in the treatises. Joan Curbet Soler's 'Justified by Whose Grace?' argues that the permanent 'sense of slippage' in late Elizabethan poetic uses of grace complicates the investigation of its origin – who grants it, be it God, king/queen, judge, literary patron, Petrarchan lady, reader – and its work – what is given *by* or *with* grace. Instances from poems by Philip Sidney, Edmund Spenser, Fulke Greville and Aemilia Lanyer demonstrate that giving and receiving grace are acts that compromise the poet's, and the poem's, worthiness. A Renaissance 'poetics of grace', particularly when its Protestant meaning of unmotivated gift is at stake, is *partly* an inquiry into the origins and essence of poetry – partly, because a later chapter on grace in this volume takes its senses in different though equally sophisticated directions. A different perspective on poetic aetiology is Emma Annette Wilson's 'The Logical Cause of an Early Modern Poetics of Action'. Wilson traces the changing meanings and roles of *cause*, with particular attention to the efficient cause in Renaissance logic and its impact in Britain. By focusing on the logicians' influence on the poets, this tactic inverts the approach of recent studies of poetry and logic, which have mainly stressed the logicians' use of poetic examples. Considering logic one of poetry's 'unwritten arts' – that is, a discipline whose written rules have an implicit bearing on the practice of poetry – Wilson sees in the Agricolan/Ramist reorientation of logic towards the study of cause the genesis of a practical poetics of action, exemplified here in sonnets by Sidney and Spenser, as well as in Marlowe's school translation of Ovid's *Amores*. The aetiological character of myth inspires Cassandra Gorman's 'Atomies of Love', an interpretation of the poetic mythography of Cupid in light of the early modern materialist philosophies' growing interest in atomic motion. In Gorman's reading of sonnets by Sidney and Drayton (and a later example by Nicholas Hookes) and the narrative poetry of Marlowe and Chapman, the multiplying, atomised Cupids of early modern poetry originate a poetics of inordinate desire. 'The legacy of Cupid's atomic beginning' empowers a 'productive and regenerative' erotic poetics. The proliferation of multiple *Cupids* and *atoms* in Renaissance poems supplies an alternative aetiology of the love poem that counters the sometimes idealising, sometimes dismissive accounts found in the major treatises.

The three chapters in the second part, 'Style: Outgrowing the Arts', share an attention to questions of poetic form arising in the intersections of theory and practice. Rocío G. Sumillera's 'Bloody Poetics' connects with the preceding chapter's interest in materiality by tracing classical and humanist sources in the English literary criticism of the sixteenth and seventeenth centuries. Sumillera scrutinises the role of blood as 'a fundamental style indicator' among other cases of similar uses of bodily lexicons. The productive semantics of blood is thus foregrounded for its contribution to a poetics of epic style, particularly in the work of the early English translators of Homer, George Chapman and John Dryden. In passing, Sumillera's attention to the critical implications of the figural language employed in the *artes poeticae* vindicates an unwritten poetics of critical praxis. The other two essays in this part embark on unconventional assessments of the fundamental notion of *eloquence* in Renaissance poetic theory. David J. Amelang's 'Figuring Ineloquence in Late Sixteenth-century Poetry' navigates between rhetorical theory and a selection of texts including poems by Sidney, Spenser, Marlowe and Drayton, as well as dramatic excepts from Shakespeare (and Lope de Vega), in search of a theory of the unpoetic and a praxis of ineloquence. Amelang pays attention to the English treatises' labelling and definition of figures of repetition and interruption – *ecphonesis, ploce, aposiopesis, parenthesis* – materialised in the proliferation of 'unpoetic' words, which constitute another version of King James's practical terms of art. This chapter also interrogates the decorum or aptness behind the apparently unelaborate (another form of the unwritten) outbursts of emotion in the context of Elizabethan ornate rhymes and stylish blank verse. Like Amelang's chapter, Sonia Hernández-Santano's 'Eloquent Bodies' is concerned with a performative poetics and the relations between eloquence and the emotions. Like Sumillera's chapter, its primary interest lies in the corporeal, although the focus now shifts from the high and mature epic to the more modest, youthful and experimental epyllion. Lodge's *Scillaes Metamorphosis* and Shakespeare's *Venus and Adonis* and *The Rape of Lucrece* provide cases for testing the value of their bodily lexicons as bases for a practical poetics of a largely untheorised genre. Embracing the recent critical trend that sees these poems as by-products of the pedagogical exercises and disciplinary practices of the grammar schools and Inns of Court, Hernández-Santano analyses the poems' promotion of a bodily rhetoric of *actio* that functions as an alternative model to traditional *elocutio*.

The third part, 'Poesis: Art's Prisoners', takes its cue from a line in Thomas Lodge's *Phillis* that depicts art's conventional snares on the poet's creative praxis.[51] Understood as praxis or process, *poesis* features here in dialogue with, as substitute for, or as complement to actual criticism about the nature, function and purposes of writing and/or reading poetry. Writing in the junctures of theoretical reflection and inventive creativity, Philip Sidney, Henry Constable and Barnabe Barnes (jointly), Thomas Lodge, Fulke Greville and George Chapman emerge in these five chapters as voicers of highly individual poetic programmes. Jonathan P. A. Sell's 'Philip Sidney's Sublime Self-authorship' reads a substitute vocabulary for the absent *sublime* in the complexly loaded lexicons of 'authenticity', 'ecstasy' and 'energy' in *Astrophil and Stella* and *The Defence of Poesy* in the attempt to solve the critical crux of the distance between Sidney the theorist and Astrophil the poet/lover. For Sell, a Sidneian unwritten poetics of the sublime not only fills a gap in his explicit, official theory of poetry; it also enables an understanding of Astrophil as Sidney's aestheticised – rather than fictionalised – self. Sidney-inspired sonnet sequences occupy the next two chapters. María Jesús Pérez-Jáuregui's 'From Favour to Eternal Life' returns to the productivity of *grace* as a poetic keyword in her analysis of the parallel trajectories of Barnabe Barnes and Henry Constable. The polysemy of 'grace' is fully exploited in both poets' transit from the secular to the religious lyric, even if their contrasting experiences – Barnes remained overtly Protestant while Constable converted to Catholicism – inspire two classically oriented though disparate career models, characterised by ascending, Virgilian self-affirmation in Barnes, and Ovidian self-denial, particularly in Constable's incorporation of his own experience as a religious exile. Cinta Zunino-Garrido's 'Thomas Lodge's "Supple Muse"' makes use of a phrase by poet John Davies to tread on well-known ground in her assessment of 'imitation', 'inspiration' and 'imagination' in Lodge's jointly published sonnet sequence *Phillis* and narrative poem *The Complaynt of Elstred*. For Zunino-Garrido, the inherent flexibility of the meanings and functions of Lodge's *Muse* epitomises an implicit poetics that claims the pre-eminence of experience over model imitation. The complex interplay of masculine and feminine voices that traverses the lyric collection and its narrative continuation reinforces Lodge's claim regarding poetry's capacity to circumvent the conventional entrapments of art. The last two chapters turn respectively to the 'difficult' poetry of Fulke Greville and George Chapman, thus sharing a sense of readerly appreciation of difficulty as a trait of the poem and of the poets' compositional processes and purposes in writing difficult, or obscure, poetry. Sarah Knight's 'The Worthy Knots of Fulke Greville' takes the centrality of *difficulty* in post-Renaissance critical discussions of Greville (Lamb via Hazlitt, Swinburne) to assess the poet's own awareness of a trait in his writing that is never named as such. Thus, Greville's poetics of difficulty is traced in the figurative language of his critical writings, but also in the knotty textures of his tragedies *Alaham* and *Mustapha*. Knight demonstrates that Greville's recognition of the intellectually and morally challenging nature of his verse entails a parallel appreciation of difficulty as an aesthetic and didactic category that presupposes its being worth the readers' effort to untie its meanings. Finally, Zenón Luis-Martínez's 'George Chapman's "Habit of Poesie"' retrieves a central keyword in this introduction from Chapman's poems and critical writings. Chapman's poetic *habit* comprises a complex array of 'creative, intellective and interpretative qualities' upon which the figures of poet, philosopher, translator and reader converge. In the paratexts to the Homeric translations, habit mediates between inspiration and labour as forces that guide the processes of composition and interpretation. It also helps explain Chapman's cultivation of *obscurity* as a vehicle to intellectual clarification in his early poetry, in which he reads his Ovidian models as representative of a misguided poetic praxis in need of discipline by habit's work.

The essays in this collection jointly subscribe to Crane's conviction that specific questions in poetics should be made meaningful in their individuality, as well as to Greene's recommendation that we look into 'untoward places' in the attempt to identify these questions. The task demands collective efforts and inevitably yields incomplete and fragmentary results. In this sense, the *unwritten* status of the poetics (plural intended) claimed here lies in the non-exhaustive and self-generating nature of the terms and questions explored. This volume is thus conceived as a contribution to a history of a Renaissance – or more amply, an early modern – unofficial poetics, but also as an invitation to further work in filling the many gaps that remain open.

Notes

This introduction has benefited from the reading and feedback offered by all contributors to the volume. I particularly wish to thank Clark Hulse for inspiring ways of readdressing important issues, and very especially Jonathan P. A. Sell for a meticulous and nuanced revision, and for digging out arguments and meanings from my draft's unwritten crevices.

1. James VI, *Essayes of a Prentise*, sig. C3v. These words can be found in the preface to James's translation of Du Bartas's *Uranie* (1574). For Gascoigne, see *Posies*, title page and sigs. T2r–U2v. For a summary of critical views of Gascoigne's influence on James, see Clewett, 'James VI of Scotland', 443–7.
2. The treatise's alternative title is 'Ane Schort Treatise, Containing some Reulis and cautelis to be observit and eschewit in Scotis Poesie'. See James VI, *Essayes of a Prentise*, sig. K1r.
3. Two very recent examples whose interests overlap with those in this collection are the essays in *Places of Early Modern Criticism*, ed. Alexander et al., and in the special issue '*Artes poeticae*', ed. Brljak and Lazarus. In the latter, see particularly Hetherington, 'Attitudes to Rule-following'.
4. Colie, *Resources of Kind*, 4.
5. Weinberg, *History of Literary Criticism*, 1:48.
6. Fraunce, *The Shepherds' Logic*, 57. For Fraunce's sources, see Piscator, *In P. Rami dialecticam animadversiones*, sig. A6v; and Lucian, *The Parasite*, 4, in *Lucian in Eight Volumes*, 3:246–7.
7. I have adapted the phrase from Purcell, *Ars Poetriae*, 56.
8. Stamatakis, 'Restful Place', 22.
9. Hetherington, 'Disciplining Creativity', 65. Hetherington's work has alerted us to the tensions in English Renaissance poetics between the systematic and the habitual. See, by the same author, 'An Instrument of Reason'.
10. Sidney, *Defence*, in *Miscellaneous Prose*, ed. Duncan-Jones and van Dorsten, 78–9. Use of the masculine third-person pronoun is in line with Sidney's text.
11. Puttenham, *Art of English Poesy*, ed. Whigham and Rebhorn, 385–6.
12. '[W]e do allow our courtly poet to be a dissembler only in the subtleties of his art; that is, when he is most artificial, so to disguise and cloak it as it may not appear, nor seem to proceed from him by any study or trade of rules, but to be his natural; nor so evidently to be descried, as every lad that reads him shall say he is a good scholar, but will rather have him to know his art well and little to use it' (ibid., 382). On *sprezzatura*, see Castiglione, *Courtyer*, trans. Hoby, sig. E2r.
13. Alexander, 'Introduction', in Scott, *Model of Poesy*, xxxviii.
14. Scott, *Model of Poesy*, ed. Alexander, 6.
15. Ibid., 10, 8.
16. Ibid., 29–30.

17. Alexander, Gilby and Marr, 'Introduction', 21.
18. Greene, 'The Lyric', 216. Greene's genre-specific argument is used here with a wider scope in mind.
19. James VI, *Essayes of a Prentise*, sig. C3v.
20. Ibid., sigs. A3r–C1r. Specific sonnets in James's short sequence are cited parenthetically in the text by number and line.
21. Ibid., sig. L4v.
22. For a detailed analysis of the dialectics of rule-making and literary practice in James's work as mediated by an eminent early modern reader, see Richards, 'Gabriel Harvey, James VI'.
23. Further discussions of *energeia* and *enargeia* can be found in this volume: Hernández-Santano, 'Eloquent Bodies', 140–1; Sell, 'Philip Sidney's Sublime Self-Authorship', 176–81; and Luis-Martínez, 'George Chapman's "Habit of Poesie"', 271–5.
24. James VI, *Essayes of a Prentise*, sig. K2r.
25. Lanyer, 'To the Queenes most Excellent Majestie', in *Poems*, ed. Woods, 3–10. Further references from this poem are cited parenthetically by line number in the text.
26. Puttenham depicts the imagination as 'a glass or mirror' offering 'all manner of beautiful visions' to the poetic or capacity or 'inventive part of the mind' (*Art of English Poesy*, 109). Scott describes poetic inventions 'grounded on likenesses' as 'crystal glasses' (*Model of Poesy*, 40). On Lanyer's use of the mirror image, see Herrold, 'Compassionate Petrarchanism', 369, 372–3.
27. Sobecki, *Unwritten Verities*, 3. Sobecki insists on the 'derogatory' sense of the phrase in the religious debates since the 1530s (109–11).
28. Crane, 'On Writing the History of Criticism'. Crane's main target was J. W. H. Atkins's series of volumes *English Literary Criticism* – the third in particular – purporting an integral history of literary criticism in England. I thank Michael Hetherington for drawing my attention to the relevance of Crane's work to this argument.
29. Crane, 'On Writing the History', 162.
30. Ibid., 166, 167.
31. Heninger, *Sidney and Spenser*, 16.
32. Bates, *On Not Defending Poetry*, 10 and passim.
33. Heninger, *Sidney and Spenser*, 369.
34. Norton, 'Introduction', 5.
35. The case of logic is particularly relevant for the present collection, as Emma Annette Wilson's chapter illustrates and references. On poetry's place among the Renaissance arts of discourse, see Weinberg, *History of Literary Criticism*, 1:2–31; see also Luis-Martínez and Hernández-Santano, 'Poetry, the Arts of Discourse', 1–14.
36. Dubrow, *Challenges of Orpheus*, 17.
37. Hulse, *Metamorphic Verse*, 34.
38. Ibid., 7.

39. Puttenham, *Art of English Poesy*, 263.
40. Lodge, *Scillaes Metamorphosis*, sig. C3v.
41. See in this respect two recent studies of the epyllion: Weaver, *Untutored Lines*; and Enterline, ed., *Elizabethan Narrative Poems*, particularly Enterline's 'Introduction: On Schoolmen's Cunning Notes', and Winston, 'From Discontent to Disdain'.
42. Williams, *Keywords*, xxvii.
43. Ibid., 9–11 ('Art'), 164–9 ('Nature'). For Williams, 'nature' owns the privilege of being 'the most complex word in the language' (164).
44. See, for instance, Jay, *Cultural Semantics*; Bennet et al., *New Keywords*; McCabe and Janacek, eds, *Keywords for Today*. A critique of the appropriation of the keyword methodology in the academic field is found in Fritsch et al., eds, *Keywords for Radicals*.
45. See Greene, *Five Words*; and Mac Carthy, ed., *Renaissance Keywords*. More recently, other scholars have resorted to similar methodologies though restricting the focus to one single word such as 'invention' or 'ingenuity': see Sumillera, *Invention*; and Marr et al., *Logodaedalus*.
46. On philology and keywords, see Scholar, 'New Philologists'. On Ramism, see Ong, *Ramus, Method*, esp. 314–18. A recent reassessment of this question is found in Hallett, 'Ramus, Print, and Visual Aesthetics'.
47. Parker, *Shakespearean Intersections*, 1.
48. See Mac Carthy, 'Grace', 76.
49. Sidney, *Defence*, in *Miscellaneous Prose*, 74–7; Puttenham, *Art of English Poesy*, 96–9.
50. Scott, *Model of Poesy*, 15–16.
51. 'Show passions in thy words, but not in heart: / Least when thou think'st to bring thy thoughtes in frame: / Thou proue thy selfe *a prisoner by thine Arte*' ('Egloga Prima', in Lodge, *Phillis*, sig. E2r; emphasis added).

Part I
Origin: Poetic Aetiologies

Chapter 1

Justified by Whose Grace? Poetic Worth and Transcendent Doubt in Late Elizabethan and Early Jacobean Poetry

Joan Curbet Soler

In Canto 10 of Book VI of Edmund Spenser's *The Faerie Queene*, Calidore, guided by attendant nymphs and having crossed an appropriately liminal river, reaches a version of the Earthly Paradise.[1] There he experiences a state of subjective blessedness (noticeably perfected by the hint of an erotic response) in witnessing the dance of a hundred naked maidens in concentric circles, around a trio of females who are gesturing towards a lady (Colin Clout's beloved) in their midst. These are the classical Three Graces, who are offering their gifts to the lady, as they do to the men they influence:

> These three on men all *gracious* gifts bestow,
> Which decke the body or adorne the mynde,
> To make them louely or well fauoured show,
> As comely carriage, entertainement kynde,
> Sweete semblaunt, friendly offices that bynde,
> And all the complements of curtesie. (VI.10.23.1–6, emphasis added)

What different forms of grace converge here on the central notion of 'curtesye'? The idea of a worldly deportment in its noblest form, to be sure; a cultivation of the self that involves 'comely carriage', 'sweete semblaunt' and 'friendly offices', which have been bestowed on men precisely as 'gracious gifts'. They have been bestowed, it must be added, by the Three Graces themselves, their classical image renewed and christianised by Spenser. The particular seduction of these Graces lies in the fact that they are only glimpsed by Calidore in their movement, though they cannot be completely apprehended either by his senses or by his intellect. Indeed, when Calidore, led away by his fascination, moves in and breaks the harmony of the dance, the piper Colin Clout is momentarily possessed by an unaccountable rage, and breaks his pipe – it is no coincidence, of course, that Colin should be an alter ego figure for Spenser in several of his poems besides *The Faerie Queene*. The mysterious operations of the Three Graces, of grace itself, must not be interrupted or disrupted by human subjects; their work, which can appear as arbitrary when seen from afar, has its own rules and its hidden yet serene order, which must not be interrogated or rationalised too deeply.

The example I have just examined provides a first hint of the poetic potential of the word 'grace' in Elizabethan and Jacobean poetry. In the first decades of the sixteenth century, the vocabulary and references of Petrarchism could fit into the English tradition with relative ease; after all, it was a cultural form created in a Catholic environment, within a mentality that was firmly based on traditional dogma and evocative of firmly institutionalised devotional practices.[2] But the development of Petrarchism and Italianate poetry in the late Elizabethan period, while retaining its value as an instrument of personal promotion and integration, necessarily involved a notion of cultural belatedness: the major sonnet sequences and narrative poems had to confront that aspect and the uneasiness that it inevitably brought about.[3] The term 'grace' operates across a palette of connotations; it has resonances in the whole field of courtly culture, where it refers to specific forms of decorum and etiquette; it designates institutionalised forms of pardon; and very specifically, it carries strong theological connotations. This is one of the terms that connect English poetry and poetics most strongly to European traditions, but also one of those that register most evidently the difficulties of cultural transmission.

The tensions thus arising explain, to a certain extent, some of the shifts and changes that make English poetry and poetics so different from their homologues in Europe at the end of the sixteenth century. There were various kinds of difficult cultural negotiations being made in England, both political and spiritual, and all of them required new forms of aesthetic transactions; a great part of our work as readers of English poetry is to register the loci, or the sites, of these transactions. Because of its peculiarly loaded nature, grace leads to peculiar situations, both within the poems and in the exchange between the poem and the reader. This implies that, at these points, there can be no completely unproblematic reading of poetry, that the relationship between the reader and the text can become strained and complicated. Readers are often brought to reconsider the terms in which their reading is made; thus, they are led to reassess the validity of the poetic performance itself. In this way, grace is not only asked of a female beloved, or of the queen, or of God, but also of readers themselves: this circumstance places them in a position that not only implies an aesthetic response but also a moral one. One of the signs of the belatedness of English Renaissance poetry is, precisely, the recurrent presence of the strong tensions manifested in the use of this term.

The consequences of this pattern bring about a variety of configurations that are relentlessly explored from a poetic standpoint, allowing both for verbal and situational irony and for serious commentary on the doubts and anxieties that are caused by the superposition of sacred and secular discourses. These doubts and anxieties respond, in the end, to a widespread doubt: the fear that the speakers might not have the capacity to assert their poetic voice on firm and self-validating aesthetic grounds, just as they do not have the capacity to reach for a full justification in spiritual terms. Poetic unworthiness or poetic doubt might thus become the sign of a deeper moral and personal worthlessness. The search for aesthetic grace (in terms of the achievement of beauty, of mastering a persuasive rhetoric, of offering a complete and coherent work) is also a quest for self-legitimation, and involves a deep interrogation of the grounds on which poetic creation occurs. There are very different outcomes to this search for poetic grace in late Elizabethan and early Jacobean poetry, and the aim of the following pages will be to explore them.

The relationship between grace and poetry is, in all the cases that will be examined here, one that cannot be fully closed, determined or categorised; to that extent, it perfectly fulfils the present volume's controlling idea of an *unwritten art*, in the sense of a poetics that can only be suggested rather than painstakingly formulated or traced. The responses given to this situation by historically canonical poets (or those who deliberately tried to assert their own canonicity) could not be more definitive, therefore, than those offered by others who have entered the canon in recent decades (Aemilia Lanyer), or by those who willingly remained in a secondary or critical position in relation to the main currents of Italianate poetry (Fulke Greville). Among the first of these groups, the work of Philip Sidney and Edmund Spenser can be seen as exploring these uncharted waters in ways that test the very limits and contradictions of the lyric and epic traditions; among the latter, Fulke Greville offers a serious interrogation of the grounds on which any assertion of poetic grace might be supposed to take place. Uniquely among my choice of examples, the work of Aemilia Lanyer showcases, in challenging and unexpected ways, the possibility of harnessing the very uncertainty and instability of the concept to new definitions of poetic legitimation and authority.[4]

Sir Philip Sidney and the Contradictions of Grace

It is not strange that the Elizabethan poets' *translatio* of European Petrarchism should be saturated with several uses of the concept of 'grace', which render this term as complex and dense with meaning as it was in theological polemics. The later canonicity of Philip Sidney's *Astrophil and Stella* (published posthumously in 1591) might prevent us from noticing its highly experimental nature, one which places the reader in the position of an observer, witnessing the speaker's movement towards a form of grace that might in itself be erroneous. From the beginning we know that the aim of the sequence is persuasive, that the speaker writes in the hope that he might 'grace' obtain from Stella (sonnet 1); but this is only the first in a long variation of uses of the term, which correspond to different gradations in a subjective quest for hope, emotional assurance and psychic security.[5] We have the 'heavy grace' (oxymoronically charged) that is dispensed to sleepers as a transient moment of rest in the final couplet of sonnet 39 (13); the breast of Stella, 'Whose grace is such, that when it chides doth cherish' (Song 1.18); the 'wel-shading grace' of the fans hiding the ladies' faces from the sun (22.7); the little sparrow that Stella's lips have kissed, and that 'Cannot such grace [its] silly selfe content', but still 'must needs with those lips billing be' (83.11–12). Like the impetuous Musidorus in the *Arcadia*, the speaker Astrophil is unable to restrain himself; instead, he keeps trying to obtain the grace or permission to approach Stella's lips, again and again, eventually succeeding in kissing her only while she is asleep (Song 2). All this takes place in an extremely rarefied and sophisticated atmosphere, which Thomas Nashe invited us to see as a 'Theater of pleasure', taking place on 'a paper stage' under 'an artificial heau'n' and behind 'christal wals', in what can be taken as one of the most perceptive early readings of the sequence.[6] Such a description emphasises the theatrical nature of Astrophil's performance and of the whole situation in which his desire for distinction leads him to project all his 'thought to highest place, / . . . even unto *Stella*'s grace' (27.13–14). The desire for preferment, for reaching the 'highest place' is a commonplace in the context of the court, and in the territory of human love.⁷ But if we understand that the term 'grace' also has religious connotations, we will see that intellectual or rhetorical power cannot be the basis on which it is obtained; humbleness and sincerity, rather, are required in this attempt.

Because of its very force, because of the conceptual weight that is put upon it, the concept itself seems to attract paradoxes or impossibilities, and as a result the act of communication is repeatedly strained, even rendered impossible (as in 93.2: 'What sobs can give words grace my griefe to show?'). To the various *oxymora* expressive of this paradox, we have to add several varieties of *polyptoton*, or lexical repetition in various inflections or grammatical forms, such as, for instance, when Astrophil, in the moment in which he manages to bite Stella's lip, refers to his admission by 'her best-graced grace' (82.10); or of *antanaclasis*, as when, earlier on, he desires to 'winne some grace in your sweet *grace* arraid' (55.4).⁸ Through the cumulative effect of all of these instances, the speaker is reaching, precisely by striving so hard to harness the concept, the realm of inexpressibility: grace approaches, step by step, the territory of what cannot be described, and since it cannot be described, it cannot be adequately delimited or clearly conceptualised.⁹ Sidney's sequence as a whole is interrogative, remains so at the end, and does not show any conclusive success on the part of Astrophil; the concept of grace is as strongly present as a topic in it as it is a source of doubt and anxiety while, in the process, losing none of its deep ambiguities.

The difficulties of defining 'grace' in the text of *Astrophil and Stella* can be understood as the effect of a larger underlying conflict: the tension between the Platonic thrust of European Petrarchism and the idealist nature of radical Protestantism. The sequence dramatises the failure of a lover who tries to think his experience through the language of the sophisticated poetry of his time, both by attempting an idealisation of the female figure and by persuading the female figure through his art. But the idealistic and Neoplatonic tendencies of Astrophil's language cannot be coherently maintained, and they have to give in repeatedly to the demands of physical desire: the reader is constantly called on to witness the difficulty of sustaining a coherent poetic project that is eroded from within, because of the speaker's tendency to give in to a form of grace that is only apparent, but not real or effective. Jean Calvin was the European theologian who exposed most consistently the doctrine of the equal degeneration of soul and body, basing his position on Paul's Letter to the Ephesians (4.23):

> It will be said, that the word *flesh* applies only to the sensual and not to the higher part of the soul. This, however, is completely refuted by the words of Christ and of the apostle . . . You see that [St Paul] places unlawful and depraved desires not in the sensual part merely, but in the mind itself, and therefore requires that it should be renewed. Indeed, he had a little before painted a picture of human nature, which shows that there is no part in which it is not perverted and corrupted.[10]

According to the Calvinist interpretation of reformed doctrine, there can be no real sense of progress in the turn from the admiration of the physical towards the contemplation of the soul, but only a shift from a kind of fallenness to another.[11] If divine grace is in fact absent, any human project (and thus, any artistic or poetic project) is bound to be fundamentally worthless. One of the dichotomies that Sidney explores in his sequence is the one between the *intellectus* (the capacity for abstract reason) and desire, in which the former tries to assert itself over the latter, only to find itself defeated in the attempt. On many occasions, the resolution of that conflict takes place at the end of the sonnets, in an abrupt movement from idealisation to reality that either seems to close off the debate permanently or to complicate the possibility of ever finding a solution (for instance, in sonnets 18, 19, 21, 47, 72). Let us take, for instance, the endings of only the first and the last of these examples:

> I see my course to lose my selfe doth bend:
> I see and yet no greater sorrow take,
> Then that I lose no more for *Stella*'s sake. (18.12–14)

> But thou Desire, because thou wouldst have all,
> Now banisht art, but yet alas how shall? (72.13–14)

These endings operate under the sign of irony, with the couplet contradicting the ostensible thrust of the quatrains, and remain very far from an idea of identification between speaker and reader. Still, it is true that the concept of humanity that underlies Sidney's collection is far more pessimistic than the one predominant in his European predecessors. For Astrophil, sin is a force that is always at work inside him, one of the basic elements that constitute his humanity and that inform the use that he makes of his poetic gifts. It is only logical, then, that the narrative structure of Sidney's sequence should be circular: at the end, Astrophil's desires and aspirations for preferment are exactly the same as they were at the beginning, and his wrongheaded attempts to find an efficient grace have exerted no significant influence on them. The fact that Sidney may have been originally writing his sonnets for the purpose of praising and/or amusing Lady Penelope Rich, or perhaps even at her direct request, does not prevent the sequence from being, on one of its many levels of signification, a serious investigation into the dangerous overlapping of sacred and secular forms of grace.[12]

Fulke Greville as Cultural Critic

The lexical item 'grace' was, as stated above, at the centre of a series of social and doctrinal tensions that informed the development of English Protestantism at the end of the sixteenth century. These tensions prevented the Church of England from reaching a complete unification of doctrine at that point in time, or attaining a full unity of religious practice across Britain.[13] The various forms of continuity with the Catholic world were seen with a watchful eye by the Church authorities, and yet they were still present, sometimes involving a return to full Roman practice (especially in areas controlled by Catholic aristocrats). The possibility of a return to iconophilia among common believers was always perceived as an ongoing threat to Protestant belief; and the confidence in *sola gratia*, with the exclusion of good works, was always poorly understood by wide sectors of the population, who adhered consciously or unconsciously to Catholic beliefs and practice in this.[14] On the other hand, there were always controversies concerning the correct uses of prayer, and the possibilities of reaching personally for grace; some forms of popular and private devotion might seem to contradict the very precepts of absolute trust in providence that reformed belief demanded.[15] All of these tensions were echoed, in one way or another, in the language of secular poetry, but it was only in the work of Fulke Greville that they were consciously and strenuously discussed, taking human love as a space in which they manifested themselves more openly, and offering a valid instance of how they might be finally solved, not by any intellectual synthesis, but by religious faith.[16]

Far more than the other sonnet writers, Fulke Greville assumes the role not only of a poet, but of a serious cultural critic through his poetic practice.[17] Greville often requires a self-conscious reader, one who is able to evaluate the text as a poetic performance and at the same time to cast a critical eye on it and judge it on moral and religious grounds. Quite often, what matters in his sequence (or perhaps his compilation) *Caelica* is not so much poetic form, but the critique of that form; not the rhetoric and figural language of Petrarchism, but the exploration of the discontents in that language. This is why Greville reads as the most consciously belated of the Elizabethan sonneteers.[18] He carries the topics of the *religio amoris* to their limits, and by doing so empties them of their previous significance and opens them to a distanced reading; he does away with the secular religion of love and makes room for a serious ethical and religious perspective. In the sections dedicated to love in *Caelica*, Greville is constantly building defences against the reader's identification with the speaker: either his language is deliberately parodic, or the situational patterns that are presented become distorted versions of those offered by the previous tradition. These strategies act as fail-safes that lead the reader away from a serious consideration of the troubles of human love. And, as a result, the perspective is reoriented towards a detached critical position, sustained on religious grounds.

In *Caelica* 69, for instance, the paradoxical patterns of Petrarchism are put to the service of a representation of deep moral uncertainty. This uncertainty goes beyond the doubt of a lover in the Petrarchan mindset; it mirrors that state closely, but at the same time it projects itself to another level:

> When Loue doth change his seat from heart to heart,
> And worth about the wheele of Fortune goes,
> *Grace* is diseas'd, desert seemes ouerthwart,
> Vowes are forlorne, and truth doth credit lose,
> . . .
> My age of ioy is past, of woe begunne,
> Absence my presence is, strangeness my *grace*,
> With them that walke against me, is my Sunne:
> The wheele is turn'd, I hold the lowest place. (69.7–10, 13–16, emphases added)[19]

There is one sense in which the clause 'grace is diseas'd' suggests the loss of favour, or the loss of preference, in front of the beloved or of a courtly or political space – a use of the term that is almost social rather than sentimental. But there is another sense, also present here and coexisting with the former one, in which the reading of the poem broadens. To experience a situation in which grace is perceived as 'diseas'd' is not unlike crossing the valley of death, in the words of Psalm 23;[20] it may mirror, very precisely, the moment of confusion in which the Protestant subject finds himself, or herself, confronting the absence of God. When 'grace' becomes 'strangeness', the whole world of the subject is turned upside down; and it must be remembered that the notion of 'strangeness', the topic of the strange and unpredictable ways of God, is one of the key topics of Lutheran theology that was readapted into English Protestantism. The thin line or the thin transition between the secular and the sacred worlds is part and parcel of the strong tension in the poem. It is by playing both hands, or by bringing both possibilities close together, that Greville explores critically the parallels between one position and the other.

In theological terms, and in the area of personal prayer, the attempts to persuade or to coerce God into granting grace were sometimes presented as proof of the subject's sincerity, and sometimes of a mistaken conception of worship. Prayer in the late Elizabethan and early Jacobean periods could often appear as a dramatic and tense situation, one in which personal subjectivity was led into an active confrontation with a silent and apparently non-responding God. In such a situation, the insistence of the worshipper might appear to be justified, or an excessive insistence might seem almost inevitable. The pastor and theologian Daniel Featley commented in 1626 on the imprudence of those who might become importunate in the search for God's approval: there are those who 'cast vp Prayers with strong lines to heauen, as it were (by force) to pul down a blessing from thence; somtimes they expostulate with *God* in a sawcie, and sometimes pose him in a ridiculous manner'.[21] This is precisely the wrongheadedness that Greville attributes to his speakers at many points in *Caelica*. Their excessive insistence is proof of their determination, but also of their incapacity to understand the nature of love and of its demands, and the kind of confidence that it requires on the part of the loving subject.

The great danger here is that of *iconophilia*: the tendency to turn human love into the worship of an idol, an idea that Greville's sequence explores again and again to the point of obsession. Greville speaks of this danger as being placed in the heart of Christianity itself, as a constant temptation that is permanently rooted in human intelligence, and that can threaten it at any moment. In his perspective, even the Cross has been historically an idol, which has been left behind in the perspective of a 'clearer faith':

> The *Manicheans* did not Idols make,
> Without themselues, nor worship gods of Wood,
> Yet Idolls did in their *Ideas* take,
> And figur'd *Christ* as on the crosse he stood.
> Thus did they when they earnestly did pray,
> Till clearer Faith this Idoll tooke away. (89.1–6)

Greville identifies the tendency to use icons in worship, to transfer the human need for grace to a purely physical vessel, as belonging to a phase in early Christian history, before a 'clearer Faith' (brought about by the Reformation) could modify and improve the forms of worship. What is more specifically Grevillean, however, is his identification of tendencies in human love that inevitably reflect or reproduce, at the level of subjective experience, these same phases. In another poem, the speaker Myraphil thinks that he sees grace itself, inscribed in the face of his beloved:

> Then he thought that in her face,
> He saw Loue, and promis'd *Grace*.
> Loue calls his Loue to appeare,
> But as soone as it came neere,
> Her Loue to her bosome fled,
> Under Honours burdens dead.
> Honour in Loues stead tooke place,
> To *grace* Shame, with Loues *disgrace*;
> Desire looks, and, in her eyes,
> The image of it selfe espies . . . (74.35–44, emphases added)

Myraphil sees a 'promis'd Grace' in Myra's face; a sense of assurance, or of the imminent fulfilment of a promise (a promise made by whom, ensured by whom?) that is soon transformed into dissimulation, because of the demands of social etiquette. As an immediate consequence, shame is 'grace[d]' (preferred, favoured) by honour, and desire can only lead to to a final self-deception for Myraphil, in the moment when it takes the image of itself, seen in her eyes, as if it were her 'owne deuotions' (74.46), while fear stops his tongue from speaking. The reader recognises this moment as the fatal mistake of narcissism, when the lover sees in the beloved only a reflection of his own wishes. And narcissism here connotes death: a spiritual death that leaves the lover unable to transcend the mutable, untrustworthy world of appearances, and condemns him to remain in it in a state in perpetual mutability, just as Narcissus was turned into a flower on the shore of a lake.

In the final analysis, Greville's *Caelica* reaches an absolute paradox, almost an *aporia*: his secular production reaches a dead end in which the topos of physical beauty and the mindset of the Petrarchan tradition have to be discarded. There can be no final assertion of a purely poetic aesthetics: in fact, this same aesthetics has been used all through *Caelica*, in order to be finally left behind in favour of the affirmation of divine grace, which can neither be accommodated nor integrated outside of a sacred perspective. To put it in Sidneian terms, the 'erected wit' of the poet can only be asserted in a radical rejection of the 'infected will' that Italianate poetry has too abundantly promoted.[22] It is between the radical assertion of transcendent grace and the rigorous questioning of any possible secular poetics that Greville's act of cultural criticism remains poised.

Edmund Spenser and the Varieties of Courtly Grace

Edmund Spenser's *The Faerie Queene* can be seen as offering a wide repertoire, or even a thesaurus, of the multiple meanings of 'grace' in late sixteenth-century poetry: here the exploration of the term and of its connotations can even be seen as one of the many recurring guidelines in the poem's intricate and proliferative plot. The allegorical narrative makes different aspects of each concept enter into a conflict with one another, both at the level of the action and at the level of its emblematic significance; in doing so, it dramatises endlessly the ambiguity of the term. In this poem, grace can adorn both the rich and the poor, it can cut across conventional distinctions of good and evil, and every time the word is mentioned it brings different and new connotations into play, depending on the contexts where it occurs.

The term can also operate across gender differences, with surprising results. This occurs at the beginning of Book III, when Redcross and Britomart are welcomed into Malecasta's inner rooms; they sit down to dinner in the hall, and Britomart removes her helmet, immediately gaining the attention of everyone around her (and it must be remembered that no one knows, at this point, that she is a woman):

> For shee was full of amiable *grace*,
> And manly terror mixed therewithall,
> That as the one stird vp affections bace,
> So th'other did mens rash desires appall,
> And hole them backe, that would in errour fall. (III.1.46.1–5, emphasis added)

The 'amiable grace' in Britomart's countenance can 'stir vp affections bace', appealing to the *vis sensitiva* of the viewer and putting in motion the mechanism of bodily desire; exactly at this point, however, the 'manly terror' she also provokes acts as a counter-effect or a safety device against this surge. If physical grace can stir up lust, fear can then counteract it; just as a physical response is elicited by one factor, the contrary one is also brought into play; both have to coexist for order to be maintained. We know, however, that this does not work for Malecasta:

> Whom when the Lady saw so faire a wight,
> All ignorant of her contrary sex,
> (For shee her weend a freash and lusty knight),
> She greatly gan enamoured to wex,
> And with vaine thoughts her falsed fancy vex. (III.1.47.1–5)

Far from being deterred by fear, Malecasta feels bodily drawn ('enamoured') towards Britomart, which will bring later on a near-lesbian scene, just before Britomart understands what her enemy wants to do with her. A physical 'grace' has almost brought about the moral corruption of its possessor, and will in fact lead her to lose her first blood in the adventure; left to itself, and occurring by itself in a fallen world that is dominated by physical desire, it is not sufficient to guarantee the welfare of its owner.

There is, therefore, an unavoidable quality of uncertainty and unpredictability about the very concept of grace, in any of its fields of signification. Grace cannot be distributed or regimented according to individual desire, either in spiritual, political or diplomatic terms. The capacity to obtain or to develop grace, in all of these fields, does not imply a capacity to measure it, to command it, preserve it or keep it. In purely courtly terms, it can define the elegance and poise that were displayed by a worthy and self-conscious gentleman – who ultimately should, as Hoby's translation of Castiglione's *Cortegiano* put it, be 'a noble progeynie',

> yf he be helped forwarde with the instructions, bringinge vp, and art of the Courtier, whom these Lordes haue fashioned so wise and good, he shall be moste wise, moste continent, moste temperate, moste manlye, and moste iuste, full of liberalitie, maiestie, holynesse, and mercye . . .[23]

And yet, ultimately, these qualities cannot depend exclusively on the will and ambition of the subject who aspired to them. Castiglione had insisted repeatedly on the innate (and therefore unmerited) disposition of the good courtiers towards the full development of their capacities. Courtesy books of Italian, French or English origin concentrated on the service to the commonwealth and the achievement of personal virtue by selected individuals, but that achievement had to be seen as the ultimate outcome of an innate predisposition that could not be caused only by the individual himself. As Pierre de La Primadauye put it in his *French Academie*, translated to English in 1586:

> And truely, the reason of man, naturally ingraffed in his hart, which so farre foorth as he is man, and according to his habilitie and maner of life he imitateth and followeth, is diuers from that which by special grace from aboue commeth to the elect, accompanieth them, and helpeth them in all their actions.[24]

The members of La Primadauye's academy of courtiers must acknowledge the difference between, on the one hand, the achievement of their intellect and personal will and, on the other, the unmerited grace that has made them 'elect' and most fit for their social position. It is only the latter that can ultimately lead them to achieve true and complete courtesy; conversely, only those who admit their human limitations can ever hope to be blessed with the capacity ('which by special grace commeth to the elect') to overcome them. Paradoxically, then, divine grace becomes a requisite for the achievement of secular, courtly grace.

But the decorum and poise that this sophisticated grace implies cannot eliminate or attenuate other aspects that complement it, and that might be less immediately palatable. On the contrary, the delicacy of the elected courtier knight can often appear to be displaced by other forces or impulses that might be required in the complex arenas of politics, religious dispute or war. And just as the very inspiration of courtly grace cannot be interpreted or motivated on purely human grounds, so the aggressive or hostile impulses of the characters who embody it can often respond to concepts of justice that operate beyond purely rational calculation.

An apparent absence of courtly grace in the field of war might thus correspond to a deeper and more transcendent grace; and the poem need not justify one in terms of the other, but may simply point to this apparent contradiction in terms that can, once again, make it deeply productive. Let us consider briefly the warlike behaviour of Britomart, whom we have just seen presented as an epitome of 'amiable grace' in her first courtly appearance. It will not do to consider the historical figure of Elizabeth I as the ultimate reference in the reading of this character's actions: the complexity of the poem does not allow for such simplifications, and recent critical developments seem to point precisely in the contrary direction, underlining the relative autonomy of the text.[25] Let us take the final confrontation between Britomart and the amazon Radigund as a case example. The possibility of grace as political pardon is conspicuously absent there, substituted by a resolute violence that seems even stronger because it is practised by two female representatives of opposite political orders (a patriarchy and a matriarchy/ *amazon*archy, respectively):

> [Where being layd,] the wrothful Britonesse
> Stayd not, till she came to her selfe againe,
> But in reuenge both of her loues distresse,
> And her late vile reproch, though vaunted vaine,
> And also of her wound, which sore did paine,
> She with one stroke both head and helmet cleft. (V.7.34.1–6)

The execution is brought about by Britomart as a triple revenge (for her wounds, for the kidnapped Artegall, for the reproaches made by Radigund against her), carried out on the spur of the moment and in the heat of a battle.[26] The obvious lack of grace (understood as pardon) does not appear here as the result of any political decision; and yet it is inevitable that this beheading of one woman by another, which brings about the recuperation of a kingdom, would call to the mind of a 1595 reader the execution of Mary, Queen of Scots, by Elizabeth, a famous historical instance of the cancellation of grace as pardon.[27] The poem does not openly identify one situation with the other, there is no direct and absolute correspondence between history and text here; and yet the text is gesturing towards history, here and throughout, suggesting parallelisms and connections, but leaving it to the reader to decide to what extent they actually apply. The operations of grace (either political or poetic) are not dogmatically established from outside the poem and projected within it; on the contrary, they are transferred to the understanding and the interpretative decisions of the reader as he or she moves through the textual patterns of the poem.[28]

Reflections and Refractions of Grace in Aemilia Lanyer

The many paradoxes at the heart of the concept of grace could also be harnessed poetically to strategies of self-justification, self-canonisation or literary promotion, especially in authors who faced particular difficulties because of predominant gender discourses.

The main example here can be found in Aemilia Lanyer, and more specifically in her fascinating poem on the Passion of Christ, *Salve Deus Rex Judaeorum* (1611): a poem that, both in itself and in its many paratexts and dedications, testifies to the existence of a complex and active network of influence and patronage among cultured women in the late Elizabethan and early Jacobean contexts. The poem itself showcases a suggestive continuity between Catholic and Protestant traditions, in which the imagery and iconography of the Passion is harnessed to a set of reformed connotations, and to an essentially Lutheran theology of redemption. Religious and literary discourses coalesce here, intertwining in favour of the self-representation of the poet.

In the passages of the poem containing Lanyer's address to the Countess of Cumberland (145–264),[29] the term 'grace' becomes a major keyword, in a carefully structured strategy that is endowed both with theological significance and political strength. After a recollection of great women whose beauty was unaccompanied by virtue, Lanyer shifts her direction and concentrates on the figure of Matilda de Brionne, who (according to legend) was sexually harassed by King John. Paradoxically, Matilda's suicide was the result of her acceptance of God's grace, sent to her and accepted by her in her moment of despair:

> By heavenly *grace*, she had such true direction,
> To die with Honour, not to live in Shame,
> And drinke that poison with a cheerful heart,
> That could all Heavenly *grace* to her impart. (245–8, emphases added)

The Countess is immediately compared to Matilda as a receiver of grace, in terms that make it clear that she is the passive recipient of it, not the active subject controlling it: on the contrary, that force ('Grace') 'possesses thy Soule', and 'all imperfect Thoughts controule / Directing thee to serve thy God aright' (249–52). Possession, control, external direction: all of these terms are specifically chosen so as to reduce the action of the will and its capacity for self-determination. Where does that overwhelming force come from? What is its source for the Christian? In good Protestant fashion, Lanyer asserts that it can come only from the Cross, where human salvation was obtained through the death of Christ. And at this critical point her lines seem to compress themselves, in order to make room for an accumulation (*copia*) of facts and objects that physically caused the death of the Saviour:

> The Speare, Sponge, Nailes, his buffeting with Fists,
> His bitter Passion, Agony, and Death,
> Did gaine us Heaven when He did loose his breath.
>
> These high deserts invites my lowely Muse
> To write of Him, and pardon crave of thee;
> For Time so spent, I need make no excuse,
> Knowing it doth with thy faire Minde agree . . . (262–8)

The density of lines 262–4 involves a self-conscious thematic anticipation of the subsequent treatment of the Passion in *Salve Deus*. But already at this point, before entering into her main subject, the poet has begun to establish herself as the adequate author for such lofty matter. The vindication of her work is based on a subtle system of continuities: Matilda's heroism was inspired by grace, the same grace that possesses the Countess of Cumberland, and which was obtained through the struggle and suffering of Christ on the Cross; this latter aspect is, at the same time, the subject of the whole poem (proleptically anticipated in the lines above) and the very cause and reason for its composition.

This interaction between the passive and active aspects of the reception of grace is carried to the limit in Lanyer's later, and bolder, justification of her *auctoritas*. Before entering the description of the Passion, and in a traditional gesture of apparent *humilitas*, the poet asks for divine inspiration. In doing so, however, she is careful to place the notion of 'merit' in its adequate place in the theology of the Cross:

> But to present this pure unspotted Lambe,
> I must confesse, I farre unworthy am.
>
> Yet if he please t'illuminate my Spirit,
> And give me Wisdom from his holy Hill,
> That I may write part of his glorious Merit,
> If he vouchsafe to guide my Hand and Quill,
> To shew his Death by which we doe inherit
> Those endlesse Joyes that all our hearts doe fill. (319–26)

The hill of Golgotha, where humanity's salvation was obtained, is the place whence illumination must come to the speaker, overcoming any sense of unworthiness that she might have. The poet's quill and hand will be guided by a force outside herself; she will be filled by it in her writing, just as the Countess of Cumberland has been filled by it in her life; any 'merit' that there mght be in her work (as any merit that both men and women might lay claim to) is to be found not in herself, but only in the grace that animates her.

The various paratexts and dedications with which Lanyer surrounds her poem offer similar patterns of refracted and reflected grace. The lengthy description of the dream in which Lanyer's destiny as a poet was revealed to her ('The Authors Dreame') ends with a dedication to Mary Sidney, Countess of Pembroke.[30] On this occasion, different 'graces' seem to come from different sources: on the one hand, the favour that Mary Sidney might bestow on the work; on the other, the worthiness of the subject, which in itself is enough to fill each of the poet's lines:

And Madame, if you will vouchsafe that *grace*,
To *grace* those flowers that springs from virtues ground . . .

Yet it is no disparagement to you,
To see your Saviour in a Sheapheards weed,
Unworthily presented in your viewe,
Whose worthinesse will *grace* each line you reade. ('The Authors Dreame', 213–14, 217–20, emphases mine)

The Countess's 'grace' favours the virtuous flowers (or poems) that Lanyer offers to her; but these are animated from within by their subject matter, whose immaculate virtue fills and 'graces', in its turn, the lines.[31] All personal merit seems elided by the poet; the value of her work is indisputably asserted, however, on the grounds of a merit that is extrinsic to herself. The problem of her *auctoritas* is thus simultaneously confronted and evaded; it is asserted inasmuch as it proceeds from outside herself, both at a political level (Mary Sidney) and at a spiritual one (Christ). The concept of grace is thus made to work in the contested area of gender politics and female authorship, establishing a network of signification within which the poet can ensure a firm and unassailable position. Religious discourse and poetic strategy can thus coalesce seamlessly in offering to the author a *solid* locus, a site from which she can proceed to write and offer her work to the public.

Grace and Poetic Worth: A Provisional Conclusion

Lanyer's poetics of grace manages to secure for the speaker a position from which she can speak, and from which the worth of her performance can be asserted. It is possible to perceive in this gesture a firm step towards a manageable *via media*, removing her both from Greville's relentless doubt about the worth of poetic performance and from Spenser's and Sidney's ambiguities about the role of grace in poetics: the rich exploration of forms of self-contradiction in Sidney, and the dense and multi-sided approach to what constitutes courtly grace in Spenser. In both of these latter authors, the assertion of the poem's worth inevitably involves a hint of doubt that is connected to the very nature of the 'grace' they seek to claim or to describe: this occurs because, in the final perspective, the poetic uses of the lexical item grace cannot be entirely disentangled from its political uses, just as these political uses cannot be wholly dissociated from its theological meanings. There is always a sense of slippage from one use of the term towards another, a difficulty in closing and restricting the chain of significations that is attached to it. But that difficulty corresponds precisely to its signifying force, its capacity to activate contrasting connotations in any given context.

Therefore, the term 'grace' cannot be entirely contained or foreclosed by any poetic system, just as it can never be completely apprehended intellectually; and yet the speakers in the poems that have been brought here as examples rely on it, depend on it, implore it, in order to assert the validity of their performance. Who, in the end, justifies by grace? Who makes the poem worthy by granting it? Is it God, the queen or king, the judicial system, the beloved lady, a network of male or female patrons? Is it each of these differently, in different circumstances and to different degrees? Or is it none of them specifically, but the very belief or need (or belief *and* need) of the poetic speaker who invokes it on every new occasion? The origin and the work of grace can never be fully apprehended or systematised, either in religious or in secular poetics: it allows itself only to be temporarily glimpsed, like the classical Graces in the vision of Calidore in *The Faerie Queene*, as it distributes its gifts and its goods to the few who have been chosen (all too mysteriously, all too arbitrarily) as worthy of receiving them.

Notes

1. All references to this poem are from Spenser, *The Faerie Queene*, ed. Hamilton et al., and are cited parenthetically by canto, book, stanza and line numbers.
2. For an illustrative reading of, among other grace-related issues, contrastive adaptations of the Lady/Saint topic in English Protestant and

Catholic settings, see Pérez-Jáuregui, 'From Favour to Eternal Life', this volume.
3. On the subject of cultural belatedness – a concept adapted from Harold Bloom's theory of the anxiety of influence – in sixteenth-century poetry, see Navarrete, *Orphans of Petrarch*, 3–15.
4. Further examples can be found in the present volume: the different approaches to grace taken by Barnabe Barnes and by the Catholic convert Henry Constable are richly explored in relation to their parallel poetic careers by Pérez-Jáuregui, 'From Favour to Eternal Life'.
5. Unless otherwise noted, all references to *Astrophil and Stella* are from Sidney, *Poems*, ed. Ringler, 163–267. Sonnet and line numbers from this edition are cited parenthetically in the text. The word 'Song' precedes the citation of songs from this work.
6. These words, from the Preface to the 1591 edition of *Astrophil and Stella*, are cited from Nashe, *Works*, ed. McKerrow, 3:329.
7. On the complex social and political mediations occurring in Sidney's sequence, see especially Marotti, 'Love is Not Love'.
8. Notice that the second 'grace' in this line is the reading of the 1598 edition of the sequence, which appeared with *The Countesse of Pembrokes Arcadia* (London, 1598). Ringler prefers to edit 'skill', and registers 'grace' in his list of variant readings (Sidney, *Poems*, 192).
9. On the subject of inexpressibility in Sidney's sonnets, see especially Miller, 'What Words May Say'.
10. Calvin, *Institutes*, II.3.1, 1:336.
11. On this specific aspect, as connected to Sidney's *Defence*, see the classic study by Weiner, *Sir Philip Sidney and the Poetics of Protestantism*, 28–50.
12. On the possible role of the sonnets as entertainment for Penelope Devereux-Rich, and on her relationship with Sidney, see Duncan-Jones, *Sir Philip Sidney*, 242–50.
13. In relation to this lack of doctrinal unity by the end of the sixteenth century, see especially Haigh, *English Reformations*, 275–85.
14. This survival of Catholic forms of belief, either in organised forms or in simple allegiance to old practice, is reviewed extensively in Dures, *English Catholicism 1558–1642*, and Pritchard, *Catholic Loyalism in Elizabethan England*. For the interplay of Catholic and Protestant meanings of grace, see Perez-Jáuregui, 'From Favour to Eternal Life', this volume.
15. See the extended and detailed study by Ryrie on the varieties of prayer, *Being Protestant*, esp. 200–38.
16. For a suggestive interpretation of Greville's perspectives on poetry, quite different from the one I offer here, but well-sustained and which takes his whole career into account, see McLean, 'Fulke Greville and the Poetic of the Plain Style'.
17. The role of difficulty and of a 'worthy' sense of complexity in some of Greville's other works, which is fully compatible with his critical

and intellectual position as I attempt to outline it here, is explored by Knight, 'The Worthy Knots of Fulke Greville', this volume.
18. The question of Greville's various attitudes to lyrical poetry and of the value he attributed to it is explored in detail in what remains the best biographical approach to his figure: Rees, *Fulke Greville*.
19. All references to *Caelica* are from Greville, *Poems and Dramas*, ed. Bullough, 1:73–153. Poem and line numbers are cited parenthetically in the text.
20. 'Yea, though I shulde walke through the valley of the shadow of death, I will feare no euil' (*Psalmes*, 23.4, in *Bible*, sig. Oo3v).
21. Featley, *Ancilla pietatis*, sig. B10v.
22. Sidney, *Defence*, in *Miscellaneous Prose*, ed. Duncan-Jones and van Dorsten, 79.
23. Castiglione, *The Courtyer*, trans. Hoby, sig. Pp1v.
24. Primadauye, *French Academie*, sig. B8v.
25. See, for instance, the reading of the 1590 parts of the poem offered by Goldberg, *The Seeds of Things*, 63–121.
26. The presence of a stronger violence and a return to assertive action throughout Book V of *The Faerie Queene* (which would include the resolution of this specific episode) have often been observed by critics; see, for instance, Sanchez, *Erotic Subjects*, 57–86.
27. A close parallelism between this episode and the relationship between Mary Stuart and Elizabeth I is traced by Stump, 'Two Deaths of Mary Stuart'.
28. For an interpretation of the signifying process offered by the poem that bases all of its operations in the external authority of Elizabeth I, and which is in fact the reverse of the one I propose here, see Greenblatt, *Renaissance Self-Fashioning*, 165–72.
29. Lanyer, *Salve Deus*, in *Poems*, ed. Woods, 57–62. All references to this poem are from this edition, and are cited parenthetically by line number in the text.
30. Lanyer, 'The Authors Dreame to the Ladie *Marie*, The Countesse Dowager of *Pembrooke*', in *Poems*, 21–31. MacBride has seen a strategy of replacement in this dedication, in which Lanyer would be going so far as to actively propose herself as a substitute Mary Sidney as a poet: 'Praise has turned to eulogy and Mary Sidney is a corpse/corpus, a fixed and finished work, a closed book, whose silencing creates the space in which Lanyer can speak' ('Remembering Orpheus', 97).
31. Benson has cleverly observed the way in which Mary Sidney's authority makes room for Lanyer's own in this poem, but without going into the religious connotations of this operation: 'The focus simply shifts to Lanyer's poetry, its quality ... Without disparaging Sidney's works, Lanyer shows the value of her own' ('The Stigma of Italy Undone', 162–3).

Chapter 2

The Logical Cause of an Early Modern Poetics of Action
Emma Annette Wilson

One of the unwritten arts underpinning sixteenth-century poetics was logic. This was the subject that gave substance, form and, crucially for this chapter, causation and agency to the world and all of its beings and entities; but without becoming acquainted with its technical apparatus, its operations are easily overlooked by modern readers. That technical apparatus was so ingrained in early modern readers and writers that it was almost automatic; it was the lens through which, since their schooldays, people were taught to analyse or to 'read', and subsequently write, the world and everything in it. I say almost automatic because there is manuscript evidence of people such as Andrew Marvell's preacher father specifically marking up his writing with analytical terms from logic textbooks, and that kind of trace evidence allows us, all too briefly, to inhabit a mindset which understood the world in terms of its logical properties and their work.[1] Early modern logicians recognised the potency of their art: repeatedly referred to as the *ars artium*, or 'art of arts', the instrument responsible for directing the mind and thoughts effectively and for finding ideas, its principles provided the foundation for all forms of eloquence and expression, but as so often happens with truly fundamental things, such as cells, micro-organisms, nerve synapses and so on, if you do not know what to look for, its elemental work goes undetected.[2]

The challenge of teaching fundamental principles was one familiar to sixteenth-century logicians: their textbooks are characterised by a flurry of innovations aimed at enhancing pedagogy, from compact digests of key principles and vernacular manuals to explorations in visual learning such as the famous branching diagrams (usually referred to as Ramistic, but in fact found in reforming logic textbooks across the pedagogical and confessional spectrum), printed Porphyrian trees, and experiments with different colours of ink to aid with memorisation.[3] In a period of heady reforms reorienting this subject at the heart of the *trivium* from a descriptive art to an art that could change the world through its actions, one of the key features used by logicians to teach their art was the poetic example. These were perhaps most famously called upon by reforming logician and pedagogue Petrus Ramus and his legions of followers, imitators, adaptors and even some competitors in the sixteenth and seventeenth centuries; but earlier work by Rudolph Agricola and Philip Melanchthon also found poetry useful as a means of explaining and illustrating logical principles.[4] In the context of this volume, we are pursuing the ways in which these 'silent' arts affect, inflect, some might say infect, and shape and drive poetry and poetic innovation in the early modern period. If logicians were interested in poetry, which they certainly were, this chapter asks how, in turn, poets were interested in and used logic.

In his vernacular manual called the *Lawyers' Logike* in 1588, Abraham Fraunce included both the Latin text and his own English hexameter translation of Virgil's Second Eclogue; he then presented a synthetic tree diagram analysis of the logic at work within the eclogue.[5] Fraunce claimed to have based his analysis on the work of Ramus's disciple, Johann Thomas Freige, although no direct source has been identified to date, and Zenón Luis-Martínez has convincingly demonstrated specific points of contact linking Fraunce's analysis with Ramus's own (non-tabulated) logical examination of Virgil's text in his 1555 *Bucolica, praelectionibus exposita*.[6] The tables in *The Lawyers' Logike* divide the Eclogue into two parts: the argument 'of the incontinency of a lover lamenting his love in solitary places' and 'the complaint and lamentation of Corydon the lover'.[7] In the analysis of Corydon's complaint, Fraunce (and by extension, Freige and Ramus) identifies the lover as 'speaking' – this is a tiny point in the context of extensive unfurling tables detailing Corydon's adjuncts, his qualities and the logical functions which inform us about these things. But it is crucial that all of this information, this substance, depends upon an action: it leans upon a cause, which is Corydon himself 'speaking'. In these diagrams, a logician uses poetry to demonstrate the principles of its unwritten art at work; poetry is transmuted into a branching tree of adjuncts, logical comparisons, qualities, contraries and corrections, and suddenly, through a poetic work which was itself a touchstone of the sixteenth-century classroom, logic itself floats up to the surface of conscious thought. It is revealed as the substrate sustaining and enabling the poetic vision, and when logic emerges as a life-giving force in poetry, we can begin to think not only about how poetry was helpful in teaching logic, but also how poets found logic to be one of the unwritten arts necessary for them to achieve their aesthetic visions.

This chapter reads sixteenth-century poetry in light of the principles of logicians, acting in effect as a twenty-first-century version of the Ramistic synthetic tree analysis of Virgil's eclogues. But in doing so it reveals the ways in which sixteenth-century poets used logic to inject a new kind of agency into their poetry. This agency has its roots in the reorientation of discursive logic in the sixteenth century which resulted in the prioritisation of personal ability, responsibility and accountability, and poetic form played a key role in generating distinctive, individualistic voices capable of creating and sustaining complex and multifaceted arguments by both fictional characters and narrative personae in verse.[8] Logic might seem like a stultifying, fundamentally unpoetic art, but reforms in this period led to its transformation into something dynamic, invested in finding and leveraging agency and possibility. It is that poetics of agency and possibility which we can recover when we learn to read sixteenth-century poetry through the lens of logic as one of its unwritten arts.

Reforming the Unwritten Art of Logic

When Petrus Ramus reoriented discursive logic in the sixteenth century, he did so by putting logical 'cause' front and centre. In a call to action (literally), the first technical logical operation which his textbooks and those of his followers explained is 'cause', insisting upon the necessity of knowing who or what is making things happen: what is the root of the root and the bud of the bud of a branch called Ramus? This decision marks a clear break from Aristotelian logic texts in the period: these perennially began by taking their readers through the descriptive operations of logic (predicaments, definitions, places, etc.), only later considering active functions such as cause, which make these things come to life. In other words, Aristotelianism can be characterised as a logic of stasis, in comparison with a Ramist logic of dynamism.[9]

The focus on cause represents not only a reordering of a standard set of principles but rather a change in worldview: a Ramist world is one predicated upon a person's ability to take action, to *cause* change, as opposed to describing a static universe and accepting his or her fate.

This chapter examines the ramifications of this reorientation towards cause for writers, whether of prose, poetry or drama, in late sixteenth-century England, tracing the evolution of the principles of logical cause in discourse manuals from early innovations by Agricola to the widely adopted reforms of Melanchthon and Ramus, and Thomas Wilson's English vernacular interpretation of this emerging culture of logical analysis and creation. Training in logic was the keystone of the *trivium*, and all writers working in the period learned their craft through studying a range of these textbooks. I refer to it as an 'invisible art', because it has no inherent vocabulary which must be present in order for its force to be at work in a piece of writing; it is an art concerned with identifying and characterising activity and passivity, cause and effect, and those might be declared in an almost infinite number of ways using an almost infinite combination of words. However, this is not to say it is undetectable: it certainly was detectable to sixteenth-century writers and readers versed in its methods, and we can likewise see it at work in their poetry if we follow in their footsteps to make connections between the discursive principles set forth in pedagogical works from the period and the ways in which writers put those ideas to use in creative contexts. We are familiar with noticing particular word orders and constructions to identify particular kinds of rhetorical technique in sixteenth-century verse: the opening 'O' of an *exclamatio*, or the symmetry of a chiasmus. This chapter explores how similar markings indicate particular types of logical activity being used by a writer in a poetic passage, aiming to make this art which would otherwise remain invisible to us visible, and to help us understand how its methods were used by poets in this period to generate meaning.

For poets, having an art purposefully designed to inject and emphasise agency and dynamic change enabled a new kind of poetics of activity and potentiality, which this chapter explores. Cause plays a key role in showing agency and motive on the part of both the speaker(s) in a poem and also the writer, and the chapter concludes by witnessing this culture of logical causation and invention in specific poems by Edmund Spenser, Philip Sidney and Christopher Marlowe. As the 'art of arts', logic is potentially detectable in any poetry from this time period, but these texts were chosen because, as love complaints, they represent a genre which is by its very nature invested in identifying and decrying agency and blame. 'It's not me, it's you' is the core refrain of all three poems, and because each writer puts questions of agency and causation in the foreground of these texts, they offer an instructive way for us to start acquaintance with logic and its cues in various modes.

While logic is ubiquitous in sixteenth-century writing and its tuition, that is not to say that all writers were simply implementing a preordained schema to produce identical results. All Renaissance logic texts teach the four causes – efficient, matter, form and end – but their order and emphasis represent very different philosophies and consequently theories of discourse. The result is a practical poetics of action, shown here through several representative examples that witness the causal reorientation taking place at this time, as a theoretical prioritising of dynamic action manifests in a poetics of agency and possibility. As is demonstrated many times over in this volume, the unwritten arts of poetry – its logic, its conscious eloquence *and* ineloquence, imitation, inspiration, grace and physiology – are constitutive of poetic praxis, rather than official poetics. The rules for this practical poetics are unwritten in textbooks about poetry itself from the period, appearing rather, in this instance, in logic books; sixteenth-century poets harnessed this different, arguably inherently unpoetic, apparatus to create a potent form of dynamic poetic praxis.[10]

Early Reforms

Before Ramus reoriented logic in the sixteenth century, in 1485 Rudolph Agricola set a new, dynamic standard for the process of invention in his *De inventione dialecticae*.[11] In Agricola's logical invention, matter and form are grouped beneath ideas of definition and description that are in and of themselves fundamentally static processes: the loci of *genus* and *species* capture the world in a photograph or at least a woodcut, freezing its players and places in names and characteristics. The activity of definition and description is inherently an attempt to see and to arrest a world of things rather than a world of actions and motions. However, there is a more active relationship at work between matter and form in Agricolan invention: matter might sound like a load of inactive 'stuff', but in Agricola's treatise we have a matter that empowers *generatur primum*, 'first generation' or 'first creation' (sig. 19r). This matter might not be active in and of itself, but it has the latent potential to enable the first, fundamental step of creation, and that ability endows it with a philosophical power and energy that belong to a world in motion. Form, too, might lack its own active creative capacity, but it holds the key for the world of things, for all of that matter, to take on specific identities and qualities and through these to lay claim to particular names (sig. 19r): *forma, est modus quidam materiae, quo sibi contingit, ut huius vel illius speciei capiat nomen* ('form is the specific type of matter by which something constitutes itself, in order that we may call it by this or that specific name'). Agricolan form holds the tacit power for everything in the world to have a name and thereby to have a particular role.

Agricola's place logic reoriented the role of loci within discursive theory and practice: he rehabilitated the places from having a final probatory role in *iudicium* to taking on an active position in creative argumentative invention. This reorientation gives a dynamic impetus to loci in the art of reasoning, taking these dialectical components from the realm of the post mortem to the birth of all forms of discourse. Agricola demonstrates his process at work not only in generic or prosaic examples, but also in poetry. Peter Mack has discussed in detail the way that, for instance, Agricola calls upon Virgil's depiction of Dido's lament to illustrate the importance of 'argumentation' in 'arousing emotions' in a reader.[12] In this example, Agricola uses Virgil's text not only to demonstrate that argumentation can be effective in inspiring a strong response in a reader, but rather to show that it is the chief, most powerful active principle making Dido's appeal effective. By calling upon poetry as well as prose and generic examples, Agricola presents a vision of a truly *universal* dialectic, applicable to and at work within any and every type of discourse in the world.

In following a Ciceronian and Boethian structure for his place logic (while also, as Marc van der Poel has pointed out, elaborating on Aristotle's predicables in an inheritance from Aristotelian manuals), Agricola treats efficient and final cause as external loci. They are *cognata*, or 'related things', necessarily entwined with the existence and nature of any subject under discussion, but coming *to* it, not from within but from without. Agricola cites Aristotle to explain the relationship that causes have with one another (sig. 28v): *materiam, ex qua res sit: formam, per quam est: efficientem, a qua sit: finem, propter quam sit* ('matter is that out of which a thing is; form, that through which a thing is; efficient cause, that by which something is; the end, for which something is'). These latter two, efficient cause and end, are the causes *cuius vi evenit aliquid* ('through whose power everything happens'). Each cause gets its own gerund, associated repeatedly and concertedly as being integral to *agendo*, or 'doing' (sigs. 28v–29r). Agricola's text is quite unusual in assigning any particular logical component a gerund, suggesting an attitudinal element to this decision. Agricola declares that *est autem potissima causarum omnium, finis* ('end is the most powerful of all of the causes'). Matter and form *rudis est et inculta* ('are rude and uncultivated'); the efficient cause might precipitate things, but it is the end which is the cause for the sake of which everything is done – *is enim cuius gratia omnia agunt* (sigs. 28v, 30r).

In 1535 Philip Melanchthon published the *Dialecticae Philippi Melancthonis libri tres*, in which he references Agricola regarding *inventio* and the loci.[13] Like Agricola, Melanchthon sets great store by the loci: he fulfils the promise of his three-book title with the sections '*Terminus*' ['Terms'], '*De propositione*' ['Of Propositions'] and '*De argumentatione*' ['Of Argumentation'], and then goes a step better to add a fourth, '*De locis argumentorum*', in which he examines all four causes just before discussing the process of invention. The rationale for Melanchthon's structure becomes evident in this final part of his text: under '*Terminus*' we learn about Aristotle's categories, predicates and predicaments in preparation for a broader discussion of definition, the principal function of all of the preceding categories. Book two covers propositions by explaining different propositional modes and division, while book three sets forth the formulaic components of argumentation, syllogisms and enthymemes. The fourth book is a synthesising move, explaining the large-scale processes of logic that demand all of the preceding components: invention, questions and demonstration. Melanchthon superadds the rhetorical *locus personarum* in this section, suggesting his participation in the humanist community that saw boundaries between logic and rhetoric as pliable or porous.

Melanchthon treats cause late in his manual, subordinating it to definitions, propositions and other static components. When efficient cause is afforded its own chapter, Melanchthon associates it with people: this is the cause *a quo primo sit motus* ('the thing by which a thing is first moved'), and because of this he defines *efficiens* as *vivendum est*, giving examples such as 'the architect who makes his building' – *Architectus cum vult aedificat* (sig. 65r). This is a cause that, Melanchthon argues, occurs naturally in people, which, in the context of his incorporation of the Aristotelian rhetorical *locus personarum*, perhaps suggests a persuasive association with *efficiens*. Melanchthon's depiction is a particularly vivid imagining of the principle of efficient cause as something living, something that brings life to all those static products of the Aristotelian categorical descriptive and defining process. This rhetorical connection, rooting these precepts in not only the rational probatory qualities of dialectic but also the persuasive qualities of its sister art, is confirmed when Melanchthon discusses final cause (sig. 65v): *et sumuntur hinc loci Rhetorici, Honestum et utile* ('they are taken from the places of Rhetoric, honest and useful'). This is a clear difference between Melanchthon's text and Ramist logics, which do not entertain this idea in their discussions of types of cause.

And Then There Was Ramus

It was Petrus Ramus who inverted the order of logic to give the causes prime position at the beginning of his treatise, the *Dialecticae partitiones*, in 1543. Ramus has been critically renowned and reviled for overhauling the relationship between logic and rhetoric, assigning *inventio* and *dispositio*, or *iudicium*, to logic, and *elocutio* and *pronuntiatio* to rhetoric, and removing altogether the traditional fifth component of oratory, *memoria*.[14] However, when it comes to understanding the early modern imagined intellectual community of logic, that through which all educated people in the period filtered their world, more important than his rearrangement of the parts of oratory is his alteration of the orientation and composition of logic.

The most striking change that Ramus makes is to bring the four causes to the forefront of his treatise. Ramus's English-language translators Roland MacIlmaine, Abraham Fraunce and Dudley Fenner open their reformed logics with only short prefatory remarks before launching into lean, clear and short chapters on cause, matter, form and end, meaning that this rearrangement is immediately apparent. Readers familiar with these texts may be caught off-guard when tracing their steps back to Ramus's first formal published treatise on dialectic, the *Dialecticae partitiones*, which begins with a lengthy 60-plus-page preface. Only after this does Ramus reveal his new way of thinking about logic, reorienting it permanently as a dynamic art based first and foremost on motion and action. If you come primed to the early editions of Ramus's textbook from an English background, it does not immediately conform to expectations of concision and clarity. It is necessary to understand the *Partitiones* as a watershed moment in which Ramus calls for an inversion of the unwritten art of arts, and that dramatic change is the reason for his lengthy and painstaking preface.

When it comes to detailing the causes themselves, while the fundamental functions remain constant (making things be; being the stuff that they are; being the particular shape that makes things individual; being the reason for things being and happening), Ramus is innovative once again in his emphasis. Whereas Agricola and Melanchthon place weight on the *finis* or end cause, Ramus gives most air time to efficient cause. Defining it in its basic form simply and efficiently as *causa est, cuius vi res est* ('cause is that by whose force a thing is or comes to be'), Ramus proceeds to identify different types of efficient cause.[15] He begins with sections on *de efficiente proceante* and *conservante*, the kinds of efficient cause which create *ab initio* and those which sustain. This creative and generative capability goes a long way towards explaining why Ramus argues that cause is the most important component of logical invention: these are the precepts that will allow you to make something, to do something with it, and to realise your purpose in doing so. In the 1592 posthumous edition of the *Dialecticae libri duo*, Virgil is called upon to bring *auctoritas* to Ramus's prioritisation of cause with his wisdom from the *Georgics* (2.490): *Felix, qui potuit rerum cognoscere causas* ('lucky is he who can understand the causes of things'). On the one hand, this is a helpful classical touchstone supporting Ramus's idea, but on the other, its introduction to the 1592 edition might indicate that this is an idea that is still in need of support. As Ramus emphasises efficient cause, he breaks it down into its different varieties and capacities, including when it works alone (*sola*) and with other causes (*cum aliis*), when it functions in and of itself (*per se*) or by happenstance (*per accidens*).[16] Ramus refers to these latter as the internal and external efficient causes respectively in a move that anticipates and perhaps seeks to participate in an uptick of interest in these two different types of agency that we can see in prominent early seventeenth-century logics by Bartholomaeus Keckermann (1602), his disciple Franc Burgersdijck (1626), Christopher Airay (1628) and more.

The Middle Man: Friedrich Beurhaus and the Consolation of Philippo-Ramism

The question of mediating between schools of logical thought was a common sixteenth-century pursuit. In 1586 music theorist and Ramist logician Friedrich Beurhaus created a dual edition and comparative commentary on the dialectics of Melanchthon and Ramus. He opens with a reflective proem which assigns the sin of our first parents as the fundamental cause requiring us to learn and to lean on the art of logic in an attempt to redeem our fallen faculties.[17] Beurhaus's text takes a bibliographic approach to logical instruction: on the verso of each page, he prints Ramus's *Dialecticae libri duo*, and this is faced on the recto by corresponding extracts from Philip

Melanchthon's *Dialecticae*. Alongside each text Beurhaus provides his own printed marginal annotations, thereby providing mediation to help us to negotiate between potential discrepancies or nuances distinguishing the two treatises. Melanchthon presented his text in a markedly different order to that invented by Ramus: Beurhaus's decision to produce a parallel comparative edition inherently, therefore, involves choosing between the authors' organisational philosophies and priorities, and in the opening chapter, Ramus wins the day with a definition that prioritises cause and that reads differently from Melanchthon's explicit definitional and argumentative discussion.

The first chapter begins with Ramus's opening question, *quid est Dialectica?* ('what is dialectic'), answered with the phrase that dominated logics in the second half of the sixteenth century: *dialectica est ars bene disserendi* ('dialectic is the art of discoursing well'; sig. B1v). Facing this remark, Melanchthon's *Dialecticae* is extracted to answer the same question with the statement *dialectica est ars recte, ordine, & perspecui docendi* ('dialectic is the art of teaching correctly, exactly and transparently'), which is elaborated upon to say that dialectic involves *recte definiendo, dividendo, argumenta vera connectendo, & malo cohaerentia refutando* ('correctly defining, dividing, constructing true arguments and coherently refuting the bad'; sig. B2r).

Beurhaus's annotations function in part by providing simple glosses. He also highlights and elaborates upon key points in his source texts, and in these we have one Renaissance reader's interpretation of these two leading theorists. Beurhaus comments that Ramus's dialectic relies upon and enables us to comprehend the essential causes of a thing, what makes it begin and come into being, the precise shape that it has (*forma*), and its goal. This is Beurhaus's first direct annotation to Ramus's text, and it immediately underscores the primary role of cause in this logic. His gloss on Melanchthon is very different, not least because he begins by glossing dialectic as *bene disserere, Logicae artis* ('to discourse well is the art of Logic'); this renaming might have its own significance, or it might speak to a broader view in the later sixteenth century that these terms were increasingly if not entirely interchangeable (sig. B1r). Due to his source text, Beurhaus's commentary debates whether definitions and divisions belong properly to invention or judgement, excluding any direct discussion of causes. However, Beurhaus seems to be making significant efforts to reconcile his duelling logics, suggesting ways in which Melanchthon's vision of an art of defining and dividing and making correct arguments fits within a Ramist umbrella of method (sig. B2v). Equally, he refers tacitly to Melanchthon's longer discussion of the role of dialectic as a tool enabling us to discourse *probabiliter* ('probably'), something that those texts by Ramus printed during his lifetime do not mention. This mediated conversation, opening lines of dialogue and contrast between two leading theorists, shows Ramus's innovation in his causal prioritising while also conjuring vivid links between that and a Melanchthonian ideal of defining and dividing. It is probably (pun intended) no coincidence that Beurhaus uses the language of defining and dividing in his commentary on Ramus in this comparative context, and here we gain a clear perspective on his reconciliatory mission to show not two competing schools of thought but two different perspectives on *the same art*.

Although Beurhaus starts by following the order of Ramus's textbook, he openly addresses the problem of the discrepancy between the structures of the two treatises in the B gathering, in a note on signature B4v, where he parallels Melanchthon's discussion of predicables and categories with an explanation that there are no dedicated chapters on these concepts in Ramus's *Dialecticae*. In the interests of fairness, Melanchthon is given the lead in the C gathering to discuss predicables. Beurhaus's notes work hard to forge a link between Melanchthon's Aristotelian predicables and Ramus's opening causal precepts. Alongside Melanchthon's discussion of *genus*, Beurhaus argues that *Ramus docet genus esse symbolum caussarum essentialium* ('Ramus teaches that genus is the emblem of essential causes'; sig. C2v). Melanchthon's text dominates the ensuing gatherings until signature H4v, and the only mention of cause is as the sixth part of a ten-part list documenting the appropriate *methodus* or method to follow when conducting logical investigations and analyses. The result of this highly interventional rearrangement of both treatises ends up skewing to Melanchthon's structure, in spite of opening with a declaration of Ramus's dynamic investment in this art. Consequently, Beurhaus's hybrid commentary text at least begins by demoting causation beneath predicables and categories.

Cause and the English Aristotelians in the Sixteenth Century

If cause is the star of the reformed logic show, it ascended to that position from a much lowlier role in Aristotelian texts, where it was at best the understudy locus to the far more important categories and predicates. Vernacular treatises might not be institutionally significant, but they do provide a useful distillation of prevailing trends in the two main competing logical factions. In 1551 Thomas Wilson was one of the first scholars to use the term 'logique' to refer to his treatise in his title, associating it explicitly with 'reason'.[18] It is not too flippant to note that he uses the noun 'reason' rather than the verbal form 'reasoning', and that interest in fixed and fixing description goes hand-in-hand with the Aristotelian structure of his textbook. However, his is a good example of the ways in which a textbook can be simultaneously innovative in some aspects and traditional or even conservative in others, contributing to a larger view of logic as a global imagined intellectual community more united by what it holds in common than divided by its differences. The choice – and choosing is an important concept in Wilson's text – to create a vernacular logic text indicates an interest in reform, and although Wilson subsumes causation beneath a heavy pile of Aristotelian categories, when he reaches it he does so with an investment not only in the ways in which it manifests, but also in why it does so, investigating its origins in the fleshy tables of the heart.

Wilson treats causes in the second part of his book, which he titles 'Inventio, that is to saie, the fyndyng out of an argument' (sig. 14v). Anyone immersed in reading Ramist logics will find Wilson's positioning of invention in the second half of his book counterintuitive, and to an extent it is the same for a modern reader: surely if we are investigating something, do we need to 'fynd' it first? But to appreciate this approach from an Aristotelian and specifically Wilsonian point of view, you could not find anything, or at least not thoroughly and correctly, without knowing what *kind of thing* you were looking for: you had to learn the categories, predicates and predicaments before you could do anything involving motion, because otherwise you would not know what you were looking at. Wilson sees causes as types of loci, allying his approach with that of Agricola. It is telling that in his preface, in a rather tortured 'declaration in meter, of the vii liberal artes', he explains how 'Logique by art settes further the truth, / And doth tel what is vayne. / Rethorique at large paintes well the cause' (sig. B2r). In this formulation, Wilson follows Agricola's coalition of causes as belonging to logic and rhetoric, or logic in a rhetorical way, but his stipulation also speaks to Melanchthon's idea of dialectic or logic as a means of establishing truth.

The four causes are explicitly associated with truth processes by Wilson, as he calls on examples both from natural philosophy and scripture to illustrate them. Wilson treats efficient cause first, and also accords it the most time in his manual. He glosses it as the 'workyng cause, by whose meanes, thynges are brought to passe', and that definition draws attention to the potency and dynamism of this locus in a way that challenges the stasis implied by that geographical motif (sig. L1v). Understanding efficient cause as something that *does work*, either because of the innate power and capacity of an agent or by compelling someone or something else to act, is to understand it as something that makes things happen. The 'workyng cause' is the mover and shaker in Wilson's treatise, yet that same potency makes it difficult to capture in its entirety, and that difficulty comes through as the terminology that Wilson uses to define it shifts. Initially, Wilson divides efficient cause into three varieties: that which functions 'by nature', 'by advisement' and 'by a fore purposed choyse'. The efficient causes working 'by nature' are internal causes which function because of the innate qualities and capacities of their agents. Wilson's examples of these causes all come from the natural world: 'the sonne, even by nature, geveth light to the daie, and cannot otherwise doo'. So too 'herbes' have their 'vertue' (although it says something about sixteenth-century medicine that Wilson does not dwell on what that might be), 'Adamant draweth Iron' and 'the bloud stone stoppeth bloud' (sig. L2r) – we will come back to that medical problem.

The key idea in Wilson's understanding of causes is whether efficient cause works on or through entities which do or do not possess 'knowledge to chuse this, or that', and which do or do not 'have judgement to discerne thynges' (sig. L2r). It is hard to read that claim without hearing a forerunner of Milton's later stipulation in his lessons in heaven that 'reason also is choice'.[19] While the predominant arrangement (and, depending on your translation, all Ramist and many other hybrid logics devoted entire books to *dispositio*, or arrangement) in *The Rule of Reason* is Aristotelian, Wilson's interest in the psychological and the internal workings and motivations propelling causal bodies allies him with logical reforms that originated with Agricola and Ramus before taking on an actively self-reflective character in the seventeenth-century works led by Keckermann. For Wilson, something may have causal dynamism from its innate qualities, but only when that dynamism emanates from a place of choosing. In the case of the 'naturall' efficient cause, Wilson argues that 'the effecte must nedes folowe': 'if the Sonne shine, the daie must nedes be, which is the effecte, or workemanship of the Sunne'; 'take away the cause, and theffect [*sic*] can not be at al: for if there be no fire, there can bee no flame, nor burning neither'. However, as soon as we reach causes through which 'thynges are dooen by advisement, and by choyse', there is no longer any 'necessitie' compelling particular outcomes (sig. L2v). In these causes, 'thynges maie aswell not bee doen, as be doen', and as soon as there is the possibility that a cause can have different effects by dint of choices made by its agent, Wilson insists that his students perceive the psychological dimension of causality. It is easy to miss the force of Wilson's claim, as he chooses a sartorial example that reads oddly today: 'if there be a Shomaker, there maie be a soue [sic] made, and contrary, if there by no Shomaker there can be no shone [sic] at all' (sigs. L2v–L3r). If cause is all-important, the driver that determines each and every happening in the world either through dumb necessity or reasoned choosing, it is hard to see that urgency in whether or not a pair of Prada shoes is created.

The quotidian example, intended presumably to allow a reader to see this conception of efficient cause at work in their everyday life, runs the risk of minimising the power of this kind of psychological motivation, but it is a lesson not to overlook the 'ordinary' examples in logic texts. For Wilson's examples of the 'voluntary' efficient cause escalate rapidly from the fickleness of a shoemaker and a carpenter who might or might not build a house to the improving qualities of books: 'if one reade good authors, and herken to the readyng of learned men, he maie come to good learnyng' (sig. L3r). When this kind of example is presented to someone who is currently reading what we might presume to be the work of one of those 'learned men', suddenly that internal psychological and emotional motivation has become our problem: what kind of reader are we each going to be? Will I learn from Wilson's learning, and succeed in *my* journey to 'good learnyng'? Or will I get to that shoemaker example and think, *Oh, I get it, no need to read the rest of those examples*, while entirely missing the gravitas that choices like this have. In a sucker punch to a cocky reader, Wilson explains 'the maner of reasonyng' underlying the voluntary efficient cause by saying that 'Christe hath reconciled mankind to his father, by suffering death upon the Crosse, Ergo suche as beleve in this saving health, shall live for ever' (sig. L3r). Now the voluntary cause determines not only whether I am clothed and housed, but the eternal clothing and housing of my immortal soul. Wilson dwells not on Christ's causal behaviour in this example, but on that of the person who chooses to believe or not believe in Christ-given divine salvation. When that example begins, there seems to be the possibility that we will be asked to understand Christ himself as exemplifying voluntary causation, but that consideration is deferred to humanity. One way to read this deferral is to question whether Wilson would see Christ's actions as voluntary, or whether these happened through necessity by his very make-up. Alternatively, perhaps as fledgling logicians we are not ready to turn our reasoning power to the choices made by divine beings, and Wilson's extended example reads as a version of 'physician, heal thyself', meaning that we need first to attend to our own internal motivations before questioning their unimpeachable equivalents in three-personed God.

Wilson firmly places the causal responsibility for salvation on each individual person under the umbrella of voluntarism, and in doing so he makes a crucial argument about the relationship between efficient cause and free will. He goes on to elaborate upon other divisions of efficient cause which explicitly deny or subjugate any such freedom, the 'commaundyng' and the 'obedient' causes. 'The Kyng is the commaundyng cause to his subjecte to doo this or that', and while rebellion is possible, it is not an option that Wilson entertains actively in his text (sig. L3r). Efficient causes 'as do obey' represent another facet of causes operating by necessity, but these are ones that derive not from a natural necessity but from necessity dictated by the free will, advisement and choosing of another agent, 'as the Mason worketh upon the stone, the Carpenter upon wood' (sig. L3v). In these instances, it is quite hard to parse the logical operations at work: it can seem as if Wilson is arguing that the stone and wood are the entities responsible for the efficient cause, as they are where its results will manifest. However, those results are products of the will (and skill) of the mason or carpenter working upon them, meaning that causal agency rests with the mason or carpenter; but Wilson does not accord them free will or voluntary power, positing them instead as 'obedient' causes who simply 'doo their woorke' in accordance with their 'maisters commaundement' (sig. L3v).

Ranked below the commanding and obedient causes is the instrument: 'hatchettes, hammers, [and] pike axes' 'are obedient' because they 'are but instrumentes of dooyng', exercising no choice and therefore no reason in their causal actions, even though they may wreak havoc (sig. L3v). These instruments, and even Wilson's workers, align with Graham Greene's blind leper with a bell roaming the world and meaning no harm. Wilson sets this causal hierarchy in a military context: 'the captain' in battle is the 'efficient commaunder' choosing – that is, reasoning – what actions his workers will take with their instruments. The soldier is the 'efficient obeyer' following the commander's reasoning by using his 'instrumentes of dooyng', the 'gunnes, dartes, bowes, and billes' to accomplish the captain's logical end or goal (sig. L3v). Wilson is unusual in dissecting agency to this degree, particularly among vernacular logics which are typically more concise than their Latin compatriots: his is a theory of logical causality in which the buck stops with the human agent. We are each responsible for the force and potency we hold. If we use that force to sin, albeit as an 'efficient obeyer' or perhaps even as an 'instrument of dooyng' acting at the will of a persuasive or coercive devil, we still in fact did that action. The devil can't be damned again – but we can.

Wilson's theory of causation is devoted to understanding personal agency and to asserting it: 'good hede ought to bee had, that in all causes wee make a difference, not confoundyng one with another' (sig. L3v). There is no danger that an attentive reader of Wilson would want for categories to distinguish different causes from one another: we are whirled through the gamut of nigh causes, farther causes, 'principall causes', causes of 'the inclinacions in man' and 'helpyng causes', and Wilson admits that 'there be other divisions, but I leave to reherse them, for feare I should be over long' (sig. L4r). However, even this more minimal list of causes reinforces the role that these play in our moral lives. The 'nigh causes and the farther causes' are exemplified by a disturbingly quick, Tarantinoesque example of a man killing his neighbour over a disagreement. The 'nigh' cause of the neighbour's death is the fact that a man dealt him 'a dedly wounde', but the man did this deadly deed because he 'fell out with his neighbour', and that act began a swift and toxic spiral of unfortunate causal consequences as 'fallyng out bryngeth chidyng, chidyng bryngeth hatred, hatred causeth fightyng, fightyng geveth blowes, blowes sone dispatche, sone dispatchyng is ready death' (sig. L3v). And just as soon as that, we have caused our own fall into perdition. Similarly, causes of the 'inclinacions' may be 'good or eivill', and which of these we will pay 'good hede' to depends upon our ability to intuit and respond to 'principall causes' such as 'the holy ghoste' 'stirryng our nature' (sig. L4r). If our causal radar is working well, we will detect the stirring of the Holy Ghost and act accordingly, heeding our best 'inclinacions' and thereby pursuing virtuous acts, and this is why Wilson takes such pains to educate us about how efficient cause works and what its power is, so that a good reader can appreciate its importance and wield it appropriately to lead a good life.

What Effect Do All These Causes Have upon Sixteenth-century Poetry?

Ramist logics are famous for incorporating poetic examples, and many scholars including Rosemond Tuve, Zenón Luis-Martínez and

Steven May have used these to illuminate the relationship between logic and literature in the sixteenth century.[20] Critics have also examined the role which Ramist logics played in the education and consequently the creative works of various prominent sixteenth-century poets, including Sidney and Spenser, whose poetry actually furnishes *exempla* for Abraham Fraunce's *The Shepherds' Logic*. Tamara Goeglein has called on William Temple's Ramist logic text to argue that, in their creative process, poets are not calling on a privileged form of *inventio* unavailable to all others, but rather that they are making a very particular use of the general category of invention found in *dialecticae artis facultate* ('the faculty of the art of dialectic').[21] Goeglein argues that '*logicians* are fiction-makers', following Temple's explanation that dialectical invention can create or find both truth and fiction.[22] By seeing cause at work in poetry and understanding it as a type of style, we can bear witness to the emergence in the sixteenth century of a dynamic unwritten poetics which originates in reformed logic texts.

Cause washes up and down the strand in Spenser's 'Amoretto 75', shifting agency between the hand writing a lover's name and the ceaseless sea erasing that work.[23] For the first two quatrains humans struggle, but are ultimately subject to the greater efficacy of nature's causal power. Only when cause is in the hands of a poet does that power dynamic shift back in favour of human creativity, as Spenser introduces another tier to the causal hierarchy of his poem, which privileges poetic invention above other human and natural activities. Spenser's sonnet begins by detailing the efficient cause, matter and form in question as he states,

> One day I wrote her name upon the strand,
> but came the waves and washed it a way:
> agayne I wrote it with a second hand,
> but came the tyde, and made my paynes his pray. (1–4)[24]

In this opening, the speaker acts as the efficient cause working upon the matter of his lover's 'name' in the form of writing upon the sand, but logic aficionados will immediately notice that we are missing the fourth part of causality: the speaker does not disclose his logical end or reason for inscribing his lover's name on the beach. Instead, he encounters causal competition as the 'waves' 'came' and acted in turn as an efficient cause upon the writing in the sand with their own end of washing it away. This pattern repeats in a wavelike causal sequence as once more the poet writes 'with a second hand' but is again defeated by the 'tyde', which denies his efforts as nature overpowers humanity in its role as efficient causal agent.

It is only in the second and third quatrains that it is made explicit that the tidal causation acts as a microcosm for a person's quest for immortality, as they work through the quarrel between the lover and her poet:

> Vayne man, sayd she, that doest in vaine assay,
>   a mortall thing so to immortalize.
>   for I my selve shall lyke to this decay,
>   and eek my name bee wyped out lykewize.
> Not so (quod I let baser things devize
>   to dy in dust, but you shall live by fame:
>   my verse your vertues rare shall eternize,
>   and in the hevens wryte your glorious name. (5–12)

Initially, it seems that efficient causal power and end belongs to the universe, as the speaker's lover sides with the waves. She and the waves parse the causal trajectory of her immortality in the same way: the name in the sand and her body are the only substance she thinks she will ever have, and are aligned in their material form to suffer the same fate. The logical poesis entwines the lover's and the sea's causal impetus, as the sea takes the name 'away', taking the upper hand to make the speaker his 'pray', and the lover likewise accuses the speaker of making 'vaine assay' to immortalise one who must 'decay'. The speaker, however, takes back logical and poetic control in the final quatrain and couplet: he creates a hierarchy of causal impetus in which 'baser things devize / To dy in dust', whereas his love 'shall live by fame'. The logical ends of dying and living are set not so much in opposition as in a hierarchy of the base and the elevated. The speaker casts 'baser things' as the architects of their own demise, as they are the ones acting as efficient causes on their own matter in order to reduce it to the logical form of dust. There is an available reading of that logic that says it is false, and that the speaker is introducing a material prejudice which taunts baser things as causing their own fall, when in fact they are victims of powers beyond their control. However, the speaker's lover is the matter and form acted upon initially 'by fame', with the end that she 'shall live' by dint of her superior material properties. Momentarily, the speaker affords logical control to fame, which selects which things are high and low. By extension, he also affords that control to poetry, as this acts as the efficient cause giving life to his love. Yet the next line reveals fame to be merely one of Thomas Wilson's helping causes, aiding his 'verse', which emerges as the principal efficient cause working to 'eternize' his lover's 'name' (which it also makes 'glorious'). To press on this logical genealogy, the speaker might be also using fame's power as an efficient cause as a cat's paw: if he argues successfully that it immortalises only the higher things, that material causation means that his poetry is of the highest order. The speaker's logic is evident in the progression of the rhyme scheme in this final quatrain, as he consigns base things to 'devize' to die while his verse shall work as the efficient cause to 'eternize' in the countermanding rhyme. This opposition in the rhyme scheme is a good example of logic both defining and also being complemented by poesis.

Spenser prioritises efficient cause as the key logical battle occurs between the competing drives of nature and poetry. In this way, his can be seen as a Ramist text, as that competition between the forces generating and shaping actions and outcomes not only provides the chief drama but also shapes the poesis as it manifests in the concatenated rhyme scheme. However, there is also a clear understanding of the Agricolan, Melanchthonian and Aristotelian conception of matter as something malleable that will ultimately be corrupted as time passes. By the closing couplet, we can see efficient cause working to counteract the corruptibility of matter by successfully challenging death and, indeed, inspiring future, generative loves. Yet in spite of the speaker's claim that it is love that makes this conquest, Spenser's logical apparatus indicates a different cause at work, as the form which that love takes is, of course, poetry. In this way, Spenser's poetic logic serves to promote and amplify the power of his theory of poetry itself.

Philip Sidney also experiments with causation to express the power and longevity of poetry in his sonnet sequence *Astrophil and Stella*.[25] Like Spenser, Sidney ostensibly puts poetry into service to declare and immortalise love. However, a causal analysis of both poets' lyrics reveals poetry as their ultimate agent and motivation. While Spenser's sonnet builds to the revelation that he and his poetry are the wonders keeping the stars apart, Sidney's opening sonnet culminates in the same revelation being experienced by Astrophil and perhaps even the poet himself, as his Muse bids him write – in other words, to take up his own efficient cause. The sonnet opens with a logical misapprehension by Astrophil:

> Loving in truth, and faine in verse my love to show,
> That the deare She might take some pleasure of my paine:
> Pleasure might cause her reade, reading might make her know,
> Knowledge might pitie winne, and pitie grace obtaine,

> I sought fit words to paint the blackest face of woe,
> Studying inventions fine her wits to entertaine:
> Oft turning others' leaves, to see if thence would flow
> Some fresh and fruitful showers upon my sunne-burn'd braine. (1–8)[26]

Astrophil occupies an efficient causal role in seeking to show his love to Stella. Like Agricola, Melanchthon and Wilson, Astrophil initially prioritises his end causes. These are defined at the end of his lines like a kind of logical rhyme scheme as he seeks first 'in verse my love to show', then hopes that the right verse might make Stella 'know' that love, and that knowledge might lead to 'pitie', and pity might 'grace obtaine' to make her reciprocate his emotion. In pursuit of these ends, Astrophil employs a series of Wilson's supporting efficient causes, from verse to pleasure to reading to knowledge to pity. While these do not achieve his desired end when Astrophil calls on them to be applied through poetry written or inspired by others, when read retrospectively this description shows what a formidable armoury of efficient causes the poet is equipped with. Here, the relationship between logic and poesis is not only one shaping this specific verse; it also informs a theory of poetry that promotes its originating power and capacity for change.

In the middle quatrain of the sonnet, Astrophil has to learn the hard way that he must be his own source of inspiration. He 'stud[ies] inventions' in the writings of others, hoping that this form of poetry will achieve his end. However, a dissection of the matter of 'Nature' (10) which generated 'invention' reveals another facet of the poetics underlying the sonnet sequence. Sidney and Astrophil identify invention as a natural phenomenon which is opposed in its very logical matter to artificial 'Studie'. Here, Sidney makes his argument in verse in favour of the privileged, untaught poetic invention which William Temple would contradict in his advocacy of logic. Yet as much as Sidney separates studied from natural poetic invention, the logic which he uses to make that separation speaks to his years of 'expensive, athletic, and prolonged' education.[27]

Reading his sonnet through the forbidden lens of studied logic raises another dimension to Sidney's dichotomy between the natural and the studied.[28] For the lesson that Astrophil learns in the final line is not to abandon his own erudition, but rather to embrace it and 'looke in thy heart and write' (14). The Muse issues Astrophil a causal instruction: draw on your own internal or, as the seventeenth-century theorists would term it, proegumenic capacity, and trust in it enough to use it to act as *your own* efficient cause producing *your own* original poetic matter and form, and that process of causal responsibility is what will allow you to achieve your end. There is a delicious irony in the fact that Astrophil must learn to rely on his inner inventive resources by being instructed and acted upon by the external cause of his Muse.[29] Yet the Muse working as efficient cause on Astrophil with the end of showing him the innate power of poetry serves as a divine endorsement of both poet and poetry.[30] It also represents a shift over the course of the sonnet from a focus on ends to a focus on efficient causes, speaking to a logical poetics of action very much in keeping with Ramist theories of causation and their potency as an agent of change.

Cause in Longer Sixteenth-century Poetry

There is a similar causal impetus at work in longer late sixteenth-century poetry. In his student translation of Ovid's *Amores* composed during his time at Cambridge in the early 1580s, Christopher Marlowe similarly plays upon causal tactics to summon and work with his Muse, and his strategy aligns with that of Spenser and Sidney to suggest a vision of poetry and poetic inspiration as agents of change.

Drawing on Peter Mack's formative reading of Agricolan invention, Robert Cockcroft has considered the ways in which Marlowe's logical training at Corpus Christi College, Cambridge, can be seen in the ways his characters combine emotional pathos and apprehension of effect at climactic moments in his plays.[31] Cockcroft explains that John Seton's *Dialectica* and Agricola's *De inventione dialectica* were probably the standard texts at Corpus Christi, though of course he notes Marlowe's familiarity with Ramus's works given his portrayal of the logician's brutal tripartite murder in his final play, *The Massacre at Paris* (1593). Scholars including Sarah Knight, Tamara Goeglein, John Ronald Green, myself and others have spent much ink examining Marlowe's explicit engagement with Ramus in that famous scene, but here I wish to suggest his wider participation in the active logical causal culture of later sixteenth-century poetry by looking at one of his student creations, the translation of Ovid's 'Elegia I' from the *Amores*.[32]

In a poem ostensibly about attributing causal accountability – that is, blaming – for poetic creation and its problems to external agents, Marlowe turns necessity into opportunity to claim his space as a light-footed innovative love poet:

> With Muse upreard I meant to sing of Armes,
> Choosing a subject fit for fierce alarmes.
> Both verses were alike till Love (men say)
> Began to smile and tooke one foote away.
> Rash boy, who gave thee the power to change a line?
> We are the Muses Prophets, none of thine. (5–10)[33]

This example differs from those considered earlier in this chapter because it is a translation. Here, if Marlowe is to insert his own sense of dynamic poesis, he must do it as part of a negotiation with his Latin counterpart, but that complication provides us with an unusual opportunity to understand some of the earliest ways in which Renaissance writers could experiment with causality and agency – by proxy. Translation of Ovid was, of course, a staple of the Renaissance classroom; here, in Marlowe's quite faithful rendition of 'Elegia I' there are small shifts in the poet's precise use of logical techniques to create a translation which both captures its inheritance but also enables the creation of a new, distinctive poetic voice.[34] The unwritten art allows Marlowe to satisfy the dual desires of fidelity in translation and innovation in poetic creativity. We can see this authorial negotiation in one of the lines which Marlowe changes, as he takes us from *quis tibi, saeve puer, dedit hoc in carmina iuris?* ('Savage boy, who gave thee the right over poetry?') to a 'rash boy' who has gained not the 'right' but the 'power' over poesy.[35] Perhaps that poetic power is what Marlowe himself is asserting through his translation, and a logic of agency would certainly advance that goal. Initially, Marlowe's Agricolan training seems to be the dominant mode, as the poet prepares to act at the behest of his 'Muse upreared' with the end 'to sing of armes', positioning both efficient and final cause as external loci working upon him. As the matter of the verse takes shape, another external efficient cause arises as Cupid interfered and 'tooke one foote away', shifting the form and the motivation of the poem from war to love. In both scenarios, the poet positions himself and, by extension, all poets as mere instruments being acted upon by divine external agents, lacking any causal impetus of their own. Even the identity of Cupid himself comes to the poet only through the things 'men say', not from direct experience or knowledge, seeming to make all poetry a second- or third-hand business. The only pushback comes as the poet tries to reassert his own instrumental qualities over Cupid, arguing that poets 'are the Muses prophets, none of thine', but this still leaves them stuck with the wills and motives of Agricola's external causal agents.

With Cupid causing creative differential chaos, the poet casts himself in a topsy-turvy world in which Ceres takes Diana's bow and Diana tills the plain, while Mars plays the Aeolian harp.[36] He conjures this list of mismatched efficient, material, formal and final causes to show the disarray which the world would have to be in for Cupid to have the right to act on the matter of poetry in the form of altering its feet with the end of changing its subject matter and aesthetic format. This central part of the translation represents a shift in agency for Marlowe's speaker, for although he is arguing that he must be subject to the Muses' causal desires, he crafts that argument with his own very compact, dense causal concatenations depicting the putative effect of Cupid's meddling. He may be claiming allegiance to a higher power, but he may also be protesting too much of his own causal helplessness. This subtle shift in causal mood begins the closing negotiation between the poet and Cupid:

> When in this workes first verse I trod aloft,
> Love slackt my Muse, and made my numbers soft.
> I have no mistris, nor no favorit,
> Being fittest matter for a wanton wit,
> Thus I complaind, but Love unlockt his quiver,
> Tooke out the shaft, ordained my hart to shiver:
> And bent his sinewy bow upon his knee,
> Saying, Poet heers a worke beseeming thee.
> Oh woe is me, he never shootes but hits,
> I burne, love in my idle bosom sits.
> Let my first verse be sixe, my last five feete,
> Fare well sterne warre, for blunter Poets meete.
> *Elegian Muse*, that warblest amorous laies,
> Girt my shine browe with sea banke myrtle praise. (21–34)

This part of the poem is an exercise in logical retrospection. At the start of writing, the poet moans that Cupid acted as an efficient cause to 'slack' his Muse with the effect of making his 'numbers soft': so far, so Agricolan, and the poet remains powerless at the mercy of external agents. However, turning inward, he considers the causal resources at his disposal to create poetry, and concludes that with 'no mistris, nor favorit', he lacks the 'fittest matter' for amorous poetry. The fact that he even inventories the matter and form which he might work on for his verse suggests an elision in causal power between the external inspiration (be it Muse or Cupid) and the maker himself, with the poem itself as a kind of syllogistic outcome resulting from their talents combined.

In thinking about his lack of 'matter' to empower 'a wanton wit', the poet turns towards Thomas Wilson's efficient causes which act by 'nature', dependent upon the innate qualities of their agents, suggesting a greater degree of causal independence and capability than we saw at the beginning of the elegy. However, Cupid is a dangerous person to equip with logical matter or its absence, as he immediately pulls out his bow and, with deadly accuracy, shoots our poet through the heart to give him ample of the 'fittest matter' to allow him to act as 'a wanton wit'. In this logical conflict, the poet is transparently the loser, becoming subject to yet another causal agent as 'love' 'sits' in his 'idle bosome', making him 'burne' in a precursor of Donne's active passivity in the holy sonnets in the next century. However, from ashes comes victory: for in what seems like a moment of abject causal defeat and subjugation, suddenly the poet steps forth to claim his creative role. He exclaims, 'let my first verse be sixe, my last five feete', and in doing so takes possession of the new matter and form that will constitute his innovative verse. He is driven by the love burning within him, and by finding (or inventing, if you will allow it) his own 'fittest matter', that once-external cause is transmuted to what Wilson would see as a causal 'inclinacion', an innate characteristic driving agency and action. As he embraces this new creative power, the poet is able to act directly *as* an efficient cause, bidding 'fare well' to 'sterne warre' and condemning it to the matter and form of 'blunter Poets', and in a final step to ascend the poetic throne it is now he, the poet, commanding the '*Elegian Muse*' to 'girt my shine browe with sea banke myrtle praise'. This precipitous causal reorientation and sublimation is the magic of Marlowe's translation, building the elegy's climactic revelation that, when the poet understands and accepts his 'inclinacions' he, not his Muse, is the ultimate creative agent.

All three poets play with causation to elevate the active role of the poet as an agent of change in the world. They are able to do so by using the principles of reformed logic which they studied at school and university, and in doing so participate in a poetic revolution that prioritised change, dynamism and the exploration of personal agency. It might not be too much of an extension to see the very early glimmers of the explorations of the self that were championed centuries later by the Romantic poets in these sixteenth-century logico-poetic experiments in agency, cause and blame. The apparatus and operations of logic can be hard for us to detect with twenty-first-century vision, but this unwritten art both used and was used by poets to create a new kind of aesthetics and practical poetics which prioritised dynamic change and thereby energised invention as the prime creative strategy.

Notes

My sincere thanks to Zenón Luis-Martínez and his colleagues at the University of Huelva, who organised the symposium where this volume began; the resulting imagined community brought the unwritten arts to life and I am most grateful for both their collegiality and their insightful comments on this chapter. Many thanks also to Maria Katsulos for her assiduous assistance in preparing the bibliography and references, and to Russell Hugh McConnell for his input during the final edit; the chapter would not be the same without their wisdom and scholarly generosity.

1. See Wilson, 'Marvell and Education'.
2. For a brief cross-period survey of this kind of definition, see Eck, *Elementarius dialectice* (1518), sig. A2v; Keckermann, *Systema logicae* (1602) 1–2; Du Moulin, *Elementa logica* (1603), 42; Airay, *Fasciculus praeceptorum logicorum* (1628), 1; Scheibler, *Opus logicum* (1651), sig. A2r; Heereboord, *Ermhneia logica* (1657), 7; Du Trieu, *Manductio ad logicam* (1678), 1; De Vries, *Logica compendiosa* (1684), 3.
3. Ramus's *Partitiones dialecticae* (1543) and its successive editions as the *Dialecticae libri duo* represent the first significant wave of abridged, reoriented 'modern' logics for the sixteenth century; Roland MacIlmaine's *The Logike of the Moste Excellent Philosopher P. Ramus Martyr* (1574), along with the English-language works of Dudley Fenner, *The Artes of Logike and Rethorike* (1584) and Abraham Fraunce, *The Sheapheardes Logike* (c. 1580s), are examples of vernacular volumes; Eck, *Elementarius dialectice*, Pedro da Fonseca, *Institutionum dialecticarum* (1597), and Keckermann, *Systema logicae*, are among those including bracketed diagrams, while Airay's 1628 textbook and several sixteenth-century Aristotles have Porphyrian tree diagrams. Friedrich Beurhaus's edition of Ramus and Melanchthon's texts, *P. Rami dialecticae libri duo* (1586), alongside others, uses different colours of ink to aid with readability and usability.
4. For one of the keystone articles on this topic, see Mack, 'Rudolph Agricola's Reading of Literature'; these ideas are expanded upon in Mack, *Renaissance Argument*.
5. See Appendix I.4 in Fraunce, *Shepherds' Logic*, ed. Luis-Martínez, 168–72.
6. Fraunce, *Shepherds' Logic*, 162; Ramus, *Bucolica, praelectionibus exposita*.
7. Fraunce, *Shepherds' Logic*, 170.
8. The emphasis on personal responsibility and capacity is closely linked to Protestant ideas about salvation *sola fide*, by faith alone, in which

a believer is responsible for their own spiritual progress. Ramus was a famous convert to Protestantism, which resulted in his murder during the 1572 St Bartholomew's Day Massacre, and the vast majority of his later followers, editors, adapters and imitators were also Protestant. Much has been written on the confessional contexts of Ramism; see Meerhoff, 'Petrus Ramus and the Vernacular'; Hotson, *Reformation of Common Learning*; Reiter, 'William Perkins: The Imagination in Calvinist Theology'.

9. Ong, *Ramus, Method*, is the seminal work bringing to modern scholarly attention the challenge made by Ramus and his followers to established scholastic Aristotelian theories of logic, rhetoric and the discursive arts in the early modern period. Feingold, 'English Ramism', discusses this division specifically in the context of early modern England, while Schmitt addresses the question of English Aristotelianism in *John Case and Aristotelianism*. More recently, Sgarbi, *Aristotelian Tradition*, surveys the relationship between Aristotelianism and empiricism in England. For an examination of Ramist and Aristotelian logical dynamics, see Wilson, 'International Nature of Britannic Ramism'.
10. My thanks to Zenón Luis-Martínez for his extremely helpful editorial dialogue on this point.
11. See van der Poel, 'Ramus and Agricola'; Mack, *Renaissance Argument*. Agricola's work appeared in manuscript during his lifetime, and in numerous printed editions posthumously in the sixteenth century (as we will see, up to and including the period of Christopher Marlowe's training at Corpus Christi College, Cambridge). The 1554 Paris edition of Agricola's *De inventione* is cited parenthetically in the text by signature.
12. Mack, 'Rudolph Agricola's Reading of Literature', 28. This indispensable article details several of Agricola's interpretations of Virgil's *Aeneid* as well as some of his discussions of Cicero, Juvenal, Horace and Plato.
13. Melanchthon, *Dialecticae*, sig. 55v. Further references are cited parenthetically in the text by signature.
14. Ong, *Ramus, Method*; Sharratt, 'Ramus 2000'; Feingold, 'English Ramism'.
15. Ramus, *Dialecticae*, 2. Ramus's text went through numerous editions, revisions and adaptations; for a full listing of these, see Ong, *Ramus and Talon Inventory*.
16. Ramus, *Dialecticae*, 2–3.
17. Beurhaus, *P. Rami*, sig. 4r. Further references to this work are cited parenthetically in the text by signature.
18. T. Wilson, *Rule of Reason, Conteinyng the Arte of Logique* (1551). Further references to this work are cited parenthetically in the text by signature.
19. Milton, *Paradise Lost*, ed. Fowler, III.108, p. 173.
20. Luis-Martínez, 'Ramist Dialectic'; May, 'Marlowe, Spenser, Sidney and – Abraham Fraunce?'; Tuve, *Elizabethan and Metaphysical Imagery*.

21. Goeglein, 'Wherein hath Ramus been so offensious?', 82–3.
22. Ibid., 85.
23. On Spenser's exposure to Ramism, see Hadfield, *Edmund Spenser*, 51–82; Koller, 'Abraham Fraunce and Edmund Spenser'; Tuve, 'Imagery and Logic'.
24. Spenser, *Amoretti*, sonnet 75, in *Yale Edition of the Shorter Poems*, ed. Oram et al., 645. Line numbers are cited parenthetically in the text.
25. On Sidney and Ramism, see Buxton, *Sir Philip Sidney*, 45–7; Ong, *Ramus, Method*, 302–3.
26. Sidney, *Astrophil and Stella*, 1, in *Poems*, ed. Ringler, 165. Further references to this poem are cited parenthetically in the text by line number.
27. I am indebted to Stella Gibbons for this ideal phrase from *Cold Comfort Farm*, 1.
28. See Sell, 'Philip Sidney's Sublime Self-Authorship', this volume, 178–9, for another reading of this sonnet.
29. On the Muse, see Zunino-Garrido, 'Thomas Lodge's "Supple Muse"', this volume.
30. For detailed readings of the role of grace in sixteenth-century poetics, see Curbet Soler, 'Justified by Whose Grace?', and Pérez-Jáuregui, 'From Favour to Eternal Life', this volume.
31. Cockcroft, *Rhetorical Affect*, 58–9. Cockcroft draws on Mack's formative interpretation of Agricolan invention in *Renaissance Argument*.
32. Knight, 'Flat Dichotomists and Learned Men'; Goeglein, 'Wherein hath Ramus been so offensious?'; Green, 'Martyrdom of Ramus'. It may be more obvious to seek Marlowe's Ramism in his passages about Ramus, but the precise importance of these causal innovations is their ubiquitous presence.
33. Marlowe, *All Ovids Elegies*, I.1, in *Complete Works*, ed. Gill, 1:13–14. References to this poem are cited parenthetically in the text by line number.
34. Marlowe and others would experiment with that voice in the epyllia of the 1590s (for example, in *Hero and Leander*). For further discussion of this practice in early modern pedagogy, see Enterline, *Shakespeare's Schoolroom*.
35. Ovid, *Amores*, I.1.5, in *Heroides. Amores*, 318–19.
36. 'What if thy mother take *Dianas* bowe? / Shall *Dian* fanne, when loue begins to glowe? / In wooddie groves ist meete that Ceres Raigne, / And quiver-bearing *Dian* till the plaine: / Who'le set the faire trest sunne in battell ray / While Mars doth take the Aonian harpe to play?' (11–16).

Chapter 3

Atomies of Love: Material (Mis)interpretations of Cupid's Origin in Elizabethan Poetry
Cassandra Gorman

They say then that Love was the most ancient of all the gods; the most ancient therefore of all things whatever, except Chaos, which is said to have been coeval with him . . . And himself out of Chaos begot all things, the gods included. The attributes which are assigned to him are in number four: he is always an infant; he is blind; he is naked; he is an archer . . . The fable relates to the cradle and infancy of nature, and pierces deep. This Love I understand to be the appetite or instinct of primal matter; or to speak more plainly, *the natural motion of the atom*; which is indeed the original and unique force that constitutes and fashions all things out of matter . . . [T]he summary law of nature, that impulse of desire impressed by God upon the primary particles of matter which makes them come together, and which by repetition and multiplication produces all the variety of nature, is a thing which mortal thought may glance at, but can hardly take in.

Francis Bacon[1]

In his 1609 publication *De sapientia veterum*, translated for later editions as *The Wisdom of the Ancients*, Bacon considers in turn thirty-one figures from classical mythology in the light of what he has termed the 'new learning'. His mission is to discover what can be derived from the allegorical meanings behind ancient mythologies. In his Preface, Bacon argues that parables and similitudes are continually necessary for the advancement of learning. They not only sweeten the pill when introducing new theories – allowing the philosopher to communicate without 'offence and harshness' – but also sustain communion with the divine in the pursuit of knowledge, evoking the very use of typological 'veils and shadows' that 'religion delights in'.[2] Allegories, although they cloak and protect their hidden significance, permit the learner a glimpse of purer, more distant truths.

Memorably, Bacon includes among his mythologies the myth of Cupid, or 'Love' – whom he equates with the 'appetite or instinct of primal matter; or to speak more plainly, *the natural motion of the atom*'. In the section 'Cupid, or the Atom', Bacon traces the cryptic history of a figure who bears two forms from his classical origins. The newest and perhaps most recognisable of these is the cherubic infant, 'youngest of all the gods, son of Venus'. According to other strands of thought, however, Cupid – or Eros, the Greek name with which he appears in Hesiod – owes his birth to primordial beginnings, as the 'most ancient of all the gods' alongside the original Chaos.[3] It is this Cupid, Bacon argues, who assumes the form of an atom. He expounds some key parallels between the god of Love and the indivisible particle to support his claim. Atoms, like Cupid's arrows, dart and pierce; like Cupid, atoms were considered 'blind', as they jostle, collide and congregate in space; like the infant god, atoms are simultaneously ancient and yet fresh from birth – the first and last of all things.[4]

This deep, layered association between Cupid and the atom does not come out of nowhere in Bacon's philosophy; nor is it a metaphor restricted to studies of natural philosophical ontology. There is, I argue in this chapter, a strong connection between the atomic particle and the influence of Cupid in late sixteenth- and early seventeenth-century English love poetry. For various reasons, this relationship has been little commented on in works of literary criticism. Allusions to Cupid, it is safe to say, are everywhere, from the lyrics of *Tottel's Miscellany* to the sonnets of Philip Sidney and the stanzas of Spenser's *Faerie Queene*. Most studies, however, have drawn attention to the classical origins, aesthetic and theological contexts of the early modern Cupid that bypass the influence of philosophical materialism.[5] Studies of atomism in poetry, moreover, have tended to focus on the influence of Lucretius in the seventeenth century, by which time theories of Epicurean materialism had enjoyed a resurgence in English literary culture and *De rerum natura* was on the syllabus at the universities.[6]

Without doubt, the most prominent of Elizabethan poets – Spenser, Sidney, Lyly – were writing with informed knowledge of Lucretius, and Lucretian tropes affected the shape of their compositions. Several studies of poesy from the late sixteenth century acknowledge the aesthetic significance of *De rerum natura*. In his *Defence of Poesy*, Sidney refers to Lucretius as one of the key classical, philosophical poets, referencing his work alongside Virgil's *Georgics* as one of the most influential 'natural' philosophical poems.[7] William Webbe's *A Discourse of English Poetry* (1586) similarly lists Lucretius, without any cause for noting his controversy, as one of several 'excellent' writers beyond the remit of his current study.[8] The link between Cupid and, as Bacon writes, the 'natural motion of the atom' according to Lucretius is a bond that permeates the movements and corporeal experiences of poetic accounts of love. Coincidentally, the Latin word for desire, *cupido*, is a word applied frequently by Lucretius to explain its physical impact on living things, something that can be paralleled easily with the innate impulse – and desire – of atoms for connection and creation.[9] The re-creation of material forms from restless atomic movement could just as easily be considered, or repronounced, recreation: Lucretius often depicts the particles mixing and dancing in 'sport'; a materialist trope echoed in the startling, and recurrent, image of Cupids jostling about and between lovers' persons in sixteenth-century poetry.[10]

Parallels between *De rerum natura* and the tropes of Elizabethan love poetry are strong.[11] The aim of this chapter, however, is to reveal a connection between material atoms (or, in several cases, elements with atomic properties) and the figure of Cupid prior to and beyond the literary influence of Lucretius. This is the bond between *atom* and *Cupid* derived from works of Renaissance mythography, the principal sources behind Bacon's scholarship in *De sapientia veterum*. By tracing this history and its influence on sixteenth-century poetics, it becomes apparent that, even when the specific term 'atom' is absent, the mischievous Cupids of love poetry display atomic characteristics that shape experiences and explanations of desire. Poets activate Cupid to address the 'impulse' towards love and poetic expression and, in so doing, to form the origin for a distinctive poetics of desire. It becomes characteristic for the poet-lover to blame the injuries of love on the external force of a destructive agent: the minuscule, invasive and materialist figure of Cupid. As the number of Cupids in a poetical work increase, however, so do the dangers of desire, with emotional disorder reconfigured as physical chaos. These dangers emerge, I argue, from rising (mis)interpretations of the Cupid myth in Elizabethan poetry. New metaphors and allegories of Cupid arise to meet, defend and explain diverse experiences of desire, with the result of enriching poetic creations at the cost of grave injury to lovers. In the following section, I introduce the mythographic background to the atomic, regenerative Cupid image, before tracing flights of the love god in action across poetic spaces. The trope of the atomised Cupid develops an aetiology for its own poetics of desire in the period, wherein physical elements and Cupids conjoin to create both powerful, multi-layered metaphors (that 'pierce deep') and natural philosophical explanations for love and lust.

Cupid and Physical Causes: Renaissance Mythography

To date, Thomas Hyde has produced the most detailed account of the Renaissance mythography of Cupid, in a study that traces the philosophical afterlife of the love god from the writings of Boccaccio to the theories of Natale Conti.[12] My introduction to this background is indebted to his research. Beginning in the fourteenth century, in *Geneologia deorum gentilium* Boccaccio interpreted the origin story of Cupid as an extended metaphor for innate, bodily compulsions of feeling. Humans may enjoy blaming the external forces of Cupid, Venus and Mars for their overwhelming and seemingly involuntary passions, but in reality these figures presented allegories of an experience that was rooted in corporeal instinct: 'Passion is not provided by Mars or Venus, but . . . men so inclined are moved to submit to passion following a bodily disposition; if this does not exist, passion is not produced'.[13] Interestingly, Boccaccio's wording stresses that this desire, while not produced by external deities or planets, still emerges as something that happens *to* the lover rather than something actively done *by* him or her. The human being is vulnerable 'to submit' to the physical crisis, suggesting a division between the self that experiences and the body that subjects it to the passion. This is parallel to the vulnerability of Petrarchan lovers, under attack by corporeal disorder and the physical forces of love – which, as Boccaccio claimed, they attribute keenly to Cupid.

From Boccaccio onwards, metaphorical understandings of Cupid expanded to create a tension in Renaissance texts, as Hyde has observed, between his appearances as 'a single god or as a multiple personification'.[14] Boccaccio's emphasis on the forces of physical passion was shared by later mythographers, who explained the multiplicity of Cupids according to the diversity of human emotional experience.[15] The scholar Grigorio Giraldi declared in *Historia de deis gentium* (1548), his study of classical mythology, that he does 'not present one Cupid, but there are said to be many because love of things are diverse'.[16] A decade later, the mythographer Vincenzo Cartari agreed that 'if Cupid is no other than loving desire directed from us toward things, love will not be one or two, but rather many'.[17] This enduring focus on the plurality of Cupids paved the way to a materialist interpretation of erotic love and its effects, a retelling of love based upon physical interactions. Importantly, however, this did not contradict the Neoplatonism that was inseparable from higher understandings of the Cupid myth. From Hesiod onwards, the multiplicity of Cupids enabled the concurrence of interpretations both primordial and divine; physical and elemental, yet spiritual. These mythographic complexities trickle down into the love poetry of sixteenth- and seventeenth-century England, in which invasive visits by Cupid activate and present a theory of cause for myriad, alternative perspectives of experiencing desire.

For these poets, the most influential sixteenth-century mythographer was Natale Conti, who affirmed 'the unity and divinity' of the love god while also acknowledging a plurality of Cupids in human experience.[18] Following Boccaccio, Conti stressed that Cupid was not responsible for inflicting violent passions, however much humankind wished to lay the blame for their own actions on his arrow: 'it would be closer to the truth to say that Cupid is not evil in himself, but actually an excuse for criminals and shiftless men to do things that are wrong'.[19] The multiple Cupids blamed by these men were all smoke and mirrors. At the heart of the myth was the essential history that influenced Francis Bacon, as Hyde has observed:

> Beneath the fable that Cupid is the eldest of the gods is concealed the fundamental force of Empedoclean physics – the primal attraction that, binding the warring elements, fashioned the universe from chaos. A physical force might seem sub-human, but it is Conti's route to a general affirmation of Cupid's divinity. The elements can obey only a 'principle more divine' (*diviniore principio*) than themselves, and this principle shortly becomes a 'divine force' (*vim divinam*) and then, 'to speak more accurately, a divine mind (*Mentem divinam*) which induces these same motions in nature itself' (412). Indeed, Conti says, this was Cupid's original meaning: only later was he 'brought in, personified as it were, from the universal nature of things because of the unrestrained appetites of individuals' (412–23).[20]

Conti outlines this theory in his *Mythologiae* (1567), which proceeded to become the most influential work of mythography in sixteenth- and seventeenth-century Europe. His scholarship shaped the work of Philip Sidney, Edmund Spenser and George Chapman, among other prominent Elizabethan poets, decades before the appearance of Bacon's *De sapientia veterum*.[21] Cupid is the origin of things and, as 'a physical force', is akin to the atom – the first and last element of creation. Conti bypasses the Epicurean (or Lucretian) understanding of chaos to evoke Empedocles and his famous theory of the elements, which were set in motion by the primal forces of Love and Strife.[22] The bond introduced between Cupid and the atom is not, therefore, merely aligned with Epicureanism. It is bare, ancient and essential, stemming from the original impulse at the beginning of time. From this starting point, as Conti explains and Hyde acknowledges, physicality emerged from divinity. The discovery of the elemental 'Cupid' confirms that all material actions are controlled by a divine mind, which marries the most physical, seemingly base of desires to a strong Neoplatonic spiritualism. That which seems 'sub-human', the frenzied particles in the minutiae of creation, comes closest in the order of things to the original divine command. Cupid is both the first material element and action, and the first 'divine force' that sets it in motion.

It is not surprising, therefore, that Conti's element-based and, by strong association, atomic interpretation of the Cupid myth influenced the imagery and metaphysics of sixteenth-century love poetry. An awareness of this background offers a new reading of the materialist and Neoplatonic energies of lyric and narrative forms. It suggests that, contrary to previous readings of, for example, Sidney's *Astrophil and Stella* and Chapman's *Ouids Banquet of Sence*, the rub of corporeal sensuality with Neoplatonic transcendence need not have produced contradictions.[23] Instead, the physical and the spiritual represent the two sides of a single experience, bound together into the unified (and atomic) symbol of Cupid. It is no coincidence that the word 'atom', while associated most readily with ultra-materialism, translates literally as 'indivisible' and has the potential to encapsulate origins both material and divine, of space and time.[24]

Conti raises, moreover, a crucial point about Cupid's plural afterlives, in poetry and other cultural media: the generative impact of misinterpretation. Cupid was 'introduced as if he were a personage who represented the way everything behaves', Conti argues, due to 'our uncontrolled sexual appetites'.[25] An increase in desires led to further needs for expression and justification, as Hyde describes – the process of *translatio* into the figure of Cupid becomes 'also the process by which wicked men translate an image of disgracefulness into a justification for it'.[26] Leaving behind for now Conti's harsh condemnation of wickedness in desirous, sensual humankind, this theory does explain the development of Cupid into such a multifaceted figurative image. The perils of interpretation are key to the influence of Cupid on sixteenth-century poetry. Misinterpretation of the myth, according to Conti, is dangerous, and a glance at the mischievous gods in poetic spaces reveals this is the case: the poet-lover runs the risk of coming under attack by Cupids and falling into physical destruction, an experience often contrasted with the nourishing, spiritual love that comes from interpreting things correctly. While misinterpretation may be the downfall of the poetic voice, however, it is often the fuel and success of the poem. Misinterpretation is reinterpretation. As acts of interpretation increase, images of Cupid multiply, enrich and extend the possibilities of amatory and poetic experience, even as they threaten the speaker. This tension, the combined fear and desirability of self-destructive (mis)interpretation, is essential to the spaces of Elizabethan poetry frequently visited by Cupid.

Atomised Cupids in Renaissance Poetry

If the original Cupid is the 'atom' of existence, the increase of Cupids in figurative imagery becomes atomised. In the setting of the love lyric or narrative poem, flying Cupids, like volatile atoms, make vulnerable the seeming solidity of human bodies, both emotionally and physically. The Petrarchan lover has already lost substantiality of self in the face of the unattainable love object, by whom they are burned and melted by fire and ice.[27] As Cupids strike, the attack on the poeticising lover is figured in terms suggestive of atomic dissolution. To demonstrate this further, I will begin by looking at a later poem by Nicholas Hookes, who references atoms and atomic movement alongside Cupids in his sonnet sequence *Amanda, a Sacrifice to an Unknown Goddess* (1653). Hookes was writing at a time when the 'atom' was a well-known and oft-used term, but a comparison between his work and poetry produced decades earlier reveals that the trope was nothing new.

Hookes reflects on the activities of the distant love object Amanda through a variety of guises, from 'Amanda putting flowers in her bosom' to 'Amanda fearing a second showre' of rain.[28] In the poem 'To Amanda undressing her', the atomic Cupids attack:

> Thy hood's pull'd off, nay then I'm dead and gone,
> Prethie, *Amanda* put thy night-coif on.
> I see a thousand am'rous *Cupids* there.
> Which lie in Ambush, lurking in thy haire;
> Look with what haste within those locks of thine,
> They string their bowes to shoot these eyes of mine?
> Look how that little *blinde rogue* there with his dart,
> Stands aiming and layes level at my heart!

> The sympthomes of my wounds, *Amanda*, see,
> Oh *I* bleed inwards, prethie pitty me.
> I am all stuck with arrowes which are shot
> So thick and fast, that there is ne'er a spot
> About me free, each distinct atome smarts
> By't selfe, pierc't with a thousand thousand darts,
> And as a man with pangs surpriz'd by death
> Struggles for life to keep his parting breath;
> My nerves and sinews stretch, and all within
> My body earne to graspe and reach thee in;
> How could I knit and weave eternally,
> And mingle limbs into a *Gordian* tie?[29]

Hookes's poem enacts many of the tropes of the seventeenth-century poetic 'atom', via the semblance of Cupid, recalling Conti and Bacon's interpretations of the mythological allegory. For Hookes, access to Amanda's undressed hair is a dangerous prospect. A 'thousand am'rous Cupids' there lie 'in ambush', ready to strike; at first, the single arrow to the heart which 'pierces deep' (Bacon) offers a familiar take on the Cupid myth. From there, however, the language becomes increasingly atomic. Hookes refers to the arrows directly, in close metaphor that borders on synonymy, as 'each distinct atome'. The shots from the Cupids in Amanda's hair are so many that they are imagined as a swarm of atoms piercing the skin and transforming the poet's corporeal properties. Hookes's poem entwines the violence of shifting forms in material, corpuscular philosophy with the agony of experiencing unrequited love. In atomic terms, material forms are created and uncreated by the congregation and dissolution of particles. Likewise, as Hookes's body absorbs the atomic Cupids' arrows, directed from Amanda's frame, he necessarily undergoes a transformation of formal identity as his atoms mingle with hers. She becomes, at the microscopic level of corpuscular formation, part of him. His 'nerves and sinews stretch' as his physical properties 'knit' and 'weave' to join with hers, resulting in the question as to whether he could mingle their limbs into a 'Gordian tie': a knot that cannot be untied, save by a bold stroke (which, in this case, could be the final stroke that will eventually scatter the atoms of both lovers).

Hookes published *Amanda* in 1653, by which time the atoms of Lucretius and Epicureanism had captured the cultural imagination of early modern England. Yet many of the poem's features descend from Boccaccio, Conti and earlier Renaissance mythographies of Cupid. The bodies of both the lover and the object of his affections are exposed to the besiegement of 'a thousand' Cupids, whose visceral interference explains the subsequent pain of Hookes's passion. Hiding in Amanda's locks, the Cupids use her hair to string their bows: it is the vision of her hair that injures the poet, but Amanda is unwitting of the trauma as malevolent Cupids take the blame. Arguably, this could be an example of humankind's tendency, according to Conti, to translate 'an image of disgracefulness into a justification for it' – the poet, spying on Amanda and wounded by his desire, transfers the agency of his infliction on to the ministers of love. His stretching 'sinews' mirror the formation of Cupid's bow: a sinew is a nerve or a tendon, the very enabler of feeling and movement in the body; it is also a key material of the traditional bow and arrow. The reference to the poet's 'sinews' following Cupid's attack emphasises the intimacy of the internal and external forces at play, a relationship between the body and the figurative assailant that characterised late sixteenth-century expressions of love.

Some sixty years earlier, a 'sinewy' Cupid cast his influence in Marlowe's *Hero and Leander*. The eponymous Hero is drawn to her lover upon hearing his arguments: the effect is such that it is as though she has 'swallow'd *Cupids* golden hooke'.[30] Marlowe's violent image likens Hero to a fish reeled in by the angler, though strikingly the 'hook' of Leander's honeyed words belongs to Cupid, not the lover himself. It 'pierces deep' – physically and figuratively – for maximum injury, as heightened by its 'golden' quality.[31] Elsewhere, in Spenser's Sonnet 47 from *Amoretti*, 'smyling lookes' are not to be trusted because they 'are lyke but unto golden hookes, / That from the foolish fish theyr bayts doe hyde' (1–4).[32] The golden sheen but disguises the weapon beneath, designed to deceive, tempt and capture the 'foolish fish'. Spenser's simile is supported by the Latin proverb 'fish with a golden hook', which recommends the 'golden' appearance to conceal and even make desirable the weapon.[33] Hero is certainly caught, to the extent that she loses free will:

> As she spake this, her tongue tript,
> For unawares (*Come thither*) from her slipt;
> And sodainly her former colour chang'd,
> And here and there her eyes through anger rang'd
> And like a planet, moving several waies
> At one selfe instant, she poore soule assaies,
> Loving, not to love at all, and everie part
> Strove to resist the motions of her hart.
> And hands so pure, so innocent, nay such,
> As might have made Heaven stoope to have a touch,
> Did she uphold to *Venus*, and againe,

> Vow'd spotlesse chastitie, but all in vaine,
> *Cupid* beats down her prayers with his wings,
> Her vowes above the emptie air he flings:
> All deepe enrag'd, his sinowie bow he bent,
> And shot a shaft that burning from him went.[34]

Following her ingestion of Cupid's hook, Hero's physical properties undergo involuntary change. A rift opens between her body and her soul, recalling Boccaccio's claim that confused and erroneous lovers attribute the passions of internal, 'bodily disposition[s]' to the external actions of Cupid.[35] The poetry follows Boccaccio's observation in the helplessness of Hero in love, overwhelmed by a transformation that is forced upon her, even as it emerges from within. Marlowe applies the extraordinary simile 'like a planet moving several ways / At one self instant' to heighten Hero's turmoil, attributing cosmic overtones to her confused, contradictory state of being, which moves in 'several ways' even while these movements unite into a single-seeming orbit. There may be torment and uncertainty beneath the surface, but Hero's path forward is set – much like the motion of a planet, which obeys extra-planetary forces. The command of 'Come thither' is a slip or trip of her tongue, caught by Cupid, which no longer belongs to her; her soul strives to protest and resist the overpowering force of desire, but to no avail. Violent Cupid 'beats down her prayers', 'flings' her vows, and is angered at his rebellious subject. The specification of 'his *sinewy* bow he bent' (italics mine) anticipates the onset of disorder at Hero's innermost core, the very origins of feeling and movement within her body. Marlowe reminds the reader that Cupid's bow, as conventional for the object, is physically formed from sinew; in doing so, he also heightens his emphasis on the corporeal and emotional vulnerability of the victim. If something is 'sinewy' it can also be twisted, which is felt in the impact of Cupid, and of the resulting tragic love, on Hero's corporeal experience and in the poetry. The general air of risk, combined with a violent vocabulary, suggests that the human loss arguably outweighs the giddy heights of desire.

Hookes's *Amanda* and Marlowe's *Hero and Leander* are very different poetical works, but they share a focus on the intense corporeal disorder wreaked by warring Cupids. This conflict comes not only from the violence of love but also from clashes of poetic (mis)interpretation, following Conti. From hooks to hair, the Cupids alter the properties of lovers and poems at the micro-level of bodies and texts. Hookes's poem demonstrates a common trope of the Cupid in early modern love lyric, whose arrows not only strike the powerless lover but creep inside their body to alter their very corpuscular properties.

Moving back a century, it is not only arrows but Cupids themselves that take over Elizabethan bodies. In *Ouids Banquet of Sence* (1595), George Chapman takes as his subject Ovid's passion for the beautiful Julia, known under the pseudonym of Corinna. The poem follows Ovid's sensory experiences as he encounters Corinna bathing in a garden: from hearing to smell, sight, taste and ultimately touch, the Roman poet's senses are awakened one-by-one until the lovers are interrupted 'with the view / Of other Dames, who then the Garden painted' (116.1–2).[36] *Ouids Banquet of Sence* has the reputation of being notoriously difficult, with its intentions unclear.[37] While the poem centres its focus on Ovid, its narrative interjections and repeated emphasis on spiritual metamorphosis have been considered, quite contrastingly, Platonic. According to Laurence Lerner, the title of the sonnets that follow the titular poem, 'Ouids Banquet of Sence', in its first edition, 'A Coronet for his Mistress Philosophy', 'is hardly Ovidian, and the poem is a twisted piece of Renaissance Neoplatonism'.[38] As a description, 'twisted' is more than appropriate, though perhaps not in the sense of Lerner's usage. Like Cupid's twisted, 'sinewy' bow, and like the concurrence of the single, primeval 'Cupid' amid the hostile swarm of multiple winged gods, the complex allusions of 'Ouids Banquet of Sence' achieve more than one thing at once. The poem attacks itself satirically from within, exposing a separation of voices: the narratorial voice directs the careful reader away from the entrapment of sensuality, even while Ovid vividly recounts the memory of his (increasingly perilous) delights.[39] Of all the texts considered in this chapter, 'Ouids Banquet of Sence' could serve as the greatest warning against poetic misinterpretation in love and desire, even as – and in part because – Ovid's unbridled sensuality demands increasingly complex expression and, by extension, compelling and pleasurable poetry. The twists and turns of Chapman's verse – as they manifest through the perspective of Ovid, the disordered lover – fit the double existence of Conti and Bacon's 'love' as both elemental origin and atomised flurry of physical, figurative representations. This is confirmed by the frequent appearances of Cupid in the poem, who is associated directly with threatening atomic activity.

Ovid proclaims love for his Corinna in the fashion of Orpheus, reflecting on the auditory quality of her singing even while exhaling his own poetic praise. Stanza 21 describes, after he has had the privilege of hearing the love object sing:

> In precious incense of her holy breath,
> My loue doth offer Hecatombs of notes
> To all the Gods; who now despise the death
> Of Oxen, Heifers, Wethers, Swine, and Goates.
> A Sonnet in her breathing sacrifiz'd,
> Delights them more then all beasts bellowing throates,
> As much with heauen, as with my hearing priz'd.
> And as guilt Atoms in the sunne appeare,
> So greete these sounds the grissells of myne eare. (21)

Her breath provides the sweet-smelling incense; her sung poetry the audible sacrifice to the gods. In the final two lines of the verse, Chapman draws a simile to relate the experience of hearing this song in explicitly materialist terms. The sounds are like 'guilt Atoms' that appear in the sun – here, Chapman recreates a common analogy for atomic movement that featured in Aristotle's corpus before Lucretius' *De rerum natura*, that of the 'motes' visible in the sunbeam.[40] His focus on the physical experience of absorbing Corinna's song takes in the minute details, to the extent of feeling the sound on the 'grissells', or cartilage, of his ear. There is a clash of the senses within the simile of these two lines, as it is not clear how envisioning particles in the sunlight is like the greeting of a sound. This could be considered in different ways: the sun comes out, the light revealing deeper layers to nature than what immediately meets the eye; perhaps this degree of natural wonder is akin to the marvel of hearing Corinna's voice. Predominantly, however, the simile operates at a materialist level. The allusion to 'grissells' in the final line, accompanied by the hard 'g' alliteration of 'guilt' and 'greete', emphasises tactility and physical impact. The musical 'Hecatombs' of Julia's song are material, like atoms. To support this reading, Chapman reuses the adjective 'guilt' from an earlier stanza, where Ovid exclaims 'Me thinks her tunes flye guilt, like Attick Bees / To my eares hives' (18.1–2). Analogies between bees and the atomic swarm were extremely popular across early modern literature, in the sixteenth as well as the seventeenth centuries.[41] The fact that Chapman qualifies these bees as 'Attick' could be a reference to ancient Greek atomism.

Ovid feels Corinna's notes as though they are particles jostling in his ear. Chapman continues to describe this phenomenon in the twenty-second stanza, where most suitably a reference to Cupid creeps in:

> Whose pores doe open wide to theyr regreete,
> And my implanted ayre, that ayre embraceth
> Which they impresse; I feele theyr nimble feete
> Tread my eares Labyrinth; theyr sport amazeth

> They keepe such measure; play themselues and dance.
> And now my soule in Cupids Furnace blazeth,
> Wrought into furie with theyr daliance:
> And as the fire the parched stuble burns,
> So fades my flesh, and into spyrit turns. (22)

Suddenly, with the reference to 'feete', this is no longer strictly an allusion to sounds and atoms. The verse continues to emphasise the atomic materiality of the experience – the 'pores' of the ear open to receive more; the sounds of the song continue to move deeper into Ovid's ear, until they 'tread' his 'Labyrinth'. Now these are atoms that 'tread', 'sport' and 'play'. 'Feet' is suggestive moreover of poetic feet, providing a quasi-materialist explanation for the composition of Ovid's verse. He hears and receives Corinna's 'sounds', which convert in 'Cupids Furnace' to the units of his poetry. Here, Chapman integrates a Neoplatonic 'twist'. The image of particles at play is a common one from Lucretius, but the reference to 'Cupids Furnace' after the dance suggests that these 'atoms' may have been Cupids all along. As with Hookes's *Amanda*, these sounds – which are atoms – which are Cupids enter in at the poet's pores and transform his material properties, but they also enact a process of chemical transmutation that inspires a higher, Platonised poetics: he burns and 'into spyrit turns'. Ovid confirms this in stanza 25 with the conclusion, following the aural reception of his love: 'Thus sence were feasted, / My life that in my flesh a Chaos is / Should to a Golden worlde be thus dygested' (25.2–4). Materialist chaos coincides in his body with the promise of a perfected, purified 'Golden worlde'. The reference to the golden age unites the Ovidian and Platonic features of his poetry into one complex dynamic, where spiritual perfection is in reach, but the means is the motion and recombination of physical properties.

Chapman's Ovid combines the Neoplatonic higher principle of love with the shattering, materialist impact of desire.[42] The narrator of 'Ouids Banquet of Sence' may be guiding the reader away from sensual materialism and towards Platonic doctrine, but this is complicated by the integral presence of Neoplatonism within Ovid's erotic experiences. Unsurprisingly, this marriage between the physical and the spiritual finds its home in the multifaceted Cupid image, which multiplies according to the (mis)interpretation of each sensorial experience in response to the love object. Much later in the poem, Ovid converses with Corinna and seeks to justify his passion according to the conventions of Renaissance mythography:

> Cupid that acts in you, suffers in mee
> To make himselfe one tryumph-place of twaine,
> Into your tunes and odors turned hee,
> And through my sences flew into my braine
> Where rules the Prince of sence, whose Throne hee takes,
> And of my Motions engines framd a chaine
> To leade mee where hee list; and heere hee makes
> Nature (my fate) enforce mee: and resignes
> The raines of all, to you, in whom hee shines. (84)

Cupid, it appears, is to blame. In line with the changeable metaphors of the Cupid figure from Renaissance mythography and the poetics of love, Chapman's agent of desire is a shapeshifter. There is some ambiguity around Cupid turning 'into' Corinna's 'tunes and odors': either the love god takes shelter in her exhalations, occupying them as the vehicle for his transition into Ovid's body; or Corinna's musical sounds and sweet smells, as received by the senses of the poet, are but Cupid(s) in disguise. This could be the deception of Cupid's 'golden hook' all over again. Chapman's materialist account of the surrender to love figures the body as both prisoner and machine. Cupid is in two places at once, seizing control of the engine room that directs all motions, the 'Prince of sence' in the brain, and dragging the lover by 'chaine' to the mercy of his Corinna. The plight of the lover enchained by sensuous desire recalls an interjection by the first-person narrator halfway through the poem, when the voice – possibly Chapman's – interrupts in stanza 57 to explain that Ovid's 'quick verse' was inspired as he was 'strooke dead' by the vivid sight of his mistress (57.7, 57.6). The description of Ovid's rapturous verses as 'quick' is highly ambivalent, and Zenón Luis-Martínez is correct to point out that it is 'perhaps ironically' that 'Chapman's authorial persona avows . . . the imitative subservience of his laborious "Art"' to that of his master.[43] This ambivalence grows in the later stanzas, where it becomes clearer that experiences of desire are not what they seem, and that both Ovid's love and his erotic poetry find their origin in acts of misinterpretation.

In the next stanza, Ovid begs, recalling Conti's condemnation of those who evoke Cupid to seek 'justification' for acting on bodily desires:

> For yeelding loue then, doe not hate impart,
> Nor let mine Eye, your carefull Harbengere
> That hath puruaide your Chamber in my hart,
> Be blamde for seeing who it lodged there. (85.1–4)

The action, Ovid claims, is all Cupid's ('Cupid that acts in you') and the suffering, besieged poet cannot be held responsible. Following Boccaccio and Conti, however, this would be a misinterpretation of the Cupid myth and denial of human responsibility, an error that might be noticed by Chapman's careful, critical reader. Ovid argued in the earlier stanza that Cupid 'makes / Nature (my fate) enforce mee' (84.7–8), stressing that his love is compulsory but not unwilling. It is his 'fate': a force of nature that applies a physical, natural philosophical explanation for his passions and behaviour. This sense of irrevocable destiny is continued with the role of the 'Eye', which has 'puruaide' Corinna's dwelling place into his heart. To 'purvey' is to arrange, prepare or supply, but it also bears the now obsolete meanings of to foresee, to have in mind, or to consider. An emphasis on foresight strengthens his case that loving Corinna is his 'fate', an irresistible force of nature – it is safe to say that he cannot get her out of his head (or heart). The eye that absorbs her beauty is her 'carefull Harbengere', but this introduces a level of uncertainty. A harbinger is a host or a lodging; it follows that Ovid's faculty of vision, once it has received an imprint of the beloved, should treasure and care for its impression of her there. The question remains as to whether the poet is harbouring part of Corinna, or the shapeshifting Cupid that may have disguised himself into her sensual qualities. Once again, the unreliable significance of Cupid exposes the perils of Ovid's materialist desire, recalling Conti's accusation that the winged god becomes 'an excuse for criminals and shiftless men to do things that are wrong'.[44] Morally, the poet-lover has fallen into the destructive act of misreading physical love. Aesthetically, these are the very acts of (mis)interpretation that not only enrich and energise the poem but produce it.

Chapman's Ovid directs his focus inwards, studying the transferral of the Cupid 'in' the love object into the lover, where the sensorial love god becomes responsible for his ruin or his bliss. Throughout the love poetry of the period, Cupid not only flies and lands 'on' loving and beloved bodies, but enters, often violently and encroachingly, 'into' them.[45] In *Hero and Leander*, Marlowe's introduction to the beautiful Hero presents Cupid's deep attachment:

> But this is true, so like the one the other,
> As he imagyn'd *Hero* was his mother.
> And oftentimes into her bosome flew,
> About her naked necke his bare armes threw,
> And laid his childish head upon her brest,
> And, with still panting rockt, there tooke his rest.[46]

As Jane Kingsley-Smith observes of the period's fine art, '[a]ccording to the conventions of Italian Renaissance art, Cupid's presence defines the naked woman as Venus, thus celebrating her peerless beauty'.[47] In a poem where the heroine is *not* Venus, however, this relationship breeds tension. Cupid mistakes Hero for his mother, thereby adding another layer to the dangerous, yet poetically productive, levels of (mis)interpretation stemming from the Cupid myth.[48] The risk is manifested in the clashes of Marlowe's poetry, which combines images of maternal comfort with a vocabulary of erotic transgression. Hero is not Venus, though her exquisite looks suggest that she is so. Cupid's flight 'into' – not merely 'on to' – her bosom hints troublesomely at violation, an atmosphere that is heightened by the heroine's 'naked neck' and Cupid's untranquil 'panting'.

Cupid's preoccupation with the internal properties of the beloved is a central trope in Elizabethan poetry, demonstrated further by his anxious activity in one of the most famous sonnet sequences of all: Philip Sidney's *Astrophil and Stella*. In the opening sonnets, Sidney traces the journey of Cupid from his mythological origin (the classical sources of 'Greece') to the magnetic presence of Astrophil's Stella, where the personification of desire is drawn by the very 'impulse' he stands for, migrating to realise his active desires for physical commotion and propagation:

> *LOVE* borne in *Greece*, of late fled from his native place,
> Forc'd by a tedious proofe, that Turkish hardned hart,
> Is no fit marke to pierce with his fine pointed dart:
> And pleasd with our soft peace, staid here his flying race.
> But finding these North clymes do coldly him embrace,
> Not used to frozen clips, he strave to find some part,
> Where with most ease and warmth he might employ his art:
> At length he perch'd himself in *Stella's* joyful face,
> Whose faire skin, beamy eyes, like morning sun on snow,
> Deceiv'd the quaking boy, who thought from so pure light,
> Effects of lively heat, must needs in nature grow.
> But she most faire, most cold, made him thence take his flight
> To my close heart; where, while some firebrands he did lay,
> He burnt unwares his wings, and cannot fly away.[49]

Fleeing the Ottoman wars of his ancient homeland, Love – or Cupid – emigrates to Sidney's England to breed his 'flying race', but the very 'peace' that attracted him becomes a deterrent to desire. Desire is bred by warmth, movement, interaction and, as Sidney's ensuing sonnets inform us, by a material conflict and (mis)interpretation of the signs that becomes both cause and effect. This traps Astrophil, Stella and Love itself into an ironic and dangerous cycle of productive self-destruction, mirroring Conti's warning of the perils of *translatio*, where so many stages in the experience of desire can go wrong. In sonnet 8, Cupid is the one committing the error of misinterpretation. Stella's 'beamy eyes' and 'joyful face' give the impression of sustaining warmth, but her actual resistance to love leaves him cold and he retreats, with violent consequences, to Astrophil's heart. Cupid is trapped, and Astrophil is trapped by him. Each seeming defeat is a consequence of misinterpreting the signs of love, which in turn breeds further metaphors for desire and further actions for Cupid.

Sidney directs his focus inwards here with the suggestion that Cupid perches not 'on', but 'in' Stella's face. As with the notes and sounds of Chapman's Corinna, it is unclear from Astrophil's perspective of Stella's features those which are innately hers, and those which are shaped by the influence – and physical residence – of Cupid. Of all her features, it is Stella's eyes that are most affected by the uncertain and dangerous forces of love and desire. Love is, of course, blind; so, Bacon reminds us, is the atom. Intrusions of atoms or atomies into the eye are frequent across late sixteenth- and early seventeenth-century literature, where they invade and disrupt the vision: Shakespeare's Phoebe, for example, refers to eyelids that 'shut their coward gates on atomies' in *As You Like It*.[50] In Elizabethan love poetry, Cupids creep in and commonly assault the sight like the dust particles of 'atomies'. Michael Drayton refers to this in his sonnet sequence *Idea* when, gazing into his lover's eyes and spying his reflection, he conflates the image of himself with the malicious Cupid responsible for the desire: 'And in your Eye, the Boy that did the Murther, / Your Cheekes yet pale, since first he gave the Wound' (2.11–14).[51] Sidney's *Astrophil and Stella* carries this association still further, where the Petrarchan emphasis on reading the love object's face collides, at times grotesquely, with an army of besieging, atomised Cupids. In sonnet 8, the influence of Cupid is no 'soft' love but a hostile takeover by foreign forces. The winged god retreats from Stella's 'joyful' yet cold face to the warmer heart of the unrequited lover where, in the same fashion as described by Chapman, he self-destructs by setting his surroundings on fire.[52]

It is not too much of a stretch to reconfigure the encroaching Cupids in Sidney's verse with the 'atome' blows dealt by Amanda's hair in Hookes's sonnet, some seventy years later. These atomic Cupids are jostling, sharp and ready to pierce and undermine the solidity of the physical self. Their movements parallel Sidney's belief in *The Defence of Poesy* that poetry should present images that 'strike, pierce' and 'possess the sight of the soul', an understanding of *energeia* that rests on material characteristics – as explored in the chapter by Jonathan Sell later in this volume.[53] In sonnet 11 Sidney writes, continuing with the narrative of Cupid in search of a new host:

> So when thou saw'st, in Nature's cabinet
> *Stella*, thou straight lookst babies in her eyes,
> In her cheeke's pit thou didst thy pitfould set,
> And in her breast bopeepe or couching lyes,
> Playing and shining in each outward part:
> But, foole, seekst not to get into her hart. (11.9–14)

Addressing Cupid, Sidney describes his attempted invasion of Stella's person in monstrous, atomised metaphor. Love 'straight lookst babies in her [Stella's] eyes': for Cupid, Stella's eyes provide a mirror, but his act of looking is no mere passive recognition of his likeness. By seeing, he actively reproduces his reflection in her features, so that her very identity comes under attack. From the eyes down, she is rapidly taken over by Cupid's infantile forces to the extent that her person, from the perspective of the stricken lover, is more Cupid than Stella. Far from the bloom of conventional blazon, her cheek is now a hollow 'pit', consumed and repurposed by the flying swarm. It is set as a trap for the unassuming lover – a 'pitfould' is, like a pitfall, unfavourable terrain where an army is made vulnerable to capture; it is moreover a term applied to traps used for catching birds or animals. However, Sidney's choice of 'fold' also implies a claustrophobic swarm of Cupids nesting in Stella's cheek, now a breeding 'pit' for desire. These 'babies' continue their activity 'in' – once again, not simply 'on' – her breast, where their game of 'bopeepe' is reminiscent of the rapid unpredictability of atomic motion (and most especially of prevalent, contemporary analogies of atoms at play and dance). Following Conti, as the number of Cupids and their movements increase, so do the desires experienced by the lover as he gazes upon the woman formerly known as Stella – now little more than a host for Love's invading forces.

Sidney continues in the next sonnet:

> CUPID, because thou shin'st in *Stella's* eyes,
> That from her lockes, thy day-nets, none scapes free,
> That those lips swell, so full of thee they bee,
> That her sweete breath makes oft thy flames to rise. (12.1–4)

As Jane Kingsley-Smith has claimed, Sidney 'constructs a kind of double blazon in which Stella's every physical perfection becomes a Cupidean attribute'.[54] It is unclear, from Sidney's cataloguing of the love object's features, which originate in Stella and which are more directly transformations enforced by Cupid. As the love god infiltrates Stella's features, her physical properties begin to change. She is no longer purely Stella. Via a process similar to atomic chemical mixture, Stella is now also Cupid, who shines in her eyes and uses her hair, her 'lockes' (with some suggestive wordplay of locking and trapping here), as 'day-nets'. Resonating with Amanda's hair as imagined by Hookes, Stella's tresses unleash a Cupid army. With a touch of physical horror, her 'lips swell' – they are full of swarming Cupids, living particles with a destructive agenda.

Stella has become the embodiment of Love, but once again all is not as it seems. Revisiting the previous sonnet, the grotesque, teeming Cupid 'babies' dominate 'each outward part' but gain no deeper access. The Cupids set a trap for the naïve lover on her face, but Stella deceives Love in turn by denying her heart. Through all this, it is ambiguous whether she, Cupid, or indeed Astrophil is to blame for this violence in perspective. It is the lover who blazons and embellishes this monstrous Stella, with more than a hint of lustful longing to become one of the minute 'Cupids' playing about her lips, cheek and breast. Once again, the lover blames Cupid for the perils of (mis)interpretation, manifested by the physical flux of personal attributes. This transference of agency, however, makes a productive model for the complexities and clashing experiences of love, and of a poetics of the love lyric. In *Astrophil and Stella*, as elsewhere in Elizabethan poetry, Cupids extend and elaborate upon the Petrarchan tropes they represent: from an elemental, corpuscular perspective, they offer a detailed explanation for the dissolving of physical properties in the grip of desire's ice and fire.

Conclusion

In his sonnet sequence *Idea*, Michael Drayton introduces his verse in 'To the Reader of these Sonnets' with expression that is inherently atomic. He writes: 'My Verse is the true image of my Mind, / Ever in motion, still desiring change; / And as thus to Varietie inclin'd' (10–12). The revolving topics of his sonnets complement the ever-changing, ever-desirous motions of his mind, which fly – like atoms, and like Cupids – from object to object. It is no surprise that Cupid flits between Drayton's sonnets, upsetting physical and emotional stability in his wake.⁵⁵ Like Bacon's Cupid, or the atom, his lyrics bear (to quote Bacon again) that 'impulse of desire ... which by repetition and multiplication produces all the variety of nature'. Drayton's self-declared poetic impulse, '[e]ver in motion, still desiring change', could be taken as a slogan for the impulsive, anamorphic figure of Cupid across Elizabethan poetry.⁵⁶

The growing poetic associations around Cupid result in an alternative take on the nature of things – *de rerum natura* – in Elizabethan and early Jacobean love poetry. These corporeal reimaginings of desire and its aftermath owe their creation to the ancient origin of Cupid as the atom, or primary material 'impulse', as explored by Natale Conti and other Renaissance mythographers. The legacy of Cupid's atomic beginning subsists in the love god's behaviour (at times constructive, mostly transgressive and destructive) within and beyond lovers' poetic bodies. As actions and interpretations of the Cupid myth diversified in sixteenth-century poetic culture, they both responded to and generated new expressions of desire, which manifested in elaborate descriptions of physical alteration and disorder. Minuscule Cupids offer an atomic perspective on the disintegration of boundaries in erotic love: in the poetry of Marlowe, Chapman, Drayton and Sidney, among others, the lover's desire to enter and combine self with the love object is transferred to the intermediary (and atomised) presence of winged love gods. These misinterpretations of Cupid, as Conti would judge them, are self-destructive and dangerous for the poet-lover, but productive and regenerative for the poem. They initiate a theory of cause for an ever-evolving, complex erotic poetics. Like the atom or elemental 'impulse of desire' associated with the ancient myth, these Cupids recreate the visceral impact of love and produce new forms of expression in poetic spaces. Also like the atom, they reconnect the physical experiences of desires with a reminder of their ancient, mystical origin: the Love that 'begot all things'.

Notes

I am very grateful to Zenón Luis-Martínez, and to his colleagues at the University of Huelva, for organising the symposium 'Unwritten Arts: Keywords in English Sixteenth-Century Poetry and Poetics' (October 2019), the point of origin for this volume.
1. Bacon, *Of the Wisdom of the Ancients* (English translation of *De sapientia veterum*), in *Works of Francis Bacon*, 13:122–3.
2. Ibid., 76–80.

3. See Hesiod, *Theogony*, 116–22, in *Theogony, Works and Days, Testimonia*, 13: 'In truth, first of all Chasm came to be, and then broad-breasted Earth ... and Eros, who is the most beautiful among the immortal gods, the limb-melter – he overpowers the mind and the thoughtful counsel of all the gods and of all human beings in their breasts.'
4. My opening comments on Bacon's 'Cupid, or the Atom' stem from a longer analysis of the passage in my recent monograph: Gorman, *The Atom in Seventeenth-Century Poetry*, 1–4.
5. Notable studies of literary representations of Cupid during the Renaissance have focused, largely, on the figure's intersections with theology. In a recent monograph, Kingsley-Smith examines the turbulent role of Cupid in early modern reformed theology: 'what unites his disparate roles and makes Cupid a controversial, often seductive, figure for poets, dramatists and polemicists alike is his adversarial relationship to English Protestantism' (*Cupid in Early Modern Literature*, 1). In 1986 Hyde drew attention to the Renaissance 'poetic theology of love', which he argued was so complex 'because the fictional or figurative cosmos it implies shares so many terms and images with the real cosmos explicit in Christian theology' (*Poetic Theology of Love*, 18).
6. On the study of Lucretius at the University of Oxford, see Feingold, 'The Humanities', 250.
7. Sidney, *Defence*, in *Miscellaneous Prose*, ed. Duncan-Jones and van Dorsten, 80.
8. Webbe, *Discourse*, ed. Hernández-Santano, 75.
9. Several examples can be taken from Lucretius' reflection on physical love in Book 4. He writes, to quote William Ellery Leonard's translation: 'Thus, one who gets a stroke from Venus' shafts – / ... that one strains to get / Even to the thing whereby he's hit, and longs / To join with it and cast into its frame / The fluid drawn even from within its own. / For the *mute craving* doth presage delight' (*On the Nature of Things*, trans. Leonard, 4.1053–7, emphasis added). Leonard translates 'craving' from *cupido*, or desire. See also the link between desire and lust (*cupido*) for life in Book 3: 'And too, when all is said, / What evil lust of life is this so great / Subdues us to live, so dreadfully distraught / In perils and alarms?' (3.1077).
10. For example, Barbour and Norbrook, in their edition of Lucy Hutchinson's translation of Lucretius, comment on the more 'light-hearted' tone of 'Armies of atoms sport in those bright beames' (2.129). See Hutchinson, *Translation of Lucretius*, 539.
11. For further reading on the influence of Lucretius on early modern poetics, see Hock, *Erotics of Materialism*.
12. See especially Hyde's chapter 'Renaissance Mythographers and Neoplatonists', in *Poetic Theology of Love*, 87–110.
13. I quote from Hyde's translation, *Poetic Theology of Love*, 89. For the original Latin, see Boccaccio, *Genealogie*, ed. Romano, IX.4, 2:453.

14. Hyde, *Poetic Theology of Love*, 105.
15. They also followed, in doing so, the words of Philostratus the Elder, who offered the following analysis of an image of numerous Cupids gathering apples: 'they are many because of the many things men love' (*Imagines*, trans. Fairbanks, 1.6). I am grateful to Zenón Luis-Martínez for directing me to Titian's study of this image, the painting *Ofrenda a Venus* (1518), which is housed in Museo del Prado, Madrid. See <https://www.museodelprado.es/coleccion/obra-de-arte/ofrenda-a-venus/42b30ed4-0e79-4f2b-aa62-091a27f895b3>.
16. Translation from Hyde, *Poetic Theology of Love*, 105. For the Latin, see Gyraldus, *Opera omnia*, 1.407E.
17. Hyde, *Poetic Theology of Love*, 105. For the original Italian, see Cartari, *Imagini degli dei degli antichi*, 102.
18. Hyde, *Poetic Theology of Love*, 107.
19. Conti, *Mythologiae*, IV.14, p. 411; trans. Mulryan and Brown, 1:336.
20. Hyde, *Poetic Theology of Love*, 109.
21. See, for example, Hartmann's note on the influence of Conti's *Mythologiae* during the sixteenth century: 'No other mythography so fully offers up antiquity to the creative uses and argumentative needs of the readers of that period' (*English Mythography*, 46).
22. See 'The Place of Love and Strife', in O'Brien, *Empedocles' Cosmic Cycle*, 104–26. See also Conti, *Mythologiae*, on Empedocles: 'Because the ancients believed that Cupid was the oldest of the gods, they seemed to be following the opinion of Empedocles, who claimed that Love and then Strife separated all of the matter that had once been amassed in a state of confusion, and which could produce nothing of its own without the help of these two' (IV.14, p. 412; trans. Mulryan and Brown, 1:336).
23. Snare comments on the ambiguity in *Ouids Banquet of Sence*, for example, as to whether Ovid 'rises to a spiritual epiphany or sinks in spiritual debauch' (*Mystification*, 118). See also Snare's acknowledgement of Chapman's debt to Conti, and a review of other critics' analysis of this influence (27–32). See also Luis-Martínez's study of Chapman's complex qualities and poetic 'habit', this volume.
24. I discuss the significance of the 'atom' further in early modern metaphysical, Platonic and poetic contexts in *The Atom in Seventeenth-Century Poetry*.
25. Conti, *Mythologiae*, IV.14, pp. 412–13; trans. Mulryan and Brown, 1:337.
26. Hyde, *Poetic Theology of Love*, 109. Conti writes: 'For foolish people actually used Cupid as an excuse for many of the bitter quarrels and terrible things that occurred both at home and abroad' (*Mythologiae*, IV.14, p. 410; trans. Mulryan and Brown, 1:335).
27. Brady re-explores the 'Petrarchan conventions of the ice-cold beloved and fiery lover' ('The Physics of Melting', 40).
28. Hookes, *Amanda*, 17 and 50.

29. Ibid., 34–5.
30. Marlowe, *Hero and Leander*, 333, in *Complete Works*, ed. Gill, 1:197.
31. The image of 'piercing' poetic words was pervasive during the period. I am grateful to Zenón Luis-Martínez for reminding me of Sidney's description of the poet who paints '[a] perfect picture . . . for he yieldeth to the powers of the mind an image of that whereof the philosopher bestoweth but a wordish description, which doth neither strike, pierce, nor possess the sight of the soul so much as that other doth' (*Defence*, in *Miscellaneous Prose*, 85). See also Wolfe: 'Chapman imagines his ideal readers as "serching" spirits capable of penetrating the subtle mysteries of his arcane texts' (*Humanism, Machinery*, 162).
32. Spenser, *Amoretti*, sonnet 47, in *Yale Edition of the Shorter Poems*, 628–9.
33. See, for example, Riley, *Dictionary of Latin Quotations*, 32.
34. Marlowe, *Hero and Leander*, 357–72, in *Complete Works*, 1:197–8.
35. Quoted previously from Hyde's translation, *Poetic Theology of Love*, 89. For the original Latin, see Boccaccio, *Genealogie*, IX.4, 2:453.
36. Chapman, 'Ouids Banquet of Sence', in *Poems*, ed. Bartlett, 53–82. Further references to the poem are from this edition, and are cited parenthetically in the text by stanza and (when necessary) line numbers.
37. Kermode referred to *Ouids Banquet of Sence* as 'one of the most difficult poems in the [English] language' ('The Banquet of Sense', 84). Editions of the poem are typically apologetic for its difficulty. For example, Braden writes that Chapman's 'ambitions inform a style . . . that can be extraordinarily difficult to untangle into ordinary intelligibility' (*Sixteenth-Century Poetry*, 430); Miles introduces Chapman's poetry as 'characteristically learned and difficult, both for its intellectual content and its compressed and knotty language' (*Classical Mythology*, 106). Snare, however, argues that it 'is not the most difficult or obscure poem in the English language, as its interpreters had proclaimed it to be' (*Mystification*, 3).
38. Lerner, 'Ovid and the Elizabethans', 131. Luis-Martínez has recently argued that 'A Coronet for His Mistresse Philosophie' 'undercuts the dialogic and narrative patterns of the Petrarchan amatory cycle', as the 'epideictic quality of Chapman's language guides the reader in the intellective process of discovering love's nature' ('Friendlesse Verse', 567–8). For the full text of 'Coronet', see Chapman, *Poems*, 83–6.
39. As Waddington has written, '[t]he critical issue of the poem hinges on whether Ovid should be regarded as Chapman's spokesman or simply as a fictive character'. Waddington argues the latter, referring to Chapman's dedication to readers with 'the "judiciall perpective" and "The actual meanes to sound the philosophical conceits" . . . The judicial reader is expected to bring this knowledge to bear upon the poem, thereby reinforcing acceptance of the narrator's negative evaluation of Ovid, expressed by narrative intrusions and admonitory

digressions' ('Visual Rhetoric', 41–2). Four years previously, Gless argued for an ironic reading of the poem in 'Chapman's Ironic Ovid'. On the poem as satire, see Weaver, who takes '*Ovid's Banquet* seriously as a satire of the English epyllion' ('Banquet of the Common Sense', 759).

40. For the reference to 'mooving attoms in the sunbeames', see Hutchinson, *Translation of Lucretius*, 2.123. Aristotle refers to Democritus' comparison between atoms and 'motes in the air which we see in shafts of light' (*De anima*, trans. Lawson-Tancred, 403b31–404a5).
41. For instance, the lyricist John Dowland associates bees with 'atomies' in 'It was a time when silly bees could speak' (*Third and Last Booke*, sig. K2v).
42. Wheeler, for example, reads Ficinian allusions into Ovid's narrative in *Ouids Banquet of Sence*, arguing that the poem overall 'espouses a Neoplatonic epistemology but rejects its impracticable puritanism and legitimizes physical love' ('The obiect', 326).
43. Luis-Martínez, 'Friendlesse Verse', 570.
44. Conti, *Mythologiae*, IV.14, p. 411; trans. Mulryan and Brown, 1:336
45. As Kingsley-Smith has observed, the 'conceit of the love-god positioning himself in a woman's eyes, on her cheek, or in her bosom was conventional'. She proceeds to argue that 'no other Elizabethan poet used it to such intense effect as Sidney' (*Cupid in Early Modern Literature*, 40).
46. Marlowe, *Hero and Leander*, 39–44, in *Complete Works*, 1:190.
47. Kingsley-Smith, *Cupid in Early Modern Literature*, 38.
48. A parallel moment can be found in Giles Fletcher the Elder's second sonnet from *Licia, or Poemes of Love*: 'Wearie was love, and sought to take his rest, / He made his choice, uppon a virgins lappe: / And slylie crept, from thence unto her breast, / Where still he meant, to sport him in his happe' (2.1–4). See Fletcher, *English Works*, ed. Berry, 82.
49. Sidney, *Astrophil and Stella*, sonnet 8, in *Poems*, ed. Ringler, 168–9. References to this work are cited parenthetically in the text by sonnet and line number.
50. Shakespeare, *As You Like It*, 3.5.13, in *Norton Shakespeare*, ed. Greenblatt, 1636.
51. Drayton's *Idea* (1619 text) is cited parenthetically in the text by sonnet and line numbers from *Works*, ed. Hebel, 2:309–42.
52. Of Drayton's many poems featuring the god of love, sonnet 23 from *Idea* reveals parallels with Chapman's corporeal attack:

> Love banish'd Heav'n, in Earth was held in scorne,
> Wand'ring abroad in Need and Beggerie;
> And wanting Friends, though of a Goddesse borne,
> Yet crav'd the Almes of such as passed by:
> I, like a Man devout and charitable,
> Clothed the Naked, lodg'd this wand'ring Ghest,

> With Sighes and Teares still furnishing his Table,
> With what might make the Miserable blest.
> But this ungratefull, for my good desert,
> Intic'd my Thoughts against me to conspire,
> Who gave consent to steale away my Heart,
> And set my Brest, his Lodging, on a fire. (23.1–12)

The 'charitable' and increasingly lovelorn poet houses beggared Love within his body, but Cupid proceeds to wreak internal disorder. While this is just one Cupid, the result is similar: the insides of the poet-lover are set on fire, incited to physical disorder via the self-destructive act of Love, the mindless 'impulse of desire'.

53. See Sell, 'Philip Sidney's Sublime Self-Authorship', this volume, 176–81.
54. Kingsley-Smith, *Cupid in Early Modern Literature*, 40.
55. See, for example, sonnet 48, where Drayton retorts 'Cupid, I hate thee, which I'de have thee know: / A naked Starveling ever may'st thou be' (1–2, in *Works*, ed. Hebel, 2:334).
56. 'Ever in motion' in fact provides the subtitle for a recent collection of essays on the early modern sonnet form: see Vuillemin, Sansonetti and Zanin, *The Early Modern English Sonnet: Ever in Motion*.

Part II

Style: Outgrowing the Arts

Chapter 4

Bloody Poetics: Towards a Physiology of the Epic Poem
Rocío G. Sumillera

William Alexander, in his possibly unfinished essay on poetic criticism 'Anacrisis: or, A Censure of some Poets Ancient and Modern' (probably written in 1634 but not published until 1711), explains that his method to 'censure any Poet', that is, to assess poetry, is to 'dissolve the general Contexture of his Work in several Pieces, to see what Sinews it hath, and to mark what will remain behind, when that external Gorgeousness, consisting in the Choice or Placing of Words, as if it would bribe the Ear to corrupt the Judgment, is first removed'.[1] In a process that resembles an anatomical dissection of the poetic body by breaking it down into its 'several Pieces', Alexander thus disregards the 'gross Staff' that serves 'to uphold the general Frame', and concentrates instead on the 'sinews' of the poem, by which he means its invention, which lies hidden beneath the poem's skin, that is, its 'language'. Alexander praises in these terms John Barclay's heroic Latin novel *Argenis* (published posthumously in 1621, and translated into English in 1625), which, he affirms, 'whether judged of in the Whole, or parted in Pieces, will be found to be a Body strong in Substance, and full of Sinews in every Member'.[2]

Alexander's observation on the strength of the poem residing in its sinewy invention recalls Ben Jonson being commended for his translation of Horace's *Ars poetica* (1640) on account of 'his *Strenuous* and *Sinewy* Labours', which explain the 'rare profundity' of his work.[3] Indeed, that the poem is envisioned as a body with bodily functions and processes that mirror those of humans and animals results in a parallelism that affects the understanding of poetics, the discipline whose object of study is the poem, its constitution and its parts, as analogous to anatomy, the science that dissects bodies and examines their inner workings and constituents. Barton Holiday, archdeacon of

Oxford and translator of Persius, establishes the poem–body, poetics–dissection dual analogy in an epode preceding Jonson's translation:

> Master of Art, and Fame! who here makst knowne
> To all, how all thine owne
> Well-bodied works were fram'd, whilst here we see
> Their fine Anatomee.
> Each nerve and vaine of Art, each slender string,
> Thou to our eye dost bring:
> Thus, what thou didst before so well collect,
> Thou dost as well dissect.[4]

Descriptions of poems as possessing a living materiality depicted in organic and bodily terms are not uncommon in early modernity.[5] Furthermore, the 'language of textual division as anatomy' has already been discussed, among others, by Jonathan Sawday in connection to ideas 'of the body as itself being constituted as text – as the *liber corporum* – the book of the body written by God'.[6] If texts are thought of as bodies (and vice versa), 'the anthropomorphic language of books' is of little wonder; authors ponder over the partition of discourse into volumes, books, chapters, cantos, in a manner 'akin to the progressive partitioning of the body in anatomical demonstration, and thus indebted to a language of the body'.[7] If physicians such as Pierre Charron in *La Sagesse* (1601) state that man is 'a Summary recapitulation of all things, and an Epitome of the world, which is all in man, but gathered into a small volume, whereby he is called the little world',[8] contemporary authors of poetics likewise think along these lines regarding matters of textual partition. Scaliger, for one, stated in his chapter 'Regulations for the various kinds of poetry: epic poetry' of his *Poetics* (Book I, Chapter 3), that for the writing of epic, 'an author should divide his book into chapters in imitation of nature, which subdivides into parts of parts, all so related that they constitute an organic body'.[9] Scaliger's belief that 'where the parts are in proportion, the body is beautiful'[10] follows Longinus's thinking about 'greatness in speech', which he argues is largely the result of 'the setting together of the members, as in living bodies', for 'though one member sheared off from the rest has nothing in itself worthy of rational speech, all combined together complete a perfect system'.[11] Beyond the linguistic matter of the poem, that is, in addition to the poem's constitution in 'letters and syllables', 'single words', 'clauses of speech' and 'perfect sentences' crafted by the poet, as George Puttenham suggests in *The Art of English Poesy* (1589),[12] the outcome of the poetic contrivance exceeds the textual realm. By some form of transubstantiation, through a mysterious process that mirrors the conversion of the word into flesh, what the poet appears to end up producing, according to many early modern accounts, is a living creature with body parts, humours and temperaments, one that eats, grows, speaks and communicates precisely because of its physical dimension,[13] and one that, most importantly for the purposes of this chapter, bleeds.

My approach to the physicality of the poem does not here address either matters of textual partition and arrangement (that is, the understanding of volumes, chapters, acts, stanzas, as bodily parts), or the ability of the poem to produce its own voice and in so doing speak and be heard. Rather, this chapter explores the early modern understanding of the poem as a living body that is run through by flows of blood that keep it alive. Blood, a highly complex structural symbol in discourses from the political to the religious, from the medical to the romantic and amatory in its relation to love and passion, one that is complicated further by being heavily gendered and by going hand in hand with definitions of identity (ethnic, racial, familial, national),[14] was used at the time as a helpful resource to explain diverse aspects of the workings of language more generally. For example, in the opening chapter of *The English Grammar* (written c. 1623, published posthumously in 1640), Ben Jonson defines grammar as 'the art of true and well speaking a language', divides it into etymology and syntax, distinguishes several constituents of language (word, syllable, letter), and concludes his introductory overview by clarifying that, even if 'Prosody and orthography are not parts of grammar', both are 'diffused, like the blood and spirits, through the whole'.[15] Jonson again resorts to the blood analogy in the last chapter ('Of the distinction of sentences') to discuss 'the breathing, when we pronounce any sentence', which he says is 'one general affection' that is 'dispersed through every member thereof, as the blood is through the body'.[16] His words echo Alexander Richardson's 1657 commentary on Ramus in *The Logicians School-Master* almost verbatim: 'Orthography and Prosody they are not part of Grammer, but common adjuncts, and run through whole Grammer as blood through the whole body.'[17]

Early modern corporeal conceptualisations of the poem continue a tradition of discussions of style in analogy with the body that can be traced back as far as Isocrates, as the first section of this chapter explores. Body-related terms, plentiful in discussions of rhetoric and oratory in Antiquity, ultimately assembled personifications of the different styles, as each style would be thought of as embodying a specific bodily constitution or type which also projected an image of the orator that would favour it in his speeches. 'Some men are tall and big, so some language is high and great',[18] says Jonson, rephrasing Juan Luis Vives, the perfecter and systematiser of this tradition. The second section of this chapter, by principally drawing on epic and heroic poetry, traditionally so rich in descriptions of human bodies in battle scenes and depictions of wounding,[19] analyses the language of corporeality in early modern accounts of the inner workings of the poem with a focus on the function that blood performs within the poetic organism. Finally, the concluding section centres around John Dryden's bodily poetics as a means to outline some of the complex variations and by-products of the poem–body analogy that expand beyond the uses of blood and into the overall humoral conception of the poem by the end of the seventeenth century.

Tracing Bodily Discourse in Discussions on Style

> Style is a constant and continual phrase or tenor of speaking and writing, extending to the whole tale or process of the poem or history, and not properly to any piece or member of a tale, but is of words, speeches, and sentences together a certain contrived form and quality, many times natural to the writer, many times his peculiar by election and art, and such as either he keepeth by skill or holdeth on by ignorance, and will not or peradventure cannot easily alter into any other.[20]

Puttenham devotes an entire chapter of his *Art of English Poesy* to style (Book 3, Chapter 5), which he succinctly defines in the sentence quoted above. Style was one of the notions shared by all the arts of discourse, and a recurrent one in reflections on language throughout the early modern period, revealing of beliefs inherited from Antiquity, including the long-standing tradition of discussing style in corporeal terms. Ben Jonson, for instance, touches upon style in his unconventional hodgepodge commonplace book *Timber: Or, Discoveries Made Upon Men and Matter* (1640), stating that 'in all speech, words and sense are as the body and the soul',[21] and defining style by being more or less replenished with blood and juice, by having more or less flesh and corpulence, and by looking more or less bony and sinewy.[22] 'A fleshy style' is said to grow 'fat and corpulent', and to have 'blood and juice, when the words are proper and apt'; it is also qualified as redundant whenever 'the blood and juice are faulty and vicious', and said to become, unless properly irrigated by 'juice' and 'blood', 'thin, flagging, poor, starved; scarce covering the bone'.[23]

Like so much in *Timber*, this is not the fruit of Jonson's own unique thinking, but rather an abridged paraphrase of long extracts from Juan Luis Vives's *De ratione dicendi* (1533). Vives here enunciates a number of general tenets in relation to style, including the principle that 'the conjunction of parts and proportion engenders the form of the discourse, which we liken to the form of a human body',[24] and that of the indissolubility of language and thought, as inseparable 'as the body and soul': 'Thoughts are as the life and soul of language, and are therefore called its mind and sense. Words without sense are lifeless and dead.'[25] In Book IV of *De causis corruptarum atrium* ('De corrupta rhetorica'), the first part of *De disciplinis* (1531), Vives had already challenged the classic, and to his mind simplistic, tripartite division of style into the categories of 'high, low and intermediate': 'there are not three but many kinds of style, and within each of these there are in turn more than three', Vives argued instead.[26] In addition, he maintained that the language often used to describe them, which metaphorically relied on parts and qualities of the human body, was too vague and imprecise:

> They [ancient authors] fashioned a speech in the form of a man, so that they spoke about the flesh, blood, sap, bones, sinews, skin, complexion, stature, bearing and proportions of style; then the inner qualities: wit, judgement, strength of soul, emotional force, breeding and character. They designate these things with the same names we use to describe parts of the human body, but with very doubtful accuracy and precision, and because none of these terms is defined or has its use delimited, they fail to say clearly what they mean by bones, blood, sap or character. And so there is an extraordinary inconsistency among them when they use these terms, with the result that they describe the same style not only in different ways, but in opposite ways.[27]

Vives therefore writes *De ratione dicendi* specifically to set in order this inherited corporeal terminology, which had thus far been used unsystematically and in a highly imprecise fashion despite its potential, if used rigorously, to explain successfully the different types of style.[28] Vives consequently dwells on a wide array of terms referring to physical qualities (*statura, figura, cutis, caro, sanguis, ossa, nervi, musculi, latera*) applied to traits of style; hence, for instance, *statura* 'has to do principally with the magnitude and sound of words and constructions',[29] *figura* with 'the form or mould of a sentence',[30] and *cutis*, that is, skin, with 'the way in which sentences are put together, whence arises their harmony'.[31] Sinews, lungs and muscles, 'inasmuch as they make for vigour and action', 'are taken as referring to the force of a style and its ability to move the feelings'; 'an abundance of flesh', to the development of a 'corpulent' style, corpulence being based on 'an over-endowment of words and longer periphrases and circumlocutions than are appropriate', which if in excess render style 'fat and obese'. 'A style rich and well-fed' is one that 'has blood and sap', for 'the words, whether natural or transferred, are proper and apt, their sound somewhat full and sweet, the diction rather elegant, and the words just sufficient to convey the thought'.[32]

In this scheme, blood becomes a fundamental style indicator, key in distinguishing different sorts, for if blood is scarce and the style seems 'without flesh and blood', then it appears 'thin, lean, starved, hardly covering the bone, and looks like bones heaped up against the skin like stones in a sack'; whereas if 'blood flows more abundantly than is necessary there is redundancy', and when in excess it is 'harmful' and results 'in triviality and affectation'.[33] The perils of a surplus in blood, as remarked by Vives, cannot be ignored, and they are ultimately based on the fact that blood is not merely a bodily fluid but also a humour which the fluid itself carries. Blood the substance is effectively the vehicle of blood the humour, which holds no pre-eminence in explanations of ingenuity and genius, a privilege indisputably held instead, since at least Aristotle, by black bile and the consequential melancholic temperament.[34] On the contrary, when in excess, blood is accountable for blockishness. Early modern physicians and natural philosophers throughout Europe, among them the Spaniard Juan Huarte de San Juan, author of the highly influential treatise *The Examination of Men's Wits*, as titled in its first English translation (1594), warned that blood the humour is a hindrance to the proper workings of the mental faculty of the imagination, to the various intellectual activities dependent on it (poetry writing among them), and, generally, to a quick wit. Given that, to operate properly, first and foremost the imagination requires heat, and 'because the blood partaketh much moisture' and 'where there is much moisture it is a sign that the heat is remiss', as Huarte explains, blood 'breedeth damage to the imagination'.[35] 'After Galen's opinion', he continues, 'all the humours of our body, which hold overmuch moisture, make a man blockish and foolish', for which reason blood is the humour 'of simplicity and dullness'.[36]

As Vives remarked, discussions of style through the language of the body were prevalent among ancient authors, who drew on similar analogies.[37] In *Orator*, Cicero describes 'plainness of style' as being 'not full-blooded';[38] Quintilian, in *Institutio oratoria*, praises Demosthenes by highlighting his 'muscular' style,[39] and in *Dialogus de oratoribus*, Tacitus affirms that 'with eloquence' it is 'as with the human frame': 'There can be no beauty of form where the veins are prominent, or where one can count the bones: sound healthful blood must fill out the limbs, and riot over the muscles, concealing the sinews in turn under a ruddy complexion and a graceful exterior.'[40] Previously, in *On Types of Style*, Hermogenes had elaborated on beauty of speech in corporeal terms. His argument was that, because harmony and temperateness guarantee not only beauty but also health, the priority for discourse is to 'be harmonious and well-tempered':

> To use an analogy with the human body, Beauty generally consists of symmetry and harmony and proportion in the various parts and limbs of the body, combined with a fresh and healthy complexion. That is also how the style is produced, whether you mix all the types together or concentrate on each one individually – for these are, as it were, the 'parts and limbs of the body'. It is also necessary that a certain healthy complexion, as it were, bloom in it, a uniform quality of expression appearing throughout, which some critics naturally call the complexion of the speech.[41]

Hermogenes then goes on to echo Socrates' statement, as recorded in Plato's *Phaedrus*, that 'every discourse must be organised, like a living being, with a body of its own, as it were, so as not to be headless or footless, but to have a middle and members, composed in fitting relation to each other and to the whole'.[42]

Similarly, Isocrates conceived of his twofold distinction of styles (namely, the polished high style versus the unpolished low style) as two distinct body types, respectively the full (ἁδρός, *hadros*) and the thin (ἰσχνός, *ischnos*), establishing in *Antidosis* the foundational comparison between rhetoric and athletics:

> In my treatment of the art of discourse, I desire, like the genealogists, to start at the beginning. It is acknowledged that the nature of man is compounded of two parts, the physical and the mental ... Since this is so, certain of our ancestors, long before our time, seeing that many arts had been devised for other things, while none had been prescribed for the body and for the mind, invented and bequeathed to us two disciplines, physical training for the body, of which gymnastics is a part, and, for the mind, philosophy, which I am going to explain. These are twin arts – parallel and complementary – by which their masters prepare the mind to become

more intelligent and the body to become more serviceable, not separating sharply the two kinds of education, but using similar methods of instruction, exercise, and other forms of discipline.[43]

When Aristotle, in his tripartite classification of styles (forensic, deliberative and epideictic), begins to replace *hadros* to refer to grand style, he does so by means of other 'terms suggesting height or size, such as *megaloprepes* and *hypselos*', thus continuing to assume bodily conceptions of speech.[44] Following this description, Isocrates' 'grand style resembles the fleshy, well-developed, and harmoniously proportioned figure of the athlete, while the low forensic style has a soldierlike tautness and lean muscularity'.[45] However, the ideal reverses in subsequent centuries, and by the third century BCE it is the soldier's physiognomy that has come to be associated with Demosthenes' grand style and regarded as grander than the athlete's.[46]

It has been suggested that this description of grand style in physical terms owes much to, and is to a large extent shaped by, 'the connotations of heroic strength and noble idealism that link it to the values of epic and tragedy'.[47] Indeed, it is hard to imagine it coincidental that these references to the body in general, and to blood in particular, in early modern sources abounded in, precisely, discussions of epic and heroic poetry.

Blood in Early Modern Accounts of the Epic and Heroic Poem

Translators of Homer and Virgil are possibly the most evident followers in the early modern period of the ancient tradition of using bodily language to discuss style-related matters, as indeed the paratextual material to the translations of epic and heroic poetry relies on, or puts forward, a corporeal poetics. Richard Stanyhurst, the Dublin-born translator of *The Aeneid* (1582), is among those who suggested that poetry is made up of a set of body parts that, when well arranged, bring to life a fully functioning body. For instance, he describes conjunctions as 'copulatiue sinnewes' which gracefully 'knit' the 'ioynctes' of Latin verse,[48] and praises Virgil on account of 'thee *barck and bodye* of so exquisit and singular a discourse' as *The Aeneid*.[49] In referring to Thomas Phaer's previous translation of Virgil's epic, typically considered 'the *Aeneid* of the English Renaissance',[50] Stanyhurst insists that, because his aim is to produce a new translation altogether, he purposely avoids Phaer's 'choise woordes' unless 'oothers could not countreuaile theyre signification'.⁵¹ Interestingly, Stanyhurst justifies some of his translating decisions by stating that

> in soō poinctes of greatest price, where thee matter, as yt were, doth bleede, I was mooued too shun M. *Phaer* his enterpretation, and clinge more neere too thee meaning of myne authoure, in slising thee husk and cracking thee shel, too bestow thee kernel vpon thee wyttye and enquisitiue reader.⁵²

The matter of a poem can of course bleed because, like George Chapman years later, Stanyhurst takes it for granted that poems have bodies. Chapman, in 'The Preface to the Reader' to his *The Iliads of Homer Prince of Poets* (1611), claims for the 'Poets' fictions' the respect that would generally be granted to true stories, for fictions abide more to 'the laws of learning' and 'wisdom' than many true stories: 'Nor is there any such reality of wisdome's truth in all humane excellence as in Poets' fictions.' The poet, being 'strictly and inextricably confined to all the lawes of learning, wisedom, and truth', consequently produces fictions by fusing sinewy matter to a soul: 'For were not his fictions composed of the sinewes and soules of all those, how could they defie fire, iron, and be combined with eternitie?'⁵³ In the dedication to his translation of the *Odyssey* (1614–15), Chapman insists, first, that 'Nor is this all-comprising Poesie phantastique, or meere fictive, but the most *material* and doctrinall illations of Truth', and, second, that 'the Poet *creates* both a *Bodie* and a *Soule*': the former 'being the letter, or historie' (that is, the argument, the plot, also perhaps the words on the page and the materiality of the phrasing), the latter, 'the sence' and 'Allegorie' (that is, the moral teachings).⁵⁴

The poet thus creates for the poem that which defines all living beings, a body and a soul, which for many authors, both ancient and modern, were not only indivisibly merged, but moreover profoundly grounded in materiality. Aristotle, for example, identified the heart as the central location of the soul, in charge of sensory knowledge, memory and the imagination, and the organ that produced the natural pneuma, 'responsible for reproduction and movement' and understood as 'the vehicle of the soul'.⁵⁵ In the same vein, John Davies, in *Nosce teipsum* (1599), records how some take the soul to mean but blood in the heart: 'One thinks the *Soule* is *Aire*, another *Fire*, / Another, *bloud* defus'd about the hart';⁵⁶ Helkiah Crooke's *Mikrokosmographia* (1615), in tune with Galen's theories, defines the 'spirit' as '*A subtle and thinne body alwayes mooueable, engendred of blood and vapour, and the vehicle or carriage of the Faculties of the soule*',[57] and John Donne, in Meditation 18 of *Devotions upon Emergent Occasions* (1624), states that, according to philosophers, the soul 'is nothing, but the *temperament* and *harmony*, and *just and equall composition of the Elements in the body*, which produces all those *faculties* which we ascribe to the *soule*; and so, in it selfe is *nothing*, no *separable substance*, that overlives the *body*'.[58]

Around two decades prior to his translations of the *Odyssey* and the *Iliad* (Books 9–12 of the former would be published in 1673, and the rest in 1675; the latter, in 1676), Thomas Hobbes discussed at length his own views on poetry, despite his remark that he was no poet, in his 'The answer of Mr. Hobbes to Sr. Will. D'Avenant's preface before *Gondibert*', included in *A Discourse upon Gondibert an Heroick Poem, Written by Sr. William D'Avenant; with an Answer to it, by Mr. Hobbs*, published in Paris in 1650. In this text, Hobbes responds to his friend William D'Avenant apropos the latter's *Gondibert: An Heroic Poem*, whose first two books would be published in London a year later, and the third in 1685, posthumously. In the Preface to *Gondibert*, considered by some 'one of the most important critical essays of the seventeenth century',[59] and 'the first ambitious piece of criticism since Jonson's *Timber, or Discoveries*',[60] Hobbes focuses on the 'Heroique Poeme', differentiates it from other sorts of poetry, and phrases what is essentially required of its author: the ability to 'make both body and soule, coulor and shaddow of his Poeme out of his owne store'.[61] Hobbes then describes *Gondibert* as a living creature thematically irrigated through veins that carry flows of stories. According to Hobbes, characters and 'the actions of these (the number increasinge) after severall confluences', 'run all at last into the two principall streames', and 'so, from severall and farre distant Sources', they flow 'into one another', this final encounter having 'the same resemblance also with a mans veines, which proceeding from different parts, after the like concourse, insert themselves at last into the two principall veynes[62] of the Body'.[63]

In this description, Hobbes thus draws on the veins as rivers metaphor, previously employed in the English tradition by, among others, Donne, who, in the opening Meditation of *Devotions upon Emergent Occasions*, likened man to '*a little world*' and his veins to '*rivers of blood*',[64] and by Phineas Fletcher, who used it extensively in *The Purple Island* (1633). Yet their working notions of the behaviour of blood in the body, be it human or poetic, radically differed from those held by Hobbes, who, by virtue of being a friend of William Harvey and an admirer and close follower of his work, no longer played by Galen's rules.⁶⁵ So, while Hobbes envisioned the heart as operating in the manner of a water pump, with blood flowing in a continuous circuit, Fletcher believed, after Galen, that the liver repeatedly produced blood then sent it out through the body. For Fletcher, then, it was not that blood circulated, but that it moved in one direction, running from the centre to the peripheries of the body:

> Nor is there any part in all this land,
> But is a little Isle: for thousand brooks
> In azure chanels glide on silver sand;
> Their serpent windings, and deceiving crooks
> Circling about, and wat'ring all the plain,
> Emptie themselves into th'all-drinking main;
> And creeping forward slide, but never turn again.⁶⁶

Even if it is undisputed that, in irrigating the body of the poem, blood ensures its life, there is no unanimous agreement as to what exactly blood represents. For Peletier, for instance, as he explains in *Art poétique* (1555), blood is a nurturing substance that corresponds to the poet's invention, which 'flows through the poem, like blood through the body of an animal'.⁶⁷ For Laurence Humphrey, by contrast, as he affirms in *Interpretatio linguarum* (1559), 'blood stands for clarity (*perspicuitas*)' and 'supremely assists understanding': 'Rather like blood, it should run through every part of what we are saying. For what is the point of language if it is so indistinct that nobody can understand it, so obscure as to be incomprehensible?'⁶⁸ Neil Rhodes observes that Humphrey's 'might seem a slightly odd metaphor to use for the principle of clarity, but its purpose is to suggest that by finding the right form of words to elucidate the meaning of the original, the good translator will produce a living imitation of his source text'.⁶⁹ Although this is a reasonable interpretation of Humphrey's use of the analogy, he may have employed it not to discuss specifically his understanding of translated texts, but rather of texts in general, which he seems to perceive as living bodies regardless of whether they have been translated or not. Perhaps not coincidentally, Humphrey was a close reader of Homer, an active participant in an edition of the Greek text of Homer's epics,⁷⁰ and the author of the edition's prefatory epistle, the 'Epistola de Graecis litteris et Homeri lectione et imitatione' (1558).⁷¹

Like Humphrey, Thomas Blount, in *The Academie of Eloquence Containing a Compleat English Rhetorique* (1654), places '*perspicuity*' at the heart of 'Epistolary Style',⁷² and, in discussing metaphors and similes, Blount in addition quotes verbatim (acknowledging his source)[73] a long extract from Hobbes's text against relying on worn-out metaphors and similitudes, for these are 'as the ayres of musique with often hearing become insipide, the Reader having no more sense of their force, then our Flesh is sensible of the bones that susteine it': 'As the sense we have of bodies, consisteth in change and variety of impression, so also does the sense of language in the variety and changeable use of words.'[74]

Other early modern authors established a relationship between blood and digestion, as is most significantly the case with Du Bellay. In *Déffence et illustration de la langue francoyse* (1549), Du Bellay puts forward his 'théorie de l'innutrition', by which he means that the Romans enriched Latin 'by imitating the best Greek authors, transforming themselves into them, consuming them, and after having digested them well, by converting them into blood and nourishment'.[75] In the English tradition, Chapman likewise argues in his 'To the Understander', prefaced to *Achilles Shield* (1598), that 'All tongues have inricht themselves from their originall (onely the Hebrew and Greeke, which are not spoken amongst vs) with good neighbourly borrowing and as with infusion of fresh ayre and nourishment of *newe blood* in their still growing bodies.'[76] The pairing of fresh air and new blood, a phrasing indicative of a pre-Harvey mindset, is certainly not accidental, as within the Galenic framework the lungs worked in close cooperation with the liver and the heart to ensure life. In Chapman's eyes, then, the English language, a young creature still growing, feeds on other tongues to produce 'new blood', ironically mostly transfused from the oldest bodies, that is, the classical languages.

Both Du Bellay and Chapman thus envision their own vernaculars, together with the poetic works produced in them, as ultimately dependent for their growth on the nourishment provided by the classical models. For Hobbes, the classical tongues in fact pertain to a different league altogether, one by definition unreachable for the vernaculars. In praising *Gondibert*, Hobbes affirms that it 'would last as long as either the *Aeneid,* or *Iliad,* but for one Disadvantage', linguistic in nature: 'The languages of the *Greekes* and *Romanes* (by their Colonies and Conquests) have put off flesh and bloud, and are become immutable, which none of the moderne tongues are like to be.'[77] Hence, in contrast to the immutability of the classical languages, which renders them perfect and incorruptible, modern tongues are doomed to continual transformation and corruption. The classical tongues, fleshless and bloodless as embalmed bodies, grant the works written in them immunity to decay and to threats to their privileged status. Bloodlessness as indicative of immutability and godliness had been traditionally accepted since Antiquity and was fully in agreement with the conventions of the Greek epic tradition, according to which the Greek gods, instead of having 'blood', have 'a special immortal fluid with a name of its own, ἰχώρ'.[78] As John Dryden explains in 'Dedication of the *Aeneis*' (1697), that godly ἰχώρ (*ikhōr*) 'was so very like our common Blood, that it was not to be distinguish'd from it, but only by the Name and Colour'.[79]

Coda: Beyond Blood. Dryden's Bodily Epic Poetics

Recent scholarship has argued that early modern poetry can be read as a process conducive to the making of knowledge through the artificial creation of small worlds or *microcosmos*.[80] From this perspective, the insight that poets offer through the composition of poems is a window into the making of a physical body, one in which blood is but one of the many bodily elements that account for the inner workings of the poem explained in accordance with prevailing medical theories and developments in the scientific realm. By the end of the seventeenth century, the views on style and bodily descriptions that Vives so profusely discussed in the first half of the previous century were still in force, as Dryden's deeply rooted body-based poetics evince. In his preface to *Troilus and Cressida* (1679), Dryden comments on the poet's 'natural robustuousness' and warns the 'Fanciful Writer' of the importance of 'managing his strength', after the classical analogy between the body of the rhetorician-orator and the wrestler: for in the poet, 'as in a Wrestler, there is first requir'd some measure of force, a well-knit body, and active Limbs, without which all instruction would be vain', Dryden states.[81] His stylistic preferences thus match the physique of the warrior-like character traditionally associated with Demosthenes' style, which Dryden knew so well, not least because of his translation into English of Plutarch's *Life of Demosthenes* (1683).[82]

Judging from 'Dedication of the *Aeneis*', Dryden did not change his mind on this point over time: his comparative analyses of the metrical choices of Italian, French and English translators of Latin heroic verse into their vernaculars make him conclude that while 'the *French* and *Italians* value themselves on their Regularity: Strength and Elevation are our [the English's] Standard'.[83] Dryden holds against French poets their addition of an extra foot to translate Latin epic, which, he argues, only proves that French is 'too weak' a language to support 'Epick Poetry, without the addition of another Foot', which has made the French run 'with more activity than strength':

> Their Language is not strung with Sinews like our *English*. It has the nimbleness of a Greyhound, but not the bulk and body of a Mastiff. Our Men and our Verses over-bear them by their weight . . . The *French* have set up Purity for the Standard of their Language; and a Masculine Vigour is that of ours. Like their Tongue is the Genius of their Poets, light and trifling in comparison of the *English*; more proper for Sonnets, Madrigals, and Elegies, than Heroick Poetry.[84]

Dryden's conclusion 'that the affected purity of the *French*, has unsinew'd their Heroick Verse' can be taken as a sample of the complex and varied uses that he gives to the analogy of the poem as a living body.[85] In Dryden's bodily poetics, these include the suggestion that the poet is a physician who either cures the body of the poem (by bettering it, as in the case of gifted translators) or administers poetry as a drug to an audience-readership that is, as a consequence, healed. In this manner, for instance, Dryden distinguishes between 'Chymical Medicines' (that is, modern medicines), which he likens to tragedies, and '*Galenical* Decoctions' (the first and earliest sort of drugs), which he compares to epic poetry. Whereas the former tend 'to Relieve oft'ner than to Cure: For 'tis the nature of Spirits to make swift impressions, but not deep', Dryden states that the latter 'have more of Body in them' and 'work by their substance and their weight' more successfully.[86] Not coincidentally, he states, 'there is more Virtue in one Heroick Poem than in many Tragedies';[87] after all, drama ultimately derives from epic poetry: 'the Original of the Stage was from the Epick Poem'.[88]

Dryden's eulogy of epic poetry is inseparable in the 'Dedication of the *Aeneis*' from his praise of Homer, the major referent for both poets and playwrights: 'Those Episodes of *Homer*, which were proper for the Stage, the Poets amplify'd each into an Action: Out of his Limbs they form'd their Bodies: What he had Contracted they Enlarg'd.'[89] At the time of the publication of his translation of *Aeneis* (1697), Dryden would have agreed with Chapman's statement, formulated in 'The Preface to the Reader' to his translation of Homer's *Iliad*, that 'Of all bookes extant in all kinds, Homer is the first and best',[90] even if previously, in his 'A Parallel, of Poetry and Painting' (1695), written while Dryden was still translating Virgil, he had argued for the superiority of Virgil over Homer.[91] By 1697, however, for Dryden as for

Chapman before, Homer is the 'great Creator' of both poetic bodies and souls: 'Nor were they only animated by him, but their Measure and Symetry was owing him.'[92]

A metaphorical by-product that Dryden develops from his understanding that the poet creates the body and soul of his poem is that, in the process, he passes down to it features of his own temperament and character, as if fathering an offspring. Hence, for instance, after contrasting the temperaments of Virgil and Homer in the preface to *Fables Ancient and Modern* (1700), Dryden concludes that the former is 'Cholerick and Sanguin', and the latter 'Phlegmatick and Melancholick', judging by how the two authors 'excel in their several Ways': for 'each of them has follow'd his own natural Inclination, as well in Forming the Design, as in the Execution of It'. If Virgil 'warms you by Degrees', Homer 'sets you on fire all at once, and never intermits his Heat', so 'You never cool while you read *Homer*'. The opposing temperaments of the authors reveal themselves in the dissimilar natures of their protagonists: 'The very Heroes shew their Authors: *Achilles* is hot, impatient, revengeful', whereas '*Eneas* patient, considerate, careful of his People, and merciful to his Enemies; ever submissive to the Will of Heaven'.[93] The implication here is that, in the composition-generation of the poem, the poet passes down to it his own temperament as humoral heritage.

Interestingly, the process of identifying the humour of the poet involves a tracing back, and hence means extrapolating to the profile of the author the conclusions drawn from the stylistic-temperamental analysis of the poem itself. Alexander Pope, in the 'Preface to the *Iliad*' that preceded the six volumes of his translation (1715–20), corroborates this method for profiling the poet:

> When we behold their Battels, methinks the two Poets resemble the Heroes they celebrate: *Homer*, boundless and irresistible as *Achilles*, bears all before him, and shines more and more as the Tumult increases; *Virgil* calmly daring like *Eneas*, appears undisturb'd in the midst of the Action, disposes all about him, and conquers with Tranquillity: And when we look upon their Machines, *Homer* seems like his own *Jupiter* in his Terrors, shaking *Olympus*, scattering the Lightnings, and firing the Heavens; *Virgil* like the same Power in his Benevolence, counselling with the Gods, laying Plans for Empires, and regularly ordering his whole Creation.[94]

Dryden takes this manner of thinking further by suggesting that this is likewise what determines the personal preference of a reader for one author or the other. In other words, Dryden suggests that the temperament of the poet, coincidental with that of the hero of the poem and the poem overall, conditions its reception, as those readers with a shared humour are more prone to appreciate it than readers with other temperaments. Dryden's theory derives from his own experience: because he believes himself 'Saturnine and reserv'd', and Homer 'Melancholick',[95] he understands Homer's 'Vehemence' to be 'more suitable to my Temper: and therefore I have translated his First Book with greater Pleasure than any Part of *Virgil*'.[96]

A century later, Samuel Johnson would describe Dryden temperamentally just as Dryden had depicted Homer, and by contrast he would portray Pope as Virgil. 'If of Dryden's fire the blaze is brighter, of Pope's the heat is more regular and constant', Johnson affirmed.[97] It would be safe to say that Dryden was, after all, and just like his beloved Homer, 'a hot spark, or man of fire', to take one of Johnson's definitions of blood.[98] Exploring perceived poetic similitudes and affiliations among early modern authors in terms of, literally, bloodlines is a topic of research also worth exploring further, as it would shed light on the process of, and criteria involved in, drawing literary genealogies, where assumptions about the circulation of poetic blood are also inevitably involved.

Notes

I am particularly indebted to Zenón Luis-Martínez for his insightful feedback on this chapter, and to Laura Bass for her endorsement of a three-month Visiting Researcher placement in 2019 at the Department of Hispanic Studies at Brown University (Consortium for Advanced Studies Abroad, CASA–UGR programme), which proved crucial for the completion of this research.

1. Alexander, 'Anacrisis', 159.
2. Ibid., 162.
3. 'To the Right Honourable Thomas Lord Windsore', in Jonson, *Q. Horatius Flaccus: His Art of Poetry*, sig. A5v.
4. 'Barton Holyday, to Ben Jonson. Epode', in Jonson, *Q. Horatius Flaccus: His Art of Poetry*, sig. A9r.
5. This interest is also evinced in Gorman, 'Atomies of Love', and Hernández-Santano, 'Eloquent Bodies', this volume, both apropos love poetry.
6. Sawday, *The Body Emblazoned*, 134–5. For more on the *liber corporum* analogy, see Josipovici, *The World and the Book*.
7. Sawday, *The Body Emblazoned*, 136.
8. Charron, *Of Wisdome*, sig. B4v.
9. Scaliger, *Select Translations from Scaliger's Poetics*, trans. Padelford, 55.
10. Patterson, *Hermogenes and the Renaissance*, 53.

11. Longinus, *On the Sublime*, ed. and trans. Arieti and Crossett, 201.
12. Puttenham, *Art of English Poesy*, ed. Whigham and Rebhorn, 245. For more on this subject, see Anderson, *Words that Matter*.
13. Smith, *Acoustic World*, 96–129.
14. Paster, *The Body Embarrassed*, especially chapter 2, 'Laudable Blood: Bleeding, Difference, and Humoral Embarrassment', 64–112; Linke, *Blood and Nation*; Bradburne, ed., *Blood: Art, Politics, and Pathology*; Zorach, *Blood, Milk, Ink, Gold*; Bildhauer, *Medieval Blood*; Greene, *Five Words*, especially his chapter 'Blood', 107–42; Balizet, *Blood and Home in Early Modern Drama*; García Hernán and Gómez Vozmediano, eds, *La cultura de la sangre en el Siglo de Oro*.
15. Jonson, *English Grammar*, ed. Britton, in *Cambridge Edition Online*, 1.10–11.
16. Ibid., 400.
17. Richardson, *The Logicians School-Master*, sig. B8v. Ramus employed blood to discuss various logical notions, including that of causality; see also in Richardson, sigs. K3v, Q4v.
18. Jonson, *Discoveries*, ed. Hutson, in *Cambridge Edition Online*, lines 1443–4.
19. Adams, 'Anatomical Terminology in Latin Epic'.
20. Puttenham, *Art of English Poesy*, 233.
21. Jonson, *Discoveries*, in *Cambridge Edition Online*, lines 1335–6.
22. Ibid., lines 1478–80.
23. Ibid., lines 1468–73.
24. Vives, *Selected Works, XI: De ratione dicendi*, ed. Walker, II.20, p. 197.
25. Ibid., I.3, p. 69.
26. Ibid., IV.14, p. 445.
27. Ibid., IV.14, pp. 445–7.
28. In Mack's opinion, '*De ratione dicendi* is potentially one of the most interesting sources for a sixteenth-century Latin vocabulary of literary criticism' ('Vives's *De ratione dicendi*', 79). See also Rodríguez Peregrina, 'Algunas consideraciones en torno al *De ratione dicendi*'.
29. Vives, *Selected Works, XI: De ratione dicendi*, II.4, p. 171.
30. Ibid., II.6, p. 175.
31. Ibid., II.7, p. 175.
32. Ibid., II.23, pp. 201, 203.
33. Ibid., II.8, p. 177.
34. See on this issue Sumillera, 'From Inspiration to Imagination'.
35. Huarte de San Juan, *Richard Carew's The Examination of Men's Wits*, ed. Sumillera, 142.
36. Ibid., 126.
37. Rodríguez Peregrina, 'Introducción', in Vives, *Del arte de hablar*, lxxxvi–lxxxvii.
38. Cicero, *Orator*, 76, in *Brutus. Orator*, trans. Hendrickson and Hubbell, 363.

39. Quintilian, *Institutio oratoria*, trans. Butler, X.1.76, 4:44–5.
40. Tacitus, *Dialogue on Oratory*, 21, in *Agricola. Germania. Dialogue on Oratory*, trans. Hutton and Peterson, 289.
41. Hermogenes, 'Carefully Wrought Style (*Epimeleia*) and Beauty (*Kallos*)', in *On Types of Style*, ed. Wooten, 54–5.
42. Plato, *Phaedrus*, 264c, in *Euthyphro; Apology; Crito; Phaedo; Phaedrus*, trans. Fowler, 529.
43. Isocrates, *Antidosis*, 180–2, in *Isocrates II*, trans. Norlin, 289. For more on rhetoric and athletics, see Hawhee, *Bodily Arts*.
44. Shuger, *Sacred Rhetoric*, 17.
45. Ibid., 21.
46. Ibid., 21–2. Interestingly, Quintilian portrays Isocrates as a 'neat and polished' orator, 'better suited to the fencing-school than to the battle-field' (*Institutio oratoria*, trans. Butler, X.1.79, 4:44–5).
47. Shuger, *Sacred Rhetoric*, 20.
48. Stanyhurst, *First Foure Bookes of Virgil his Aeneis*, sig. B1v.
49. Ibid., sig. A2r; emphasis added.
50. Lally, 'Introduction', in *The Aeneid of Thomas Phaer and Thomas Twyne*, xi–lxii. Phaer translated 'nine and a third books from 1555 to 1560', and Thomas Twyne, who subsequently revised Phaer's rendering, 'translated the remaining three and two thirds books from 1568(?) to 1583'; 'the completed translation . . . was read and enjoyed immense popularity as a unified work', and from its first printing of the seven books translated by Phaer, it 'ran in its various stages of completion to eight editions during a period of sixty-two years, which ended in 1620' (xii).
51. Stanyhurst, *First Foure Bookes of Virgil his Aeneis*, sig. A2v.
52. Ibid., sig. A3r.
53. Chapman, *Iliads* (1611), 'The Preface to the Reader', in *Chapman's Homer*, ed. Nicoll, 1:14.
54. Chapman, *Odysseys* (1616), 'To the Earle of Somerset', in *Chapman's Homer*, 2:5. For more on Chapman's poetics, see Luis-Martínez, 'George Chapman's "Habit of Poesie"', this volume.
55. Furley and Wilkie, 'Introduction', in *Galen: On Respiration and the Arteries*, 19.
56. Davies, *Nosce teipsum*, 209–10, in *Poems of Sir John Davies*, ed. Krueger, 13.
57. Crooke, *Mikrokosmographia*, 174. On Galen on blood, see Brain, *Galen on Bloodletting*.
58. Donne, *Devotions upon Emergent Occasions*, 91. See in this regard Park, 'The Organic Soul'; Byatt, 'Feeling Thought: Donne and the Embodied Mind'; and Schoenfeldt, 'Eloquent Blood and Deliberative Bodies'.
59. Harbage, *Sir William Davenant*, 196.
60. Dowlin, *Sir William Davenant's Gondibert*, 16. See also De Witt Thorpe, *Aesthetic Theory of Thomas Hobbes*; Dumouchel, 'Hobbes on Literary Rules and Conventions'.

61. Hobbes, 'The Answer to Sr. Will. D'Avenant's Preface', 50.
62. Perhaps the superior vena cava and the inferior vena cava.
63. Hobbes, 'The Answer to Sr. Will. D'Avenant's Preface', 50.
64. Donne, *Devotions upon Emergent Occasions*, 7–8; original emphasis.
65. Harvey's *Exercitatio anatomica de motv cordis et sangvinis in animalibvs* was published in Frankfurt in 1628, and the first translation of this work into English, *The Anatomical Exercises of Dr. William Harvey [. . .] on the Motion of the Heart and Blood in Animals*, carried out anonymously, dates from 1653. The Galenic model would nonetheless predominate into the eighteenth century. See Erickson, *The Language of the Heart*, 10–11.
66. Fletcher, *The Purple Island*, Canto II.9, ed. Hope, 73. Hope's 'Introduction' comprehensively summarises the different and often opposed scholarly readings of Fletcher's knowledge of anatomy (12). Early modern anatomists also used the veins-as-rivers analogy for their own purposes; see, in this regard, with a focus on Realdo Colombo's *De re anatomica* (1559), Cunningham, 'Columbus: The Revival of Alexandrian Anatomy', in *The Anatomical Renaissance*, 143–66.
67. In the original French: 'est répandue par tout le Poème, comme le sang par le corps de l'animal: de sorte qu'elle se peut appeler la vie ou l'âme du Poème' (Peletier, 'Art poétique', 252).
68. Humphrey, *Interpretatio linguarum*, 272. Aristotle discusses perspicuity (σαφῆ εἶναι, *saphē einai*) in connection with style (*Rhetoric*, III.2, 1404b, trans. Freese, 351), although he never compares it to blood.
69. Rhodes, 'Introduction', in *English Renaissance Translation Theory*, 38.
70. The full title of this edition is Κέρας Ἀμαλθείας, ἡ Ὠκεανός των ἐξηγησεων Ὁμηρικῶν: *copiae cornu sivae oceanus enarrationum Homericarum, ex Eustathii in eundem commentariis concinnatorum, H. Junio autore* (Basel, 1558).
71. For more on Humphrey's epistle, see Merchant, *Laurence Humphrey and Reformed Humanist Education*, 74–6.
72. Blount, *Academie of Eloquence*, sig. G12v.
73. Ibid., sig. H1v.
74. Hobbes, 'The Answer to Sr. Will. D'Avenant's Preface', 53.
75. Du Bellay, 'Defence and Illustration', 50.
76. Chapman, *Achilles Shield* (1598), 'To the Understander', in *Chapman's Homer*, 1:549, emphasis added.
77. Hobbes, 'The Answer to Sr. Will. D'Avenant's Preface', 54. The poet and playwright Nahum Tate quotes Hobbes almost verbatim in his preface to the 1697 edition of John Davies's *Nosce teipsum*, published under the title *The Original, Nature, and Immortality of the Soul*. Tate uses Hobbes's words to praise Davies's book: 'the Poem, on account of its intrinsick Worth, would be as lasting as the *Iliad*, or the *Aeneid*, if the Language 'tis wrote in were as Immutable as that of the *Greeks* and *Romans*' (sig. A7v).

78. Pulleyn, 'Homer's Religion', 63.
79. Dryden, 'Dedication of the *Aeneis*', 315.
80. See Spiller, *Science, Reading, and Renaissance Literature*, especially her chapter 'Model Worlds: Philip Sidney, William Gilbert, and the Experiment of Worldmaking', 24–58.
81. Dryden, 'The Preface to the Play [*Troilus and Cressida*]', 241.
82. See Dryden's translation in Plutarch, *Lives of the Noble Grecians and Romans*, Vol. II, 387–408.
83. Dryden, 'Dedication of the *Aeneis*', 331.
84. Ibid., 322.
85. Ibid., 331.
86. Ibid., 270.
87. Ibid., 270.
88. Ibid., 269.
89. Ibid., 269.
90. Chapman, *Iliads* (1611), 'The Preface to the Reader', in *Chapman's Homer*, 1:14.
91. Dryden, 'A Parallel, of Poetry and Painting', 50–1, 72.
92. Dryden, 'Dedication of the *Aeneis*', 269.
93. Dryden, 'Preface to *Fables Ancient and Modern*', 29–30.
94. Pope, 'Preface to the *Iliad*', 12.
95. Dryden, 'A Defence of *An Essay on Dramatic Poesy*', 8.
96. Dryden, 'Preface to *Fables Ancient and Modern*', 30.
97. Johnson, 'Life of Pope', in *Works of Alexander Pope*, 61. Twentieth-century scholarship has also studied Dryden's temperament; see Fujimura, 'The Temper of John Dryden'.
98. Johnson, *Dictionary of the English Language*, sig. L4r.

Chapter 5

Figuring Ineloquence in Late Sixteenth-century Poetry
David J. Amelang

On his first appearance in Shakespeare's *Hamlet*, the titular character suffers what we would now describe as an emotional meltdown. After some quick-witted repartee with his mother and his newly crowned uncle, Hamlet is left all alone on the stage for his first soliloquy, during which he tries to put into words his feelings regarding the recent death of his father and his mother's hasty marriage to his uncle. Throughout the prince frequently chokes up and is often unable to finish his sentences. His speech breaks down, blunting the melodious cadence of the underlying iambic pentameter with sudden arhythmic outbursts and screeching track changes in his train of thought:

> But two months dead – nay, not so much, not two –
> So excellent a king, that was to this
> Hyperion to a satyr, so loving to my mother
> That he might not beteem the winds of heaven
> Visit her face too roughly! Heaven and earth,
> Must I remember? Why, she should hang on him
> As if increase of appetite had grown
> By what it fed on, and yet within a month –
> Let me not think on't; frailty, thy name is woman –
> A little month, or ere those shoes were old
> With which she followed my poor father's body,
> Like Niobe, all tears, why she, even she –
> O God, a beast that wants discourse of reason
> Would have mourned longer! – married with my uncle,
> My father's brother, but no more like my father
> Than I to Hercules . . .[1]

The prosody of this soliloquy stands out for its raw emotional verisimilitude and iconicity.[2] It convincingly reads and sounds not as words written by a poetic dramatist but rather as speech, which at times appears to be somewhat spontaneous and with flickers of improvisation. This is not the first instance of what I have elsewhere described as Shakespeare's rhetoric of iconic distress, in which he moves away from ornate and musical verse in scenes depicting overwhelming anguish and suffering in favour of a more realistic and pain-stricken linguistic style. It is, I argue, one of the first conscientious attempts to deploy systematically a series of tropes and figures of speech that artificially mirror the natural disruptions language suffers when a speaker is overcome by such grief and sorrow that words fail altogether.[3] Shakespeare employs the same rhetorical devices and strategies – perhaps even more effectively – in other well-known scenes in his plays, such as Othello's handkerchief-laden rant, the dying words of Lear, Leontes' fit of jealousy towards the beginning of *The Winter's Tale*, and a long and sustained roster of other scenes.

Others of Shakespeare's contemporary dramatists, especially beginning in the early years of the seventeenth century, also endowed characters undergoing intense emotions and distress with this style of language. This clearly suggests that there was a slow yet growing attraction for linguistic verisimilitude on the Elizabethan-Jacobean stage, a period broadly defined by strongly codified poetic forms and highly ornate rhetoric, and that a series of tropes and figures of speech facilitated the disruption of these otherwise firmly established expectations. But can the same be said of the non-dramatic literature of the time? Did the English poets of the final decades of the sixteenth century resort to the same rhetorical devices that their playwriting counterparts used? This chapter seeks to answer these questions by exploring representations of ineloquence in the poetry of late Elizabethan England. In particular, it analyses the relationship between theory and practice during this period with regard to a short list of tropes and figures ideally suited to mimicking inarticulate speech. To that end, the first half of the chapter focuses on the descriptions of these under-scrutinised linguistic devices in the most prominent rhetorical treatises and manuals of the time. Thereafter follows an analysis of a selection of poems from the period that reveals not only how different writers resorted to these devices, but also the different ways in which they deployed them.

Towards a Poetics of Ineloquence

'When a construction recurs often enough', writes John Porter Houston, 'it begins to constitute a rhetoric.'[4] While undoubtedly many tropes and figures can be deployed in order to imbue language with apparent ineloquence and incoherence, Shakespeare and his contemporary dramatists relied on a short list of devices when characterising their speeches of overwhelming distress. The recurring nature of these choices speaks directly to Houston's observation, as one is witness in these scenes to the development of a pattern. And these choices do not seem to be coincidental. In fact, if one reads descriptions of these figures in the most prominent manuals of rhetoric from the period, they are consistently singled out as the most effective vehicles for transmitting emotional turmoil. The following pages concentrate on the tropes in question, along with descriptions and examples derived directly from three of England's most important and widely read treatises and manuals from the late sixteenth century: Henry Peacham's *The Garden of Eloquence* (1592), George Puttenham's *The Art of English Poesy* (1589) and Angel Day's *The English Secretary* (1592).[5]

The most frequently used trope in speeches depicting emotional ineloquence is *ecphonesis*. Puttenham explains that he translated this into English as 'the Outcry' because 'it utters our mind by all such words as do show any extreme passion, whether it be by way of exclamation or crying out, admiration or wondering, imprecation or cursing, obtestation or taking God and the world to witness, or any such like as declare an impotent affection'.[6] In other words, it is a sudden exclamatory outburst that results from the speaker's emotional state. Peacham echoes Puttenham when he defines *ecphonesis* as 'a forme of speech by which the Orator through some vehement affection, as either love, hatred, gladnesse, sorrow, anger, marvelling, admiration, feare, or such like, bursteth forth into an exclamation or outcrie, signifying thereby the vehement affection or passion of his mind'.[7] Both rhetoricians highlight the trope's ability to convey extreme passions and affections; Angel Day shares their opinion, and succinctly describes *ecphonesis* as an exclamation 'which hath signification of griefe or indignation of a thing, as of grief'.[8] Outcries of this nature are extremely common in Elizabethan plays, and are a constant presence in speeches such as Hamlet's first soliloquy shown above.

Two other figures that are directly related to *ecphonesis* and that also feature prominently in these passages are *epizeuxis* and *ploce*. Day describes *epizeuxis* as the 'redoubling of a worde, by vehemencie to express a thing'.[9] That is, it is the immediate repetition – whether once or multiple times – of a single word. Puttenham's definition falls along the same lines as Day's, and Peacham simply adds to it that the figure is used 'commonly with a swift pronunciation'.[10] *Ploce* is like *epizeuxis* except that the repetition is not immediate; as Puttenham explains, it is the 'speedy iteration of one word, but with some little intermission by inserting one or two words between'.[11] These two figures, especially when combined with *ecphonesis*, imbue the language of characters with fixation and redundancy and directly challenge its eloquence and flow. This is precisely the point Puttenham puts forth in his account of other figures of repetition, whose effects he describes as

> nothing commendable, and therefore are not observed in good poesy, as a vulgar rhymer who doubled one word in the end of every verse ... These repetitions be not figurative but fantastical, for a figure is ever used to a purpose either of beauty or of efficacy; and these last recited be to no purpose, for neither can ye say that it urges affection, nor that it beautifieth or enforceth the sense, nor hath any other subtlety in it, and therefore is a very foolish impertinence of speech and not a figure.[12]

Repeating the same word – in Puttenham's opinion – adds neither beauty nor coherence to the line of verse; a bad poet, he claims, would rely on such figures to come up with a rhyme and there is no place for such 'foolish impertinencies' in good poetry.

Puttenham's opinion notwithstanding, dramatists such as Shakespeare often lined up a series of repeated shouts in their passages of distress:

> Lie with her? Lie on her? We say 'lie on her' when they belie her. Lie with her? 'Swounds, that's fulsome! Handkerchief – confessions – handkerchief. To confess and be hanged for his labour. First to be hanged, and then to confess! I tremble at it. Nature would not invest herself in such a shadowing passion without some instruction. It is not words that shakes me thus. Pish! Noses, ears, and lips! Is't possible? Confess? Handkerchief! O devil![13]

> And my poor fool is hanged. No, no, no life!
> Why should a dog, a horse, a rat have life
> And thou no breath at all? O thou'lt come no more,
> Never, never, never, never, never!
> Pray you undo this button. Thank you, sir. [O, O, O, O!].
> Do you see this? Look on her, look, her lips,
> Look there, look there![14]

In these particularly painful scenarios centred on Othello's discovery of his wife's apparent affair and Lear breaking down after the death of his daughter and his jester, the combined deployment of *ecphonesis* with either *epizeuxis* or *ploce* helps convey effectively the characters' inability to cope with what has just happened to them. It is precisely because these passages seek not verbal eloquence but quite the opposite, the handicapped language of an anguished mind, that the eye and ear find these figures to be well placed and put to good use.

Another perhaps less obvious but even more effective figure in this sense is *aposiopesis*. Peacham describes this syntactic device as 'a forme of speech by which the Orator through some affection, as either of fear, anger, sorrow, bashfulnesse or such like, breaketh off his speech before it be all ended'.[15] Elizabethan writers resorted to *aposiopesis* relatively frequently in passages of distress, but more often than not they did so while following a very specific formula: a performative utterance, in which the speaker declares his or her inability to speak.[16] A perfect example of this trope in action is Cleopatra in Mary Sidney's *Antonius* (1592) uttering with her final breath 'I can no more, I die'.[17] Another unrelated sub-genre of poetry in which this technique was used with relative frequency is the erotic epyllion, in which early modern poets often resorted to the Ovidian *cetera quis nescit?* ('who does not know the rest?') refrain as a way of hinting at the lovers' consummation. The following two examples come from Christopher Marlowe's translation of Ovid's *Amores* (c. 1580s) and John Marston's *Metamorphosis of Pygmalion's Image* (1599):

I cling'd her naked body, downe she fell,
Judge you the rest, being tird she bad me kisse;
Jove send me more such after noones as this.[18]

Who knowes not what ensues? O pardon me
Yee gaping eares that swallow vp my lines
Expect no more.[19]

Returning to representations of distress, some writers also employed *aposiopesis* in a more literal sense, with a speaker's train of thought derailing mid-sentence and switching to a different syntactic construction in the manner of what descriptive linguists refer to as *anacolutha*. This second interpretation of the classical trope, which I term 'literal *aposiopesis*' to distinguish it from the 'performative' version, comes closer to Puttenham and Day's definitions; the latter wrote of *aposiopesis* that it is 'when by passing to another matter, we stop our speech on a sodaine, as it were in an interrupted or discontented moode'.[20] Such levels of linguistic disruption went against all precepts and conventions of poetic discourse in late sixteenth-century England, which emphasised linguistic elegance and rhythmic harmony. And yet, despite its unorthodox and disruptive intent, poets and playwrights alike occasionally relied on this technique due to its potential effectiveness to capture the pathology of emotional strain, as depicted perfectly in Hamlet's soliloquy cited above. Gavin Alexander explains it best in his analysis of *aposiopesis* in the poems of Philip Sidney:

> At the same time as rhetoric contains aposiopesis, aposiopesis threatens it ... Elocutio, the rhetorical choosing of words and figures of speech, means eloquence, and is opposed by ineloquence. And elocutio means speaking, which is opposed by silence. But it also, literally, means speaking out, and that is opposed by significant silence, speaking in, aposiopesis. Silence therefore runs the risk of being taken for insignificance, and it is this flirtation with ineloquence which gives aposiopesis its force.[21]

The last figure to be included in this overview of rhetorical ineloquence, and very closely connected to this literal interpretation of *aposiopesis*, is *parenthesis*. A 'figure of tolerable disorder' in the words of Puttenham, *parenthesis* 'is when ye will seem for larger information or some other purpose to piece or graft in the midst of your tale an unnecessary parcel of speech, which nevertheless may be thence without any detriment to the rest'.[22] Both Peacham and Day agree with Puttenham in describing the use of parenthetical interjections as tolerable if slightly distracting disruptions of syntactic harmony. 'It is a form of speech', Peacham writes,

> which setteth a sentence a sunder by the interposition of another, or thus: When a sentence is cast between the speech before it be all ended, which although it giveth some strength, yet being taken away, it leaveth the same speech perfect enough.[23]

As is the case with *aposiopesis*, the basic premise behind *parenthesis* is an alteration of natural and complete syntax. Parentheticals also resembled *aposiopesis* in that if deployed with enough bluntness, writers could use them to deviate and disrupt the underlying coherence in the speech of characters.

If so desired, all these figures – whether used in isolation or combined with each other – can help recreate the acute and brisk jumps and jolts warranted by certain scenes in which the mind's regular flow of thought is disturbed. Writers from the late Elizabethan period could turn to the rhetorical manuals of the time to find the necessary tools to elaborate a discourse built around the notion of poetic ineloquence. Or at least they could attempt to free discourse from the constraints of linguistic embellishment and artificiality, not unlike the psychological stream of consciousness narrative style that modernist novelists developed from the turn of the twentieth century. Most of the evidence of late sixteenth-century authors pursuing this conscious ineloquence so far put forth comes from the sphere of drama; the following section explores how Elizabethan England's poets engaged with the (un)rhetorical figures of speech that contemporary theorists mobilised in order to convey overwhelming passion, grief and sorrow.

Syntactic Disruption, Rhythmic Consonance

During a brief stint in prison in 1537 for slapping a courtier, Henry Howard, Earl of Surrey, wrote the sonnet 'The Geraldine'. It was dedicated to then 10-year-old Elizabeth Fitzgerald, the future Countess of Lincoln, whose beauty had infatuated him to the point of poetic action. A little over sixty years later, in 1597, Michael Drayton included his own rendition of Surrey's predicament in a love-torn letter as part of his *Englands Heroicall Epistles* collection. In its closing lines, Drayton's earl turns to well-worn imagery to express his love for the young Countess:

> Love did us both with one-selfe Arrow strike,
> Our Wound's both one, our Cure should be the like;
> Except thou hast found out some mean by Art,
> Some pow'rfull Med'cine to withdraw the dart;
> But mine is fixt, and absence being proved,
> It stickes too fast, it cannot be removed.
>
>   *Adiew, Adiew*, from *Florence* when I goe,
> By my next Letters GERALDINE shall know,
> Which if good fortune shall by course direct,
> From Venice by some messenger expect;
> Till when, I leave thee to thy hearts desire,
> By him that lives thy vertues to admire.[24]

Throughout the poem, Surrey occasionally finds himself doubling words and phrases at moments of peak emotionality, such as the parting farewells highlighted above. A combination of *ecphonesis* (the outcry) and *epizeuxis* (the doubling of words) alerts the reader to the vehemence of the speaker's passion, as prescribed by Peacham,

Puttenham and Day. Nevertheless, the use of these figures of ineloquence does not affect the prosody and melodic cadence of the poem: the repeated *adieus* fit hand in glove into the epistle's iambic pentameter, and their position at the beginning of the line allows the sequence of rhyming couplets to continue without disruption.

The doubled outcry is one of the most recurrent and visible expressions of melodramatic anguish in Elizabethan poetry. As it relates to the topic at hand, Drayton's poem is in no way exceptional; far from it, his use of *ecphonesis* could be described as archetypical. The exact same technique can be seen deployed continuously throughout the lyrical productions of sixteenth-century England, such as in the induction to Thomas Sackville's *The Mirror of Magistrates* (1563) and in the anonymously written 'The Seafarer' included in *Tottel's Miscellany* (1557):

> Nor worthy Hector worthiest of them all,
> Her Hope, her Ioy, his Force is now for naught.
> *O Troy, Troy*, there is no boote but bale,
> The hugy Horse within thy Wales is brought:
> Thy Turrets fall, thy Knights that whilome fought
> In Arms amid the Field, are slayne in Bed,
> Thy Gods defilde, and all thy honour dead.[25]

> Shall I thus ever long, and be no whit the neare,
> And shall I still complain to thee, the which me will not heare?
> *Alas say nay, say nay*, and be no more so dome,
> But open thou thy manly mouth, and say that thou wilt come.
> Wherby my hart may thinke, although I see not thee,
> That thou wilt come thy word so sware, if thou a lives man be.[26]

Sackville's induction is a perfect mirror of Drayton's technique; 'The Seafarer' is written in iambic hexameter instead of pentameter and the doubling device used is *ploce* instead of *epizeuxis*, but its underlying effect and purpose remain the same. These rhetorical choices represent the broader trend of how most Elizabethan poets engaged with figures of ineloquence. Rather than placing these potentially disruptive elements in positions that would challenge the flow of the verse, they capitalise on the repetitiveness of the doubling to enhance the line's musicality. While figures such as *epizeuxis* or *ploce* in their essence distort the inner logic and conventions of language, examples such as these show that they need not be at odds with regular poetic rhythm.

Far from it, Elizabethan poets seemed to hold the rhythmic cadence of doubled outcries in particularly high regard. It is not uncommon to see these figures deployed in positions of significant musical importance.

Thomas Proctor, in his 'A Proper Sonnet, how Time Consumeth All Things' (1578), begins every first and third line of each quatrain with the same repeated shouts:

> *Ay me, ay me!* I sigh to see the scythe afield;
> Down goeth the grass, soon wrought to withered hay.
> *Ay me, alas! Ay me, alas!* That beauty needs must yield,
> And princes pass, as grass doth fade away.
>
> *Ay me, ay me!* That life cannot have lasting leave,
> Nor gold take hold of everlasting day.
> *Ay me, alas! Ay me, alas!* That time hath talents to receive,
> And yet no time can make a sure stay.[27]

Within this pattern, the anaphoric cries play the role of anchors that bind the poem's different stanzas together; effectively, they serve the same purpose as the end-of-stanza refrain that one often sees in poems and songs. And, not coincidentally, refrains are another recurrent locus for ineloquent figures in sixteenth-century English poetry, which yet again highlight the musical value that poets of the period placed on these devices. In the following excerpts – the first from a song attributed to Thomas Wyatt (1530s) and the second from Philip Sidney's fourth song in *Astrophil and Stella* (1580s), separated by a fifty-year span in which many lyrical conventions changed – the refrains follow the same pattern, presumably with the same musical purpose in mind:

> Heaven and earth and all that hear me plain
> Do well perceive what care doth cause me cry,
> Save you alone, to whom I cry in vain
> 'Mercy! Madame, alas! *I die, I die!*'
>
> If that you sleep, I humbly you require
> Forbear a while, and let your rigour slake –
> Since that by you I burn thus in this fire –
> To hear my plaint, 'Dear heart, *awake! awake!*'
>
> Since that so oft ye have made me to wake
> In plaint and tears and in right piteous case,
> Displease you not, if force do now me make
> To break your sleep, crying '*Alas! alas!*'[28]
>
> Onely joy, now here you are,
> Fit to heare and ease my care:
> Let my whispering voyce obtaine,

Sweete reward for sharpest paine:
Take me to thee, and thee to me.
'*No, no, no, no, my Deare, let be.*'

Night hath closd all in her cloke,
Twinckling starres Love-thoughts provoke:
Danger hence good care doth keepe,
Jealousie it selfe doth sleepe:
Take me to thee, and thee to me.
'*No, no, no, no, my Deare, let be.*'[29]

It is clear, thus, that English poets were not shying away from using *epizeuxis*, *ploce* and other disruptors of prosody: Sidney goes even further by quadrupling the *no*'s, doubling down on the conventional single-repetition schemes. What is also evident is that they did not allow these figures to create bumps in the melody of the iambic verse. Quite the contrary, their strategic placement of repetition-based emotional outbursts more often than not imbue the lines with an incantatory quality that strengthens the poems' musicality as opposed to weakening it; indeed, the fact that the formula used in these repetitive patterns is internally built as markedly iambic sequences effectively reinforces the overall pattern. Whereas Shakespeare's use of these devices in the aforementioned passages cause rhythmic glitches and syncopations, that is not the case in these poems, in which one can read and intellectually perceive the anguish and distress of the lyrical I while the beat of the verse marches on, uninterrupted.

This observation, here presented as a miscellany of poetic excerpts, is based on the reading of several hundred poems written throughout the sixteenth century. With little variation over time, Tudor England's poets turned to these conduits of ineloquence with relative frequency. Yet they rarely resorted to them so as actually to cripple the flow of the verse: they operate instead as signals of emotional instability within an otherwise unwaveringly stable line. As one can see below, however, in the final decades of the century some poets did start to experiment with more overt challenges to the sanctity of the eloquent line.

Hearing Sense in Nonsense

In a particularly provocative essay, Stephen Booth once argued that Shakespeare was England's most underrated poet because he – unlike most of his contemporaries – was able to write linguistically unintelligible yet emotionally comprehensible speech. In certain passages of the playwright's canon, Booth writes, 'one is hearing sense in nonsense'.[30] Booth's description of what he deems a uniquely Shakespearean talent makes clear the connection that he establishes between the works of the Elizabethan-Jacobean dramatist and the narrative style of some early twentieth-century novelists who aimed to recreate the chaotic nature of one's inner monologue. Indeed, at least from the turn of the seventeenth century onwards, Shakespeare did develop an idiolect of distress and mental anguish that does share some similarities with the Joycean stream of consciousness. The two language patterns inhabited the same common ground, one that could be described – in a general way – as a conscious disregard for the linguistic principles of order and clarity, with particular emphasis on the disruption of conventional syntactic structures. A jumbled sentence reflects a jumbled mind, and a character's inability to communicate properly and elegantly speaks to their emotional turmoil.

While Shakespeare reaches the high point of the rhetoric of distress in the so-called major tragedies discussed previously (*Hamlet*, *Othello* and *Macbeth*), it is important to recognise that he explored less intense iterations of the same formula both in earlier and later stages of his career as well, as the following passages from *Richard III* (1593) and *The Winter's Tale* (1610), two plays separated by almost two decades, underline:

> Give me another horse! Bind up my wounds!
> Have mercy, Jesu! – Soft, I did but dream.
> O coward conscience, how dost thou afflict me?
> The lights burn blue. It is now dead midnight.
> Cold fearful drops stand on my trembling flesh.
> What do I fear? Myself? There's none else by.
> Richard loves Richard; that is, I am I.
> Is there a murderer here? No. Yes, I am.
> Then fly! What, from myself? Great reason. Why?
> Lest I revenge. Myself upon myself?[31]

> . . . Come, sir page,
> Look on me with your welkin eye. Sweet villain,
> Most dear'st, my collop! Can thy dam? – may't be? –
> Affection, thy intention stabs the centre.
> Thou dost make possible things not so held,
> Communicat'st with dreams – how can this be? –
> With what's unreal thou coactive art,
> And fellows't nothing.[32]

These are two completely different scenes, one in which the embattled and terrified Richard is fending off both soldiers and ghosts in the middle of a battlefield and another in which Leontes is becoming consumed with unwarranted jealousy over his wife Hermione's imagined infidelity, featuring the same incoherent and rambling style that so quickly jumps off the page. And presiding over the centre of this stylistic detour is *aposiopesis*, the rhetorical device Puttenham vernacularised as 'the Figure of Silence, or of Interruption'.[33]

As we saw above, there are two completely different ways of understanding and deploying *aposiopesis*. The first is as a performative utterance in which speakers verbally express their inability or lack of will to carry on. This technique was a favourite with Philip Sidney and his admirers, for instance, as the heroic couplet in Samuel Daniel's 42nd sonnet to Delia exemplifies:

> When thou surcharg'd with burthen of thy yeeres,
> Shalt bend thy wrinkles homeward to the earth,
> When time hath made a pasport for thy seares,
> Dated in age the Kalends of our death
> *But ah no more*, this hath beene often tolde,
> And women grieue to thinke they must be olde.[34]

This is not, however, the figure that anchors what Booth describes as Shakespeare's sensical nonsense. It is the other interpretation of *aposiopesis*, the literal interruption of a syntactic structure, that lies at the centre of the passages of turbulent inner monologue featured throughout this chapter.[35] Unlike its performative counterpart, literal *aposiopesis* breaks off the end of a syntactic unit without providing any form of semantic closure. In doing so, writers convey the emotional turmoil of speakers not by what they are saying, but by their inability to speak coherently. And while it is virtually impossible to find examples of this usage of the trope in poems from the late Elizabethan period, it appears only rarely in the plays either, including Shakespeare. That said, some of the other devices that play a significant role in Shakespeare's idiolect of distress also feature in lyrical works to a similar, if perhaps less dramatic, effect.

In the type of literal *aposiopesis* that ends up deriving into an anacoluthon, a speaker abruptly interrupts what they are saying, leaving the sentence incomplete and moving on to a different utterance. It is precisely that dispersal of thought and lack of discipline that so effectively transmits the speaker's inner turmoil. When employed with this same intent, *parenthesis* can also convey a similar level of psychological meandering. Instead of interrupting a thought never to return and flesh it out, the parenthetical digression inserts a second utterance in between the two halves of a full and self-sufficient sentence; by doing so the poet recreates the speaker's lack of mental focus or of ability to remain composed and coherent throughout the entirety of the pronouncement:

> I might, *unhappie word, (woe me)* I might,
> And then would not, or could not see my blisse.
> Till now, wrapped in a most infernal night,
> I find how heavenly day *(wretch)* did I miss.
> Hart rent thy self, thou doest thy selfe but right,
> . . .
> And yet could not by rising Morne foresee,
> How faire a day was near, *(ô punisht eyes)*
> That I had been more foolish, or more wise.[36]

This excerpt from Sidney's sonnet 33 of *Astrophil and Stella*, and especially its first line, provides a poignant representation of what is meant by *parenthesis* here. It might refer to the actual use of parenthetical punctuation markers, or it might appear in between commas as an embedded clause; regardless of its visual presentation on the page, it is the syntactic digression that concerns us. In scenes and poems of emotional distress, these interpolations – more often than not outcries à la *ecphonesis* – become more and more frequent, especially in the poems from the 1580s onwards. They do not challenge the formal expectations of verse, with both metre and rhyme staying steady and on course, but they definitely add hiccups – and draw attention – to the prosody and intelligibility of the line. Moreover, a sliver of emotional iconicity imbues the pathos of the highly codified written language, as if one were spontaneously shouting instead of meticulously writing these words. This is the case in many passages of Spenser's *The Faerie Queene*, including this stanza from the Mask of Cupid:

> Her brest all naked, as nett yuory,
> Without adorne of gold or siluer bright,
> Wherewith the Craftesman wonts it beautify,
> Of her dew honour was despoyled quight,
> And a wide wound therein *(O ruefull sight)*
> Entrenched deepe with knife accursed keene,
> Yet freshly bleeding forth her fainting spright,
> *(The worke of cruell hand)* was to be seene,
> That dyde in sanguine red her skin all snowy cleene.[37]

These are clearly not instances of sensical nonsense, at least not in the way Booth meant. What Shakespeare achieves in those passages goes beyond the strategic deployment of rhetorical devices, and even only in the most heightened of circumstances can one really assert that all channels of verbal communication have truly broken down. Nevertheless, it is through the conscious use of these often under-scrutinised figures of speech that poets and playwrights alike season their words with a waft of natural spontaneity, despite the unapologetically artificial and ornamental nature of verse writing in this literary period. It is 'unpoetic poetry', to repurpose Maurice Charney's term:[38] occasional outbursts, unprompted repetitions of words or phrases, unfinished syntax and sentences complicated by meandering thoughts and interjected digressions . . . these are what one witnesses in real-life moments of distress. Considering the medium in which they appear, one can and should immediately acknowledge that these devices seem somewhat out of place, and yet they sound and read and feel right, especially when considering their circumstances.

Conclusion

Under the auspices of a volume that aims to shed new light on under-scrutinised and neglected elements of sixteenth-century English poetry, this chapter offers at least two points of contact with its broader themes of analysis. The first is that the rhetorical devices at the core of what I have described as the poetics of ineloquence have for the most part been neglected not only by literary critics, but also by the poets and lyricists of the Elizabethan period. Clearly these should not be counted among the most popular or recurrent figures of speech in late sixteenth-century poetry, in terms of both writing as well as of critical reading. And for good reason, which leads to the second point of contact: these devices, when used ably, can recreate a style of writing that appears to be improvised and unscripted. Or, to capitalise on one of the keywords of this volume, unwritten.

There does not seem to have been much of a market in Elizabethan England for unpoetic poetry. It was served in small bites and appeared only in (some, not all) situations of maximal emotional distress. One witnesses an increase in the use of iconic ineloquence in the poems of the Jacobean and Caroline periods, which can confidently be attributed to the philosophical and artistic trends that distinguished the Baroque from the Renaissance: artists and writers in sixteenth-century Europe – including England – demonstrate a stronger propensity for order, balance and elegance than their more disruptive and chaos-curious successors. What is less easy to explain, however, is the disparate presence of the rhetoric of distress in the writings of late Elizabethan poets and their dramatic counterparts. Not only do both belong to the same period and to the same cultural and literary current, in some cases they are the same people. Moreover, most of the dramatic output of this time also appeared in verse. And yet there is an indisputable difference between the levels of iconicity found in the two.

Two possible explanations occur to me. The first is that in late Elizabethan drama, and especially in scenes that feature instances of poetic ineloquence, the use of blank verse is much more common than rhyming verse. The lack of rhyme automatically reduces the artifice and musicality of the line, and lends itself more comfortably to further explorations of arhythmic prosody and mid-line hitches. On the other hand, most poems follow strict metrical and rhyme patterns, and thus the poet would have to work harder than the playwright to make the peg fit the hole. The second explanation involves the nature of the medium itself. Dramatic texts are generally composed as dialogue spoken among characters with some degree of verisimilitude; consequently, there is a certain expectation – or at least potential – for iconic speech. Since poetry is inherently an artificial apparatus, much more so than drama, the presence within it of verisimilar (and in this case ineloquent) language is harder to justify. Unlike in drama, there is little conceit of spontaneity in poetry, which renders out of place any writing technique that simulates an inability to speak due to shock.

These formal and essential considerations aside, it is nevertheless noteworthy that poets still found ways of inserting these rhetorical figures into their works without using a shoehorn. The need to appease the rhythm and rhyme constraints does diminish their disruptive quality, but only to a point. When I found the first instances of syntactic interruptions and emotional outbursts in these poems, seamlessly integrated into the artifice of the rhyming verse, it immediately reminded me of the way in which early modern Spanish playwrights engaged with these figures as well. Golden Age Spanish plays, unlike English ones, follow strict metre and rhyme conventions, which leaves precious little room for anacolutha and similar linguistic disruptions. However, Spanish dramatists figured out a way to have these broken sentences complement each other as fragments of a shared line of verse, as can be seen here in the opening lines of Lope de Vega's *Los locos de Valencia* (*Madness in Valencia*):

FLORIANO: ¡Oh, amigo en amistad; en sangre, hermano!
    Yo he dado...
VALERIO: ¡Hablad!
FLORIANO: *Yo he dado...*
VALERIO: ¡Decid!
FLORIANO: *Muerte...*
VALERIO: ¿A quién?
FLORIANO: ¿Óyenos alguien?
VALERIO: Nadie.
FLORIANO: A un hombre,
    que por mi mal ...
VALERIO: Decidlo; ¿qué os divierte?[39]

The ingenuity of Spanish playwrights, much like that of English poets with whom they share the more formal medium of rhymed verse, shines through in such instances of poetic innovation. By using these rhetorical figures occasionally to chip away at both the eloquence as well as the linguistic correctness of their otherwise dependably prosodic verse, writers were able to communicate more viscerally the emotional despair of those moments in life in which words inevitably fall short.

Notes

1. Shakespeare, *Hamlet*, 1.2.138–53, in *Norton Shakespeare*, ed. Greenblatt, 1676.
2. Derived from the term 'icon', the notion of iconicity was developed by Olga Fischer and Max Nänny to refer to instances in literature that have a high degree of lifelike aesthetics; an icon, Fischer explains, is 'an image that more or less reflects a situation, concept, or object in the real world' ('Iconicity in Language and Literature', 65). See also Fischer and Nänny, 'Introduction: Iconicity as a Creative Force in Language Use'; 'Introduction: Iconicity and Nature'.
3. For more, see Amelang, 'A Broken Voice'; and Sacks, 'Where Words Prevail Not'.
4. Houston, *Shakespearean Sentences*, 45.
5. For *The Garden of Eloquence* I have relied primarily on the 1593 edition, an expanded and more detailed revision of the original 1577 publication; similarly, while the first edition of *The English Secretary* was published in 1586, I cite from the second edition of 1592 in which Day included for the first time an appendix with the different figures and their definitions. I would also like to credit here the importance of the digital project *Silva Rhetoricae*, <http://rhetoric.byu.edu>, an online

Figuring Ineloquence in Late Sixteenth-century Poetry 137

compendium of sources and explanations on the art of rhetoric, in the development of this essay.
6. Puttenham, *Art of English Poesy*, ed. Whigham and Rebhorn, 297.
7. Peacham, *Garden of Eloquence*, 62.
8. Day, *English Secretarie*, 96.
9. Ibid., 93.
10. Peacham, *Garden of Eloquence*, 47; Puttenham, *Art of English Poesy*, 285.
11. Puttenham, *Art of English Poesy*, 285.
12. Ibid., 286.
13. Shakespeare, *Othello*, 4.1.34–41, in *Norton Shakespeare*, ed. Greenblatt, 2147.
14. Shakespeare, *King Lear*, 5.3.304–10, in *Norton Shakespeare*, ed. Greenblatt, 2552. Bracketed interjections added from the Quarto text, ed. Greenblatt, 2472.
15. Peacham, *Garden of Eloquence*, 118.
16. The concept of performative utterance was first discussed by British philosopher J. L. Austin. See his seminal work *How to Do Things with Words*.
17. As cited in Alexander, 'Sidney's Interruptions', 192.
18. Marlowe, *All Ovids Elegies*, I.5.24–6, in *Complete Works*, ed. Gill, 1:19.
19. Marston, *Metamorphosis of Pigmalions Image*, 38.1–3, sig. B7r.
20. Day, *English Secretarie*, 87.
21. Alexander, 'Sidney's Interruptions', 194–5. For another thought-provoking study of the figure of *aposiopesis*, see Sell, 'Terminal Aposiopesis and Sublime Communication'.
22. Puttenham, *Art of English Poesy*, 252.
23. Peacham, *Garden of Eloquence*, 198.
24. Drayton, *Englands Heroicall Epistles*, 'Henry Howard, Earle of Surrey, to the Lady Geraldine', 241–52, in *Works*, ed. Hebel, 2:283–4; emphasis added.
25. Sackville, *The Last Part of Mirour for Magistrates*, fol. 136v; emphasis added.
26. 'The ladie praieth the returne of her lover abiding on the seas', 1–6, in *Tottel's Miscellany*, 172, emphasis added.
27. Proctor, 'A Proper Sonnet, how Time Consumeth All Things', 1–8, in *Oxford Book of Sixteenth Century Verse*, ed. Chambers, 149, emphasis added.
28. Wyatt, XCIX.1–12, in *Complete Poems*, ed. Rebholz, 134–5, emphasis added.
29. Sidney, *Astrophil and Stella*, Song 4.1–12, in *Poems*, ed. Ringler, 210, emphasis added.
30. Booth, 'Shakespeare's Language', 3.
31. Shakespeare, Richard III, 5.5.131–40, in *Norton Shakespeare*, ed. Greenblatt, 590–1.

32. Shakespeare, The Winter's Tale, 1.2.137–44, in *Norton Shakespeare*, ed. Greenblatt, 2888.
33. Puttenham, *Art of English Poesy*, 250.
34. Daniel, *Delia*, sonnet 42.9–14, in *Poems and a Defence of Rhyme*, ed. Sprague, 31.
35. The expression 'turbulent inner monologue' was first used in this context in Houston, *Shakespearean Sentences*, 97. Very similar to Houston's own are the words with which Kermode described Hamlet's soliloquy cited at the beginning of this chapter (1.2.138–53), to which he refers as a 'new way of representing turbulent thinking' (*Shakespeare's Language*, 16).
36. Sidney, *Astrophil and Stella*, sonnet 33.1–5, in *Poems*, ed. Ringler, 181, emphases added. Punctuation has been altered, and Q1-Q2 variants such as '(woe me)' in line 1 preferred over Ringler's text.
37. Spenser, *The Faerie Queene*, ed. Hamilton, III.12.20, emphasis added.
38. Charney, 'Shakespeare's Unpoetic Poetry'.
39. Lope de Vega, *Los locos de Valencia*, 1.6–9.

Chapter 6

Eloquent Bodies: Rhetoricising the Symptoms of Love in the English Epyllion

Sonia Hernández-Santano

In *The Rhetoric of the Body* (2000), Lynn Enterline initiated the scholarly tendency to analyse the English epyllia in light of the connections established in Ovid's *Metamorphoses* between the voice – understood as a trope for the verbal and cognitive articulation of the self – and the body as the vehicle that 'dramatize[s] language's vicissitudes'.[1] Enterline argues that it is upon the complicated relation between language and the flesh that Ovid displays his reflections about the shortcomings of both rhetoric and poetry when it comes to the expression of inwardness. The violence exerted on the metamorphosed body, whose verbal abilities are maimed by literal or metaphorical mutilation of its vocalic instruments (tongue), renders it not only a 'bearer of meaning', but also a 'linguistic agent' and 'a place where representation, materiality and action collide'.[2] Among the many aspects that the Elizabethan poets imitated from Ovid's epic poetry, the most evident are the stylistic exuberance and the elaboration of images of corporeal violence and change that, according to Clark Hulse, stand for a society in flux.[3] However, the pervasive occurrence in these poems of disabled voices and the recurrent metaphor of what Enterline calls 'speaking bodies'[4] strike us when reading poems such as *Scillaes Metamorphosis* (1589), *Venus and Adonis* (1593) and *The Rape of Lucrece* (1594), among many others, and suggest that the cultural significance that underlies this Elizabethan genre has meta-poetic and meta-rhetorical connotations. The multiple allusions in the poems to the performative potential of bodily parts are intended to counteract the characters' ineloquence in what might be interpreted as the epyllion's response, by means of poetic praxis, to unsolved theoretical issues concerning eloquence. As stated by Zenón Luis-Martínez in the introduction to this volume, the potential of the sixteenth-century epyllion to generate a poetics of genre through the strategies developed in its linguistic praxis is due to the fact that it still remained in the margins of theory.[5]

Taking its cue from Enterline's analysis of the ways in which the principles of humanist rhetorical training are imprinted in Shakespeare's works, and also from William Weaver's recent study of the epyllion as representative of 'the rites of passage' that Elizabethan boys had to go through in the context of the humanist grammar school,[6] this chapter aims to circumscribe the scope of interpretation of this genre to two specific aspects of the humanist conception of rhetoric and poetics on which the Elizabethans based the boys' education: one is the practice of rhetorical delivery, or *actio*, through the command of corporeal language; the other is the emphasis given to the cultivation of style as a means of making words enact the emotions. Although they seem to be disparate aspects, both derive from the same principle of classical rhetoric: effective discourse, be it written or oral, should create in the readers' and auditors' imagination a vivid image of the idea exposed. Both style in written poetry and delivery in oratory aim at achieving *enargeia*, which, as defined by Quintilian in *Institutio oratoria*, refers to the ability of words 'not so much to narrate as to exhibit'.[7] Frustrated Ovidian voices function as the convergence point on which the metaphorical relation between formal artifice (*elocutio*) and rhetorical declamation (*actio*) in the epyllia is articulated, as has already been hinted by Enterline: 'That an intensely rhetorical poem written by a former student of declamation should focus on the voice so frequently cannot surprise when we remember such training.'[8] The extravagant attempts to make bodies dramatise the passions appear as a sort of mimicry of the poems' formal artifice, while at the same time they seem ironic about the humanist practice of rhetorical *actio*.[9] When commenting on the Pythagorean opposition between *anima* (mind, soul) and *figura/forma* (body), Enterline affirms that the latter two nouns designate both the form of the body as well as forms in language, and explains that bodies in Ovid stand for style:

> But as the rhetorical undercurrent in both stories [Daphne and Pygmalion] about beautiful female 'forms' should also alert us, *forma* also refers to style of composition and generally to poetic or rhetorical forms of speech ... And finally, *forma* also came to designate the grammatical quality, condition, or 'form' of a word.[10]

Assuming this correspondence, this chapter contributes to this volume's aim of unveiling the ways in which poetic praxis formulates *unwritten* critical approaches to Renaissance theoretical assumptions, in this case regarding rhetorical delivery and the cultivation of style.

However, the profusion of bodily allusions should not be approached exclusively from the perspective of rhetoric without taking into consideration the Elizabethan assumption of the connection between the psychological and physiological dimensions of the self, derived from Galenic humoral theories. During the 1990s and the first decade of the present century, critical approaches to Elizabethan poetic displays of emotion focused exclusively on the influence of humoral theories which, as Michael Schoenfeldt has shown, basically established a correspondence between the body and the soul, and made mental and emotional health largely depend upon the health of the body.[11] This critical trend, referred to by Brian Cummings and Freya Sierhuis as the 'turn to the body', and by Sibylle Baumbach as 'the body-boom' and 'the corporeal turn', provided a deterministic approach to the construction of the self, ascribing the exterior signals of emotions exclusively to physiological processes and disregarding the individual's cognitive sphere and will.[12] However, recent criticism has pointed to more conscious experiences of emotion, suggesting that this 'new humoralism' produces a conservative picture of the period that denies any kind of human agency, and emphasises the repressed and anxious side of Elizabethan culture.[13] Cummings and Sierhuis propose an approach to the emotions from a wider perspective:

> Thus rather than putting to the fore the framework of Galenic physiology or that of faculty psychology, as many recent studies have done ... we regard it as a realignment both with the ancient concerns of rhetoric and with contemporary reflections on intersubjectivity and self-reflection.[14]

This chapter aims to continue to widen the scope of the analysis of the perception and expression of inwardness in Elizabethan poetry, specifically shedding light on the extent to which interaction between the rhetorical principles that the poets assimilated during their grammar school formation, the influence of Ovidian imagery of the voice, and the Galenic theories of humours determined their articulation of emotions in the minor epic poems. Almost two decades before Enterline highlighted the force that Ovidian imagery gave to the Elizabethan rhetoric of the body, Clark Hulse had already pinpointed that the images of corporeal transformation were meant to connect the two levels of experience of the self, that is, flesh and thought, and therefore challenged our ability to categorise experience.[15] Hulse distinguished between the metaphysical image, which finds an unexpected equivalence in two things that have no apparent resemblance, and the metamorphic image, which renders the vehicle of the metaphor as its own tenor: 'a woman is like a tree and becomes identical to that tree'.[16] Therefore, in the linguistic praxis of the minor epic poems, metamorphosis and the metaphors dealing with the body's potential to display emotions function as 'analogous strategies' for the self-generated poetics of the genre, as hinted in the introduction to this volume.[17]

This chapter focuses specifically on the difficulties of the characters in the Elizabethan epyllia in giving expression to their passions in order to transfer them to their auditors, whether by means of language or, when their voices are muted, through the rhetoric of the body and the involuntary alteration of their physiology – tears, sighs, blushing, temperature and other symptoms. In considering *Scillaes Metamorphosis*, *Venus and Adonis* and *The Rape of Lucrece*, I observe that Lodge's and Shakespeare's rhetorical and poetic concerns take two directions: first, behind the pervasive and thorough descriptions of gestures and bodily movements, which on occasion take a humorous and ironic tone, is the imprint left by the humanist tutors' insistence on the performance of public exercises of declamation, which put the schoolboys under the threat of physical punishment. Second, the Elizabethan poets' penchant for giving detailed explanations for the inward and outward symptoms of love and grief derives directly from the Galenic idea that the mind is revealed in the flesh, and obliquely implies the humanist premise that perfect eloquence is attained through the fusion of matter and form, idea and word; in other words, that style should function as the vivid materialisation of ideas. Hulse's concept of the metamorphic image is approached here not so much in relation to the corporeal mutation of the characters, but in relation to how words and bodies struggle in parallel to function as the material element into which ideas and emotions respectively are metamorphosed in order to become perceptible to auditors.

The Schoolroom

One of the premises of Galenic medicine that most influenced the treatment of bodies in Elizabethan literature is the consideration that outward physical appearance denotes the health of an individual, not only concerning their physiological well-being but also the balance of the mind. Thomas Wright in *The Passions of the Minde in Generall* (1601) implies that a good physical condition was in part a result of the control of the passions of the mind.[18] The perception of the body as a prolongation of the cognitive side of the individual was also assimilated by humanist tutors in their treatises concerning the acquisition of learning. Describing the profile of an ideal student, Roger Ascham argues in *The Scholemaster* (1570) that only those boys with a natural disposition to learning, the *euphues*, were worth giving instruction in schools. To be an *euphues* obviously implied having the necessary intellectual potential, the wit, together with the will to learn; but a good learner was also required to possess 'all other qualities of the minde and partes of the body, that must an other day serue learning'.[19] The way in which a learned man could 'serve learning' with the parts of his body other than the mind in Elizabethan society was, besides having the behaviour of a good citizen, to make good use of his oratorical skills in spreading the knowledge that he had acquired in his youth. That Ascham was thinking of learning as a faculty to be transmitted mainly through the command of the performative part of rhetoric (delivery) is evinced when he enumerates the physical attributes that best fit that task. First, he mentions the tongue as a tool of *pronuntiatio*: 'a tong, not stamering, or ouer hardlie drawing forth wordes, but plaine and redie to deliuer the meaning of the minde'. Second is the voice, which should not be 'softe, weake, piping, womannishe, but audible, stronge and manlike'. Third, the 'countenance' required to be 'faire and cumlie'. Finally, the shape of the whole body, not 'wretched and deformed' because, he argues, 'a cumlie countenance, with a goodlie stature, geueth credit to learning'.[20] He concludes the section dedicated to describing the traits of a good learner by underlining the necessary cooperation between the psychological and physiological dimensions of the individual: 'And thus, by *Socrates* iudgement, a good father, and a wise scholemaster, shold chose a childe to make a scholer of, that hath by nature, the foresayd perfite qualitites, and cumlie furniture, both of mynde and bodie.'[21]

The participation of the corporeal self in the processes that concern learning is manifested in more fleshly terms when it comes to the punishments that the tutors of Latin rhetoric used to employ to motivate their students. Flogging, or 'learning by the rod', was a common practice in Elizabethan schools, especially in the public exercises of grammar, translation and declamation that boys had to perform in front of their masters and schoolmates.[22] Beating, as Richard Halpern explains, was not just a method for controlling groups, but also a way of testing the capacities of the boys to develop social and political attitudes; it became a sort of 'political ritual, in which the pedagogue both assumed and reinforced the sovereign authority of the monarch or magistrate'.[23]

As a genre that has been regarded as a means for poets to practise and display their recently acquired skills in imitation and eloquence, the English epyllion is informed by the ideology and anxieties that Elizabethan pedagogy had instilled in its authors.[24] To this we may add that poems such as Lodge's and Shakespeare's denote their authors' sense of belonging to a homosocial community of learned citizens, and also their will to contribute with their compositions to an elitist corpus of poetic works. When in 1589 Lodge allowed his second work to come to public light, it was under the threat of unauthorised appropriation, and not because he had had any interest in publishing, as he acknowledges in the dedicatory. What actually confirms that Lodge conceived his epyllion as a wink to the men with whom he had in common the hardships of school learning and of the formative discipline of the Inns of Court is the fact that he addresses his work to 'his especiall good friend Master Raph Crane, and the rest of his most entire wellwillers, the Gentlemen of the Innes of Court and Chauncerie', signing as 'Thomas Lodge of Lincolnes Inne'. Jessica Winston's contention that Lodge would be mainly addressing those members of the Inns with an interest in literary activity rather than in legal studies (the 'revellers') sheds further light on the figure of the narrator of Lodge's epyllion as a poet in search of poetic maturity.[25]

Finding inspiration in Lodge's model, Shakespeare composed *Venus and Adonis*, published in 1593, followed one year later by *The Rape of Lucrece*. Both poems were dedicated to the Earl of Southampton, who by that time was on the threshold of his twenties, had graduated from St John's (Cambridge) in 1589, and had entered Gray's Inn in 1588. He seems to have had an interest in forming a literary circle with the status of the Sidneys'.[26] Although neither Lodge nor Shakespeare was as young as Southampton when they composed their poems – both were in their very early thirties – the principal characters in their epyllia are in the process of transition to rhetorical maturity. It goes without saying that the stories of Ovid's torn bodies and their meta-rhetorical symbolism constitute a rich source of inspiration for depicting these problematic transits, which seem to evoke the authors' educational backgrounds through the convergence of irony and pathos.

While in the case of Venus, Adonis, Lucrece and even Glaucus, the transition towards ripeness is rendered figuratively in the frames of frustrated Petrarchan love (Venus and Glaucus) and of aggression against their innocent bodies (Adonis and Lucrece), Lodge introduces into his poem a peculiar persona for this genre who seems literally to represent the transition from oratorical apprenticeship to expertise.[27] *Scillaes Metamorphosis* is recounted by a young poet-narrator who participates in the events and accompanies Glaucus in his love complaints, experiencing in first person the muteness that passions cause in lovers, and acquiring eloquence after witnessing the violence of Glaucus's vengeance on Scylla. The whole poem contains several biographical details that encourage a reading in line with the pedagogical context mentioned above, starting with the fact that Lodge makes Glaucus characterise the narrator as a learned youth when the former rebukes the latter for not taking advantage of his knowledge to avoid his current sorrow: 'Thy bookes have schoold thee from this fond repent' (*Sci.* A2r, 4.3). It is also significant that Lodge locates the mythological scene in Oxford, where the narrator breaks into action while 'walking alone (all onely full of griefe) / Within a thicket nere to Isis floud' (*Sci.* A2r, 1.1–2). It is a commonplace in the English epyllia to depict young men and women whose passions, whether love or grief, hinder the fluency of their discourse, in a clear allusion to the Ovidian mutilated tongues, but who, after experiencing trauma, achieve command of their rhetorical skills. In the case of Lodge's narrator, the young poet experiences an epiphany after the episode of Scylla's metamorphosis that makes him evolve from the immature poet of the first stanzas to a mature composer whose compositional skills can control his formerly 'wandring lines' (*Sci.* B4r, 73.1): 'What neede I talke the order of my way? / Discourse was steeresman while my barke did saile, / My ship conceit, and fancie was my bay' (*Sci.* C3v, 115.1–3). This contrasts with the numerous allusions to his and Glaucus's inarticulate discourse prior to Scylla's change: 'And leave us two consorted in our gronings / To register with teares our bitter monings' (*Sci.* A3v, 18.5–6). Moreover, Glaucus, whose tongue had been 'charm'd by dread' (*Sci.* A2v, 8.3), recovers in the final stanzas his Orphic power, symbolised in the act of riding one of the dolphins whose control he had previously lamented having lost, and gains the skills of composition. The narrator puts it thus: 'And by the way, such Sonnets song to me / That all the Dolphins neighbouring of his glide / Daunst with delight, his reuerend course beside' (*Sci.* C4v, 129.4–6).

Similarly, Lucrece's innocence is depicted in the scene of the rape in terms of her incompetence to interpret the rhetoric of Tarquin's bodily text:

> But she that neuer cop't with straunger eies,
> Could picke no meaning from their parling lookes,
> Nor read the subtle shining secrecies,
> Writ in the glassie margents of such bookes. (*Luc.* B3v, 99–102)

As regards her production skills, Lucrece herself is aware of the weakness of her words to persuade her aggressor and invokes the eloquence of her body: 'My sighes like whirlewindes labor hence to heaue thee. / If euer man were mou'd with womans mones, / Be moued with my teares, my sighes, my grones' (*Luc.* E3r, 586–8). Similarly, Lodge's narrator trusts his and Glaucus's sighs to do the job that their words are not able to perform:

> The Nimphes to spie the flockes and shepheards needing
> Prepare their teares to heare our tragicke storie:
> Whilst we surprisde with griefe cannot disclose them,
> With sighing wish the world for to suppose them. (*Sci.* A3v, 20.3–6)

The skill of dissimulation, like that of simulation, is key in early modern texts as a tool for rhetorical persuasion and implies awareness of the art of physiognomy and command of body language.[28] Thus Lucrece acknowledges being ignorant of the art as she has never exercised it, in contrast to Tarquin's expertise, and her words reveal Shakespeare's notion of the eloquence of gestures as a skill that needs to be exercised: 'And my true eyes haue neuer practiz'd how / To cloake offences with a cunning brow' (*Luc.* F2r, 748–9).

In what seems to be Lodge's ironic allusion to the Petrarchan love code, Glaucus also recognises that, despite his efforts to implement the commonplaces of the lovers' discourses, his eloquence lacks efficacy:

> But short discourse beseemes my bad successe,
> Eache office of a louer I performed:
> So feruently my passions did her presse,
> So sweete my laies, my speech so well reformed . . . (*Sci.* B3r, 62.1–4)

The characters' anxiety as regards their rhetorical incompetence evokes the poets' concerns about their oratorical skills or about the actual success of their passage to rhetorical proficiency. However, in the three cases – Lodge's narrator, Glaucus and Lucrece – this passage does satisfactorily bestow on the orators the command of either poetic or bodily eloquence. While the former two, as already mentioned, gain the faculty of composition, it is Lucrece's body that, after being deprived of its purity, increases its communicative and persuasive force in a clear echo of Ovidian and other Shakespearean mutilated bodies, as can also be seen in *Titus Andronicus* (1594). But this only happens after the tapestry episode, where intertextuality provides her with the *exempla* of Hecuba and Philomel as models for her own transition towards eloquence. Prior to that moment, in her apostrophe addressed to Night, Time and Opportunity, Lucrece shows her scepticism regarding the efficacy of words to change the course of deeds, ironically associating rhetoric with the uselessness and tediousness of school training:

> Out idle wordes, seruants to shallow fooles,
> Vnprofitable sounds, weak arbitrators,
> Busie your selues in skill-contending schooles,
> Debate where leysure serues with dull debators . . . (*Luc.* H1r, 1016–19)

Nevertheless, she finds in Philomel's rhetorical resourcefulness and in the eloquence of the painted Hecuba's expression of grief the inspiration to endow her body with the force that her words have lost as a consequence of the aggression. Enterline sees in the scene of the tapestry Shakespeare's echo of the humanist practice of action in schools by the imitation of the instructors' gestures and body movements.[29] This passage of the poem contains the awakening of Lucrece's body to poetic composition as she learns how to turn her groans and tears into an articulate lyric account of her disgrace:

> So I at each sad straine, will straine a teare,
> And with deepe grones the Diapason beare:
> For burthen-wise ile hum on Tarquin still,
> While thou on Tereus descants better skill. (*Luc.* H4r, 1131–4)

She uses writing, 'paper, inke, and pen', to summon her husband back home, advancing in the letter just 'her griefe, but not her griefes true quality', because now she trusts the eloquence of her *actio* more than her words (*Luc.* I3v, 1289; I4r, 1313):

> Besides the life and feeling of her passion,
> Shee hoords to spend, when he is by to heare her;
> When sighs, and grones, and tears may grace the fashion
> Of her disgrace . . .

To shun this blot, shee would not blot the letter
With words, till action might becom them better. (*Luc.* I4v, 1316–23)

Shakespeare continues with a meditation on the efficacy of delivery in the terms of classical rhetoric:

To see sad sights, moues more then heare them told,
For then the eye interpretes to the eare
The heavie motion that it doth behold,
When euerie part, a part of woe doth beare.
Tis but a part of sorrow that we heare,
Deep sounds make lesser noise then shallow foords,
And sorrow ebs, being blown with wind of words. (*Luc.* I4v, 1324–30)

The fact that these characters acquire rhetorical proficiency after experiencing violence to their hearts or bodies recalls, as Weaver argues, the hardships faced by students in their years of training in rhetoric at Elizabethan schools. Weaver distinguishes two stages in this process of initiation: the rudiments of eloquence and the first exercises in rhetoric.[30] He contends that the formation in rhetoric was first aimed at endowing boys with multiple resources to develop their verbal abundance, and then at teaching them how to control and discipline that skill. Weaver explains that '"a perfect man", in Erasmus' terms, is a man who has first cultivated and then disciplined verbal abundance'.[31] The characters of the epyllia seem to go through these two stages, displaying first their abundant and then their disciplined rhetoric. Glaucus's ungovernable discourse gains in moderation and poetic propriety, and Lucrece takes control of her *actio* after moments of overflowing passion. Shakespeare describes thus her previous lack of control of her discourse: 'Somtime her griefe is dumbe and hath no words, / Sometime tis mad and too much talke affords' (*Luc.*, H3r, 1105–6).[32] A flagrant example of the incontinence of words is Venus's verbosity when she is possessed by her passion, which becomes less frantic after Adonis's death. Her young beloved complains about it with a hyperbole: 'If loue haue lent you twentie thousand tongues, / And euerie tongue more mouing then your owne' (*Ven.* F1r, 775–6).

One of the most relevant aims of humanist pedagogy when it came to Latin rhetoric was to form students not only in knowledge but also in manners and morality. The early moderns assimilated from Plato and the Stoics the idea that the government of the passions was an essential target in the formation of morally healthy citizens.[33]

Ong explains that boys were required to strengthen their courage (for instance, by enduring flogging) in order to get ready for the transition into adolescence, when they would be required to 'practice what one practices after crossing the threshold of maturity, namely, control'.[34] Courage and control implied a right use of reason, and Roger Ascham argues that the effort of choosing the right words for their exercises on rhetoric is an efficient method for training the students' judgement. He explains that his method's purpose is to 'haue them [i.e., boys] speake so, as it may well appeare, that the braine doth gouerne the tonge, and that reason leadeth forth the taulke'.[35] Similarly, Thomas Wright contends that one of the symptoms of passion is uncontrolled speech or 'Much talke'.[36] Undisciplined eloquence, therefore, is what makes these characters on occasion appear grotesque, like Venus, or emotionally out of control, like Lucrece. Glaucus's fable of the geese which, with the aim of silencing their cackling when flying over the eagles' territory, filled their beaks with pebbles, refers to that relation between reason and the command of eloquence:

> Ah Nimphes (quoth he) had I by reason learnt
> That secret art which birdes haue gaind by sence,
> . . .
> You then should smile and I should tell such stories,
> As woods, and waues should triumph in our glories. (*Sci.* B1r, 39.1–6)

This state of verbal incontinence would correspond to Weaver's 'rudiments of eloquence', the phase in which the characters' verbosity shows an undisciplined use of their rhetorical skills. Only when they have gone through the traumatic experience do they seem to have their rhetoric under control and become ready to initiate the 'first exercises', which, for instance, Lucrece performs in her narration of the rape for Collatine and her father.[37]

The characters' acquired maturity seems to be, in the case of *Scillaes Metamorphosis*, transferred to the author himself, as Lodge, in the last stanza of the poem, shows his intention to advance one degree in the *gradus virgilianus*, giving up the writing of plays, which he now considers to be the delight of rude audiences ('Pennie-knaues'), and taking up more prestigious genres:

> . . . and then by oath he bound me
> To write no more, of that whence shame dooth grow,
> Or tie my pen to Pennie-knaues delight,
> But liue with fame, and so for fame to wright. (*Sci.* E4v, 130.3–6)

As Hulse affirms, these stories of transformation also seem to deal with the 'search for growth of the individual poet' who composed them, and I would add that the self-reflexivity displayed in Elizabethan minor epic poems as regards questions of eloquence denotes the authors' conscious or unconscious tendency to reveal the discrepancies they came across when they strove to put the learned precepts into poetic practice.[38] Although we cannot affirm that there is a purposeful symbolism of grammar school training in the epyllia, we may state that the pedagogical principles that governed the process of acquisition of rhetorical skills are imprinted in the imagery and discourse of the poems and, what is more, also in the formal experimentation carried out through their lines.

The Body: 'When every part a part of woe doth bear'

Prior to attaining a certain control of verbosity and the passions, the characters in the epyllia are depicted in a constant struggle to find the appropriate means of creating a lively image of their emotions that will facilitate their transfer to the auditors. According to classical rhetoric, there are two ways for an orator to imprint an image on the listeners' minds: one, vivid description through words (*enargeia*); the other, the dramatisation of the passions through bodily language (*actio*). In Book V of *Passions of the Minde*, dedicated to the rhetorical potential of the body, Wright highlights that both methods are complementary in the act of persuasion:

> Orators, whose proiect is perwasion, haue two principall parts wherewith they endeuour to compasse their purpose, *Ornate dicere, and concinne agere*, To speake eloquently, and to act aptly: That consisteth specially vpon proper words and sound reasons, this in a certaine moderation of the voice and qualifications of gestures.[39]

Nevertheless, in a previous passage he had stated that 'the presence of any visible obiect, moueth much more vehemently the passion, than the imagination or conceit thereof in the absence', to come later to the following conclusion: 'usually men are more moued with deeds than words, reasonable persuasions resemble words, affectual passions are compared to deeds'.[40] Wright's contention derives from Cicero's and Quintilian's idea that the orator actually needed to feel the emotions he intended to transfer. The profusion of allusions to bodily parts, gestures and physiological reactions such as tears or blushing to the detriment of words in the narration of the characters' emotional crises seems to imply the authors' questioning of the infallibility of words and verbal eloquence in communicating emotions that overcome reason and logic. As seen above, Lucrece trusts more in the persuasive effect of enactment than in speech and reasonable arguments. And Venus perceives Adonis's rejection when his 'rubi-colourd portal opend', before he has even started to articulate any words of refusal: 'His meaning strucke her ere his words begun' (*Ven.* D2v, 451, 462). This can also be interpreted in relation to the prominence that humanists in general, and Ciceronians in particular, gave to style and poetic form as a means of materialising emotions through aural and visual effects. As George Puttenham states, style is 'the image of man (*mentis character*)'.[41] In this regard, Miller has highlighted that 'tropes and figures of rhetoric are themselves fashioned in imitation of the way men naturally give voice to feelings'.[42]

It might seem ironic that two of the most defining traits of this poetic genre, the emphasis given to the eloquence of bodies and the sophistication of stylistic features, function as textual strategies for an *unwritten* theoretical formulation of their authors' critical positions regarding received poetics.[43] In this and the following section, I intend to disentangle the ways in which the discourse of emotions conveys the humanist poets' anxiety regarding the perfect cooperation of image and speech, and of form and words, which is a fundamental premise in Elizabethan poetics. I undertake in this section an analysis of the rhetoric of the body in the light of the two main cultural factors that may have conditioned its articulation: the authors' training in rhetorical delivery and their assimilation of humoral theories.

Echoing Ovidian mutilated tongues and muted voices, the epyllia depict characters whose words are unable to attain *enargeia* or construct lively images of their passions in the minds of the auditors, whether this be due to the annihilation of their speaking faculties by a violent act, or because of their vulnerability to overwhelming passions, which produces muteness as much as uncontrolled verbosity. In Lucrece's case, it is Tarquin who 'with her own white fleece her voice controld' (*Luc.* F1r, 678). Likewise, the violence of Venus's desire stops Adonis's speech with murderous kisses: 'What followes more, she murthers with a kisse' (*Ven.* B2r, 54). But a frequent cause for the failure of speech in the epyllia is the characters' immaturity and lack of command over their passions. For instance, Venus's 'impatience chokes her pleading tongue', and her pain stops her speech: 'her wordes are done, her woes the more increasing' (*Ven.* C1v, 217; C2r, 254); while Glaucus's tongue 'was charm'd by dread' or, on another occasion, by Ate, the goddess of derangement: 'Whilest thus he spake, fierce Ate charmde his tongue' (*Sci.* A2v, 8.3; B3r, 70.1). In both examples, the verb 'charm' contributes to connecting the Galenic idea that passion hinders speech with the supernatural intervention of gods and goddesses in the silencing of voices in Ovidian tales.

It goes without saying that the fact that stylistic sophistication is a defining trait in the epyllia facilitates the reduction of verbal argumentation and the dominance of descriptions in minute detail. Wright's 'proper words and sound reasons', which are central to the Petrarchan conceit and economy of persuasion, are replaced by gestural argumentation.[44] When words are stuck, corporeal language acts in their stead, performing through material images what figurative images should have represented (in the same manner that figures of speech predominate over figures of thought and argumentation). In episodes dealing with overwhelming emotions, the characters entrust the narration of their disgrace to the eloquence of the outward reactions of their bodies. Thus, Glaucus hopes that his and the poet's sighs can tell their 'tragicke storie' to the nymphs: 'Whilst we surprisde with griefe cannot disclose them, / With sighing wish the world for to suppose them'. Allusions to the semantic potential of bodily reactions are also constant in Lodge's poem: 'his prettie teares betokening his annoy' (*Sci.* A3v, 20.4–6). Moreover, gesticulation and the output of internal physiological and mental processes are usually treated as agents in the act of communication, appearing as speaking subjects through personification: Lucrece's 'pittie-pleading eyes' (*Luc.* E2v, 561); and, similarly, they are also endowed with the capacity to feel the emotion they denote: 'enuious blushes' and 'enuious teares' (*Sci.* A3r, 15.1; C2r, 98.2). As Hillman and Mazzio explain,

> the part [of the body], in the 'Historicall' and 'Scientificall' texts of the period, is a subject, both in the sense that it is increasingly marked and elaborated upon in a range of visual and textual spaces, and in the sense that it is frequently imagined to take on attributes of agency and subjectivity.[45]

These meticulous descriptions of bodily movements and reactions in the epyllia are inspired by the performances of passion in Elizabethan drama as, for example, the dumb-shows, which, as John Roe suggests, were intended 'to give formal expression to the emotions'.[46] For instance, the narrator refers to Venus and Adonis's enactment of the Petrarchan dispute of courtship and denial as a 'warre of looks' and as 'this dumbe play': 'Her eyes petitioners to his eyes suing, / His eyes saw her eyes, as they had not seen them, / Her eyes wooed still, his eyes disdaind the wooing' (*Ven.* C4v, 356–8). The principal narrative technique employed in the epyllia for the descriptions of intense moods is their dramatisation through gestures and spasms of the body, while the cognitive processes that originate those reactions are commonly taken for granted. There is a penchant in these poems for creating theatrical representations of the characters' mental states through allusions to the physical reactions they provoke. As hinted above, this practice is related to the authors' experience as playwrights, while at the same time both have rhetorical training as their foundation. Shakespeare refers to the communicative potential of facial expression as a skill that needs to be taught in what seems an allusion to this Elizabethan school practice: 'Thy eyes shrowd tutor, that hard heart of thine, / Hath taught them scornfull tricks, and such disdaine' (*Ven.* D3v, 500–1). This is likewise a telling example of the cooperation of the rhetorical and the humoral discourses in the understanding of the passions during this period. The heart is said by Wright to be the place where passions arise; in reaction to those passions, the humours run from other parts of the body towards the heart in order to protect the principal organ from the alterations that it might suffer.[47] Therefore, as Shakespeare suggests, outward reactions to passions also have their root in the heart. By alluding to the heart both as physiological cause of the eyes' expression and as their 'tutor' in eloquence, Shakespeare reveals how humoralism and rhetorical *actio* converge in the Elizabethan poetic manifestations of emotions.

In the absence of words (or out of the inefficacy of uncontrolled speech), the epyllia exploit bodily language to the extent that descriptions of the effects of the passions become exaggerated, reiterative and even grotesque. A large proportion of stanzas contain allusions to parts of the body and to the external manifestations of inward processes, such as tears or sighs. William Keach refers ironically to the abundance of tears in *Scillaes Metamorphosis* when affirming that the whole poem is a flood, and he contends that this and other traits make of the poem a 'humorously entertaining vignette'.[48] On occasion, prosody contributes to make the dramatic overreactions of the characters appear more vehement. When Lodge's narrator makes his entrance, this is achieved through alliteration: 'Weeping my wants, and wailing scant reliefe, / Wringing mine armes (as one with sorrowe wood)' (*Sci.* A2r, 1.3–4). The fact that the young poet needs to clarify in a parenthesis that the bodily reactions depicted correspond to those conventionally expected from a sorrowful person is rendered almost redundant and highlights the rhetorical and theatrical intention that corporeal manifestations have in the poem. The narrator presents himself as an imitator of the natural economy of bodily language, just as Philip Sidney proclaims that a good orator such as Cicero would: 'he would have his words (as it were) double out of his mouth, and so do that artificially which we see men in choler do naturally'.[49] A few stanzas later, Glaucus's compulsive gestures also seem redundant and grotesque, particularly if we take into account that his physical appearance, according to mythology, would have been that of a half man with a fish tail and green hair, as he had been turned from a fisherman into a sea god: 'Here gan he pause and shake his heavie head, / And fould his armes, and then unfould them straight' (*Sci.* A2v, 8.1–2). As regards Venus, Shakespeare resorts to descriptions of her extravagant bodily postures to dramatise her desperate attempts to force Adonis to accede to her will and to denote the irrational nature of her passion: 'Ouer one arme the lusty coursers raine, / Vnder her other was the tender boy' (*Ven.* B1v, 31–2). And also to impulsive performances of conventional signs of passion: 'Sometime she shakes her head, and then his hand, / Now gazeth she on him, now on the ground' (*Ven.* C1v, 223–4).

In his approach to the study of Latin as a puberty rite, Walter Ong contends that the ultimate goal of the methods used in the formation of boys in classical rhetoric, as for instance flogging those students who failed in their exercises of rhetorical delivery, was to endow them with the courage and judgement that characterised standards of manliness in the period.[50] When Lodge and Shakespeare question conventional expressions of gender, they also take advantage of the characters' clumsiness regarding bodily communication. Adonis's tenderness, for instance, is denoted by his womanlike reactions: 'the maiden burning of his cheekes' (*Ven.* B2r, 50), and by his disadvantage in the skirmishes with Venus, as she is described lying over him or forcing him to the ground. Glaucus also appears reposing his head on the narrator's 'faintfull knee' (*Sci.* A2r, 3.3).

Besides the conventional gestures in the enactment of emotions, when the passions described in the epyllia are extremely visceral, allusions to bodily language focus to a greater extent on the involuntary output of the humours' flow in the interior of the body, such as the excretion of fluids and variations in the temperature and colour of the skin. On these occasions, the poets reveal how their interpretations of the body's responses to intense emotions are biased by the humoral assumptions of the Galenic medical treatises of the period. The more fleshly the passions described, the more focused on the corporeal fluids are the depictions of the bodily reactions, as when we are informed about Venus's sweat ('by this the loue-sicke Queene began to sweate'), a reaction that will later be directly related to her sexual appetite: 'sweating Lust' (*Ven.* B4v, 175; F1v, 794). Such is Venus's lust that she seems to have a penchant for cannibalism, awakened not by Adonis's flesh, but by his fluids and exhalations: 'Panting he lies, and breatheth in her face; / She feedeth on the steame, as on a prey' (*Ven.* B2r, 62–3). Variations in skin colour, which were commonly ascribed to the oscillation of humours, are also frequently treated as eloquent signals of the emotions that cause them, as in 'anger ashie pale', or where the emotion is directly assigned a colour as a natural quality: 'crimson shame' (*Ven.* B2v, 76).

In Wright's description of 'the manner how passions are moued', he states that they appear when the senses or the memory present the image of an object to our imagination.[51] Through mysterious channels that image reaches the heart, where desire for or rejection of that object arise; in accomplishing this task, the heart demands that the bodily humours abandon the rest of the organs and come to its assistance, thus provoking outward reactions such as blushing, paleness and trembling of the legs, among other symptoms that are commonly mentioned in poetic descriptions of the passions. As seen in Wright, humoralism implied that the immaterial and material selves were very narrowly connected. Conscious of these internal responses to the passions, and intending to provide a more vivid image of them, the authors of the epyllia not only observe their external manifestations but also peep into the body through the boundaries of the flesh. An example of this is Lodge's explanation of the languidness of Glaucus's 'feeble head and arme': 'Herewith his faltring tongue by sighs oppressed / Forsooke his office, and his bloud resorted / To feede the hearte that wholly was distressed' (*Sci.* A4v, 33.1–3, 5). Shakespeare also describes the workings of the passions, from the perception of the stimulus by the senses until the moment when the members of the body become affected, in the passage where Venus, after hearing the boar's groans, is overwhelmed by fear:

> This dismall crie rings sadly in her eare,
> Through which it enters to surprise the hart,
> Who ouercome by doubt, and bloudlesse feare,
> With cold-pale weaknesse, nums ech feeling part . . . (*Ven.* F4v, 889–92)

Words: *mentis character*

The Elizabethan poets' penchant for adapting Ovid's tropes of the voice to their own rhetorical and poetic concerns accords with the fact that in their time, language was primarily conceived in oral terms; this 'primacy of speech' led the early modern writers to find in Ovidian mutilated tongues and muted voices a potent source of images for the hardships that the search for eloquence posed for them.[52] Moreover, the fact that the 'metamorphic images' represented Ovid's reflections on language by referring to bodies as both vehicles and tenors provided an ideal frame for the humanist poets, who conceived of language in close connection with the body. In a passage dedicated to style in *Timber: or Discoveries* (1641), Ben Jonson draws a parallelism between the physical traits of the body on the one hand, and style on the other: 'No glass renders a man's form, or likeness, so true as his speech. Nay, it is likened to a man: and as we consider feature, and composition in a man; so words in language: in the greatness, aptness, sound, structure, and harmony of it.'[53]

When trying to find a cultural connection between such an ornamented style and the profusion of allusions to corporeal eloquence in the epyllion, it is essential to bear in mind this early modern notion of the 'physicality of the poem'.[54] In his discussion of the Renaissance uses of the terms 'expression' and 'articulation', Neil Rhodes argues that both had physiological connotations, as the former refers to 'the livingness of speech', while the latter alludes to the bodily parts that make vocalisation possible. And when it comes to rhetorical action, the distinction between both 'collapses', because 'here the articulated body is itself a voice, its different parts working in concert to express inward thoughts and feeling'.[55] Therefore, the correspondence between language and body would not only be understood in terms of speech, but also as a reflection of the form of the written text, as Jonson's analogy of the body and style shows. When describing the variations of style, he mentions *statura*, alluding to the gravity and sound of words, *figura*, referring to the shape of sentences, and *cutis*, or 'the skin, and coat, which rests in the well-joining, cementing, and coagmentation of words'.[56] As Sumillera pinpoints in this volume, Jonson is here paraphrasing Juan Luis Vives's *De ratione dicendi* (1533), where he complains about the vagueness of the corporeal language traditionally used to describe the variety of styles, and provides a series of concrete correspondences between physical qualities and traits of style.[57] It is evident that the epyllia not only capture the poets' anxieties regarding the efficacy of rhetoric, but also reflect the pressure of the humanist conception of style as a distinctive feature of true poetry. The analogy of the body and style underlies a critical discourse that stems from the cooperation in these poems of textual strategies, such as their prosodic elaboration and the numerous allusions to bodily language, which correspond respectively to the Elizabethan anxiety about the sophistication of style and the efficacy of rhetorical delivery.

The outward expression of the passions through physiognomy, gestures and parts of the body in the epyllia is frequently sustained by images that have written discourse as their vehicle. The most pervasive of these is the Ovidian image of the tongue, which appears at the same time as a metonym for language and a synecdoche for the body, and is revealed as the principal example of the idea that words also belong to the corporeal. Carla Mazzio explains that 'the very invocation of the word [i.e., tongue] encodes a relation between word and flesh, tenor and vehicle, matter and meaning'.[58] Regarding the expression of emotions, the association of word and flesh is, by extension, articulated through other parts of the body within the frame of the *liber corporis* motif. Besides the tongue, the face is the most pervasive element in the construction of images of the corporeal essence of written language, due in part to the popularity that the art of physiognomy had gained through treatises such as Thomas Hill's *The Contemplation of Mankinde* (1571). In her study of the impact of this pseudo-science on Elizabethan culture, Sybille Baumbach quotes Sir Thomas Browne's reference to the equation face/words as regards eloquence:

> there are mystically in our faces, certain Characters which carry in them the motto of our Souls, in which he that cannot read ABC may read our natures . . . The Finger of God hath left an Inscription upon all His works, not graphical, composed of Letters, but of several forms, constitutions, parts, and operations, which, aptly joined together, do make one word that doth express their nature.[59]

Shakespeare establishes this relation between facial gestures and the disposition of words in a text in almost identical terms, as can be seen in the passage where Lucrece laments that the terrible deed would remain forever recorded on her brows and her eyes:

> The light will shew, characterd in my brow,
> The storie of sweete chastities decay,
> . . .
> Yea the illiterate, that know not how
> To cipher what is writ in learned bookes,
> Will cote my lothsome trespasse in my lookes. (*Luc.* F4r, 807–12)

The narrator in *Scillaes Metamorphosis* also perceives how Glaucus's mind is embodied on his brow: 'And whilst the God upon my bosome slept, / Behelde the scarres of his afflicted minde, / Imprinted in his yvorie brow by care' (*Sci.* B4r, 70.3–5).

But as mentioned above, the images that associate the material essence of the body with the indelible nature of words are also concerned with other elements such as corporeal fluids, tears being the most abundant. I have previously stressed that, while sighs denote grief, tears replace words: 'To register with teares our bitter monings' or 'Whilst I with teares my passion was a telling' (*Sci.* A3v, 18.6; B2v, 56.6). Blood is also endowed with the property of permanence attributed to written language in the passage in which Lucrece determines that her suicide will become the testimony of Tarquin's crime:

> My stained bloud to Tarquin ile bequeath,
> Which by him tainted, shall for him be spent,
> And as his due writ in my testament.
> . . .
> How Tarquin must be us'd, read it in me. (*Luc.* I1r–I1v, 1181–3, 1195)

As mentioned above, the relation of the body to words not only alludes to the common property of materialising emotions, but also to their potential to present an image of those emotions that fulfils the humanist penchant for aestheticism. Thomas Wilson in *The Art of Rhetoric* (1560) highlighted that eloquence 'beautifieth the tongue with great change of colors and variety of figures'.[60] It is remarkable that, on occasion, the bodily reactions of the characters in the epyllia are referred to as fulfilling the aesthetic function of style, as can be inferred from these lines from *The Rape of Lucrece*: 'Her modest eloquence with sighes is mixed, / Which to her Oratorie addes more grace' (*Luc.* E2v, 563–4). By using verbs that denote blending, such as 'mix' and 'mingle', Shakespeare seems to insist on the role of bodily expression in reinforcing speech: 'Mingling my talk with tears' (*Luc.* F4r, 797). If bodily gestures and reactions stand for tropes and figures of speech, we may therefore conclude that the sometimes hyperbolical and grotesque physical expressions in the epyllia could be perceived as parodic winks not only to the early modern obsession with rhetorical delivery, but also with elaborated style. The functions of gestures and figures of speech – that is, to embody the passions and to embellish discourse – are all one. As when in the initial lines of *Scillaes Metamorphosis* alliteration of the sound 'w' reinforces the successive affected gestures of the poet-narrator, the epyllion as a genre literalises this cooperation.

Notes

1. Enterline, *Rhetoric of the Body*, 3.
2. Ibid., 6.
3. For Hulse, metamorphosis is not only related to the subject matter of the minor epic poem, but also to 'its narrative principles, its mode of symbolism, its ability to combine and remake other genres, and its power to transform the poet'. Hulse argues that 'it is a system where recurring instances of flux build toward a view of a world in process, a view that always threatens to break down into the chaos of its part' (*Metamorphic Verse*, 4).
4. Enterline, *Rhetoric of the Body*, 4.
5. See Luis-Martínez, 'Introduction', this volume, 17.
6. Enterline, *Shakespeare's Schoolroom*; Weaver, *Untutored Lines*, 3. For approaches to the study of Latin rhetoric in Elizabethan schools in the light of political and social goals, see Ong, 'Latin Language Study'; and Halpern, *Poetics of Primitive Accumulation*, 19–60.
7. Quintilian, *Institutio oratoria*, trans. Butler, VI.2.32, 2:435.
8. Enterline, *Rhetoric of the Body*, 49.
9. In her rhetorical analysis of the emotions in the Renaissance, Miller affirms that 'tropes and figures serve to express passions' ('The Passions Signified', 412).
10. Enterline, *Rhetoric of the Body*, 63.
11. See Schoenfeldt, *Bodies and Selves*.
12. Cummings and Sierhuis, *Passions and Subjectivity*, 5; Baumbach, *Shakespeare and the Art of Physiognomy*, 13.
13. See Strier, *Unrepentant Renaissance*, 6–7.
14. Cummings and Sierhuis, *Passions and Subjectivity*, 6–7.
15. Hulse, *Metamorphic Verse*, 7.
16. Ibid.
17. See Luis-Martínez, 'Introduction', this volume, 13.
18. Wright, *Passions of the Minde*, II.3, 'How Passions alter the body', 59–68.
19. Ascham, *Scholemaster*, sig. D2v.
20. Ibid., sig. D4r.
21. Ibid., sig. E1r.
22. For detailed descriptions of the pedagogical system, see Ong, 'Latin Language Study'; and Enterline, *Shakespeare's Schoolroom*.
23. Halpern, *Poetics of Primitive Accumulation*, 26, 36. See also Ong, 'Latin Language Study'.

24. In *Untutored Lines*, Weaver provides an illustrative account of how these poems recreate some of the rhetorical exercises performed in Elizabethan schoolrooms.
25. Winston, 'From Discontent to Disdain', 147. For a similar argument on Lodge's *Phillis*, see Zunino-Garrido, 'Thomas Lodge's "Supple Muse"', this volume.
26. Akrigg, *Shakespeare and the Earl of Southampton*, 184–5; see also the 'Introduction' in Shakespeare, *Poems*, ed. Roe, 13.
27. In line with my treatment of Lodge's and Shakespeare's epyllia as cultural products of their time, I am citing from the original editions of *Scillaes Metamorphosis* (1589), *Venus and Adonis* (1593) and *The Rape of Lucrece* (1594). Parenthetical citations from these editions in the text are by abbreviation (*Sci.*, *Ven.* and *Luc.* respectively) and signature. Additionally, stanza and/or line numbers from modern-spelling editions are also provided. For Lodge, readers are referred to *Sixteenth-Century Poetry*, ed. Braden, 408–29. For Shakespeare's *Ven.* and *Luc.*, to *Poems*, ed. Roe, 3–20 and 21–40 respectively.
28. For a detailed account of the influence of the art of physiognomy on Elizabethan emotions, see Baumbach, *Shakespeare and the Art of Physiognomy*.
29. Enterline, *Shakespeare's Schoolroom*, 125–6.
30. See Weaver, *Untutored Lines*, 1–13. In Weaver's opinion, '[i]f the purpose of the rudiments is to give free rein to eloquence, the purpose of the first exercises is to restrain eloquence and direct it into certain channels of verbal and social competency' (9).
31. Ibid., 7.
32. Weaver contends that Lucrece performs the first exercises of rhetoric in the second half of the poem. It is interesting to note that he specifies that, despite the fact that Lucrece is neither a male adolescent nor 'an allegory of the schoolboy', the poem contains echoes of the social process of the *progymnasmata*. After her invective to Night, Opportunity and Change, she prepares herself to tell the incident to her husband and father, a speech that reproduces the exercises of *narratio* and *confirmatio* (*Untutored Lines*, 123–47).
33. Cummings and Sierhuis, *Passions and Subjectivity*, 3.
34. Ong, 'Latin Language Study', 117. Ong explains that one of the reasons for flogging in schools was 'the courage which [the master] hopes to develop in his pupils'.
35. Ascham, *The Scholemaster*, sig. C3r.
36. Wright, *Passions of the Minde*, 107–8.
37. See note 30 above.
38. Hulse, *Metamorphic Verse*, 4.
39. Wright, *Passions of the Minde*, 172.
40. Ibid., 158, 175.
41. Puttenham, *Art of English Poesy*, ed. Whigham and Rebhorn, 233.

42. Miller, 'The Passions Signified', 412.
43. Zunino-Garrido observes a similar pattern in the inherent poetics of Lodge's *Phillis*, where 'Lodge tacitly interrogates the meaning of creativity in a work where, ironically enough, translation and imitation are primary *raisons d'être*'. See 'Thomas Lodge's "Supple Muse"', this volume, 217.
44. Wright, *Passions of the Minde*, 172.
45. Hillman and Mazzio, 'Introduction: Individual Parts', xii.
46. Roe, note to lines 359–60 of *Venus and Adonis*, in Shakespeare, *Poems*, 98.
47. Wright, *Passions of the Minde*, I.7, 'The seate, place, and subiect of the Passions of the Minde', 26–30.
48. Keach, *Elizabethan Erotic Narratives*, 45, 376.
49. Sidney, *Defence*, in *Miscellaneous Prose*, ed. Duncan-Jones and van Dorsten, 117–18. As Miller notes, '[a] genuine passion is formed by imitation of the signs of another's passion; and it is expressed by imitation as well' ('The Passions Signified', 417).
50. Ong, 'Latin Language Study', 114–17.
51. Wright, *Passions of the Minde*, 45.
52. Rhodes, *Shakespeare and the Origins of English*, 22.
53. Jonson, *Discoveries*, ed. Hutson, in *Cambridge Edition Online*, lines 1441–3. See Sumillera, 'Bloody Poetics', this volume, for a nuanced account of discussions of style in terms of bodily analogies in the early modern period.
54. Sumillera, 'Bloody Poetics', this volume, 103.
55. Rhodes, *Shakespeare and the Origins of English*, 8, 17–18, 28.
56. Jonson, *Discoveries*, in *Cambridge Edition Online*, lines 1464–5.
57. Sumillera, 'Bloody Poetics', this volume, 105.
58. Mazzio, 'Sins of the Tongue', 93.
59. Browne, *Religio Medici*, 98, quoted in Baumbach, *Shakespeare and the Art of Physiognomy*, 24.
60. Wilson, *Art of Rhetoric*, 3.188.

Part III

Poesis: Art's Prisoners

Chapter 7

Philip Sidney's Sublime Self-authorship: Authenticity, Ecstasy and Energy in *The Defence of Poesy* and *Astrophil and Stella*

Jonathan P. A. Sell

Sir Philip Sidney's sad demise in 1586 was followed by one of England's first celebrity burials. Already to many the ornament of the English aristocracy, his premature death only fanned the flames of his popularity and meant that immortality of some sort was already on the cards. Unlike pop stars and Romantic poets cut off in their prime, Sidney was rewarded with three afterlives, two in his own name – the bloodied champion of the hawkish anti-Spanish Protestants and the model of Elizabethan chivalry and courtesy[1] – and a third as his literary self-image, Astrophil. The reverential homage rendered to Sidney *sub specie* fictional alter ego was as unprecedented as it was unusual, since the self-image of the sonnet sequence was quite at odds with the virtuous and chivalric Protestant – Walter Raleigh's 'A spotlesse friend, a matchles man, whose vertue euer shinde'[2] – who died as the hero of Zutphen. The emulable Sidney whom Raleigh apotheosised 'To sit in skies, and sort with powres diuine'[3] is a far cry from the anxious, scurrilous, querulous Astrophil of the sonnets.

Unsurprisingly, *Astrophil and Stella* was ignored in the hagiographic memorial literature. Neither Fulke Greville's *A Dedication to Sir Philip Sidney*, William Alexander's *Anacrisis* nor Thomas Moffet's *Nobilis, or a View of a Life and Death of a Sidney*, written to reform Sidney's wayward nephew, William Herbert,[4] mention it, while it only serves to illustrate a minor metrical point in William Scott's *A Model of Poesy* (1599), albeit Scott was 'one of Sidney's best-attuned and most sympathetic readers'.[5] However, the largely unedifying and non-existent Astrophil was arguably more keenly emulated by Sidney's contemporaries than the Protestant martyr or flower of chivalry. Indeed, in the short term, Astrophil/Sidney provided a role model for subsequent English lyric poets, an authoritative exemplar of the productive ambivalence of the poet/poetic persona conflation, even if what those poets/poetic personae wrote, said or thought was often distinctly un-Sidneian;[6] and of course, that teasing, liberating ambivalence was in frank defiance of the official or officialistic doctrines of pedagogical Protestant poetics that Astrophil's creator had, however seriously, purveyed. When all is said and done, there is much that is *dulce*, but little *utile*, in *Astrophil and Stella*.

The poetic achievement of Sidney is, then, its contribution to reconceptualising the notion of poetic authorship. This chapter contributes to a new poetics of Elizabethan poetry by proposing a Sidneian model of authorship that helps to solve two of the enigmas of *Astrophil and Stella*. The first enigma, of authenticity, has to do with the vexed issue of the sequence's relationship to the biography of the historical personage we know as Sir Philip Sidney. The second enigma, of exemplarity, has to do with the sequence's apparently vexed relationship to Sidney's own poetics. Both these enigmas hinge on the image Sidney presents of himself under the name of Astrophil. At first sight, Sidney's *Astrophil and Stella* unwrites the written art – or a large portion of it – that Sidney himself compiled in *The Defence of Poesy*. It is an extreme case of poetic praxis contradicting poetic theory, with the added spice that the practitioner and the theorist were one and the same person. Yet I shall suggest that, in its model of the sublime poet, the written art of Sidney's theory is more consistent with his practice than is often thought, while the unwritten art that transpires from that practice partially completes the theoretical model. If Astrophil is viewed as a sublimation or sublime reconstitution of Sidney rather than an imitation of him, both enigmas might be solved. This chapter is, then, a further contribution to the spate of recent publications that assert the existence and importance of an early modern discourse of the sublime, since it attributes to Sidney a 'Longinian' model of ecstatic and energetic self-authorship, which in turn derives from a theory of poetry as something aboriginal, organic and self-regulating.[7] This is by no means to claim that the *Defence* or *Astrophil and Stella* or both are exclusively Longinian, much as it would be futile to argue for an entirely Aristotelian, Platonic or Horatian Sidney, a point to which I shall return in my conclusion. It is, however, to throw into relief a vital strand of Sidney's poetic theory and practice which has been relatively neglected.

There is now no need to apologise for using the term 'sublime' in connection with early modern English literature. It is clear that well before Nicolas Boileau Despréaux's translation of Περὶ ὕψους (*Peri hupsous*) in 1674 there was a thriving European tradition of sublime poetic discourse and practice. Three editions of the Greek text were published in 1554, 1555 and 1569–70, the first by Francesco Robortello, while Latin translations followed in 1566, 1572 and 1612 (two others are lost), and an Italian one in 1575.[8] Longinus was the principal force behind Francesco Patrizi's *Poetica* (1586), Lorenzo Giacomini's *Discorso del furor poetico* (1587) and Torquato Tasso's *Discorsi del poema eroico* (1587, pub. 1594).[9] In France, Marc-Antoine Muret, who had planned to produce an edition of *Peri hupsous*,[10] disseminated Longinian ideas in his own works, as did his students and friends, among them the poet Pierre Ronsard, the playwright Étienne Jodelle, the essayist Michel de Montaigne and the historiographer Joseph Scaliger.[11] The popularity in France and elsewhere of Torquato Tasso's *Gerusalemme liberata* (1575) and his *Discorsi* meant that Longinian ideas were imbibed across Europe by poets, playwrights and painters.[12]

Not only has the sixteenth- and early seventeenth-century reception of the Longinian treatise been charted more accurately, but the centrality – indeed the necessity – of Longinus to discourses about the sublime has been roundly challenged by his greatest contemporary reader, James I. Porter: with or without *Peri hupsous*, '[t]he sublime was consistently available and exploited . . . from antiquity to the present', with Renaissance and early modern periods lying somewhere between the two, closer in time to us but peopled with much 'closer readers of the ancients than modern students of the sublime have shown themselves to be'.[13] Plato and the Neoplatonists were one obvious alternative source of an aesthetic-philosophical model of sublimity which was eagerly tapped by Renaissance theorists such as Julius Caesar Scaliger or Cristoforo Landino, both of whom Sidney cites. Another was Aristotle, whose *Rhetoric*, long before Longinus, had found room for 'Extreme pathos, *enthousiasmos* [possession] *ekstasis* . . . divine inspiration, complete subjugation of the hearer – all the ingredients of a Longinian experience'.[14] For its part, Christianity had its own sublimity which Augustine did much to define.[15] As for practical manifestations of sublimity in poetry, there was a continuous line linking Homer with Dante, two of Sidney's favourite authors, and embracing the Greek tragedians, Virgil, Lucretius and Ovid, the medieval mystics and a whole host of others.[16]

Nonetheless, there is a distinctly Longinian slant to some of Sidney's less orthodox poetics. This is not to say that Sidney had read *Peri hupsous*, and there was more than a whiff of Longinus in Scaliger's *Poetices libri septem* (1561), which Sidney knew. There was even an exiguous but not negligible tradition of English comment and translation of Longinus before Gerald Langbaine's parallel Greek–Latin edition (1636) or John Hall's English translation (1652). Evidence has come to light of two copies of Longinus in a Cambridge bookshop in 1578.[17] John Rainolds, who would become 'a close acquaintance of Sidney',[18] was lecturing on Longinus at Oxford in 1574–75.[19] George Chapman's poetry of the 1590s was markedly Longinian before his discussion of Longinus in the dedicatory epistle (1614) to *The Whole Works of Homer*, a point which Luis-Martínez's chapter in this volume confirms.[20] In view of the pre-existing classical, Christian and medieval traditions and the contemporary continental Longinus fad, it would be odd if Sidney had remained aloof to the allure of a long-standing sublime poetics that was enjoying a new lease of life. Assertions to the effect that 'Sidney, of course, did not know Longinus, but intuitively grasped his principles'[21] are no longer tenable. Patrick Cheney has ably demonstrated the pertinence of the sublime, particularly the Longinian sublime, to late Elizabethan and Jacobean literature in studies of Edmund Spenser, Christopher Marlowe, Willliam Shakespeare and Ben Jonson.[22] Yet Cheney has no room for Sidney in his canon of sublime authors and is dismissive of his sublimity, detecting only a 'potential Longinian trace' in Astrophil's use of the otherwise alchemical verb 'sublime' (*AS* 77.8);[23] Sidney, we are told, 'never engages fully in a sublime poetics of rapture', by which Cheney means that Sidney, like Skelton and Wyatt before him, never – or only very rarely – '*represent*[s] rapture'.[24]

We shall return to rapture later. What requires comment here is Cheney's insistence that the sublime must be represented and that therefore poetic sublimity must imitate a phenomenally sublime object or experience. It is this misprision which limits his understanding of sublimity and his reading of early modern writers. According to Cheney, the members of his quartet write themselves sublime either by transcribing sublime matter or by investing themselves in the topical accoutrements of sublime authorship: thus, to write of witches or goddesses or to write of oneself as divinely inspired is to be sublime. But this is to confuse the literary simulacrum with the phenomenon that that simulacrum purports to represent: a fridge-magnet Matterhorn is not sublime, even if it is a representation of a sublime thing, nor are all tropes of flight or topical thunderstorms necessarily sublime. Sublimity can, but need not, involve representations: the Matterhorn itself represents nothing but is still sublime; so too, Mozart's Clarinet Concerto or Strauss's Four Last Songs, the sublimity of which may derive in part from the very unfathomability of what, if anything, they represent or even evoke. If for the sublime to be generated there must be a mimetic relationship between the sublime phenomenon and the simulacrum that represents it, one will indeed be hard put to extrapolate backwards from peevish, anxious, neurotic Astrophil to the phenomenon known to history as Sir Philip Sidney.

Three Types of Authenticity

Astrophil is misconstrued if read mimetically, as if the poetic self-image necessarily bore some autobiographical relation to the historical referent of Philip Sidney. Of course, as the clues Sidney teasingly drops suggest, some such relation exists, although its exact nature continues to baffle critics. The very name Astrophil has been as a red rag to a bull for those readers who in some way or another engage with 'Sidney's self-inquisition, his scrutiny of his own poetic veracity'[25] or with the extent to which what he writes matches what he is. The nub of that engagement is authenticity, a notion which attracts some and repels others. The more candid read *Astrophil and Stella* as charting the ups and downs of the true romance between Sidney and Penelope Devereux; the more sophisticated as the pursuit of a courtly career by other means or the covert release of pent-up frustrations regarding thwarted ambitions. Some will take Astrophil's psychological disarray, instability or fragmentation as mirroring Sidney's own fluctuating mental states or subjection to competing Petrarchan and Protestant discourses on love, competing public and private duties, imperatives and protocols, and so on. Non-foundationalists or postmodernists will celebrate, liberal humanists lament, the dispersal of the self into a void at the heart of subjectivity. And yet others will diagnose in the rift between 'language . . . [and] internal cognitive and affective emotional states' Sidney's self-alienation and the inauthenticity that inevitably obtains in so far as the 'produced thing' is not the 'producer's own'.[26] All take Sidney as the poet of his own psyche and notice a mimetic disjunction or shortfall between self-image and historical person, between the aesthetic object produced and the producer poet. In that sense, all are hung up on a loosely

Romantic conception of authenticity despite the powerful reservations Rosemond Tuve registered over seventy years ago.[27] What is more, all disregard Sidney's animadversion in the *Defence* against the pettifogging particularisation of history, and Astrophil's warning against applying 'allegorie's curious frame' (*AS* 28.1) to his poems.[28]

But if the mimetic relationship between producer and produced thing, between poet and poetic persona, between historical phenomenon and aesthetic simulacrum is replaced with another of identity, then the two enigmas with which we commenced can both be resolved. In his essay *Sincerity and Authenticity* (1974), Lionel Trilling picks out some of the strands in the history of the anxious discourse of moral authenticity or being true to oneself. Hegel's *Phenomenology of Spirit* (1807) looms large,[29] and the Hegelian model of self-alienation consisting in the 'base' or 'disintegrated soul's' knowing detachment from the 'honest' or 'noble soul' is of ready application to the institutionalised early modern practice of courtly dissimulation and social performance familiar to us from George Puttenham and Thomas Hobbes.[30] Sidney did not wholly identify with court culture, politics and religion. His chequered, generally disappointing career and the documentary record testify to the fact that he was no Hegelian 'obedient servant' and was averse to the Hegelian heroism of flattery. He would not have graduated with honours from Puttenham's finishing school for dissembling gentlemen, while some of his sonnets display a jaundiced or mocking attitude towards courtly life. For its part, the doctrinal flaw in the *Defence* is the outcome of Sidney's chronic incapacity to pay 'obedient service' to the imperatives of a wholesome, Protestant pedagogical poetics: he allows it space, but cannot repress his own more dangerous counter-theory of the sublime. Nor does the sonnet sequence afford Sidney any escape from the dilemmas of existence, for Astrophil as Petrarchan lover and Elizabethan courtier oscillates too between the nobility of obedient political and religious service and the baseness of heroic flattery. In the Hegelian, moral sense, neither Sidney nor Astrophil are authentic.

However, Trilling does help us to see how Sidney's Astrophil might be authentic in a different way, which is neither mimetic (Sidney is what his self-image shows him to be) nor moral (Sidney and Astrophil are true to themselves). This third type of authenticity is in compliance with the primary Wildean duty 'to be as artificial as possible', the first aphorism of 'Phrases and Philosophies for the Use of the Young' (1894), which condenses the thinking of the 'Tired Hedonist' Vivian in Oscar Wilde's dialogue, *The Decay of Lying* (1891). What looks like a cynical vindication of self-serving Puttenhamian, Hobbesian or

Hegelian social and political performance also contends quite seriously that the only authentic self is the aestheticised self. Performance, story, even art itself becomes the real thing, or at least an authentic manifestation of it: it is a lie rendered truth. To shore up the aphorism's philosophical credentials, Trilling follows the lead of André Gide and Thomas Mann to find one authority in Nietzsche, while turning up another in Ralph Waldo Emerson.

When Sidney was writing the *Defence*, 'aestheticised' was a keyword that had yet to be coined; he did not have the semantic wherewithal to tidily designate a concept that was crucial to his creation of Astrophil. But there are words in Wilde's critical lexicon that Sidney would have readily recognised and understood. It is part of Vivian's aesthete's credo that 'Art never expresses anything but itself', two related corollaries of which are the severance of 'that vital connection between form and substance' and that 'The highest art rejects the burden of the human spirit.'[31] In contrast, as we shall see, the whole point of Sidney's self-sublimating art is to maintain 'that vital connection between form and substance' and to squarely shoulder the weight 'of the human spirit'.[32] The relationship between producer and production, phenomenon and simulacrum, poet and self-image is not one of mimesis but of identity. Astrophil is Sidney reconstituted aesthetically, made poetry, aestheticised. He is therefore Sidney transported from the realm of history to the realm of art; and by working this ontological transfer on himself, Sidney offers an instance of the Longinian poet's hallmark ability to 'carry us off, to ravish us, and to transport us'.[33] It was that ἔκστασις (*ekstasis*) that underlay the very notion of the godlike poet whose aboriginal creativity, independent of external inspiration, may have been revived with the mid-sixteenth-century rediscovery and circulation of *Peri hupsous*.[34] As we shall see, in a novel twist, Sidney and Astrophil ravish themselves.

The Sidneian Sublime

In *The Advancement and Reformation of Modern Poetry* (1701), John Dennis, dramatist and pioneering theorist of sublimity, wrote: 'Take the cause and the effects together and you have the Sublime.'[35] The Longinian effects Dennis referred to are those that sublimity 'produces in the minds of men', namely, 'admiration and surprise; a noble pride, and a noble vigour, an invincible force, transporting the soul from its ordinary situation, and a transport, and a fulness of joy mingled with astonishment'. Some such 'transport', though less 'joyful', is mapped in Stella's route in sonnet 45 from 'hearing of late a fable' to bursting into tears. The psychopathology of an emotion – here, 'pity' – literally swelling, to adopt Prospero's term, sea-like within her to the point that tears are forced from her lachrymal ducts is as consistent with early modern psychological accounts of imaginative apprehension as with literary representations of extreme experiences.[36] Stella's deeply imagined, somatically externalised reading is a measure of the fable's energy (see below) and the sort of response that Hamlet so admired in the players and that characterised a histrionic age.[37] It is also the readerly counterpart to the orator's spontaneous shows of emotion when possessed or enthused by the power of his own words.[38]

Evidence of *Astrophil and Stella*'s sublime effects on the minds of real men is available in the post-mortem tributes thst his fellow poets paid Sidney under the alias of Astrophil: their keywords or master concepts, typically brushed under the carpet in the written arts, are the godlike poet and rapture that are hallmarks of the Longinian sublime. According to Matthew Roydon, Astrophil was so touched by the Muses that 'his personage seemed most divine'. His listeners were transported: 'To heare him speake and sweetely smile / You were in Paradise the while'; clad in armour, 'heauen admired' him.[39] Of all tributes, Michael Drayton's, written perhaps in 1587, most emphatically and exhaustively sublimates its subject, who is 'the God of poesie', 'A heavenly clowded in a humaine shape', 'immortal made' by 'fame', 'The essence of all Poets divinitie' and 'Immortall mirror of all Poesie'. One stanza seems almost to paraphrase Sidney's well-known discussion of the term *vates*:

> Spel-charming Prophet, sooth-divining seer,
> O heavenly musicke of the highest spheare,
> Sweet sounding trump, soule-ravishing desire,
> Thou stealer of mans heart, inchanter of the eare.[40]

The *Defence* (76.22–5.8)[41] speaks of 'charms', 'prophet' and 'foreseer', and Sidney's coinage 'heart-ravishing' is evoked by the 'souleravishing' of Drayton, who is so keen on the idea of rapture that he glosses his own portmanteau as 'Thou stealer of mans heart'. This sort of praise is undoubtedly conventional, which is perhaps one reason why its sublime key is so easily overlooked. Yet the memorial literature's emphasis on Astrophil's divinity and the effect of transport or rapture that his poems caused in his listeners nonetheless calls for some consideration of how *Astrophil and Stella* might be sublime and whether its sublimity finds some theoretical specification in the *Defence*.

The enigma of exemplarity mentioned above can be revamped as follows: 'All told, the figure of the poet Sidney described in this sequence so closely resembles the portrait one finds in antipoetic texts that much of *Astrophil and Stella*' seems designed 'to replicate and therefore confirm antipoetic discourse'.[42] However, the *Defence*, an extremely equivocal and, perhaps, deliberately equivocating work, is 'a text terminally in conflict with itself'.[43] Among other things, its overarching, essentially Horatian ethical project[44] is undermined by the competing, or imperfectly reconciled, spirit of a poetics which combines elements of the Platonic and the Longinian sublimes. Indeed, in its initial *narratio*, the treatise sets out its stall as taking a distinctively sublime view of the poet. We have just referred to the *Defence*'s discussion of the Roman '*vates*, which is as much as a diviner, foreseer, or prophet ... so heavenly a title did that excellent people bestow upon this heart-ravishing knowledge. And so far were they carried into the admiration thereof' (D 76.22–6). The speaker's subsequent remark that the Romans fell into the 'very vain and godless superstition' of using randomly selected gobbets of poetry to predict the future need not be read as timorous backtracking.[45] The term *vates* is just a title 'bestowed' by the Romans; to take it as pledging the speaker, or Sidney, to the sacrilege of taking poets for actual gods is to be as misled as the superstitious Romans themselves, who took the poems' 'knowledge' as literal future truths. The point is that some special power is detected in poetry for which the most serviceable analogy is with godlike creation: the claim is not that the poet is divine,[46] but that his 'high flying liberty of conceit proper to the poet, did *seem* to have some divine force in it' (D 77.7–8, emphasis added).

Sidney's implicit reprimand of the credulous Romans draws attention to the pitfalls of the same misuse of poetry, this time at the receiving end, that he censures at the producing end in his later treatment of comedy (D 96.18–19). Similarly, there is no self-cavilling or niggling hesitancy in the speaker's appraisal of '[holy David's] heavenly poesy, wherein *almost* he showeth himself a passionate lover of that unspeakable and everlasting beauty to be seen by the eyes of the mind, only cleared by faith' (D 77.10–24, emphasis added). The 'almost' merely indicates the approximateness of the analogy;[47] if 'heavenly' is reckless blasphemy, Petrarch and his myriad line would all be languishing in the seventh circle of Dante's hell. Again, when the poet outdoes Nature 'with the force of a divine breath'

(D 79.22), the efficient cause is 'the force', which is assimilated to that of '*a* divine breath' (emphasis added) – not necessarily *his* (the poet's) or *the* (i.e., God's) 'divine breath'. The upshot is that both Sidney and the speaker have a sublime conception of the poet; neither conflates or equates the sublime poet with the godhead. Rather, in the absence of any technography of sublimity, they turn their hand to the closest available analogy with divine creation, excusing themselves along the way for what otherwise might 'be deemed too saucy a comparison' (D 79.17).[48]

In both sublime conception and terminological difficulty, Sidney and the speaker were by no means alone. Their invocations of a special poetic power, a *furor poeticus* that was so readily aligned with a *furor divinus*, were only among the latest effusions of a venerable tradition[49] reaching back to Plato's *Phaedrus*, which had received the Ovidian stamp of approval, and was referenced by, among others, Elyot, Lodge, Spenser, Puttenham, Webbe and Chapman.[50] In his notes on literature, Ben Jonson, for example, handles what he calls 'the poetical rapture' under the heading of '*Ingenium*' or 'natural wit'. 'The poet,' Jonson tells us,

> must be able by nature and instinct to pour out the treasure of his mind ... Then [the poet's natural wit] riseth higher, as by a divine instinct, when it contemns common and known conceptions. It utters somewhat above a mortal mouth. Then it gets aloft, and flies away with his rider, whither before it was doubtful to ascend.[51]

Jonson's stated authorities are Seneca, Plato, Aristotle, Ovid and Justus Lipsius; he runs together two different passages from Ovid as if they were one, and borrows Plato and Aristotle (in fact, pseudo-Aristotle) from Seneca, whom he misquotes.[52] This ragged collage would deter all but the most foolhardy from pinning one or other philosophical persuasion on Jonson; and the warning might not be ill-applied to students of Sidney. However that might be, two thousand years after Plato, *furor poeticus* and divine authorship smack less of serious analytical categories than clichés culled from an untidy scrapbook of generally received notions. Jonson's is an exercise in the same sublime discourse as Sidney's: his 'poetical rapture' is the first step of *ingenium*'s ascent to 'the zodiac of [Sidney's poet's] own wit' (D 78.29–30), his equine source of energy as indebted to the *Phaedrus* as Sidney's opening in the riding school of Vienna. And of course, those clichés are still handled warily: '*as* by a divine instinct' and '*somewhat* above a mortal mouth' (emphasis added) remind us in their respective comparison and cagey quantifier that Jonson's is a way of putting things for which better definitions are unavailable.

The horse metaphor surfaces again in the *Defence*'s classic definition of idealist mimesis, in the process of which poets 'borrow nothing of what is, hath been, or shall be; but range, only reined with learned discretion, into the divine consideration of what may and should be' (*D* 81.3–6). Here 'divine' is subjected to no qualification and forms part of no analogy. This may be an oversight, or it may be a subtle means of upping the poet's credentials now that the speaker has rolled his sleeves up and is immersed in the serious business of the three-hander *paragone* between philosophy, history and poetry. At the same time, the poet is not given free rein to range as far into that 'divine consideration' as he might perhaps like; rather, he is Phaethon with his foot on the brake pedal. This tempering defuses some of the apparent danger of Sidney's ambivalent poetics: poetry's fictions will only be taken for self-authorised truths of the same status as divine laws by poor readers such as the superstitious Romans or poets who have so lost their judgement or discretion that their 'wit abuseth poetry' (*D* 104.13). Significantly, too, Sidney's reiterated riposte to the 'arguments of abuse' (*D* 95.31–2), namely that poetry is not to be censured for the faults of those who produce it or consume it ('shall the abuse of a thing make the right use odious?', *D* 104.24),[53] has a very Longinian pedigree.[54]

Sidney's care to qualify adverbially or defuse through comparison the full, potentially sacrilegious implications of *furor poeticus/divinus* may answer in part to genuine Protestant reserve, but it is also consistent with the Longinian sublime's emphasis on instrumentality in the human here-and-now; and the Longinian sublime has been argued to be particularly congenial to Protestant poetics.[55] Thus, Sidney and his speaker water down the fully apotheistic charge of the Platonic transcendental sublime, the conquest of which requires superhuman powers of meditation, denial of the flesh and even annihilation in death; instead, it is diluted into a more accessible Longinian sublimity in which man is instinct with a natural aspiration towards great things (*S* 35.2–5).[56] That aspiration drives writers of genius towards the production of sublimity whereby they are raised '*towards* the spiritual greatness of god' (*S* 36.1, emphasis added), not becoming gods but comparable with them (ἰσόθεοι, *isotheoi*; *S* 35.2). What is more, if writers were gods there would be no need for treatises such as Longinus's which taught the art or technique of sublimity. Sidney's reminder that poetry is a combination of 'industry' and 'genius', that even 'the fertilest ground must be manured' and that 'the highest flying wit [must] have a Daedalus to guide him' (D 111.33–112.1), replicates the Longinian refutation of the view that sublimity is a natural product needing no teaching: genius requires the guiding hand of art or technique (S 2.1–3). Worth noting too is the second of Sidney's three pillars of acquired or learned poetry, 'art, imitation and exercise' (D 112.3), which remits us to the Longinian emphasis on and practice of taking other authors as models.[57] Also Longinian is the Sidneian poet's enjoyment of a certain freedom: 'freely ranging only within the zodiac of his own wit' (D 78.28–9), he enjoys 'high flying liberty of conceit' (D 77.7). This should not give wings to those who, misreading the closing dialogue between Longinus and the philosopher, herald *Peri hupsous*, and too often sublimity itself, as a force for democratic progress.[58] If the basic meaning of 'free' is free of subjections, in the *Defence* it also carries social-ethical connotations of nobility, honour and magnanimity,[59] as well as the lofty scorn of the 'poet, disdaining to be tied to . . . subjection' (D 78.22–3). Sublimity is the exclusive preserve of ennobled minds, much as in Longinus it was off-limits for those with 'low or ignoble thoughts' or whose 'thoughts and habits are trivial and servile' (S 9.3).[60] Sidney's Longinian sublime is an aristocratic mode, literary excellence practised by the socially excellent and, as Sidney's disdain for those born in the mud of the Nile suggests, for consumption by the excellent alone.[61]

Kelly Lehtonen is too reductive in assimilating Sidney's prioritisation of the feigning of images to the centrality of *phantasia* in Longinus:[62] φαντασία (*phantasia*) or image-making was crucial, too, in Cicero's and Quintilian's accounts of affective rhetoric and Plutarch's comments on Thucydides.[63] For Sidney, it is not 'rhyming and versing that maketh a poet' (D 81.33–4), but 'that feigning notable images of virtues, vices, or what else' (D 81.36–7); such images 'strike, pierce' and 'possess the sight of the soul' (D 85.28–9); 'the lofty image [of the epic poets] . . . most inflameth the mind with desire' (D 98.14–15). Sidney is writing in a tradition of sublime rhetoric, in which metaphors of fire and inflammation were rife. As fire breeds fire it was a useful metaphor for the working of *energeia*, 'that same forcibleness or *energia*' (D 117.8–9), as Sidney puts it, which is felt first by the speaker then conveyed linguistically to be felt anew by the audience. In *The Arte of Rhetorique* (1560), Thomas Wilson makes the point well: 'There is no substance of itself that will take fire except ye put fire to it. Likewise, no man's nature is so apt straight to be heated except the orator himself be on fire and bring his heat with him.'[64] That transmission of the energy of passion was, for Sidney, 'the material point of Poesy', which was just what he missed in contemporary 'writings as come under the banner of irresistible love' (*D* 116.35–117.1). Sidney's implication is that *energeia* should be the driving force or the essence of a love poetry which had a material and potentially sublime effect on its readers.

Sidney's is the first use in English of the term *energia*, borrowed in Scaliger's Latin form of the original Greek ἐνέργεια (*energeia*),[65] as coined by Aristotle. When not confused or assimilated to ἐνάργεια (*enargeia*, or *enargia*) – Puttenham's 'glorious lustre and light' – it is still often taken as designating some or other 'clarity of expression'[66] in the presentation of subject matter, as if it were an ancillary component of mimesis. This is not the case. Scaliger's alternative term for *energeia* is *efficacia*, which Puttenham picks up in his explanation of *energeia*, carefully distinguished from *enargia*. Puttenham considers the etymology of Aristotle's coinage to provide a definition: '*energeia* of *ergon*, because it wrought with a strong and virtuous operation',[67] which is exactly the meaning of Sidney's 'forcibleness'.[68] In Aristotelian metaphysics, *energeia* denotes the force or energy inside a body which tends towards a body's fulfilment or completion; entelechy is generally regarded as synonymous. Energy is a thing's active essence, its vital spirit, its 'being-at-work' or 'is-at-work-ness'.[69] It is not therefore a rhetorical figure but a physical property, which poses a presentational challenge and sets a pragmatic goal in that the poet endeavours to capture it in words which, in a 'reciprocal dynamic', will then enable readers to experience it as he did.[70] Aristotle theorises *energeia* in the *Physics*, *Metaphysics* and *Nichomachean Ethics*; in the *Rhetoric*, he applies *energeia* to poetry in his discussion of metaphor:[71] after stating that effective metaphors bring things 'before the eyes', he explains that this is done 'by words that signify *actuality*' (emphasis added).[72] 'Actuality' is the Loeb translator's word for *energeia* and conveys the sense of an active, actualising essence or being-at-work of a body. Importantly, 'actuality' is something that is expressed or created, not a way of expressing or creating something, and Aristotle pre-empts Longinian methodology by offering various instances of metaphors expressing or failing to express it. He is particularly impressed by Homer's facility for speaking 'of inanimate things as if they were animate'; it is, he tells us, 'to creating actuality in all such cases that his popularity is due'. Finally, Homer 'gives movement and life to all, and actuality is movement'.[73] By implication, then, Aristotelian *energeia* is a property of living things; it is the continually sparking force which actuates their being. And it was inevitable that the sublime metaphor of fire was invented to describe it.

Sidney's understanding of *energeia* is Aristotelian: what love poets fail to communicate is what makes them tick, or better, the ticking inside them, or that energising fire of cupidity which is documented in Cassandra Gorman's chapter in this volume.[74] Sidney wants his readers to tick or smoulder alongside him, as the energy in his mind is transmuted into words which, on entering a reader's imagination, generate further energy, diminished but sufficient to stimulate the sort of somatic response depicted in sonnet 45. *Energeia* permits genuinely sympathetic reading. In this sense, Sidney calls for poems which, like Thomas Watson's, are 'love passions'.[75] Sidney's comments grow more specifically Longinian in the ensuing discussion where budding orators are urged to take 'Tully and Demosthenes' as their models and 'devour them whole, and make them wholly theirs' (*D* 117.25–8). Cicero ('Tully') and Demosthenes feature in Longinus's famous comparison likening the abrupt intensity of the latter with 'a thunderbolt or a flash of lightning', the lasting, rolling burn of the former with 'a spreading conflagration' (*S* 12.4). In Sidney – a Jonsonian cut-and-paste of misremembered or half-recalled *Peri hupsous*? – the 'thunderbolt of eloquence' is Cicero, but his fiery *energeia*, permitting him, 'inflamed with a well-grounded rage ... [to] do that artificially which we see men in choler do naturally' (*D* 117.34–118.2), is Demosthenic and Longinian.

The Ecstatic Self

Transport, rapture and ravishment are close cognates in the Longinian sublime. As noted, early on in the *Defence* Sidney mentions the 'heart-ravishing knowledge' of the *vates* (*D* 76.25). Later, on the authority of Plato and Cicero he speculates that 'who could see virtue would be wonderfully ravished with the love of her beauty' (*D* 98.5–7) and, when differentiating delight from laughter, explains 'we are ravished with delight to see a fair woman, and yet are far from being moved to laughter' (*D* 115.22–3). In *Astrophil and Stella*, of the three cognates, 'ravish' alone is represented, and that only once, when Stella's 'beauties so devine / Ravisht' the 'wanton winds' (*AS* 103.5–6). The sequence's fundamental, indeed seminal, act of ravishment occurs outside its pages, but can be deduced from sonnet 1 where Astrophil's pregnancy is significantly foregrounded. 'Great with child', Astrophil, like his 'spotted' creator,[76] is presumably, and despite the Marian allusion,[77] no virgin. If he is 'helpless in his throes', there has been a prior act of conception and the most likely candidate for putative father is Astrophil himself – or Sidney if, in the end, poet and self-image need not be separated or if, less controversially, poet may be supposed to share similar views on poetic creation as his poetic self-image. Sonnet 37 specifies the symptoms of pregnancy as childbirth nears: 'My mouth doth water, and my breast doth swell, / My tongue doth itch, my thoughts in labour be' (*AS* 37.1–2); while sonnet 40 prescribes writing as an antidote to or, as an act of poetic delivery, release from the pangs of the obstetric table: 'As good to write, as for to lie and grone' (*AS* 40.1). That Astrophil's poems are stillborn – their incapacity to 'portrait that which in this world is best' means 'those poore babes their death in birth do find' (*AS* 50.8, 11) – is beside the point. The procreative autonomy of this metaphorical self-rapture and self-midwifery is one way of declaring the aboriginality of the poetry: not divinely inspired, it is all Astrophil's own work, fruit of his self-sown and self-germinated seed: or, as the *Defence* tells us, 'The Poet only bringeth his own stuff, and doth not learn a conceit out of a matter, but maketh matter for a conceit' (*D* 99.7–9). William Scott's rhetorical question concerning *furor poeticus* hits the note with precision: 'is this instinct, fury, influence, or what else you list to call it, is this, I say, divine seed infused and conceived in the mind of man in despite of nature and reason, as you would say by rape?'[78] Scott is wary of such anti-natural and unreasonable poetic mitosis – unreasonable in the sense that the wit is not reined in by discretion but hurtles along like Phaethon, foot off the brake, or Icarus heedless of Daedalian imperatives. It is the rape which in the *Defence* Sidney himself confesses to have fallen victim to, quite possibly in his sonnet sequence, when 'overmastered by some thoughts, I yielded an inky tribute to them' (*D* 111.23–4). From the very first sonnet, Astrophil is the self-infusing, self-fertilising Longinian poet, godlike in his immaculate conceptions and providing another aetiology of poetry to sit alongside those unpicked in the first part of this volume.

In this respect, Sidney can be situated among those such as Lodovico Castelvetro who rejected theories of poetic inspiration and hived invention off from imitation to make it an index of the poet's creative autonomy and originality. For this reason, Homer gradually came to replace Virgil as the pre-eminent poet, since what Chapman called the Greek's 'free furie' was set at a higher premium than Virgil's borrowing.[79] French Huguenot Guillaume Salluste du Bartas provided in *La Sepmaine, ou Création du monde* (1578) a magnificently rugged and sublime riff on Genesis 1, which had not left Longinus unmoved, with particular emphasis on God's *ex nihilo* primordial making. Here was a model for the human maker, Godlike in his creative originality but not divine or divinely inspired. For Heninger, in early modern England, 'maker' – Sidney's 'high and incomparable' title (*D* 77.36–7) – as opposed to 'author' had lofty, transcendental overtones and suggested original creativity, on the analogy with God the maker, rather than imitation. Alongside Sidney's *Defence*, Spenser's *Shepheardes Calendar* was crucial to advancing this meaning.[80] Whether or not claims for such a watertight distinction can be sustained, Du Bartas's work was extremely popular. Sidney's translation, registered with the Stationer's Office in 1588, was never printed and has not survived;[81] William Scott's version of the first two days has.[82] It has even been suggested that Sidney gleaned his notions of 'idea' and 'fore-conceit' from a manuscript reading of Du Bartas's *La seconde sepmaine*;[83] certainly, when Josuah Sylvester translated the relevant passage in 1603, he drew on Sidney's terminology ('l'avant-conceu portrait' = 'th'*Idea* fore-conceaved'), which suggests that in his mind at least there was a theoretical affinity between both writers. Further evidence of conceptual coincidence is Du Bartas's God's and Sidney's poet's reliance on the zodiac in their creative efforts, the difference being that in Du Bartas it is above the human, whereas in Sidney it is within the human's mind. Again, the fact that both authors – as well as Scott in his *Model* – deploy metaphors of gestation in their accounts of creation suggests that they were tapping into a shared conceptual economy.[84]

The poem that the self-ravished poet gives birth to is flesh of his flesh, tied umbilically to him. Inspiration, composition and end product constitute a watertight, organic process, the end product of which is organically of a piece with its producer. This poet–product organicity reminds us of the Wildean aestheticised subject and enables the generation of authenticity. What is more, it may underlie the several grammatical slippages in the *Defence* which cause poet to blur into poem, or poem into poet. A case in point is the grammatical equation of poet and art in 'the poet, with that same hand of delight, doth draw the mind more effectually than any other art doth' (*D* 94.9–10), which is followed almost immediately by the equal and opposite metamorphosis of poetry into workman: 'so poetry . . . is the most excellent workman' (*D* 94.13–15). Sidney is so struck by this anthropomorphism that for the whole of the following paragraph he refers to poetry with masculine 'he', 'him' and 'his' instead of neuter 'it' and 'its', a change of person drawn from the Longinian armoury (*S* 23) of sublime figures: 'I am content not only to decipher him by his works . . . but more narrowly will examine his parts, so that (as in a man) . . . Now in his parts . . .' (*D* 94.16–22). We have already been told that Sidney's subject is the art itself;[85] now, that art has absorbed the artificer into itself and acquired a human agency as the result of a theoretical U-turn from a poet-driven to a poetry-driven art, which is recorded in a well-known sentence whose pivotal 'or rather' captures a change of mind as surprising to its author as to his readers: 'For Poesy must not be drawn by the ears; it must be gently led, or rather it must lead' (*D* 111.28–9). Moreover, it plays by its own rules: 'a tragedy is tied to the laws of Poesy, and not of History; not bound to follow the story, but, having liberty, either to feign a quite new matter, or to frame the history to the most tragical conveniency' (*D* 114.3–6). In short, poetry has attained an ontological status as an independent and self-regulating dynamic force,[86] some primordial *energeia* that ravishes the poet and is guaranteed perpetuity in the poem to which the poet gives birth and through which his readers are transported in grateful reciprocation.

Aestheticised self-images in *Astrophil and Stella* include Astrophil as Sidney's heraldic device ('Thou bear'st the arrow, I the arrow head', *AS* 65.14) or as his own story ('I am not I, pitie the tale of me', *AS* 45.14). The story of Astrophil's own self actually has the power to transport him in a special case of self-ravishment: when Stella reads to him 'the anatomy of all my woes' he has recently penned 'in piercing phrases', 'most ravishing delight / Even those sad words even in sad me did breed' (*AS* 58.9–14). 'Piercing' is Longinian, and its sexual connotations – we might recall Cupid's piercing arrows from Gorman's chapter in this volume – are activated in the presence of 'ravishing' and 'breed' to recreate the procreative process of poetic production, now transposed to that of poetic reception: the poem ravishes its audience, and the fruit of that ravishment is a replica of the originary emotion which the poet had first conveyed through an *energeia* now communicated and felt by the receiver. The irony here is that Astrophil's response is not the intended one. He takes delight where he had 'wooed woe'; instead of ravishing her, he has ravished himself, but gratifyingly so, and there is comfort, one supposes, in that. When, as in this case, poet is poem and also reader, a solipsistic, self-reflexive ecstasy is the logical outcome.

Elsewhere, Longinian grammatical slippage, this time of pronouns, once again engineers some further ecstasies. The final stanza of the Eighth Song suddenly abandons a third-person narration of Astrophil and Stella's conversation when, like a gentle thunderbolt, the first-person possessive intervenes: 'Therewithal away she went, / Leaving him so passion rent . . . / That therewith *my* song is broken' (*AS* Song 8.101–4, emphasis added). Here, Sidney ecstaticises himself from his poetic self-image. In contrast, in the Ninth Song, it is Astrophil who self-ecstaticises as first-person shifts to third:

'*Stella* hath refused me; / *Astrophil*, that so wel served . . .' (*AS* Song 9.26–7). The most sublime self-ecstasy in a technical Longinian sense is staged in sonnet 83. Straight out of the Longinian toolkit (*S* 26), its opening vocative is remarkable enough, more so in its surprising shift of focus on to the real-world poet responsible for the fictional speaker: 'Good brother Philip' (*AS* 83.1). Producer is ecstaticised from product, although the assertion of fraternity suggests a process of gemmation and the consequent genetic identity. What is more, since it is the fictional character Astrophil who addresses Sidney, the poet is transported into the realm of his own creation, while readers are ravished to wobble disconcertingly between the here-and-now of reality and the there-and-then of art. It immediately transpires that the Philip of the poem is Stella's pet sparrow and that the sonnet, Longinian in its intertextuality, is a new variation on an old theme stretching back through Skelton to Catullus. But the damage has been done: Sidney will be forever his aestheticised self, while his readers, once transported, will never forget the experience.

In Sidney's sonnet sequence, self-aestheticisation is an ecstasy in which the energetic essence of the producer is sublimated and preserved in the product; self-ravishment thus guarantees a Wildean authenticity. This helps to solve the biographical enigma: Astrophil may or may not bear a mimetic relationship to Sidney, but both share an ontological identity since the poetic product is, or is in Aristotelian fulfilment of, the poet's *energeia*. In this sense, too, Sidney is a sublime poet whose 'own Example strengthens all his Laws, / And Is himself that great sublime he draws', as Pope wrote of Longinus.[87] What interpenetrates and intercommunicates poet, product and reader is *energeia*, which in modern argot is uploaded from poet to poem for subsequent downloading by readers. The *energeia* the reader captures is a trace or vestige of, in early modern parlance, the poet's quintessence, his active, vital spirit, 'sublimed' into his poetry much as Stella's words 'do sublime the quintessence of bliss' (*AS* 77.8). If the primary reference here of 'sublime' is to alchemy, as a process in which elements undergo a change of state, alchemy involved its own chemical transport and was in that sense metaphysically sublime as well. Alchemical and metaphysical sublimes are brought together in sonnet 28: 'Looke at my hands for no such quintessence; / But know that I in pure simplicitie / Breathe out the flames which burne within my heart' (*AS* 28.11–13). In a poem that eschews the ambivalent duplicities of allegory, the 'simplicitie' Astrophil avows is untouched by 'eloquence' or 'the hid ways' of occult 'philosophy' (*AS* 28.9–10), but is his own quintessence, figured here as the flames that heat the alchemist's crucible, the flames that run through the Petrarchan and, ultimately, the Sapphic lover anthologised in *Peri hupsous*, the flames of rhetorical *energeia* and the fire, finally, of the sublime.

Conclusion: Energetic Instrumentality

None of this is to say that Sidney is a sublime poet. Although a coherent theory and model of sublime poetry can be derived from the *Defence* and *Astrophil and Stella*, neither work is consistently sublime in conception, execution or effect. The former is eclectic in its amalgam of Aristotle, Plato, Horace and, now, elements of Longinian sublimity; the latter, a kaleidoscope of moods and modes in which sonnets 3 and 6 may be read as poking fun at sublime poetry, among other kinds, or at least at the sublime topographies replicated *ad absurdum* by the Petrarchan sonneteers: the paradoxes of their 'heav'nly beames, infusing hellish paine: / . . . living deaths, dear wounds, fair storms and freezing fires' (*AS* 6.3–4) serve only to banalise natural sublimity and remind us that the sublime must always be more than mimesis – indeed, when Sidney's sequence is most mimetic or factually autobiographical (for instance, sonnets 30, 41, 53), it is least potentially sublime. At the same time, the eloquent taciturnity of the dumb swans which Sidney prefers to the chatter of 'Pies' (*AS* 54.13) – as in the reductive compression of all he feels to the plain statement that 'I do *Stella* love' (*AS* 6.14) – has, too, its Longinian legitimation in the silence of Ajax. One problem with pinning down the sublime is its very multimodality.

In the *Defence*, Sidney grafted on to flagging Aristotelian mimesis a transcendental Platonic superstructure, which had the additional advantage of satisfying the Horatian requirement of utility. However, Castelvetro's spurious theory of the unities would in the longer term prove more successful in restoring Aristotle's health, until its slow decline during the long eighteenth century. As far as the history of aesthetics is concerned, that century commenced with the publication in 1674 of Nicolas Boileau's translation of Longinus and terminated with the Romantic consolidation of the cult of authorship and original, human creative genius. In that consolidation, once it had evolved through the Leibnizian metaphysics of perfect worlds and Herder's organicism, Sidney's theory and model of aboriginal, organic and self-regulating poetry achieved its historical fulfilment; in the amalgam of now conflicting, now complementary aesthetic postulates that is

Sidney's *Defence*, the emergent aesthetic discourse of the sublime is as yet a faint presence, although its impact on Sidney's model of authorship, as exemplified in certain passages of *Astrophil and Stella*, is, for the reasons set out here, decisive.

Sidney's model of authorship offers an alternative to the corporeal views of poetry explored in Rocio Sumillera's chapter in the present volume, or what might be called the 'mental imprint' view, which took style to be the textual impression or character of the writer's mind.[88] A closer parallel to Sidneian self-ravishment is the Marlovian self-annihilation which results in 'a sublime coupling with the literary image' or relocation of the transcendent in 'the temporal immanence of authorship'.[89] More prosaically, Sidney's self-aestheticisation and its Astrophiliac aftermath found a counterpart in the fad for euphuism and 'Lylian emulation' sparked by the publication in 1578 of *Euphues: The Anatomy of Wit*.[90] An attack on Lyly has been detected in Sidney's remarks on 'similitudes, in certain printed discourses' (*D* 118.13),[91] while the final remarks of the *Defence* ('Thus doing, your name shall flourish in the printers' shops', etc., *D* 121.19) can be read as a broadside against print culture and the nascent, bourgeois cult of the author, to which his own untimely death was soon to contribute. Yet it is also uncannily prescient of Sidney's immediate afterlife. He, too, was to 'dwell upon superlatives' (*D* 121.22), and be remembered as author of 'Highest conceits, longest foresights, and deepest works of wit' by Raleigh who, instead of placing his soul with 'Dante's Beatrice, or Virgil's Anchises' (*D* 121.25–6), honoured him as '*Scipio, Cicero*, and *Petrarch* of our time'.[92]

That an expressive vocabulary for the sublime effects of Sidney's authorship already existed – after all, the sublime as a constant of human experience has existed in supreme independence of Longinus, Boileau, Burke and the rest – is attested in the commonplaces of sublime poetry and authorship rehearsed in the memorial literature that proliferated on Sidney's death, which can leave little doubt regarding the efficacy and energetic impact of his poetry. In that sense, poetic praxis compensated for the technographic shortfall of the written arts. Contemporary readers of *Astrophil and Stella* felt something unprecedented as they intuited the communication of the poet's 'essence of divinity' and, more broadly, the emergence of a new model of aboriginal, organic and autonomous poetry of which the self-ravishing author was a part. Thus, Sidney's theory of sublime poetry and model of sublime self-authorship maintained 'that vital connection between form and substance' which Wilde's Vivian claimed most art severed, and shouldered 'the burden of the human spirit' – admittedly far less onerous once sublimated – which, Vivian asserted, 'The highest art rejects'. To that extent, the counter-Hamletian thesis of Wilde's Vivian was proven: 'Life imitates Art . . . Life in fact is the mirror, Art the reality.'[93] Thus, too, the enigma of exemplarity is solved, for even the unlikeliest of fictional models can inhabit the most profitably emulable works of art. It was in that sense a practically efficacious, utilitarian, Longinian sublimity, the ultimate and actually realisable end of which was literary immortality.[94] Furthermore, to the extent that emulation implies a degree of real or desired identification, the early reception of *Astrophil and Stella* amplifies the truth of Longinus's dictum: 'Filled with joy and pride, we come to believe we have created what we have only heard' (*S* 7.2). Not only did Sidney's readers participate in the sublimity of *Astrophil and Stella* by receiving its energy and Sidney's essence like grateful communicants, but, in emulation, they went on to regenerate what they had read in their own sequences. And in so doing, they replicate the same slippage between reader and poet which, around the pivotal 'Thus doing' of the *Defence*'s peroration, enunciates the completion of the Longinian process by which poetry is ultimately and energetically instrumental in breeding poets.[95]

Notes

1. Hager, 'The Exemplary Mirage', 3–4.
2. Raleigh, 'Another of the Same', 13, in Spenser, *Poetical Works*, ed. de Selincourt, 559.
3. Raleigh, 'An Epitaph upon the right Honourable sir Phillip Sidney knight: Lord gouernor of Flushing', 20, in Spenser, *Poetical Works*, 558.
4. Matz, *Heroic Diversions*, 56–87.
5. Alexander, 'Introduction', in Scott, *Model of Poesy*, lii.
6. Despite his lack of humour, Henry Constable is one of the more Sidneian sonneteers; so too, though much less so, Samuel Daniel and Michael Drayton. Barnabe Barnes, John Davies, George Chapman and Fulke Greville were decidedly not Sidneian; neither, in general, was Edmund Spenser. Giles Fletcher was more Sidneian in theory than in practice. My thanks to the editor of this collection for conversations on this point.
7. Consent is almost unanimous that Cassius Longinus was the author of *Peri hupsous*; see Heath, 'Longinus and the Ancient Sublime', 15–16; and Porter, *Sublime in Antiquity*, 1–2.
8. Weinberg, 'Translations and Commentaries of Longinus'. Even earlier, three manuscript copies circulated in fifteenth-century Italy, France and Britain; see Eck, Bussels and Delbeke, 'Introduction', 1.

9. On Longinus and Patrizi, Giacomini and Tasso, see, respectively: Platt, *Reason Diminished*, 12–17; Refini, 'Longinus and Poetic Imagination'; and Lehtonen, '*Peri Hypsous* in Translation', 454–7.
10. Chang, *Into Print*, 111.
11. Martin, '"Prehistory" of the Sublime', 78.
12. Ibid., 78–9.
13. Porter, *Sublime in Antiquity*, 49.
14. Porter, 'The Sublime', 395.
15. See Auerbach, *Literary Language*, 181–233.
16. See, for instance, Boitani, *The Tragic and the Sublime*; Hardie, *Lucretian Receptions*; and Jaeger, ed., *Magnificence and the Sublime*.
17. Cheney, *English Authorship and the Early Modern Sublime*, 13.
18. Lehtonen, '*Peri hypsous* in Translation', 458.
19. Ringler, 'An Early Reference to Longinus'.
20. Cheney, *English Authorship and the Early Modern Sublime*, 14–15. See also Luis-Martínez's chapter, 'George Chapman's "Habit of Poesie"', this volume.
21. Dundas, *Sidney and Junius on Poetry and Painting*, 254 n.22.
22. Cheney, *Shakespeare's Literary Authorship, Marlowe's Republican Authorship*; 'The Forms of Things Unknown'; and *Reading Sixteenth-Century Poetry*.
23. Cheney, *English Authorship and the Early Modern Sublime*, 6. All references to *Astrophil and Stella* are from Sidney, *Poems*, ed. Ringler, 163–267, and are cited parenthetically in the text by sonnet/song and line numbers.
24. Cheney, *Reading Sixteenth-Century Poetry*, 156–7, original emphasis. In *Sidney and Spenser*, Heninger notices in passing a Sidney who 'strives for sublime effects' (457).
25. Conrad, *Everyman History of English Literature*, 98.
26. Lowrance, 'Sidney's Strangers', 18.
27. Tuve, *Elizabethan and Metaphysical Imagery*, 3–26.
28. Defending allegory in *Ouids Banquet of Sence*, Chapman helped himself to Sidney's phrase: 'So in the compasse of this curious frame / Ovid well knew that there was more intended' (117.7–8, in *Poems*, ed. Bartlett, 82). My thanks to the editor for this reference.
29. Trilling, *Sincerity and Authenticity*, 34–9.
30. See Hobbes, *Leviathan*: 'a person, is the same that an actor is, both on stage and in common conversation' (106). Identity as social performance has a long history, stretching at least from the sixteenth century through David Hume, Friedrich Nietzsche and Herbert Mead, to Erving Goffman and Judith Butler.
31. Wilde, *Complete Works*, 4.44–5.
32. Sidney would also have understood the three further aphorisms Trilling quotes from Wilde, Emerson and Nietzsche, respectively: 'Man is least himself when he talks in his own person. Give him a mask and he

will tell you the truth'; 'Many men can write better in a mask than for themselves'; and 'Every profound spirit needs a mask' (*Sincerity and Authenticity*, 119). Astrophil's manifesto of poetic sincerity consigns the concealments of dissimulation and disguise to 'dainty wits . . . / That bravely maskt, their fancies may be told' (3.1–2); his honest obedience to the protocols of courtly behaviour renders them *de rigueur*: 'My friend, that oft saw through all maskes my wo' (69.5).

33. Porter, *Sublime in Antiquity*, 45.
34. Refini, 'Longinus and Poetic Imagination', 39. In *Poetica d'Aristotele vulgarizzata e sposta* (1570), Lodovico Castelvetro rejected theories of poetic inspiration; see Sumillera, *Invention*, 87–8.
35. In *The Sublime: A Reader*, ed. Ashfield and de Bolla, 34.
36. For example: 'It is clear that the mind . . . by reason of the apprehensions both sensible and imaginative doth diversely change and alter the body with sensible alterations, by varying the accidents thereof, and producing sundry qualities in the members' (Lomazzo, *Artes of Curious Painting, Carvinge and Building*, II.10); 'Th'idea of her [Hero's] life shall sweetly creep / Into his [Claudio's] study of imagination . . . / Then shall he mourn' (*Much Ado About Nothing*, 4.1.223–9, in *Norton Shakespeare*, ed. Greenblatt, 1427). In the case of Antonio and the rest, it was their 'understanding' that 'begins to swell' (*The Tempest*, 5.1.79–80, in *Norton Shakespeare*, ed. Greenblatt, 3100).
37. On the cultural praxis of performed emotion, see Enterline, *Shakespeare's Schoolroom*, 173 n.48, 174 n.49; Hobgood, 'Feeling Fear in Macbeth'; and MacNeil, 'Weeping at the Water's Edge'. Shakespeare's Bolingbroke was sceptical of such energetic shows of imagined emotion, or mind over matter (*Richard II*, 1.3.257–66, in *Norton Shakespeare*, ed. Greenblatt, 965).
38. For example, Quintilian, *Institutio oratoria*, VI.2.35–6; see original text and Butler, trans., 2:436–9.
39. 'An Elegy; or, Friend's Passion for his Astrophel', 98, 101–2, in Spenser, *Poetical Works*, 557.
40. Drayton, *Idea: The Shepheards Garland*, 'The Fourth Eglog', 58, 61, 110, 62–5, in *Works*, ed. Hebel, 1:60–4.
41. All references are by page and line number to Sidney, *Defence*, in *Miscellaneous Prose*, ed. Duncan-Jones and Van Dorsten, and are cited parenthetically in the text.
42. Herman, *Squitter-wits and Muse-Haters*, 96.
43. Bates, *On Not Defending Poetry*, 10.
44. Reisner, 'The Paradox of Mimesis', 335.
45. Pace Bates, *On Not Defending Poetry*, 14–15.
46. On a weaker but unnecessary sense of 'divine' as meaning beautiful, perfect or excellent, see Bates, *On Not Defending Poetry*, 16 n.24.
47. Shepherd takes 'almost' to mean 'indeed'. See Sidney, *Apology*, ed. Shepherd, 152 n.19.

48. Puttenham shows similar reticence, not about how poets may be conceived but about the best way to put that conception into words: 'they be (by maner of speech) as creating gods' (*Art of English Poesy*, ed. Whigham and Rebhorn, 94).
49. See Curtius, *European Literature*, 474–5.
50. Bates, *On Not Defending*, 171 n.186. See also Luis-Martínez's chapter, 'George Chapman's "Habit of Poesie"', this volume.
51. Jonson, *Discoveries*, ed. Hutson, in *Cambridge Edition Online*, lines 1713–21.
52. For details of sources and misquotation, see Vickers, ed., *English Renaissance Literary Criticism*, 584 nn.117–20.
53. The poet is to blame for offences against 'the right use' of poetry, a phrase which sounds as a leitmotif throughout the *Defence* (see, e.g., 94.32, 96.20, 104.31, 117.10–11, 119.13); the audience is to blame for failing to suspend its disbelief when confronted with violations of the dramatic unities of time and place (113.14–26).
54. In his expectation that there be abuse in sublime language, Longinus differed from Sidney, but he agreed on abuse by audiences. See Heath, 'Longinus and the Ancient Sublime', 22.
55. Till, 'The Sublime and the Bible', 59–61. On the religious nonconformity of Longinus's sixteenth-century disseminators, see Martin, '"Prehistory" of the Sublime', 79.
56. All references, by the conventional chapter and section divisions, are to *On Sublimity*, trans. Russell, in *Ancient Literary Criticism*, ed. Russell and Winterbottom, and will be cited parenthetically in the text using the abbreviation *S*.
57. On the quotational nature of the Longinian sublime, see Porter, *Sublime in Antiquity*, 143; on intertextuality as a key component of sublime literary authorship, see Cheney, *English Authorship and the Early Modern Sublime*, 17–18, 37–8.
58. 'A "democracy" is crucial for providing a home to the world's greatest artistic achievement, and sublimity is the highest mark of a democracy' (Cheney, *English Authorship and the Early Modern Sublime*, 43).
59. For the economic implications, see Bates, *On Not Defending Poetry*, 19–20.
60. On connections with the Protestant doctrine of salvation by grace alone (as with sublimity, work or industry is not enough), see Lehtonen, '*Peri hypsous* in Translation', 459. Lehtonen (460) also compares the *Defence*'s concluding slur of those 'born so near the dull-making cataract of Nilus' that they 'cannot hear the planet-like music of poetry' etc. (*D* 121.27–31) with Longinus's remarks on those who, given over to the vices of materialism, 'spend their admiration on their mortal parts and neglect to develop the immortal' (*S* 502.8).
61. In his letter to Roydon that accompanied *Ouids Banquet of Sence*, Chapman (*Poems*, 49–50) inverts Sidney's courtly poetics as practised

62. Lehtonen, 'Peri hypsous in Translation', 459–60. On phantasia, see Cheney, *English Authorship and the Early Modern Sublime*, passim.
63. For an overview of the vast literature on psychological, philosophical and rhetorical accounts of *phantasia*, see Webb, *Ekphrasis, Imagination and Pleasure*, 115–19. On Plutarch, see Goldhill, 'What is Ekphrasis For?', 5.
64. Wilson, *Art of Rhetoric*, ed. Medine, 163:28–30.
65. 'Efficaciam Graeci ἐνέργειαν vocant' (Scaliger, *Poetices libri septem*, III.27, p. 116).
66. Bates, *On Not Defending Poetry*, 216. Compare Shepherd's gloss of Sidney's *energia* as 'the intellectual clarity with which the poet distinguishes or apprehends the fore-conceit or Idea' (Sidney, *Apology*, 226).
67. Puttenham, *Art of English Poesy*, 227.
68. Maslen is right to associate Sidney's *energia* with 'Herculean energy' ('Introduction', 73).
69. See, for instance, Sachs's translation of *energeia* in Aristotle, *Metaphysics*, passim.
70. Craik, *Reading Sensations*, 41–2.
71. Aristotle, *Rhetoric*, III.9.1–4, 1411b, trans. Freese.
72. Aristotle's use of *energeia* in the same breath as references to the sense of sight might explain why it is often confused with *enargeia*. For a definitive disentanglement, see Westin, 'Aristotle's Rhetorical *Energeia*'; see also Plett, *Rhetoric and Renaissance Culture*, 195–6.
73. This seems to be what Chapman means when he called Homer's ekphrasis of Achilles' shield '*autokinestéos*' or self-moving, consisting 'not of hard and solid mettals but of a truely living and moving soule' (*Achilles Shield*, 'To the Earle Marshall', in *Chapman's Homer*, 1:543).
74. See Gorman, 'Atomies of Love', this volume, esp., 89–92.
75. Watson, *Hekatompathia*, 'To the frendly Reader' sig. A4r.
76. The 'spotted', sexually voracious Sidney/Philisides is a fourth afterlife to vie with the militant Protestant, the chivalric flower and the poetic Astrophil. See Hager, 'The Exemplary Mirage', 10–11, 13–14.
77. 'To be taxed with Marie that was giuen him to wife, that was with childe' (Luke 2.5, in *Bible*, sig. Gg3r).
78. Scott, *Model of Poesy*, 7.
79. Chapman, *Achilles Shield*, 'To the Earle Marshall', in *Chapman's Homer*, 1:543. See Sumillera, *Invention*, 87–9; also Luis-Martínez, 'George Chapman's "Habit of Poesie"', this volume, 267–9.
80. Heninger, *Sidney and Spenser*, 285–6. See also Heninger, *Touches of Sweet Harmony*, 288–90, 296, 315; and Healy and Healy, 'Introduction', 4. The early modern sublime was reinstated too late for Heninger to consider the potentially Longinian associations of making.

81. See Ringler's note to this lost translation in Sidney, *Poems*, 339.
82. Auger, 'William Scott's Translation'.
83. Heninger, *Sidney and Spenser*, 60ff.; Mack, *Sidney's Poetics*, 76–80.
84. Du Bartas, *Divine Weekes*, trans. Sylvester, 140. Heninger cites the first three lines of this passage as the best way of glossing Sidney's use of the term 'idea' (*Touches of Sweet Harmony*, 320). On gestation, see Auger, 'A Model of Creation?', 76–80. Du Bartas conceived of the poet as only fashioning creatively a God-inspired idea, whereas for Sidney, the idea was what remained of the divine essence inside the poet's mind; see Stillman, *Philip Sidney and the Poetics of Renaissance Cosmopolitanism*, 117.
85. '[Y]et say I and say again, I speak of the art and not of the artificer' (*D* 89.34–5).
86. Lehtonen, '*Peri hypsous* in Translation', 459.
87. Pope, *An Essay in Criticism*, 680, in *Poems*, ed. Butt, 165.
88. See Sumillera, 'Bloody Poetics', this volume.
89. Cheney, *English Authorship and the Early Modern Sublime*, 258, 153.
90. See Kesson, *John Lyly and Early Modern Authorship*, 74–5, 180–1.
91. See Maslen's note in Sidney, *An Apology*, 246.
92. Raleigh, 'Another of the Same', 16, 58, in Spenser, *Poetical Works*, 559.
93. Wilde, *Complete Works*, 4.56.
94. Porter, *Sublime in Antiquity*, 616–17.
95. 'I conjure you all that have had the evil luck to read this ink-wasting toy of mine . . . Thus doing your name shall flourish in printers' shops . . . your soul shall be placed with Dante's Beatrice, or Virgil's Anchises' (*D* 120.36–121.26).

Chapter 8

From Favour to Eternal Life: Trajectories of Grace and the Poetic Career in the Sonnets of Henry Constable and Barnabe Barnes
María Jesús Pérez-Jáuregui

In the summer of 1591, poets Henry Constable (1562–1613) and Barnabe Barnes (1571–1609) joined the Earl of Essex's expedition to France.[1] The rising star Robert Devereux could not have failed to attract two men who had started out with promising prospects and were making their way in a world that was notoriously difficult for the unknighted heir of a knight and a bishop's third son.[2] Their acquaintance is uncertain, but their lives and careers yield some striking points of convergence that have so far been unexplored. They turned to writing poetry as a means of seeking patronage and protection, but their efforts yielded mixed results. Constable converted to Catholicism, gave up everything he had been working towards and lived in exile for over a decade, unable to benefit from his fledgling literary reputation.[3] Barnes, apparently the boisterous type, was ridiculed by literary rivals, made a bad choice of enemies and later even stood accused of attempted murder.[4] As writers, both men performed a shift of interest from the secular to the sacred at about the same time, when they were living abroad between 1594 and 1595.[5] They died unmarried and without issue.

Constable's reputation largely rested on *Diana. The praises of his Mistres, in certaine sweete Sonnets* (1592), an edition of twenty-three amatory sonnets that is nevertheless only a sample of a much vaster collection that survives in manuscript.[6] Barnes's *Parthenophil and Parthenophe* saw the light a year later. Often considered a medley of poetic forms of inconsistent quality, it was still a remarkable achievement for a man of 22, displaying a wide range of formal experimentation.[7] As far as religious poetry is concerned, Constable's *Spiritual Sonnets*, very obviously the work of a Catholic, were unpublishable in England and had a limited circulation.[8] Barnes's *A Divine Centurie of Spirituall Sonnets* was more palatable to Protestant tastes and was printed in 1595 by John Windet.

Barnes's voyage from secular into religious themes parallels Constable's. Both redeploy language in a way that is consistent with deliberate moves in their poetic career; the same words are often used and made to acquire different layers of meaning to serve a new, more elevated purpose. A salient key term that is explored in all its semantic possibilities and nuances throughout and across the four collections is *grace*. The shared secular connotations of the word, arisen from the common ground of Petrarchan sonneteering, give way to the poets' expression of divergent religious beliefs, according to which the workings of divine grace vary.[9] For Barnes, grace is linked with the doctrine of *sola gratia* by which human beings are saved; his Protestant notion of predestination determines all aspects of life, his poetic gift included. In Constable's verse, the repentant speaker, under the influence of prevenient grace, undertakes a journey to merit salvation with the help of the Virgin and saints.

In both Constable's and Barnes's sonnets there is a despairing lover who hopes to win the favour of an angelic lady. Confessional differences notwithstanding, the poet later transcends his worldly subject matter and enters a one-sided conversation with the divine, and does so by articulating the various meanings of grace. This chapter will trace the trajectories of grace in the sonnets by Constable and Barnes in an attempt to uncover parallels and points of discrepancy. It ultimately aims to chart an upwards move through which each poet reaches not only for the divine but also for transcendence and the fulfilment of literary ambition. Both authors develop a practical poetics that is surprisingly similar as an attempt to change course, *un*writing a career that, at an early stage, had looked to earthly matters only.

Grace and the Lady-Saint in the Secular Sonnets

Parthenophe, the lady addressed in Barnes's amatory collection, is presented as the most inaccessible sort of Petrarchan mistress. Her name evokes her chastity, which is seen as an insurmountable obstacle by the frustrated Parthenophil, driving him to voice an array of emotions ranging from melancholy to jealousy or rage.[10] She is exceedingly beautiful; her 'graces', that is, her attractive attributes, are frequently invoked. Indeed, they open the sequence:

> Mystrisse behold in this true-speaking Glasse,
> Thy beauties Graces of all women rarest,
> Where thou maist finde how largely they surpasse
> And staine in glorious louelynesse the fayrest. (1.1–4)[11]

The poet's verse is said to function as a mirror of her beauty, which was a conventional enough trope. It is no coincidence that he should have chosen the same mirror motif to conclude the sequence. His poetry, he insists, fails to encompass the totality of Parthenophe's beauty, which escapes the powers of his Muse. 'Graces' occurs both in the second and the second-to-last line in his sonnet collection, and can be considered a key word in terms of structure:[12]

> Hold (matchlesse myrrour of all womankind)
> These pennes, and Sonnettes, seruaunts of thy prayse,
> ...
> Thine endlesse graces are so amiable,
> Passing the spirite of my humble muse,
> So that the more I write more graces rise
> Which myne astonish't muse cannot comprise. (104.1–2, 11–14)

The lady's beauty is often equated to or connected with the mythological Graces, as in sonnet 64, in which the love complaint is rife with allusions to gods and goddesses, and the term 'graces' appears three times in as many consecutive lines:

> If all the loues were lost, and should be founde,
> And all the graces glories were decayde,
> In thee the graces ornamentes abounde,
> In me the loues by thy sweet graces layde. (64.1–4)

In sonnet 71, her eyes are 'two cleare springs of graces gratious named, / There graces infinite do bathe, and sporte' (4–5). The mythological sisters bathe in them; metaphorically, Parthenophe's beauty and charm streams from her eyes as a source or fountain. Barnes employs the rhetorical devices of polyptoton and antanaclasis in this sonnet and the next, in which goddesses Phoebe and Juno compare the nymph-like Parthenophe with the graces and find her superior in beauty, to the extent that 'in her cheekes the graces blush for shame' (72.13).

Grace becomes a locus of tension when it is used to refer to the lady's lack of favour and pity. When the two meanings are presented together to refer to the good-looking but pitiless Parthenophe, the word stands in an oxymoronic relationship with itself. Sonnet 73 is one of the best examples and deserves to be quoted in full:

> Why did rich nature graces grant to thee,
> Since thou art such a niggard of thy grace?
> Or how can graces in thy body bee
> Where neither they, nor pittie finde a place?
> Ah they bene handmaydes to thy bewties furie,
> Making thy face to tyrannise on men.
> Condemn'd before thy bewtie by loues Iurie,
> And by thy frownes adiudg'd to sorrowes den.
> Graunt me some grace, for thou with grace art wealthie
> And kindely mayst afforde some gratious thing,
> Mine hopes all as my minde weake and vnhealthie,
> All her lookes gratious, yet no grace do bring
> To me poore wretche, yea be the graces theare:
> But I the furies in my brest doe beare.

'Grace' and derived words mean beauty in lines 1, 3, 9 (second instance), 12 ('gratious') and 13. They stand for the lady's favour in lines 2, 4 ('they'), 9 (first instance), 10 and 12 ('grace'). This means that there are five occurrences of the word in each sense throughout the sonnet, creating a perfect balance – or unresolved tension. Additionally, in line 9 the lover presents himself as a man condemned before a 'jury', so grace takes on the additional meaning of pardon or an act of clemency. In the final couplet, the mythological allusion to the Three Graces and the Three Furies serves to contrast her beauty with the poet's state of mind. Parthenophil voices no melancholy acceptance of his fate but bitter anger.

In the Petrarchan tradition, the poetic mistress is often presented as a divine creature, a *donna angelicata*. Hence grace is an attribute ascribed to the lady-saint in Barnes's sonnets. The words that come out of her mouth are described as angelic: 'And from loues rubie portall louely rushes / For euery word she speakes an Angels grace' (26.11–12).[13] However, Parthenophe's divinity is undermined by her lack of mercy towards the poet, given that this quality is associated with Christian *caritas*. In sonnet 28, the lover complains that the lady is stonehearted and she ignores his plight:

> When I begge grace, thou myne intreatie spurnes:
> Mine hart with hope vpheld, with feare returnes
> Betwixt these passions endlesse is my fit
> Then if thou bee but humaine grant some pitie

> Or if a saint sweet mercies are there meedes
> Faire louely chast sweet-spoken learned wittie
> These make thee saint-like and these saints befit
> But thine hard hart makes all these graces weedes. (7–14)

Pity could be expected of a human woman, and mercy of a saint. Despite her many heavenly attributes, duly enumerated in line 12, her cruelty – understood as a lack of grace towards the lover-devotee – essentially offsets them, and she is portrayed in strikingly negative terms in the final line. The implication is that, in order to be truly divine, the lady should take pity on the poet and yield to his desires, which seems ironic in that giving in to lust would ruin the chastity that makes her a saint in the first place. This fundamental conflict simply cannot be resolved.

Among the amatory sonnets of Henry Constable, the closest parallel to Barnes's sonnet 73 is one in which the word 'favour', synonymous with 'grace', takes on different meanings; this is Constable's own exercise in antanaclasis:

> Ladye in beautye and in favoure rare,
> Of favoure, not of due, I favoure crave;
> Nature to thee beautye and favoure gave,
> Fayre then thow arte, and favoure thow mayst spare. (10.1–4)

The word 'grace' is also used to contrast the lady's attributes and her lack of compassion – albeit Constable's persona exhibits considerably less bitterness than Barnes's. This does not happen within the same sonnet but across his amatory production. His mistress is praised for her 'gratiouse lookes' in sonnet 49, which contrast with her 'hard and disgratious words', mentioned in the heading to an occasional piece. In the text the poet complains that his 'hope laye gasping on his dying bed / slayne with a word' (64.1–2).[14]

As in Barnes, grace is perceived to be a quality of the lady as a divine being in Constable's amatory poetry. In sonnet 20, the speaker persuades her to show him favour. After explaining that a friend has urged him to give up on his love because the lady cannot be moved, the poet asks her to prove his friend wrong and do something apparently impossible, which is what a god or goddess would do:

> Gods only doe impossibilityes;
> Impossible, sayth he, thy grace to gayne.
> Shew then the powers of devinityes

> By graunting me thy favour to obtayne.
> So shall thy foe give to himselfe the lye;
> A goddesse thow shalt prove, and happie I. (20.9–14)

If his mistress's grace is bestowed on him, the poet's friend will be figuratively defeated, she will prove that she is a goddess – having worked a miracle – and the poet will achieve his heart's desire.

In Constable's secular sonnets, 'grace' acquires another – unique – layer of meaning, which is woven together with religious overtones. The introductory sonnet in the MS Dyce 44 collection dedicates the whole sequence 'To his Mistrisse', and opens with a curious apostrophe:

> Grace, full of grace, though in these verses heere
> My love complaynes of others then of thee,
> Yet thee alone I lov'd . . . (1.1–3)

It evokes the apostrophe to the Virgin Mary, 'Hail Mary, full of grace', and thence a form of Catholic prayer; the lady is praised as a Mary-like figure – whereas Barnes, a Protestant, never goes that far. The possibilities for wordplay are enhanced by the fact that Constable's addressee is called Grace; she was Grace Pierrepont, a young lady whom he might have intended to marry.[15] The sonnet may work as a preface, but it reads almost like a farewell. It is the poet's last attempt at romantic love, written about the time of his conversion. If unsuccessful, he promises to give up love altogether and turn to God, who – unlike the lady – will have mercy on him and save him from further lovelorn suffering:

> To him I flye for grace that rules above,
> That by my Grace I may live in delight
> Or by his grace I never more may love. (1.12–14)

Similar wordplay is found in a sonnet to Grace's aunt, Mary Talbot, Countess of Shrewsbury, in which he complains about his unrequited love for her niece, possibly lodging with Mary at the time, and asks for her intercession. This is all the more significant considering that the Countess was a devout Catholic:

> A warrioure of youre campe by force of eyes
> Mee pris'ner tooke, and will with rigor deale
> Except yow pity in youre heart will place,
> At whose white hands I only seeke for grace. (38.11–14)

If the possessive 'youre' is correct, and not a scribal error replacing third person 'her', the poet is pinning his faith on being able to move the Countess so that she will sanction his courtship. His desire for 'grace' is as much a plea for mercy or intercession as a direct, literal allusion to his mistress.

In both Barnes's and Constable's secular sonnets, the speaker presents himself as disconsolate, irate or – at most – mildly hopeful in his attempt to woo a lady who is fundamentally out of his reach. She emerges as a contradictory figure in that she boasts every positive physical and psychological attribute but one, the willingness to return the speaker's affections and thus metaphorically spare him the suffering of unrequited love. Grace is ascribed to the lady in all its multiplicity of meanings through the use of rhetorical devices such as antanaclasis; what emerges is a *donna angelicata* who is, at the same time, full of grace and utterly devoid of it; she can only preserve her sanctity by denying the poet her mercy.

Recantation as a Career Move

The final manuscript collection of Constable's secular sonnets can be holistically appraised as a landmark in his career or, rather, a conscious career move.[16] On the verge of, or perhaps fully immersed in, a process of conversion, he gathers together the fruits of his poetic efforts, neatly organises them under sections and subheadings, and adds the introductory sonnet, his parting gift to 'Grace', and some materials that both serve as a conclusion and give the sequence – and the first part of his poetic career – closure.[17] A short prose inscription between the second-to-last and last sonnets records a momentous decision:

> When I had ended this last sonnet and found that such vayne poems as I had by idle houres writ did amount to the climatericall number 63, me thought it was high tyme for my follie to die and to employe the remnant of wit to other calmer thoughts lesse sweete and lesse bitter. (42v)

It is significant that Constable the poet does not give up writing altogether. The climacteric number seems to manifest to him as some sort of revelation, a signal urging him to change direction; it could hardly have been accidental, given his concern with balance and proportion, but he seems to want his prospective readers to think otherwise.[18] Here he is manifesting an intention to move on to the next stage of his poetic career, leaving behind the frenzies and the despair of his amatory endeavours in verse, now seen with hindsight as the product of his foolishness – the old meaning 'lewdness' is perhaps implicit. By doing so he joins a tradition of written recantation of earlier, or youthful, poetry and his career takes an Ovidian turn in that, like the Roman poet, he expresses a regretful attitude towards his former works.[19] As Prescott puts it, 'Renaissance poets could think the love sonnet a beginner's genre', whereas 'divine poetry was . . . both an alternative to secular literature and a means of ascent to something new'.[20]

That Constable's move is going to be upwards, to God, is perhaps hinted at in the very last sonnet, number 63, which functions as a petition to Lady Arbella Stuart, a potential candidate for the English throne, to protect his book:

> So, like twin byrds, my Muse bred with her fame,
> Together now doe learne theyre wings to use.
> And in this booke which heere yow may peruse
> Abroad they flye, resolv'd to try the same
> Adventure in theyre flight; and thee, sweet dame,
> Both she and I for oure protectoure chuse. (3–8)

The avian conceit by which he and his mistress, his poetic reputation and her eternal fame, fly safely under Arbella's wing can be read in the light of Cheney's notion of 'the myth of the winged poet', used by poets 'to communicate the workings and goals of their art'.[21] With some wistfulness, Constable the poet imagines a scenario in which his sociopolitical aspirations and romantic desire could come together, fulfilled in the same space and time: 'O happie if I might but flitter there, / Where yow and shee and I should be so neare' (63.13–14). If the feeling of disillusionment with earthly affairs is to be taken seriously and deemed consistent with his prose renunciation, the envisioned destination of this flight upwards may be heaven, where souls are reunited after death, and the next stage in his career religious poetry. Failing to obtain grace literally and figuratively, the poet readies himself to embrace a life devoted to spiritual matters. He seems bent on a Virgilian career path, a self-conscious ascent; however, it is hard to forget that the poet's progress in terms of public literary achievement and fame was thwarted by the exile ensuing from his conversion, rendering Constable an Ovidian figure with an 'after-career' charged with plaintiveness and a sense of displacement.[22] The word 'abroad' in the sonnet quoted above points at this tension between fame and fleeing; it means 'in public' or 'in general circulation', which hints at his poetry being read by a wider audience, and it also means away from home, perhaps in the current 'overseas' sense, in a thinly veiled allusion to his contemplation of exile.

Like Constable, Barnes comments on the former stage of his career and expresses an intention to write in the praise of God. The shift is expressed textually. In the epistle to the reader that prefaces his *Divine Centurie of Spirituall Sonnets*, the poet refers to Du Bartas and describes the writing of religious poetry as elevating; it brings the poet closer to God and renders him 'more then man', whereas other poetic endeavours are the product of 'humane furie', which debases man.[23] It is not surprising that the first sonnet in the collection should have an avian conceit depicting the metamorphosis of the poetic muse from a baser kind of winged creature, a sparrow, into one endowed with angelic wings:[24]

> No more lewde laies of Lighter loues I sing,
> Nor teach my lustfull Muse abus'de to flie,
> With Sparrowes plumes and for compassion crie,
> To mortall beauties which no succour bring.
> But my Muse fethered with an Angels wing,
> Diuinely mounts aloft vnto the skie. (1.1–6)

It is Him alone, and not a lady, that kindles his desire, and he promises to make 'Thy loue my theame and holy Ghost my Muse' (1.14). This series of substitutions confirms the renunciation of his amatory poetry and sets the tone for the collection.

In their recantations, both Constable and Barnes seem to accomplish two things at the same time. They reflect on a stage in their poetic career that they deem to be over and express a desire to unwrite it by moving on to a loftier subject matter. Nevertheless, their denial amounts to emphasis. The use of expressions such as 'high time', 'now' and 'no more' leaves the reader to ponder what exactly is being renounced; the fundamental shift cannot be understood without knowledge of the love sonnets which the poets purport to be dispensing with. Despite the two poets' changing feelings towards their previous self-image, the poems remained in circulation; they were left behind, not buried.[25]

Grace in the Religious Sonnets

Reading Constable's and Barnes's religious sequences side by side reveals obvious differences but also common ground. Barnes's

Divine Centurie was published in print and dedicated to Tobie Matthew, Bishop of Durham, to whom he writes in the prefatory epistle that the sonnets were composed during his travels in France and devoted to God 'daily to his honour by prescribed taske' (sig. A2v).[26] There is the sense of an intention to undertake a project; as Marcy North notes, 'the task is disciplined and focused, not occasional or casual'.[27] In terms of organisation, Barnes himself admits that his sequence 'may to some readers seem disordered and straunge', with an 'unequall coherence' (sig. A3v). Earl takes this at face value, but nevertheless identifies some landmarks or 'cardinal points', and loosely delimited thematic groups.[28]

Constable's *Spiritual Sonnets* were largely unknown; they were kept close, copied in manuscript and probably shared with a reduced Catholic coterie only.[29] The copy at Berkeley Castle, a booklet containing twenty-one sonnets, is the most perfect in terms of organisation. The poems are intricately arranged in groups and triads informed by strong numerological and hierarchical concerns.[30] The same careful structuring that Constable applied to his secular sonnets in their last, definite compilation seems to be at work in the sacred, lending authority to the manuscript's readings.

Besides the poets' choice of medium and its implications, another fundamental difference lies in the religious landscape presented in the sonnets themselves. In Constable's *Spiritual Sonnets*, that landscape is populated by the Trinitarian God, the Virgin Mary and a panoply of saints, perfected human beings who, having merited salvation, are capable of aiding the poet, and are thus petitioned for spiritual succour and intercession. The Virgin and the female saints honoured, in particular, effectively replace the earthly mistresses of the secular sonnets. In the tenth sonnet, St Catherine of Alexandria is presented as a female paragon; the term 'grace' is used with multiple meanings:[31]

> Because thou was the Daughter of A kinge,
> whose beautie did all natures wourkes exceede
> and wysedome wonder to the wourlde did breed,
> a muse might rayse it self on Cupids winge.
> But sithe these graces which from nature springe
> were grac'd by those which from grace did proceed
> & glory have deserv'd, my muse doth neede
> an Angelles feathers when thie prayse I singe. (10.1–8)

In this instance of antanaclasis, the first occurrence of 'graces' refers to her natural attributes: nobility, beauty and wisdom, which would make her a worthy Petrarchan mistress (4). But these qualities were embellished by God's divine 'grace' (6), which made her an exemplary Christian and a martyr who has deserved 'glory' (7). Constable returns to the avian or flight conceit in this sonnet, with angels' wings far surpassing Cupid's and enabling the poet's muse to soar higher.

The landscape in Barnes's *Divine Centurie*, on the contrary, is populated by God alone. His grace is all-encompassing, unmerited and bestowed directly on the believer. Barnes's sonnets are informed by a specifically Protestant rationale, which Lewalski summarises in her volume on John Donne in the following way:

> [M]an's salvation is wholly the work of God ... Because the image of God in man is almost wholly destroyed by original sin its restoration must be wholly God's work, effected by the merits of Christ and apprehended by a faith which is itself the gift of God.[32]

This Protestant view is fully illustrated in sonnet 53, which begins with a powerful question – 'Didst thou redeeme my soule, my sole saluation?' (1) – and provides an account of the human soul's original purity and later regeneration enacted by Christ's sacrifice:

> Because at our forefathers first creation,
> Hee in his breast by sacred inspiration,
> From his owne mouth (which did so well beseeme it)
> Breathed a soule diuine, then let vs deeme it
> A gracious, precious and deare immolation,
> For him to saue our soules with his bloodshed. (53.3–8)

No intercession is necessary or possible in Barnes's view; therefore, there is no place in the sequence for anyone but God, and the Virgin and the saints are excluded as addressees.[33] Only God replaces earthly mistresses as the object of devotion and praise. In sonnet 2, the poet muses on Christ's sacrifice and His blood comes to replace the eyes of the Petrarchan mistress as the source of all love to which the wretched sinner needs to respond; Barnes juxtaposes the conventions proper to love poetry, so familiar to him, with renewed spiritual concerns:

> In steede of lustfull eyes with arrowes fillde:
> Of sinfull loues which from their beames abound.
> Let those sweete blessed wounds with streames of grace,
> Aboundantly sollicite my poore spirite:
> Rauish'de with loue of thee that didst debase
> Thy selfe on earth that I might heauen inherite. (2.7–12)

The 'streames of grace' effectively cleanse and heal his soul in the final couplet, and render the poet aware of and grateful for this freely bestowed salvation.

Grace is described by Halewood as 'God's inexplicable benevolence' that 'passes all distances and overcomes all obstacles'.[34] Its healing properties pervade Barnes's sequence. It is often imagined in a liquefied state to emphasise its permeating capabilities, with phrases such as 'thy graces louely Riuer' (26.5), 'siluer streame of grace' (68.2); it distils from God 'in full aboundance' (15.6), compared to an 'Antidote' (2.2), a 'nectre' or elixir that purifies (2.14). The state of the sinner's soul, or heart, is constantly depicted as wounded: 'my wounded hart with pearsed conscience bleedes' (25.7). This 'wound', emphatically described with epithets such as 'foule' (19.9) and 'desperate' (77.3), or with gruesome images of festering or rotting (77.3), can only be cured with grace by way of an ointment: 'gracious oyle' (10.10), 'oyle of mercies and sweete grace' (19.10), 'his gentle graces Oyle, his mercies balme' (64.2).[35] The epithets 'Gracious shepheard' (9.1), 'gracious bridegroome' (5.9) or 'bounteous giver of all graces' (75.6) are employed to refer to God. His grace is, of course, 'endless' (38.13) or 'eternal' (87.3), 'lively' in that it is life-giving for the spiritually dead sinner (15.12), and, above all, unmerited – men are deemed 'worthlesse' (65.7) or 'not worthie' (56.5). The musical quality and repetition of some of these phrases is reminiscent of the language in the Psalms, which have been identified as the main source for Barnes's sonnets.[36]

One particular description of grace as incense or perfume is shared by Constable and Barnes. In Constable's 'To God the Father', which opens the sequence, the poet beseeches God to let his soul become a true *imago Dei*, 'and sence my harte with sighes of holie love / that it the temple of the sprite may prove' (1.13–14). Barnes's appeal is strikingly similar: 'O let my soule (thy Temple) be perfum'de / With sacred incense of thy vertuous grace' (4.9–10).[37] This evidences that biblical references worked cross-confessionally, and some metaphors came from a shared pool of knowledge at the disposal of both Catholic and Protestant writers.[38] In this instance of comparison of divine grace to incense the underlying notion could be what Manley refers to as an 'infusion . . . *de sursum descendens*, which allowed the soul to perceive the beauty of god'.[39]

A major preoccupation in both sequences is the status of the sinner. The two poets mournfully repent their sinful life focused on earthly passions, and, by extension, on amatory poetry. The speaker in Barnes expresses sorrow over his many shortcomings, for instance in sonnet 40:

> My daies bee few, my sinnes past number bee,
> Adde to my daies (Oh God) more time of grace,
> And mercy to my sinnes: behold my case,
> With eyes of gracious pittie looke on mee:
> My wounded and afflicted conscience see,
> My soule afraide to stand before thy face. (1–6)

Grace is the divine gift that the poet longs for; he presents himself as 'him that penitently sues for grace' despite his sins (40.4), which he depicts in colourful terms such as 'the large blacke bill / Of my dead sinnes' (3.7–8); they 'sting' or prick his soul (e.g., 19.4, 34.5). In true Protestant fashion, the sinner cannot work towards his salvation. In her study of Donne, Papazian has referred to the 'irony' that arises in the *Holy Sonnets*: 'as readers of Donne's divine poems of religious anxiety – if not the speakers themselves – know, the very ability of these speakers to contemplate their sinfulness is itself a sign of God's presence with them'.[40] Regardless of his momentary lapses in confidence throughout the sequence, the speaker in Barnes knows that his 'very ability . . . to call out to God', not only in prayer but also in writing, is a sure sign of grace being at work in him.[41]

As a Catholic convert, the speaker in Constable has no such assurances. He must undergo the different stages of the sacrament of penance, from contrition to confession and satisfaction, and he asks for assistance during his journey along the *via penitentiae*. In a sonnet meditating on the Blessed Sacrament, he asks God to 'quench' in his heart 'the flames of bad desire' following His assimilation into the communicant's body during the Eucharist (4.14). His best explorations of the theme of penitence take a woman saint, Mary Magdalene, as the exemplary penitent worthy of emulation. In the seventh sonnet in the sequence, the poet muses on the Magdalene's legendary penance in the desert and the metaphorical wasteland in which his sinful soul lives:[42]

> In suche a place my soule doth seeme to bee
> when in my boddye she laments her synne
> and non but brutall passions findes therein,
> excepte they be sent downe from heaven to me.
> Yet if those graces god to me imparte
> which he inspir'd thy blessed brest withall,
> I may finde heaven in my retyred harte.
> And if thou change the objecte of my love,
> the wing'd affection which men Cupid call
> may gett his sight and like an Angell prove. (7.5–14)

Inspired by the success story of the Magdalene, the poet prays that divine grace will be the inspiration he needs to overcome sin and be reconciled with God and infused with a holier type of love through penance. Struggle lies ahead: the poet is not certain of salvation; he hopes to become worthy of it so that he may go to heaven, and faith must go hand in hand with actions. In a collection fraught with longing and anxiety, the Virgin and the female saints, in particular, are asked to point the way. He petitions St Margaret for chastity mirroring hers: 'Give me then puritie, in steed of powre / and lett my soule, made chaste, passe for a mayde' (11.13–14); the Virgin will inspire him, through contemplation of her 'lovely face' (13.6), to leave worldly ambition behind and transcend into the only true court in God's realm.

The above sonnet presents the theme of the conflict between body and soul, which is common to Constable and Barnes, although with significant nuances. In *Divine Centurie*, the poet states in his address to the reader that his sequence arises out of 'inseperable combat betwixt earth and my spirite' (sig. A3r). The recurrent image remains one of violent strife:

> My soule through manifold assaults of sinne
> (In grieuous combate with my flesh retain'de)
> Declining faintes, vnlesse it bee sustain'de:
> Then send thy mercies which might enter in,
> To seuer them least further broyles beginne (97.1–5)

God's grace is invoked as that which can intervene and settle the matter. There is a certain dynamic quality to this struggle: the Devil works incessantly to corrupt the sinner's soul, but God can – and indeed does – succour him:

> Mee swallowed in the gulfe of sinne behold:
> A Lambe amongst wilde wolues (once of thy fold)
> Whom Sathan now doth for his porcion craue:
> Deare sonne of Dauid helpe, yet helpe with speede (13.6–9)

In the *Spiritual Sonnets*, the body is a prison for the soul, holding back its purification and progress towards God. The speaker's soul is portrayed as 'shutt in' his 'bodies Jayle' (11.9); it is at odds with a body overcome with 'brutall passions' (7.7).

Earl has observed that, despite the obvious influence of the penitential Psalms, in particular, Barnes 'undertakes the penitential mode only to a limited extent' and expends more poetic energy on the praise of God:

Barnes proclaims his repentance in a more subtle Calvinist fashion and seeks the means of newness of life and the chance . . . to praise his Maker and Redeemer. To that extent, in looking for new life upon earth, his poetry is life-affirming, and . . . the final intution in the reader's mind must be optimistic, and so hopeful in the deeper Christian sense.[43]

There are indeed moments of great joy and confidence in the sequence, such as sonnet 43, in which Satan tempts the poet as he travels abroad but fails to doom him because grace is already at work within him:

> But now behold Gods mercie to mee showne.
> Hee gracious, louing, mercifull, and wise,
> Declar'd expressely that I was ordaind
> Vnto saluation, for that enterprise
> Of Sathans mou'de my soule (before profaind)
> To purge it selfe, with that repentant grace,
> Which mee shall saue from hell, and him displace. (8–14)

Whereas Barnes's religious poetry, like his theology, is life-affirming, Constable's can be read as life-denying. A core idea is that happiness is not to be found in this life but in the next. In a little-known sonnet to St Colette, the patron saint of his birth day, grace is the resulting state of the poet's perfected soul after purification is complete:

> Yf I to longe in earthes affection staye,
> lett this thy better liffe teache me to see
> howe I muste strive to sett my spiritt free
> before true lyffe and Joye I purchase maye.
> When I was borne, I lefte with grieffe and woe
> my mothers wombe, & for to lyve againe
> I muste with payne from my owne bodye goe;
> firste from the lustes thereof to live in grace,
> then from it self before I cann obtayne
> a lyfe of glorye in thy dwellinge place. (12.5–14)

Life on earth is depicted as a vale of tears and a transitory state, and the poet must undergo a double pain – that of renouncing earthly passions and the more literal one of illness and death – before achieving eternal life. The tone is markedly sombre. The only moments of true joy in Constable's religious sonnets are those in which the emphasis shifts to life in heaven and the soul's union with God is imagined. He draws upon erotic or marital imagery to describe the state of bliss associated with the mystical ascent and union.[44]

> My boddy is the garment of my sprite
> while as the daye time of my liffe doth laste;
> when death shall bringe the night of my delighte
> My soule, uncloth'd, shall rest from labours paste
> and, clasped in the arms of god, enjoye,
> by sweete conjunction, everlastinge Joye. (18.9–14)

There is little mysticism in Barnes's poetry and erotic language is used more sparsely. He nevertheless anticipates John Donne's depiction of God's ravishing of the soul in *Holy Sonnets*, for instance in *Divine Centurie* sonnet 2, 'rauish'de with love of thee' (11). Later in the sequence grace inflames the poet with divine love, which drives the poet to praise Him:

> Kindle my spirit with that sacred heate,
> Which me may rauish with an heauenly Loue:
> Whil'st I thy ceaselesse graces doe repeate (8.10–12)

Barnes's protestations that the *Divine Centurie* arose out of his own spiritual conflict and in 'especiall occasions and in earnest true motions of the spirite' (sig. A3v) are deemed 'an interesting ploy' by Serjeantson, who notes their relatively impersonal, universal character and use of widely available, ready-made images.[45] Barnes offers an account of the spiritual life of the Protestant believer to which the notion of justification is central; his sequence is safely conventional in its theology, publishable and published, available to readers who might benefit from it. Constable's religious sonnets, as a whole, have an air of privacy or sincerity which, as has been argued, 'is rare in the secular sonnets'.[46] There was little immediate social gain to be expected from writing fiercely Catholic sonnets; the poet knows it, and he trusts that his ultimate reward will be reaped in the life to come.

Self-affirming and Self-denying Poetics

Constable and Barnes made a conscious decision to devote their energies to religious verse that replaced their earlier secular lyrics. Drawing upon Cheney's classification of career models, they stand at a crossroads between the Virgilian and the Augustinian models. The former traces the ascent from lower to higher genres. The latter 'emphasizes the poet's need to end such a career by turning from youthful, courtly, erotic poetry to aged, contemplative, divine poetry'.[47] As in the case of Spenser, their shift took place in the mid-1590s, when the influence of

Du Bartas was at its peak.[48] In the French poet's invocation to Urania, poetry is a God-sent gift and an unequivocally Christian divine fury rightfully replaces the more pagan *furor poeticus*.

Barnes deploys this notion of divine gift; in the *Divine Centurie* it is a state of heavenly rapture resulting from the inspiration of the Holy Spirit on the poet, as in the final couplet in sonnet 29: 'Rayons of comfort through my Temples pearse, / And consecrate my Muse to sacred verse'. In another, the speaker, grateful for God's redemption, turns his talent 'to praise the Lord' and compels fellow poets to do the same: 'Nay try (vain Poets) try, that King, that place, / If God, and heauen, giue not your Muse most grace' (39.13–14). He reflects upon his own literary prowess and asserts its connection with divine grace in sonnet 50: 'that facultie / with which thou didst mee worthlesse beautifie' (2–3). The poet seeks to return God's gift by devoting all his energy to His praise, in an act of reciprocation or gift exchange which further proves the life-affirming character of Barnes's poetics – the act of writing is to be carried out on earth:

> That all my thoughts thy Testament embrace,
> That all my wits thy tearmelesse grace set out,
> That by thee praising I may shew thy grace
> Which in large Talent thou to mee let out (26.9–12)

'Talent' is a key term here, and its equation with grace is paramount; in its original fifteenth-century meaning, it referred to an ability granted by God to a person. It was therefore linked to godliness in the Protestant sense.[49]

Barnes is not only looking to Du Bartas but also drawing on a concept central to Renaissance sacred rhetorics; in Shuger's words, 'to express one's own feelings is to express one's response to the inner presence of the Spirit'. These feelings are articulated by means of 'figures of thought'.[50] At certain points in the *Divine Centurie*, rhetorical devices fall short and the poet despairs at the inadequacy of language, leading to 'conventional aphasia'.[51] Sonnet 22 is an enumeration of epithets given to God but language fails him in the very last line: 'What man can giue due glorious Epithites?' (32.14). God's grace is such a gift that no degree of gratefulness suffices:

> Oh where shall I finde to my spirite voice?
> Where to my voice sufficient choyce of words?
> To shew how much my spirite doth reioyce
> In those large blessings, which thy grace affords? (65.8–11)

Despite the limitations of language, from a Protestant standpoint poetic talent and its rightful application confirm the poet's status among the elect. The connection between poetry and eternal life is made explicit in sonnet 70, in which the winged poet motif and the idea of ascent return:

> Vnto my spirite lend an Angels wing,
> By which it might mount to that place of rest,
> Where Paradice may mee releeue opprest.
> Lend to my tongue an Angels voice to sing (1–4)

Towards the end the poet imagines himself 'In spotlesse white', bound to wear 'an Angels Crowne' in the afterlife (13–14). He is to become one of God's 'Saints' (e.g., 16.9, 33.12) a term that does not refer to the men and women from Catholic hagiology, but to God's chosen.

In the *Spiritual Sonnets* Constable also enacts the career shift he promised in the conclusion to his secular collection. In Augustinian fashion, 'mastery of the word' is turned to the praise of God instead of being used as a means to fulfil his earthly ambitions.[52] He does not articulate the notion of divine *furor*, but turns to the heavenly court and its king as an alternative to fallible monarchs and ungrateful patrons – whose protection he had sought and failed to achieve in any lasting way. He reflects on the futility of his desires for material gain in a sonnet to the Virgin:

> Soveraigne of Queens, yf vayne ambition move
> my harte to seeke an earthly princes grace,
> shewe me thy sonne in his imperiall place
> whose servants raigne, o're kinges & Queens, above. (13.1–4)

The use of 'grace' here is significant; the implication is that God's grace, unlike earthly monarchs' favour, will be everlasting:

> Soe by ambition I shall humble be
> when in the presence of the highest kinge
> I serve all his, that he may honnor me. (9–12)

If the poet successfully atones for his sins and purifies his soul, he will merit a 'highe rewarde' (9.14) such as no monarch can bestow; it is described as 'true lyffe and Joye' (12.8) or 'everlasting Joye' (18.14), and as a 'place' or position in the heavenly court (16.1). Whereas the speaker in Barnes's sequence confidently asserts his own talent as a divine gift, what is transcendent in Constable's religious sonnets is his displacement of 'the urge for his own fame . . . into an urge to glorify God'.[53] In drawing upon the exact same conventions he had employed in his secular verse, Constable unwrites his career, only to rewrite it by denying ambition and fame – and, by extension, earthly life. His later poetics could therefore be termed self-denying. This denial is, on the page, merely a rhetorical ploy which stands at odds with the biographical facts surrounding the *Spiritual Sonnets*, which may indeed have been partially intended to curry favour with prospective Catholic patrons.[54]

Grace in Exile

Barnes's and Constable's voyage from secular into religious themes went hand in hand with their literal removal from home. Sonnet 41 in *Divine Centurie* links a 'forren nation', France, with temptations of the flesh, so much that the poet turns his 'sinfull eyes' towards God (1, 6). In the final lines, temporary displacement from his country makes the poet wish to be done with earthly matters altogether, and his literal change of language is made to prefigure the shift in his literary concerns:

> That (as I haue my natiue Countrie changed)
> So likewise from the world I may bee weaned:
> And as my weede with nation is estranged,
> I so may shine in Christian armes vnfeyned:
> And as I leaue my nations true language,
> My Muse may change for a diuiner rage. (9–14)

The circumstances surrounding Barnes's stay in France are obscure, although they were likely political rather than religious in nature.[55]

Constable's exile was much longer and was self-imposed – but it remained irrevocable for years, as he was not allowed back home. The sense that exile is equated with death pervades his poetic production. In the secular collection, the poet distances himself from the lady in order not to die, only to find out that 'absence' cannot save him (59.5) because he is doomed to endure a living death. In the *Spiritual Sonnets*, the poet is both alone and isolated, with only his language, poetic talent and faith to hold on to. He is dead to his country and his former friends. His poetry is life-denying not only because there is a better, eternal life to come but also because, like Ovid, he can 'only cope with his loss of identity by understanding exile as a living death'.[56] This renders Constable a peculiar figure as far as career poetics is concerned: following Virgil, he moves upwards; like Augustine, conversion elevates the nature of his concerns; lastly, as an Ovidian figure, exile brings his career and all his former aspirations to an abrupt halt, which forces him to find the rhetorical modes to deal with his expulsion from his former community and with his after-career. There is no ready comfort for a Catholic convert who, unlike Barnes, cannot seek solace in the idea of divine grace and his status as one of God's chosen, but must work tirelessly for his own salvation. Much as Ovid appealed to relatives and friends in his *Tristia* and *Epistulae ex Ponto*, Constable petitions a series of silent interlocutors to keep him company along his penitential journey. In this sense, grace recovers its former meaning of mercy, or favour, in that the poet asks for succour to cope with his sense of displacement and disconnection.

Conclusion: A Poetics of Grace

Never before has the poetry of Barnes and Constable been juxtaposed, perhaps due to the traditionally clear-cut division between Protestants and Catholics in historiography and literary criticism. Within the last two decades, this polarisation has begun to be transcended, with scholars emphasising the 'remarkable degree of cross-pollination of ideas, imagery, and texts across confessional divides'.[57] Indeed, the two authors inhabited the same political and cultural milieu, and it is possible to look for similarities and, in particular, shared keywords in their poetic production.

The semantic multiplicity of the term 'grace' is fully exploited in Barnes's and Constable's secular and religious sonnet sequences. Their shift from worldly concerns, articulated around petitions for the angelic lady's favour, to a focus on the divine is not only thematic but also a deliberate career move clearly seen at, and after, a turning point based on renunciation. The poets' perception of divine grace and its attainment is as different as could be expected of their opposed confessional stances, Barnes's firm belief in *sola gratia* contrasting with Constable's penitential course and his reliance on intercession. Grace is also central to their consideration of their own poetic talent and the purpose of their art: Barnes is grateful for the God-given gift of poetry, which he wants to devote to His praise; his poetics is affirming as much as Constable's is life-, self-, and even career-denying in that his *Spiritual Sonnets* unwrite his earlier courtly pieces, and he trades a concern with secular love, social ambition and earthly reward for a longing for communion with God and eternal life. Whereas the career move of both poets can be seen as Augustinian, and, to a limited extent, Virgilian in their ascent from a lower to a higher or more enlightened genre, Constable's exilic poetry can also be appraised in Ovidian terms; the isolated poet who has lost everything he knew is left to lament and petition for help and some form of intercession that will earn him grace.

This chapter has shown that neither Constable nor Barnes articulates the tenets underlying the unwriting of their poetic careers and the avowed rehabilitation of their self-image as poets in a prose manifesto or treatise on *ars poetica*. Instead, their poetics of grace remains unwritten, woven into the textual fabric of the sonnets through the deployment of shifting, contradictory and often irreconcilable meanings.

Notes

1. Essex led a contingent meant to aid the Huguenot Henri of Navarre in the suppression of rebels. See Sutherland, *Henry IV of France*, 405–8.
2. Henry Constable was the son of Sir Robert Constable, who had served the Crown in various capacities and held the positions of Marshal of Berwick and Lieutenant of the Ordnance; see Wickes, 'Henry Constable', 272. Sir Robert's good connections with court personages such as Sir Francis Walsingham and Lord Burghley kick-started his son's career. For an extensive, updated biography, see Constable, *Complete Poems*, ed. Pérez-Jáuregui. Barnes's father was Dr Richard Barnes (1532?–1587), bishop of Durham; see Dodds, 'Barnabe Barnes'.
3. Constable declared his Catholicism publicly while he was in France and deserted before he could be sent to England. He lived abroad until James I's accession, when he was allowed to return home.
4. He was drawn into the quarrel between Gabriel Harvey and Thomas Nashe and became a target of Nashe's satirical pen. See Cox, 'Barnes, Barnabe'.
5. See Dodds, 'Barnabe Barnes', 24; Wickes, 'Henry Constable', 278.
6. A second, augmented edition including sonnets by Sidney and unknown authors saw the light in 1594. The most comprehensive collection of Constable's sonnets survives in the miscellany MS Dyce 44, in the National Art Library, Victoria and Albert Museum (London), also known as the Todd MS. Quotations are from my own edition of its text (Constable, *Complete Poems*), which the publishers at the Pontifical Institute of Mediaeval Studies have kindly allowed me to reproduce.

7. Blank praises Barnes as a 'metrical experimentalist surpassed only by Spenser and Sidney', following the model of Petrarch and other continental poets in terms of metrical variety and range (*Lyric Forms*, 31).
8. MS Harley 7553, in the British Library, contains seventeen sonnets, whereas the later collection at Berkeley Castle, Gloucestershire, Select Books 85, has twenty-one. I am quoting from my edited text of the latter.
9. For a more general exploration of 'grace' as a keyword in the Renaissance, see Mac Carthy, 'Grace'.
10. The name derives from *parthénos*, 'virgin', an epithet given to the Greek goddess Athena.
11. Barnes, *Parthenophil and Parthenophe*, ed. Doyno, 3. All quotations are from this edition, containing a critical old-spelling text edited from the sole extant copy of the 1593 edition, with an apparatus and notes. Further references are given parenthetically in the text by sonnet and line number.
12. Note that sonnet 104 concludes the 'Sonnets' section of the 1593 volume, yet it is not the very last sonnet in the volume. One more sonnet serves as a prelude to the infamous 'Sestine 5', which concludes the book. It seems that Barnes was concerned about the structural integrity of each section; see Doyno's introduction in Barnes, *Parthenophil and Parthenophe*, lxvii–lxviii.
13. The poetic mistress's voice is described as angelic in other sonnets. See, for instance, Watson, *Hekatompathia*, sonnet 12, sig. B2v, and Constable's sonnet 11, 'Of the excellencye of his Ladies voice', the latter of which compares the singing lady to the angelic choir.
14. This sonnet survives only in an earlier manuscript, MS Z3.5.21, in Marsh's Library, Dublin, 25r. It is numbered 64 in my edition.
15. For the first identification of Grace with a real woman, see Lyall, 'Stella's Other Astrophel', 200. Grace was niece to the Countess of Shrewsbury, Mary Talbot, who was one of Constable's most esteemed relations. She would have been around 18 and unmarried at the time Constable was at court, in 1588–89.
16. The sonnets in MS Dyce 44 were copied by the miscellany compiler; despite being removed from the lost holograph, their integrity as a sequence is beyond doubt.
17. This career perspective rests on Lipking's statement that 'every major Western poet after Homer . . . has left some work that records the principles of his own poetic development'. Lipking extrapolates the argument to so-called minor poets, who, perhaps, had to prove themselves not only to merit a laurel garland but also to survive in the highly competitive world of patronage and thwarted ambitions (*Life of the Poet*, viii).
18. Parker focuses on Constable's concern with numerology as an organising principle in his sequence and discusses the significance of the numbers 63 and 21 (*Proportional Form*, 147–67).

19. See Cheney, 'Literary Careers', 179.
20. Prescott, 'Divine Poetry as a Career Move', 228 n.15, 223. Ferry mentions Petrarch's collection and its narrative 'development in distinctions between poems to Laura in life and in death', and Sidney's *Certaine Sonnets* and Barnes's sequences as version of Petrarch's 'pattern' (*The 'Inward' Language*, 217). Cheney centres on Spenser's renunciation of erotic poetry in *Fowre Hymnes* (*Spenser's Famous Flight*, 195). Constable was heavily influenced by French poets, and Du Bartas's 'L'Uranie' offered another secular-to-sacred poetic career model.
21. Cheney, *Spenser's Famous Flight*, 12.
22. Ovid was banished to Tomis by Augustus in 8 CE for obscure reasons that were at least partly related to the circumstances surrounding the *Ars amatoria*. Banishment interrupted Ovid's career trajectory, which had been one of ascent in terms of literary genres, following the Virgilian model; he stepped backwards from the epic *Metamorphoses* into the elegiac poetry with which he had started out, and his post-exile poetics has been termed one of 'unending lament'. See Barchiesi and Hardie, 'The Ovidian Career Model', 59–60; also, Hardie and Moore, 'Introduction', 6.
23. Barnes, *A Divine Century*, sig. A3v. As there is no contemporary edition of this collection, quotations are from the original edition. Further references are given parenthetically in the text by sonnet and line number. Prose is cited parenthetically by signature.
24. Catullus's poems on his lover Lesbia's sparrow were well known and the bird itself was often interpreted as a symbol for the intimate relationship that the poet longed for. See Mulroy, 'Introduction', in *Complete Poetry of Catullus*, xxviii.
25. In a recent essay, Vuillemin has stressed the continuity between Barnes's profane and spiritual sequences. He views the poet's 'recantation' as 'a strategic move the purpose of which was to modify his image as a poet' regardless of what Barnes's feelings 'about his life or about the subject matter of his poetry' might have been ('Barnabe Barnes's Sonnet Sequences', 133).
26. On the immediate publication context of Barnes's book, of which no manuscript survives, see Earl, 'Late Elizabethan Devotional Poetry', 223–4. This context included an array of Protestant devotional works but also some pertaining to the genre known as the literature of tears, eminently Catholic in character, by Jesuit priest Robert Southwell.
27. North, 'The Sonnets and Book History', 214.
28. Earl, 'Late Elizabethan Devotional Poetry', 225. A longer hymn serves as conclusion to the one hundred sonnets.
29. Marotti has pointed out that the manuscript medium favoured Catholic writers whose works could not easily fit into 'the censored public sphere of print' (*Manuscript, Print*, 44).
30. The sacred number three lies at the core of the sequence; an example of the hierarchical principle at work is the fact that the sequence opens

with three sonnets to the Trinity and the next follow the order in which the Virgin and the saints are mentioned in the Confiteor. The number 21 is also a third of 63, which seems hardly coincidental.
31. The numbers given are the order in which the sonnets appear within the sequence, as they are not individually numbered.
32. Lewalski, *Donne's Anniversaries and the Poetry of Praise*, 126.
33. This idea is emphasised by Earl: 'The Hebrew God who can achieve more lasting victories than his rivals has become the Protestant omnipotent Deity who alone, to the implicit exclusion of the Virgin and saints, deserves the ascription of might and majesty' ('Late Elizabethan Devotional Poetry', 238).
34. Halewood, *Poetry of Grace*, 54.
35. Christ's own wound is also invoked in contrast with sinners' 'wounded soules' (45.14), as He purchased the redemption of humankind with His blood.
36. Serjeantson observes that 'the individual sonnets of the *Divine Centurie* draw on the language and imagery of the psalms' and 'the sequence presents itself as a model of the Psalter' ('The Book of Psalms and the Early Modern Sonnet', 635).
37. The metaphor of the heart as a temple goes back to 1 Corinthians 6:19. Donne also employs it throughout *Holy Sonnets*, as in 11.3–4: 'How God the Spirit, by angels waited on / In Heav'n, doth make his temple in thy breast'. See Donne, *Complete Poems*, ed. Robbins, 556.
38. As a trend, 'biblical poetics' has been regarded 'exclusively as a component of Protestant poetics' since the 1970s. See Lewalski's discussion of biblical tropes in the third chapter of *Protestant Poetics*, 72–110. Nevertheless, even she admits that these tropes are not 'peculiar . . . to Protestants' (87).
39. Manley, 'Introduction', 27.
40. Papazian, 'The Augustinian Donne', 81.
41. Ibid., 82. Halewood notes that, in Protestant doctrine, 'emphasis on sin is not in itself morbid or negative . . . To recognize man's inherent sinfulness is to cease self-blame for failure to achieve righteousness and to appreciate the immense generosity of the gift of grace' (*Poetry of Grace*, 53).
42. This legend has its roots in the ninth century. After Christ's Ascension, 'Mary Magdalen fled to the solitude of the desert and for thirty years lived as a hermit without food or clothing' (Jansen, *The Making of the Magdalen*, 37–8). The image evoked in this sonnet is perhaps more poignant considering that Constable was living in literal self-exile at the time.
43. Earl, 'Late Elizabethan Devotional Poetry', 238, 235.
44. An important influence at work here is St Bernard, who draws an analogy between carnal and mystical union in his exegesis of the Song of Songs; see, for instance, Wimsatt, 'St. Bernard, the Canticle of Canticles, and Mystical Poetry', 80.

45. Serjeantson, 'The Book of Psalms', 644.
46. Wickes, 'Henry Constable's Spiritual Sonnets', 33.
47. Cheney, *Spenser's Famous Flight*, 5.
48. For an overview of the publication of Du Bartas's works in Scotland and England in the late 1580s and 1590s, see Shell, *Catholicism, Controversy*, 65–6.
49. See, as an instance, Milton's sonnet 'When I consider how my light is spent', which refers to poetic talent as God's gift, in Milton, *Complete Shorter Poems*, 304.
50. Shuger, *Sacred Rhetoric*, 235–6, 239.
51. Earl, 'Late Elizabethan Devotional Poetry', 230. On aphasia and figures of speech that attempt to portray disruptions of language, see Amelang, 'Figuring Ineloquence', this volume.
52. See Braudy, *Frenzy of Renown*, 172, 169.
53. Ibid., 169.
54. Three final sonnets honouring the late Mary, Queen of Scots, render the *Spiritual Sonnets* a far more politically charged collection than it might appear. See Pérez-Jáuregui, 'A Queen in a "Purple Robe"'.
55. He could have been involved in the activities of the Essex circle abroad; see Dodds, 'Barnabe Barnes', 24.
56. See Grebe, 'Why Did Ovid . . .?', 508.
57. See Shagan, 'Introduction: English Catholic History', 2.

Chapter 9

Thomas Lodge's 'Supple Muse': Imitation, Inspiration and Imagination in *Phillis*
Cinta Zunino-Garrido

Published in 1593, Thomas Lodge's *Phillis: Honoured with Pastoral Sonnets, Elegies and Amorous Delights* comprises forty sonnets, two eclogues, an elegy and an ode which, though not precisely set in the conventional pastoral setting that the title promises,[1] portrays shepherd Damon's unrequited wooing of Phillis, followed by a long poem entitled *The Complaint of Elstred*. The layout of the poems – inclusive of the complaint – closely follows other coeval sonnet cycles, thus fuelling the fad for Petrarchan lyric sequences after Philip Sidney, Giles Fletcher the Elder, Samuel Daniel or Barnabe Barnes. However, of all the works of Lodge, *Phillis* is possibly the one that was greeted with the least enthusiasm by his contemporaries, as well as by modern critics. As it happens, at variance with the sonnets of Philip Sidney, Samuel Daniel, Michael Drayton or Henry Constable, *Phillis* was published in only one edition and was never after reissued or reprinted. Perhaps the main reason for this inattention has to do with the fact that *Phillis* is not entirely the product of Lodge's own inventiveness. The silent debts to French and Italian poets such as Petrarch, Desportes, Ronsard, Ariosto and Paschale are recognisable in about half of the sonnets, many of which are, in reality, imitations and fairly close translations or paraphrases of the European originals, as several scholars have striven to show.[2] Suspicions of plagiarism thus affected the response to *Phillis* not only among Lodge's contemporaries but also among modern scholars. By attesting to 'Lodge's servile dependence on Ronsard' and other European poets, Sidney Lee affirmed that 'it is a misuse to describe him [Lodge] as an original poet seeking to give voice to his individuality', whereas

Charles W. Whitworth has suggested that Lodge's sequence is just the result of having randomly gathered a series of unconnected poems, composed during a long period, with the sole intention of adhering to the popular trend of the sonnet cycle.[3] In general, led by this inclination to accept *Phillis* simply as a clear case of literary imitation, modern scholars have largely focused their efforts on ascertaining the sources of the poems.

As it stands, it is a fact that in *Phillis* Lodge silently echoed French and Italian poets. However, his original poems are, on the contrary, evident exemplars of his own invention – embodied in that 'Genius of my Muse' he invokes in the 'Induction'. As I argue in the following pages, the original sonnets constitute a productive space for the exploration of the poetics of this kind of sonnet compilation. These poems establish the basis on which Lodge tacitly interrogates the meaning of creativity in a work where, ironically enough, translation and imitation are primary *raisons d'être*. For all this, I contend that a reassessment of these poems could at the very least help enrich the critical response to *Phillis* and re-evaluate it as something more than a random collection of imitative verses lacking a real 'method' or intended *dispositio*. As stated above, Whitworth has been very assertive in this regard, and no less than him were the two modern editors of the text, Sidney Lee and Martha Foote Crow, who coincided in excluding *The Complaint of Elstred* after considering it a later addition totally unrelated to the sonnets.[4] However, while there might be reasons to suppose that Lodge did not arrange his poems as conscientiously as the authors of other sonnet collections,[5] the sequence's structure and its concern with the nature of poetic creativity appear to evince an internal plan that counters the received idea of *Phillis* as an unoriginal and incongruent assemblage of poems.

At first glance, a comparable incongruity seems to characterise other works by Lodge, yet research has proven their internal coherence. For example, published only two years after *Phillis*, *A Fig for Momus*, similarly 'containing Pleasant varietie, included in Satyres, Eclogues, and Epistles', shows unity in the diversity of its poems. As Arthur F. Kinney explains, Lodge's concern with a humanist poetics of felicity serves to 'bind together all the disparate works of this Momus', as well as to progressively transform the classical god of mockery into a more transcendent character.[6] Another of Lodge's works that at first reading appears to have an unsystematic structure, comparable to that presumed in *Phillis*, is *An Alarum against Usurers*, published in 1584. Conceived as a warning against the misuse of moneylending, *An Alarum* 'seems to be an odd collection of juvenile *imitatio* of deliberative declamation, Alexandrian romance, and allegorical satire'.[7] But an attentive analysis of the three sections discloses the logic of the sequence. In Kinney's words,

> the exhortation and pastoral serve as humanist precept and illustration, while the concluding poem serves to reconcile the dialectic by partaking simultaneously of both. Lodge thus gives us a new kind of triadic art in which each of the three parts, separately and together, responds to the Latin motto on the title page of this and other works by Lodge.[8]

This combination of narratives provides the key to understanding the meaning of *An Alarum*, a formula that Lodge would repeat in *Rosalynde* (1590), 'where pastoral romance in Arden realizes the precepts of Sir John of Bordeaux'.[9] That the closing poem in *An Alarum* is a complaint – entitled *Truth's Complaint over England* – that helps bring together the debate as explored in the previous two sections might also give a clue about the significance of the final complaint in *Phillis*. Although Lee and Crow omitted it in their respective editions, when *Phillis* is compared to other sequences, one can infer that *The Complaint of Elstred* is most probably not an addition to the sonnets, but a coherent part of the whole sequence, just as, for example, *The Complaint of Rosamond* is a part of Samuel Daniel's *Delia* (1592) or *Truth's Complaint over England* is a decisive element of *An Alarum*.

In any case, even if the pattern of *Phillis* is the most arbitrary – in which the varied interspersed poems perhaps only serve to 'anticipate and complicate their relationship to the poems that succeed them'[10] – in the poems of Lodge's own invention there is an evident interest in recurrent issues of literary creativity that were similarly discussed by other coeval authors, and that accordingly turn *Phillis* into a site as valuable for the exploration of Elizabethan poetics as the sonnet cycles of Sidney, Fletcher or Daniel. In fact, by maintaining that in the line of succession of *Astrophil and Stella*, *Phillis* plays an important role comparable to that of *Delia*, *Licia* (1593) or even Drayton's *Ideas Mirror* (1594), Joel B. Davis has pointed to its tripartite structure and use of trochaic verse in the ode and second eclogue as decisive choices in the evolution of the English sonnet sequence:

> If Lodge's trochaic poems extend the trend of simplifying the flexible experiments with trochaic meter emphasized in the 1591 quartos of *Astrophel and Stella* – with a purpose and not out of incompetence – then his *Complaint of Elstred* extends and sophisticates the meditation of succession and decay begun in *Delia* and *Rosamond*.[11]

All this makes the more sense when one recalls that, along with Sidney's *Defence of Poesy* (c. 1580) and Daniel's later *Defence of Rhyme* (1603), Lodge also led the way in theorising about literature – and drama in particular – when, as early as 1579, he anonymously published *A Reply to Stephen Gosson's Schoole of Abuse in Defence of Poetry, Musick, and Stage Plays*. That is why I presume that a new reading of *Phillis*, with an emphasis on its immaterial as well as material features, will help the understanding of its poetic nature or what, in accordance with the premises of this volume, we could perhaps describe as a kind of *unwritten* poetics. Just as Jonathan Sell argues in this volume that Sidney's 'unwritten art' emerging from *Astrophil and Stella* completes the theoretical model that he renders in *The Defence of Poesy*,[12] we could similarly argue that *Phillis* exhibits a comparable attitude in also functioning as a kind of test case for a practical poetics of imitation. After all, in his sonnet sequence Lodge silently tackles questions of poetic invention likewise recurrent in the works of other Elizabethan poets such as Sidney – an undertaking that might help us to reassess his part in the evolution of Elizabethan poetry and his position as a forerunner in the publication of sonnet sequences. Such a claim seems necessary in order to appraise the general reaction to *Phillis*, which since its publication has repeatedly been listed solely for its imitative nature, and virtually ignored for its other literary attributes.

To such an extent has *Phillis* been considered a mere replica of French and Italian poetry that Michael Drayton's dedicatory sonnet in his *Ideas Mirrour* (1594) has been presumed to sneer at Lodge's imitative habits:

> Yet these mine owne, I wrong not other men,
> Nor traffique further than thys happy Clyme
> Nor filch from *Portes* nor from *Petrarchs* pen,
> A fault too common in thys latter time.
> Divine Syr *Phillip*, I avouch thy writ,
> I am no Pickpurse of anothers wit.[13]

Contradicting Kastner, Burton Paradise and Whitworth maintain instead that Drayton's lines are vague, and could as well refer to any other poet as to Lodge, as the sonnet sequences of Thomas Watson, Samuel Daniel and Henry Constable, among others, similarly bristled with comparable echoes of French and Italian poetry.[14] Whether or not Drayton's charges of plundering were indeed addressed to Lodge, it is a fact that, despite the success of *Rosalynde* (1590), at some point in his career Lodge had to confront serious accusations of plagiarism and inefficiency that overshadowed his literary reputation. In the epistle to the reader of the aforementioned *A Fig for Momus*, Lodge justified the title of this work by stating that

> vnder this title I haue thought good to include Satyres, Eclogues, and Epistles: first by reason that I studie to delight with varietie, next because I would write in that forme, wherin no man might chalenge me with seruile imitation, (wherewith heretofore I haue beene vniustlie taxed).[15]

The real cause for such a vindication remains unknown, but evinces that, not long before the publication of *A Fig for Momus*, some of Lodge's works had been – 'vniustlie', he retorts – singled out as examples of literary theft. This is a question to which Lodge again returns in *Wits Misery* (1596), where he denounces the fact that, merely out of spite or envy, some authors are systematically and wrongly blamed either for extensive borrowing or lack of creativity. He protests that if for whatever reason a work fails to gain other scholars' favour, these will indict its author of piracy, or else insufficient originality: 'Let a scholler write, Tush (saith he) I like not these common fellowes: let him write well, he hath stollen it out of some note booke: let him translate, Tut, it is not of his owne.'[16]

Copious referencing of other writers was a sign of the times. Otherwise, in *A Reply to Gosson's Schoole of Abuse* (1579), Lodge would not have invited Gosson to disclose the sources of his arguments:

> Tell me Gosson was all your owne you wrote there: did you borow nothing of your neyhbours? Out of what booke patched you out Ciceros oration? Whence fet you Catulins inuective? Thys is one thing, *aliena . . . olet lucerni non tuam*, so that your helper may wisely reply vpon you with Virgil.[17]

Additionally, in the epistle to the reader of *A Fig for Momus*, in what seems to be, as Harold Ogden White suggests, a critical remark on E. K.'s glosses to *The Shepherd's Calendar*, Lodge maintains that 'for my Eclogues, I commend them to men of approved iudgment, whose margents though I fill not with quotations, yet their matter, and handling, will show my diligence'.[18] Our poet thus claims that in his eclogues he had followed the classical models just as other writers such as Spenser had done, which shows that his practices did not significantly differ from those of other authors of the period. He further explains that there was no need to mention the sources of his poetry; educated readers, imbued as they were with the Renaissance praxis of imitation, would be able to recognise these or, at best, appreciate the imitative quality of his poems. Moreover, in the epistle to the reader of *The Divel Coniured* (1596), he laments that his works, when praised for their rhetoric, were contrariwise criticised for the way matters were handled – that is, with the *dispositio* of his arguments, if in the following statement we understand 'iudegement' as comparable to the second division of rhetoric: 'If the handling [makes you suspect], I repent me not, for I had rather you should now condemn me for default in Rhetoricke, then as in times past, commend my stile, and lament my iudegement.'[19] Comments such as these corroborate Paradise's assertion about the difficulty of ascertaining Lodge's actual relations with his literary contemporaries, while they nourish the belief that 'Lodge seems to have been always on the doorstep of Parnassus, but never to have quite succeeded in entering the company of the elect'.[20]

Taken as a whole, the rejection of these accusations of plagiarism impelled Lodge to contend that his poetry simply put into effect the conventional practice of *imitatio*, to which he was inevitably pushed by the trends, as he indicated in *William Longbeard* (1593):

> Taylors and Writers nowadays are in like estimate, if they want new fashions they are not fancied: & if the stile be not of the new stamp, tut the Author is a foole. In olde time menne studied to illustrate matter with words, now we strive for words beside matter. Since therefore the time is such, and iudgements are so singular, since the manners are altred with men, and men are in thraldome to their fashionate manners, I will with the Diar prepare my selfe to washe out the spots as soone as they are spied, and borrow some cunning of the drawer, to colour an imperfection so well as I can, till such time I have cunning to cut my garment out of the whole cloath.[21]

Without arguing any further, this excerpt stands comparison with the ideas about art and imitation endorsed in Puttenham's *The Art of English Poesy* (1589) and quoted in the introduction to this volume. In this regard, it is remarkable that, like Puttenham, Lodge also dissociates poetic imitation from mere imitative practices regulated by 'example or mediation or exercise'.[22] That the 'Diar' and the 'drawer' are then preferred over the painter, who counterfeits 'the natural by the like effects',[23] is quite revealing. In line with Puttenham, Sidney or even George Chapman, Lodge also suggests here a kind of poetic imitation which, though 'measured by the efficacy of poetic style',[24] should deliver a 'high, and harty invention exprest in most significant, and vnaffected phrase'.[25] In accordance with these general attitudes in Elizabethan poetics, Lodge similarly rejects an idea of imitation solely based on the observation of patterns and models established by modes.

These explanations should be evidence enough to prove, as he complains in *A Fig for Momus*, that he is not 'a servile imitator'. What is more, by additionally affirming that 'I have so written, as I have read',[26] Lodge implies that his – 'vniustlie taxed' – method of composition simply ties in with the practice of *imitatio* endorsed by Renaissance scholars, and, above all, with the kind of emulation that results from individual reinterpretation of celebrated models.[27] This is where the real value of *imitatio* rests, as he makes Ergasto affirm in 'Eclogue I' of *A Fig for Momus*:

> Let yong men boast what art they list,
> Mine eares chiefe pleasure doth consist,
> In hearing what concentfull laies
> Our Fathers chaunted in their daies;
> For often have I found this true,
> The sence is olde, the words be newe:
> What ere the yonger boast and brave,
> Their worth, and wit, from eld they have.[28]

Although no one can deny that in *Phillis*, Lodge imitated other European poets, the poems of his own invention corroborate that these imitations functioned indeed as the basis and inspiration for his own poetry, for which his Muse proved to be 'enfranchis'd from forgetfulnesse'.[29] Taking Ergasto's words into consideration, one can presume that, as in the eclogue, so in *Phillis*, while 'the scene is olde, the words be newe'.[30] The idea visibly emerges in the last sonnet of *Phillis*, where, in spite of acknowledging the use of others' poetry as model, Lodge explains that these paradigms have ultimately proved ineffective for his own poetic enterprise:

> Resembling none, and none so poore as I,
> Poore to the world, and poore in each esteeme,
> Whose first borne loues, at first obscurd did die,
> And bred no fame but flame of bace misdeeme.
> Under the Ensigne of whose tyred pen,
> Loues legions forth have maskt, by others masked:
> Thinke how I lyve wronged by ill tonged men,
> Not Maister of my selfe, to all wrongs tasked. (40.1–8, sig. H3r)

For Lodge, the real substance of poetic creativity rests on the poet's literary experience, an experience that springs from his own aptitudes and the practice of *imitatio*, and that is necessarily enmeshed with a discussion of the real significance of imitation, inspiration and poetic imagination for literary creation. Ironically enough, perhaps the meaning of *Phillis* could lie in the blending of exercises in *imitatio* with poems triggered by Lodge's particular Muse. In this regard, it is perhaps no coincidence that, in the first and last sonnet of the sequence, Lodge confirms that his poetry, albeit grounded in the verse of other writers, certainly needs to have its own essence, its own Muse. The formulae employed by other poets cannot be valid to depict the particular situation of Damon and Phillis. Therefore, in the same way that he claims to 'lyve wronged by ill tonged men, / Not Maister of my selfe, to all wrongs tasked', he can also admit that, if he wants to produce the singularising poetry that Phillis deserves, only his own experience will permit his muse to rise 'beyond our Poets pitches' (1.7, sig. B2r) – even if this implies his literary creation to be inferior in quality when compared to other models. Overall, as Sidney similarly urged in sonnet 1 of *Astrophil and Stella*, Lodge advocates a poetry inspired by true feeling:

> Oh pleasing thoughts, apprentises of loue,
> . . .
> Rowse you my muse beyond our Poets pitches,
> . . .
> Show to the world tho poore and scant my skill is,
> How sweet thoughts be, that are but thought on *Phillis*. (1.1, 7, 13–14, sig. H3r)

In this first sonnet, Lodge confirms that the distinctive character of his sonnet sequence is achieved because the real experience of the poet prevails over a deluding idea of inspiration and the works of the 'poetic predecessors responsible for some sort of "anxiety of influence", from whose "pre-text" a poet will emancipate his own heart-felt writing'.[31] As Harbicht explains, this is something that Sidney, Daniel and Drayton do with 'no small degree of self-assurance',[32] and Lodge, absorbed by the tradition, clung to the same idea. Not only is this evident in *Phillis*. In one of the 'Sundrie sweete Sonnets' appended to *Scillaes Metamorphosis*, Lodge shuns others' poetry not simply because it is inadequate to depict his love, but because it has proved deceptive: 'Goe lying books, cease fooles to boast your art, / And marke the cause: my Mistres smiles and lowres / Makes cleere the heauens, & clowdes my heart with showers'.[33] In sonnet 16 of *Phillis* Lodge similarly concludes that, as it stands, poetical conventions cannot offer the devices and acuteness needed to give shape to the hardship suffered by the poet:

> I part (oh death) for why this world containes,
> More care, and woe then with dispaire remains,
> Oh loath depart wherein such sorrowes dwell,
> As all conceites are scant the same to tell. (16.17–20, sig. D2v)

At any rate, the belief that experience is the sustenance of poetry is what really marks *Phillis* in the same way that it marks, for instance, the opening of *Astrophil and Stella* or *Licia*. Only the 'pleasing thoughts' on Phillis that open the sequence can really rouse Lodge's 'muse beyond our Poets pitches'; otherwise the poet would be unable to display his poetic competence. No matter if this is 'poore and scant', what counts is its authenticity, because it is grounded in true sentiments and in Phillis as the only possible source of inspiration. As he affirms in sonnet 4, 'none wrights [writes] with truer faith, or greater love' (4.13, sig. B4v), and it is this love that precisely commands him to write, as he also suggests in sonnet 1: 'and working wonders yet say all is duty' (1.8, sig. B2r).[34] Sonnet 8 is the most comprehensible example illustrating the pre-eminence of experience in writing poetry. In this sonnet, after displaying a clear Petrarchan blazon, Lodge suggests that literary creation directly depends on the material experience of the poet:

> No starres hir eyes to cleere the wandering night,
> But shining sunnes of true divinitye:
> That make the soule conceiue hir perfect light:
> No wanton beauties of humanitie
> Hir prettie browes, but beames that cleare the sight
> Of him that seekes the true Philosophie:
> No Corrall is hir lippe, no rose hir faire,
> But even that crimson that adornes the Sunne
> No Nimph is she, but mistresse of the ayre,
> By whom my glories are but newe begunne,
> But when I touch and tast as others do,
> I then shall wright and you shall wonder to. (8, sig. C2v)

In this sonnet Lodge has imitated the convention of the blazon, describing Phillis's beauty in the Petrarchan style. However, the last two lines imply that this imitation is far from perfection, for it is founded on a pretended idea of Phillis's beauty. In imitating this model, Lodge has created a conventional literary image of Phillis, but this image is dependent on a stereotyped – and to some extent worn-out – pattern that constrains Lodge's invention and aspirations to surpass mere theoretical and multifunctional models. It is not the Petrarchan idealised image of Phillis on which the force of his poetry should be based, but on touching and tasting her, that is, on real and material experience. Only his own experiences – based on, though emancipated from, convention – can really imprint a distinctive quality on his poetry, the distinctiveness needed to validate its own essence, as he claims in the first and last sonnet of the sequence.

The relevance given to experience is a subject likewise examined by other Elizabethan writers. In canzon 3 of *Parthenophil and Parthenophe* (1593), after displaying a sort of Petrarchan blazon, Barnes explains that his Muses feed on the nectar that seeps through the beloved's lips. By comparing Parthenophe's lips with grapes, Barnes thus develops a conceit that proves how a kiss substantiates the dependence of poetry on actual experience, just as Lodge does.[35] Madrigal 18 likewise illustrates that physicality stimulates inspiration. In this particular example, Barnes's inspiration is fired up by the materiality of a flower that symbolises the loving encounter. When the poet is able to touch, taste and smell the bud, his Muse is encouraged to preserve this experience as its substance or 'theames': 'Whose fauour, sappe, and sauour my sence reaues. / My muse hath these for theames, / They to my muse, my muse to the defence'.[36] A kiss from Parthenophe is again the cause for the literary response of the poet in madrigal 16. However, Barnes introduces here a slight variation, because the joy caused by the kiss must be kept secret as part of the *furtivus amor* topos: 'No man can speake those ioyes, / then muse be mute: But say, for sight, smell, hearing, tast, and tuch, / In any one thing, was there ever such?'[37] Though contrary to the formula employed in canzon 3, the restraint of the Muse in the madrigal similarly corroborates that experience is the trigger of poetry. In a similar, yet sardonic way William Percy asks his Muse in *Coelia* to be silent in order to conceal an episode that immediately kindled his inventiveness. When Coelia treads on the poet in sonnet V, he interprets this as a love encounter that once more is cause for poetical inspiration. Still, like Barnes in madrigal 16, Percy must restrain this enthusiasm to conceal the excitement caused by this experience.[38] And as in *Licia* Fletcher coincides with Lodge and Barnes in ascribing to the poet's own experiences the stimulus to write, so in the epistle to the reader he attributes the amorous tone of his poetry to his state of mind. Because he is in love, he feels inclined to write exclusively love poems, which 'I did it onlelie to trie my humour'.[39]

Though more indirectly and in a different manner, the first eclogue of *Phillis* also examines this notion of the poet's experience as essential for poetical invention. There Damon and the old shepherd Demades debate on the value of love and its function as fuel for poetry. Demades's age and experience have made him sceptical about the actual worth of love, whereas Damon, deeply captivated by Phillis, argues for the contrary by affirming that 'Spring flowers, sea-tides, earth grasse, skie stars shal banish, / Before the thoughtes of loue or *Phillis* vanish', and so he is determined to keep his love alive even if this only makes him 'weep thy [his] woes unto the winde' ('Egloga Prima', 143–4, sig. E3v). Damon finds in his love for Phillis a sound reason for his invention: 'All hope (but future hope to be renouned, / For weeping *Phillis*) shall in tears be drowned' ('Egloga Prima', 113–14, sig. E2r). Damon thus validates his affection as the basis for his literary creation, a creation whose material fruit will prove perpetual.

Although – if obviously more implicitly than in sonnet 8 – this dialogue evinces the relevance of experience for literary creation, what really calls our attention is the manner in which the conversation defines this experience. Demades affirms that it is Damon's own arrogance as potential lover – and accordingly poet – that envisions the experience that prompts him to write. He argues that Damon pretends to be in love so as to have a good excuse for writing – just as Fletcher also wrote 'onelie to trie my humour':

> The vaine Idea of this dietie
> Nurst at the teate of thine Imagination:
> Was bred brought, vp by thine owne vanitie,
> Whose being thou mayest curse from the creation:
> And so thou list, thou maiest as soone forget loue,
> As thou at first didst fashion and beget loue. ('Egloga Prima', 49–54, sig. E1r)

With these lines, Demades argues that poets simulate affections with the sole purpose of having an apparently solid and real basis on which to found their poetry. Whether Damon's love is actually feigned or not is not the question here, but the concern shown by Demades with the real nature of this feeling and its connection to poetry certainly interrogates the creative nature of lyric and, more significantly, contradicts what is maintained in sonnet 8 and the other excerpts quoted above. Demades implies that poetry is fiction, and as such it does not necessarily need to depend on real experience. Poetry can feign passions without the need of feeling them, for, if poetry is only sustained by real affections, poets might then have their inventions curtailed, not being able, as a result, to yield any further kind of lyric not dependent on states of mind:[40]

> If *Phillis* loue, loue hir, yet loue hir so:
> That if she flye, thou maiest loues fire forgo.
>
> Play with the fire, yet die not in the flame,
> Show passions in thy words, but not in heart:
> Least when thou think'st to bring thy thoughtes in frame:
> Thou proue thy selfe a prisoner by thine Arte.
> Play with these babes of loue, as Apes with Glasses,
> And put no trust in feathers, winde, or lasses. ('Egloga Prima', 131–8, sig. E2r)

Demades's contention ties in with what is also articulated in the sonnet preceding the eclogue. Despite being quite a literal replica of Ariosto's sonnet 15, Lodge introduces in sonnet 20 a couple of lines of his own invention – indicated below in italics – that could be read as a preamble to the old shepherd's idea of poetic discourse:

> Some praise the looks, and other praise the lockes,
> Of their faire Queenes, *in loue with curious words*:
> Some laud the breast where loue his treasure locks,
> All like the eie that life and loue affordes.
> But none of these fraile beauties and unstable
> Shall make *my pen ryot in pompous stile*. (20.1–6, sig. D4v, emphases added)

In this sonnet, the lover distances himself from poets 'in loue with curious words' who praise the outward beauty of their beloved by rioting 'in pompous style'. Just as in other moments of the sequence or even as Sidney in sonnet 1, Lodge rejects 'the letter for the spirit, or the appearance for the reality'[41] with the sole intention of valuing the moral beauty of his mistress. Yet these lines are particularly revealing when read in connection with Demades's claim, for the phrase 'in loue with curious words' besides suggests, as Luis-Martínez explains, that poets are 'endowed with the ability to rehearse "love's use", to make desire the subject of *delocution*'.[42] In short, the love displayed by these other poets is simply reduced to an exhibition of their poetic skills, thus insinuating, as Demades equally maintains, that poets pretend to be in love so that they have an excuse to write poetry. Hence Demades's demand for a poetry disenfranchised from sentiments. In consequence, it is not surprising that he urges Damon to use his lyrical abilities with other aims, advising him to 'bende thy [his] Muse to matters farre more fitte' and

> Cast hence this Idle fuel of desire,
> That feedes that flame wherein they heart consumeth:
> Let reason schoole thy will wich doth aspire,
> And counsel coole impatience that presumeth:
> Driue hence vaine thoughtes which are fond loues abetters;
> For he that seeks his thraldoome merits fetters. ('Egloga Prima', 43–38, sig. D4v)

On the whole, Demades's protest functions as counterpoint to the idea that poetry should emerge from authenticity, a notion similarly considered, for example, by Watson, who in *Hekatompathia* revealed 'that his passions were invented' and 'his borrowings of them from other writers', or Sidney, who exploited the arbitrary fictionality of literary texts in *The Old Arcadia* and *Astrophil and Stella*.[43] Demonstration of this idea also occurs in sonnets 100 and 101 of *Wittes Pilgrimage* (1605) by John Davies of Hereford: 'Why sing I then in this too loving Straine / When Loue, and I do so vnkindly iar?'; 'Thus far may Speculation help a Wit / Unapt for Love, to write of Loves estate / Thus far can Art extend his Benefit / Past Natures Bounds, in shew of Love, or Hate'.[44] Even Giles Fletcher interrogated the validity of such a principle when he suggested that it is possible for an author to write about things unknown to him: 'Yet take this by the waie, though I am so liberall to graunt thus much, a man may write of love, and not bee in love, as well as of husbandrie, and not goe to plough: or of witches and be none: or of holinesse and be flat prophane.'[45] A poet's invention is not necessarily triggered by actuality, because poetry, ultimately being a mental fabrication, proves in itself a genuine subjective experience. Demades's remarks therefore upend the idea that, for poetry to acquire a distinctive touch, the poet should draw on personal experience. In so doing, Lodge interrogates the real nature of poetic invention, rendering it a genuinely subjective experience: it is as genuine when it depends on the writer's lived materiality as when it is a product of the imagination. Similarly, when Drayton concluded that 'My Verse is the true image of my Mind',[46] he could not have defined with more accuracy the subjective quality of poetry.

It has been already argued that *The Complaint of Elstred* has been taken by modern scholars as an unconnected poem, added later to the sequence solely in order to participate in the Elizabethan craze for sonnet sequences. Recent research on Elizabethan poetry has drawn attention to the 'early modern predilection for bringing out volumes that link sonnet sequences to other texts, especially narratives',[47] and has endeavoured to explain the logic of this structure. Modelling the term on Daniel's sequence, Katherine Duncan-Jones and John Kerrigan called this the 'Delian' structure, which, characterised by the combination of a sonnet sequence with an ode and a closing narrative complaint, served as the basis for the analogous tripartite structure of other sonnet series such as *Phillis*, Fletcher's *Licia*, Richard Barnfield's *Cynthia* (1595) or Robert Lynche's *Diella* (1596).[48] Scholars such as Duncan-Jones, Kerrigan, Thomas P. Roche, Stephen Guy-Bray, Georgia Brown and Marcy L. North have attempted to read a thematic progression in these sequences.[49] These authors have underscored, for instance, the relevant function of introductory sonnets that 'acknowledge the scope and labor of the project',[50] and of the long closing poems that, as a sort of coda, either abound in the subject matter of the sonnets or propose a resolution to the problems previously posed in the sequence – especially evident in the different readings of *The Complaint of Rosamond*.[51]

Additionally, the materiality of the sequences reinforces these assumptions. Kavita Mudan Finn has stressed, for example, that in the particular case of *Phillis*, its printer, John Busby, closely followed the typographical choices employed in *Delia*, 'deliberately placing Lodge's poems within the same visual framework as Daniel's'.[52] Moreover, with the focus placed on the relation between gender and paratext in Elizabethan complaints, Danielle Clarke has argued that *Phillis*, as well as the sonnet sequences of Daniel or Drayton, 'carry title-pages that suggest the integral importance of these poems [the complaints] to the volumes'.[53] Juliet Fleming has further suggested that, although ornament borders were frequently used by Elizabethan printers to separate short poems from the rest of the sequence, 'in other cases the use of borders is continued, in whole or in part, across some or all of the other textual units in the same volume'.[54] Fleming thus claims that such a practice suggests that 'flowers were used, not to mark the single page as the territory of a single sonnet, but to articulate the composition and identity of the entire printed volume as something more than the sum of its parts'.[55] In agreement with Fleming, Clarke maintains that the layout of *Phillis* – which is partly characterised by the use of arabesques – gestures towards this combinatorial pattern to mark the transition between the diverse poems and the complaint, which, as she explains, becomes an integral part of the whole sequence:

> The transition to 'The Complaint of Elstred' is marked by a mediating 'Ode', and the use of a different flower, but is concluded not with another flower, but with 'FINIS'. In this way, the female-voiced text is presented as having a coherence and integrity of its own, and as having a loosely defined relationship to the rest of the volume.[56]

In line with these assumptions, I would like to underscore, however, that not only the tripartite structure and the materiality of the sequence justify the internal coherence and the integrity of *The Complaint of Elstred* in *Phillis*. I also believe that *Elstred* is an integral part of the sequence because it builds upon the questions about poetic creativity discussed in the previous poems. As the title indicates, the closing complaint tells the story of Elstred, who, as a result of the vicissitudes of life, becomes King Locrinus's concubine. Elstred begets an illegitimate daughter with Locrinus, Sabrina, who, like her mother, is sentenced to death when Gwendoleen, Locrinus's lawful wife, becomes queen after fighting and defeating the king in an attempt to preserve her honour and position. Most of this tragic story is told by Elstred herself, whose spectre and that of her daughter surface at the river where the poet – who in the fictional context of the sequence we presume to be Damon[57] – bemoans his unrequited love.

Although Elstred is the unquestionable protagonist of the story, for the present purposes I would like to draw attention to Sabrina, as her brief though relevant part in the narrative enters into a conversation with Damon and Demades, and extends the enquiries into creativity, experience and imagination previously examined in the sequence. From the moment Sabrina is first introduced, she is objectified as a trophy of Locrinus and Elstred's 'tryumph and good speede' (*CE*, 328, sig. K3v) and, significantly enough, as a text written by her father: 'Looke how in royall characters inchased, / She beares the records of his [Locrinus] haughty hart' (*CE*, 523–4, sig. L3v). Thus reified, Sabrina is not allowed to take an active part in the story. When Locrinus is slain, the most she can do, as Elstred tells it, is to literally replicate her mother's words and gestures:

> I faynting fell, enfeebled through my sufferaunce,
> My child that saw me fall, for griefe fell by me:
> I wept, she cryde, both gaue griefe sustenaunce,

> *I* fainted, and she fainting layd her nie me.
> Euen what I kyst, she kist, and what I sayd
> She sayd, and what I fear'd, made her afrayd.
>
> For euery sigh, a sigh, for euery teare,
> A teare, she was no niggard of her moane. (*CE*, 433–40, sig. L1r)

As a text, Sabrina can only echo Elstred's actions and words until, at the end of the narration, she demands to speak for herself and give her own account of the story, which she does in the last ten stanzas:

> Yea Mother so *I* cry'd, said *Sabrine* tho.
> Oh let me now no longer sorrow smother,
> But by my selfe capitulate my woe:
> Since none are fit, or meetest to reueale it,
> Then those who like my selfe, doe likewise feele it. (*CE*, 542–6, sig. L3r)

What Sabrina experiences somehow mirrors Lodge's practice in the composition of *Phillis*, especially as described in sonnets 1, 8, 40 and the first eclogue. On the one hand, Lodge openly – yet without making specific reference, in contrast to, for instance, Fletcher – imitates other European writers, just as Sabrina mimics Elstred. However, on the other hand, our poet also reveals the efforts made to furnish his poetry with a distinctive flavour, acknowledging as part of this process both the usefulness and ineffectiveness of others' poetry. As text, Sabrina similarly paraphrases Elstred's discourse until she is eventually empowered to report the events by herself. Sabrina demands a voice of her own and, as a consequence, argues that only a first-person narrative voiced by the protagonist of the story – or, at least, by someone who has endured a comparable situation – can truly convey her experiences. With this assertion, Sabrina brings into focus the two shepherds' dialogue about the real nature of poetic invention and whether this should be based on real experience. Sabrina insists that her story needs to be told from her lived experience.

Nonetheless, paradoxically enough, her story is actually told by a mediating poet. After all, the voice that Sabrina claims for herself is the voice which must arise from the poet's compassion:[58]

> I thus we dyed, yet not with selfe like same,
> For floting *Seuerne* loues *Sabrinaes* name.
> So may he prattle still vnto his vvaue,
> *Sabrinaes* name, whilst brine salt teares sea weepeth:

And if the Gods or men compassion haue,
Compassion that vvith tender hearts nere sleepeth,
We both shall liue. (*CE*, 593–9, sig. L4r)

Despite her efforts to have their story told from her own perspective, Sabrina knows that only the work of a poet can guarantee the perpetuation of their tale. In this sense, the passage also stresses the conviction that poetry is the instrument to make stories permanent, as permanent as Sabrina has become thanks to the jingle resonating in the Severn. Not without reason, she is the only character to be objectified as a text in the complaint. Sabrina's name has been perpetuated by the river, while her story will subsist through poetry. It is this poetic materialisation of Elstred and Sabrina's tale that ultimately serves to prove – as Demades explains to Damon – that a poet's invention does not need to emerge from his own experiences. By recognising that the poet is the one who will eventually convey their tragedy, Elstred's daughter incidentally underscores the subjectivity of poetical invention. Sabrina, we presume, addresses her plea to Damon, who closes the complaint – and indeed the sequence – with the promise of recording their story: 'And I gotte home and weepingly thus pend it, / Carelesse of those that scorne and cannot mend it' (*CE*, 605–6, sig. L5v). With this assertion, Damon boosts the debate on the actual origin of poetic invention. His account of Elstred's story ratifies, as Demades implied, that the work of a poet does not need to arise from experience. Yet it is no less true that these lines actually result from his personal reaction to Elstred and Sabrina's report and are the product of his own feelings towards the two women.

By literally exemplifying the preceding discussion on poetic invention, the end of *The Complaint of Elstred* thus strengthens the internal logic of *Phillis*, while it confirms that the whole sequence can certainly be measured from a perspective that helps to uncover Lodge's interrogations into poetic theory. Whereas in *Astrophil and Stella* Sidney was 'faced with the irony that what each sonnet represented as the truth of his love had not happened at all' and with the fact that 'the cries of despair and black fits of woe had not been uttered as he wrote them',[59] Fletcher, on the other hand, justified the amorous mood of *Licia* on the grounds that he 'onely had leasure to growe passionate', and excused the poor literary value of his sonnet sequence by arguing that 'if any man measure my affection by my style, let him say, I am in Love'.[60] In a similar vein, by likewise approaching these two opposing attitudes in *Phillis*, and literally materialising them in the final complaint, Lodge shows a concern with the creative basis of poetry, whose substance, he seems to propose, rests on a complex combination of imitation, experience, creativity and subjectivity.

Overall, this idea of poetry derives from what in the title of this chapter, using John Davies's expression from *Orchestra, or A Poeme of Dauncing* (1596), I call the poet's 'supple muse'.[61] This expression condenses the major points of what could be considered Lodge's unwritten poetics. On the one hand, the idea of the Muse comprises questions about inspiration, creativity and experience alluded to in a number of his poems. On the other hand, the adjective 'supple', meaning either obedient or flexible, actually defines the standpoint from which these questions are tackled. In *Phillis*, Lodge confirms that regular imitation in poetical composition has limitations that can only be overcome by creativity, experience and innovation, that is, by the idea of a Muse, or imaginative competence, as 'Camelion-like' as, in the words of Davies, Astrophil's 'supple muse'. In this context, the dissatisfaction with the Muses that Lodge displays in the second eclogue is all the more revealing. The eclogue begins with the traditional invocation to the Muses similarly used in other moments of the sequence:

> Muses helpe me, sorrow, swarmeth,
> Eyes are fraught with seas of languish:
> Heauie hope my solace harmeth,
> Mindes repast is bitter anguish. ('Egloga Segunda', 1–4, sig. E4r)

However, although the poet paradoxically allows his lines to run free, he shortly after protests that the Muses seem reluctant to offer him their guidance: 'Muses if you please to tarry, / Further helpes I meane to borrow' (19–20, sig. E4r). With these lines Lodge seems to suggest that the role of the Muses as the incarnation of art grounded in tradition and as the sole providers of artistic inspiration is a convention that is by no means inviolable. In its place, what basically prevail in poetical composition are those 'further helpes' which, as implied in certain passages of the sequence, materialise in the poet's own capability and experience. In letting his lines flow without the assistance of the Muses, the poet proves that his state of mind is ultimately the impelling cause for the writing of poetry, just as Damon in the eclogue or Fletcher in the preamble to *Licia* argued. Yet it should not be overlooked that Fletcher's contention conversely rests on a 'pretence to authenticity of emotion'[62] similarly stressed by Demades when he hints at the fictional nature of poetic creation.

Taken as a whole, Lodge's implicit reflections in *Phillis* on the significance of inspiration, imitation and imagination certainly enter into conversation with Elizabethan readings of the nature of poetry, while they also unveil an internal logic for his sequence, especially measured by the materialisation of this discussion in the final complaint. After all, just like his contemporaries, Lodge discards a notion of poetic imagination grounded merely in the execution of pre-established models elucidated in treatises of poetry or in the works of celebrated authors, and engages instead in offering perspectives on the meaning of experience with regard to poesis. Inventive creativity ceases to be decided by models and worn-out conceits that prove insufficient for the poet's lyrical project, because, as indicated in sonnet 1, Lodge's Muse certainly must rise 'beyond our Poets pitches'. Whether this imaginative competence should be based on real experience or on poetical precepts disenfranchised from affection is the question that Lodge tries to answer in *Phillis*. Hence, when he affirms in the dedication to the Countess of Shrewsbury that in his poems he promises 'as much in affection as any other can perform in perfection' (sig. A3r), he is perhaps solving the dilemma, and, like Damon, ignoring the opinion of those who, like Demades, 'scorne and cannot mend it'. The entire debate in *Phillis* then rests on whether good poetry can truly emerge from affections: whether his Muses, as the poetic voice concludes in the second eclogue, really 'leave their wonted uses' when the poet 'leave[s] to bee a lover' ('Egloga Secunda', 63–4, sig. E5r), or whether this masquerade is just part of the poetic fiction, as Sidney, Fletcher, Watson and other sonneteers similarly whispered in their verses.

Notes

1. Whitworth, *Literary Career of Thomas Lodge*, 158.
2. See Lee, ed., *Elizabethan Sonnets*; Walker, 'Italian Sources of Lyrics of Thomas Lodge'; Kastner, 'Lodge as an Imitator of the Italian Poets'; Scott, *Sonnets élisabéthains*, and 'Parallels to Three Elizabethan Sonnets'; Holmes, 'Thomas Lodge's *Amours*'.
3. Lee, ed., *Elizabethan Sonnets*, 1:lxxvi; Whitworth, *Literary Career of Thomas Lodge*, 161.
4. Lee, ed., *Elizabethan Sonnets*; Crow, *Elizabethan Sonnet Cycles. Phillis. Licia*.
5. See Neely, 'Structure of English Renaissance Sonnet Sequences'; see also Webster, 'The Methode of a Poete'.
6. Kinney, *Humanist Poetics*, 367.
7. Ibid., 368.

8. Ibid.
9. Ibid, 371.
10. Dubrow, 'Dressing old words new?', 97.
    Ibid., 92.
11. Davis, *The Countesse of Pembrokes Arcadia and the Invention of English Literature*, 110.
12. See Sell, 'Sidney's Sublime Self-Authorship', this volume, 166.
13. Drayton, *Ideas Mirrour*, 'To Ma. Anthony Cooke, Esquire', 8–14, in *Works*, ed. Hebel, 1:96.
14. Apparently, Lodge had good relations with Drayton, to whom he addressed one of the epistles included in *A Fig for Momus* (1595), sigs. H3v–H4r, and whom in 1596 he described as 'diligent and formal' (*Wits Misery*, sig. I1r).
15. Lodge, *A Fig for Momus*, sig. A4v.
16. Lodge, *Wits Misery*, sig. I1r.
17. Lodge, *A Reply to Gosson*, sigs. C6r–C6v.
18. Lodge, *A Fig for Momus*, sig. A4v. See White, *Plagiarism and Imitation*, 110.
19. Lodge, *The Divel Coniured*, sig. A4r.
20. Paradise, *Thomas Lodge*, 180–1.
21. Lodge, *William Long Beard*, 'To the Gentlemen Readers', unnumbered.
22. Puttenham, *Art of English Poesy*, ed. Whigham and Rebhorn, 386. See the discussion of this passage in Luis-Martínez, 'Introduction', this volume, 4–5.
23. Puttenham, *Art of English Poesy*, 386.
24. Luis-Martínez, 'Friendlesse Verse', 587–8.
25. Chapman, *Ouids Banquet of Sence*, 'To Mathew Royden', in *Poems*, ed. Bartlett, 49. See also Luis-Martínez, 'George Chapman's "Habit of Poesie"', this volume, 271–2.
26. Lodge, *A Fig for Momus*, sig. A4r.
27. This is a topic amply discussed by Puttenham in *The Art of English Poesy* (1589) and by John Harrington in the preface to his version of *Orlando Furioso* (1591). Both writers draw attention to the flaws of imitation and coincide in explaining that the shortcomings of imitation happen when authors use imitation as plain misappropriation in place of the kind of borrowing which, through individual reinterpretation, rewriting and adaptation – procedures which definitely involve invention – should be actually enmeshed in the practice of imitation – or we should rather say emulation – as endorsed by the Elizabethans.
28. Lodge, *A Fig for Momus*, 'Eclogue I', sig. B4v.
29. Lodge, *Phillis . . . Where-unto is Annexed, The Tragicall Complaynt of Estred*, 'The Induction', 28, sig. B1v. Further references to this volume are given parenthetically in the text. For *Phillis*, sonnet and line numbers, or poem title and line number, are followed by signature. For *The Complaint of Elstred*, the abbreviation CE is followed by line number and signature.

30. These lines from the eclogue somehow resume the theme of Shakespeare's sonnet 76, in which, in words of Duncan-Jones, he apologises 'for the stylistic monotony of his verse' (*Shakespeare's Sonnets*, ed. Duncan-Jones, 262). Although his intention is to carry on writing about his love, Shakespeare complains that the best he can do is 'dressing old words new, / Spending again what is already spent' (76.11–12). As instigator of poetry love eschews innovation because it is an unmovable and constant feeling, not inclined to change or novelty. In a similar way, as Ergasto implies, the substance of poetry remains unalterable, being only modified on its appearance.
31. Habicht, 'My tongue-tied Muse', 196.
32. Ibid.
33. Lodge, *Scillaes Metamorphosis*, sonnet 3.8–10, sig. E4r.
34. Ibid., sonnet 1.8, sig. B2r.
35. See Barnes, *Parthenophil*, canzon 3.20–6, ed. Doyno, 113.
36. Ibid., madrigal 18.9–11, p. 60.
37. Ibid., madrigal 16.26–8, p. 58.
38. Percy, *Coelia*, 5.6–14, sig. B1r.
39. Fletcher, *Licia*, 'To the Reader', in *English Works*, ed. Berry, 78. On the basis of what George Chapman describes as 'pretence', 'a term that puns on the fictional nature of the poetic invention and the legal/rhetorical posture supporting the lover's petition', Luis-Martínez suggests that 'Fletcher makes his own "pretence" to authenticity of emotion rest on his readers' judgement of the quality of his writing' ('Friendlesse Verse', 586). The efficacy of the poetic style thus justifies the authenticity of the poet's passion.
40. This is a pivotal question for Sidney's idea of poetry, whose matter, as he affirms, is '*quodlibet* indeed'. See Sidney, *Defence*, in *Miscellaneous Prose*, ed. Duncan-Jones and van Dorsten, 112.11.
41. Evans, 'In Love with Curious Words', 125.
42. Luis-Martínez, 'Shakespeare's Wicked Pronoun', 141.
43. Spiller, *Development of the Sonnet*, 106–7.
44. Davies (of Hereford), *Wittes Pilgrimage*, sonnets 100.1–2, and 101.1–4, sig. H3r.
45. Fletcher, *Licia*, 'To the Ladie Mollineux', in *English Works*, 75–6.
46. Drayton, *Idea*, 'To the Reader of his Poems', 9, in *Poems*, 2:310.
47. Dubrow, 'Dressing old words new?', 90.
48. See *Shakespeare's Sonnets*, ed. Duncan-Jones, 44–5; and Kerrigan, 'Introduction', 13–14.
49. Roche, *Petrarch and the English Sonnet Sequences*; Guy-Bray, 'Rosamond's Complaint'; Brown, *Redefining Elizabethan Literature*, 225–31; North, 'The Sonnets and Book History'.
50. North, 'The Sonnets and Book History', 212.
51. See Guy-Bray, 'Rosamond's Complaint'; Davies, *The Countesse of Pembrokes Arcadia and the Invention of English Literature*; and Fleming,

'Changed Opinion as to Flowers'. Heather Dubrow has suggested instead that this design is perhaps more amorphous than has customarily been assumed, since a publisher's or printer's decisions could have easily altered authorial intentions in establishing structure. Dubrow maintains that 'the critical tendency to impose on collections of sonnets the type of linearity that encourages us to think in terms of "sonnet sequences" rather than "sonnet cycles" ... not coincidentally mirrors the desire to read such collections of sonnets in terms of a linear relationship with the poems or poems that follow them'. As an alternative, she argues that 'always based on a structure in which texts offer substitute visions and genres, often impelled by a latent agenda of replacing one emotion or interpretation with a more acceptable one, the books not only stage but also thematize many visions of surrogacy', and so, she continues, one can conclude that the closing poem in a 'volume offers not a resolution of the problems in the sonnet sequence but rather a demonstration of the problematic process of attempting to effect that resolution' ('Dressing old words new?', 95–7).

52. Finn, 'Of Whom Proud Rome', 86.
53. Clarke, 'Signifying', 136. The particular case of Drayton seems more problematic. As a result of his constant revision of the sonnets, there must have been copies where the sonnets were not bound with his poem *Matilda*. For a detailed discussion of this, see *Shakespeare's Sonnets*, ed. Duncan-Jones, esp. 13–17.
54. Fleming, 'Changed Opinion as to Flowers', 56.
55. Ibid.
56. Clarke, 'Signifying', 145.
57. The setting is unquestionably similar to that described at the end of the 'Egloga Secunda'.
58. A similar situation occurs in Daniel's *The Complaint of Rosamond* (1592). In this poem, Rosamond asks the poet to write her story so it is not forgotten and can work as an example to Delia: 'Which seene with griefe, my myserable ghost, / ... Comes to solicit thee, since other faile, / To take this taske, and in thy wofull Song / To forme my case, and register my wrong' (29–35, in Daniel, *Poems and the Defence of Rhyme*, ed. Sprague, 40).
59. Spiller, *Development of the Sonnet*, 111.
60. Fletcher, *Licia*, 'To ... the Ladie Mollineux', in *English Works*, 75.
61. 'Yet Astrophell might one for all suffize, / Whose supple Muse Camelion-like doth change / Into all formes of excellent devise' (Davies, *Orchestra*, 130.1–3, in *Poems*, ed. Krueger, 125).
62. Luis-Martínez, 'Friendlesse Verse', 586.

Chapter 10

The Worthy Knots of Fulke Greville
Sarah Knight

> As to Fulke Greville, he is like nothing but one of his own 'Prologues spoken by the ghost of an old king of Ormus', a truly formidable and inviting personage: his style is apocalyptical, cabalistical, a knot worthy of such an apparition to untie; and for the unravelling a passage or two, I would stand the brunt of an encounter with so portentous a commentator![1]

We can all name authors we find difficult, whether that means difficult to read, difficult to teach, politically and morally difficult, difficult to translate or edit; and the sense of what seems difficult to us in particular arises from our preferences, educational experiences and the many other filters through which literature reaches us. Sometimes as readers we are inclined to make the effort to work through that difficulty, if we find an author's writing to be – to quote Charles Lamb via William Hazlitt on Fulke Greville – 'a knot worthy . . . to untie'. To over four centuries' worth of readers, the poems and plays of Fulke Greville (1554–1628) have sometimes been thought difficult, and we see here how Hazlitt – ventriloquising Lamb – singles out the Prologue to *Alaham* as an especially knotted example, calling Greville's writing 'apocalyptical' and 'cabalistical'. Hazlitt's version of Lamb admires Greville, and wants to untie the knots of his writing, although Lamb himself wrote less favourably about Greville in *Specimens of English Dramatic Poets* (1808), complaining instead about the speech of the characters in his plays that 'it requires a study equivalent to the learning of a new language to understand their meaning when they speak'.[2] For this particular cluster of early nineteenth-century readers, Greville's difficulty is his fundamental quality, but their emphasis shifts from prizing to becoming occasionally frustrated by it.

It is helpful to consider how Greville writes about difficulty and poetics in what we might think of, however obliquely, as his most autobiographical work, known in manuscript as *The Dedication to Sir Philip Sidney*, and in print as *The Life of Sir Philip Sidney*, and also in his discussion of '*Poesie*' in the philosophical poem 'A Treatie of Humane Learning', where he represents it as one of the 'Arts of Recreation'.[3] These works idiosyncratically combine theoretical and practical poetics, and in their epistemological and didactic considerations the *Dedication* and the 'Treatie' seem at times strenuously and at other times obliquely argued. In terms of this volume's thematic concerns, Greville's ideas about poetry, drama and rhetoric are not 'unwritten', but his readers have sometimes argued that they need 'unravelling' (to adapt Lamb's term again). Those readers have also consistently found in Greville's writing qualities such as openness to intellectual debate, wit, strenuous tests of knowledge and imagination and intellectual sustenance, responding to the rhetorical personae he constructs as they seek to decipher the writing. The question of how invested Greville was in questions of difficulty becomes more complicated too when we realise that he created a first-person speaker in works such as the *Dedication* (as an ostensibly autobiographical prose work) as well as in philosophical poems such as 'A Treatie of Humane Learning', which creates the illusion of directness, but usually tends to offer a more complicated and fraught point of view. These perspectives vacillate and shift across different works – and sometimes within the same one – to create a prismatic view on both the difficulty and the broader intentions and reception of his own poetics, as we shall see from what Greville writes about his approach to fiction in the *Dedication* and the representation of '*Poesie*' in the 'Treatie'. We will consider in detail the Preface to *Alaham* cited at the start as an example from Greville that manifests those qualities singled out by both early modern and later readers.

A history of the challenges and rewards of reading Greville can be traced from the early seventeenth century onwards, and often the intellectual and imaginative reward is framed as a *result* of the challenge. This chapter will chart some of this history, and consider the extent to which Greville himself both articulated awareness of the potential difficulties of his work for future readers, and framed such complexity and obscurity as pivotal aspects of his poetics. We will consider the views articulated by Greville's contemporaries, including acquaintances and readers such as the philosopher Giordano Bruno and the satirist John Davies, as well as the much-satirised Richard Flecknoe writing later in the seventeenth century. Davies and Flecknoe wrote poetic responses to Greville, respectively entitled 'To the immortall memory, and deserued honor of the Writing of the Tragedy of *Mustapha* (as it is written, not printed) by S^r: Fulk Greuill, Knight' (1610) and 'On the Works of Fulke Grevil, Lord Brook' (1671), two sonnets which constitute intelligent responses to a philosophically challenging writer articulated in correspondingly complex poetic forms and language. The adjectives and metaphors we see in those early responses suggest that Greville became associated with a monumental, enigmatic style that we see evoked by much later readers too: Davies rhapsodises that each line of 'this Buskin-Poet . . . reaches to the *Firmament* / Of highest *Sense*, from surest Ground of *Wit*', while Flecknoe sees the poetry as 'Food, for strong minds!'[4] We have already had a glimpse of how nineteenth-century readers such as Lamb and Hazlitt represented Greville, but will return as well to Swinburne's alignment of Greville with George Chapman as 'the two most genuinely obscure in style upon whose works I have ever adventured to embark'.[5] Perhaps the most forthright characterisation of Greville's writing in this regard is that of Robert Southey, who bluntly called him 'certainly the most difficult of all our poets'.[6]

In the 'Treatie' and in his plays, Greville articulates misgivings about contemporary educational practice, and it is striking, therefore, that his writing has often been interpreted as particularly intellectually challenging, as requiring significant educational capital to be able to understand it. One of the earliest accounts of Greville is found in the dialogue *La Cena de le Ceneri* (*The Ash Wednesday Supper*, 1584) by the Neapolitan philosopher Giordano Bruno, a dialogue set in London in which Greville features as a speaking character. Bruno starts the 'Dialogo Secondo' with Greville asking him to enlighten him about one of the central cosmological questions of the age: 'All'hora gli disse il Sig. Folco Grivello. Di gratia S. Nolano, fatemi intendere le raggioni per le quali stimate la terra muoversi' ['Then Sir Fulke Greville said to him: – "Signor Nolano, please explain to me the reasons which lead you to think that the earth moves"']. To debate this point with him, Bruno asks Greville to find 'persone, le quali fussero giudicate sufficiente a' questa impresa' ['persons whom he judged equal to such a task'] and the character of Greville, relishing such discussion, gladly accepts: 'disse, voi mi fate gratissimo officio' ['you ask me to do something which gives me the greatest pleasure'].[7] Bruno's representation gives us insight into how Greville was involved not only in contemporary courtly life, but also in wider European intellectual circles. The delight that Bruno's Greville takes in the 'gratissimo officio' of listening to knowledgeable people debate the nature of the cosmos substantiates the evidence, offered by the poems and plays, that Greville was a polymath who took a keen interest in science, especially cartography and cosmology, as well as in the poetics and rhetoric so central to the cultural exchanges of the Sidney circle.

For his interest in science as an applied as well as a theoretical discipline, which we see too in the 'Treatie', we can compare Greville with his contemporary Francis Bacon, whose *Advancement of Learning* (1607) places both a moral and intellectual value on difficulty that can chime with arguments that we find in Greville's fictions. Bacon, while arguing for a clarification and a rationalisation of knowledge, also maintains that complexity is epistemologically necessary and desirable: even 'a little superficiall learning . . . taketh away all leuitie, temeritie, and insolencie, by copious suggestion of all doubts and difficulties'.[8] As we have already suggested of the Preface to *Alaham*, the density and obscurity of Greville's writing can seem to exemplify that 'copious suggestion of all doubts and difficulties', but what Bacon's epistemological model argues is that such suggestion is salutary, even intellectually necessary. If we do not doubt, our 'insolencie' remains and so we do not think clearly or humbly enough: for Bacon, as for Greville, thinking through 'doubts and difficulties' is fundamental to intellectual and ethical development. It was perhaps in writing the 'Treatie' that Greville considered most carefully Bacon's ideas about how the human mind is formed and how its processes can be improved. In the 'Treatie', Greville represents people's minds both as limited and often ignorant, and as compulsively generating complications and fictions, introducing a central theme of his writing about the human capacity for thought. To exemplify this tension, we can compare how the first stanza ends, stating that 'Knowledge doth it selfe farre more extend, / Than all the minds of Men can comprehend' (1, p. 154), with the later argument that rather than conceiving of '*Ideas*' and '*Science* [here, knowledge] of the Godhead', 'in their stead we raise, and mould Tropheas, / Formes of Opinion, Wit, and Vanity, / Which we call *Arts*; and fall in loue with these' (25, p. 160). For Greville, 'art', so often used in the late sixteenth and early seventeenth centuries to denote skill and refinement, is often a pejorative term: here '*Arts*' turn people into deluded idolaters.

Some of Greville's contemporaries, however, chose to foreground his authorial skill and elite status as a courtier close to the monarch over this kind of Baconian striving or the challenges posed by reading his work. The French botanist Carolus Clusius (Charles de l'Escluse) kindly if somewhat blandly called Greville a *Generosus Adolescens* (noble young man), in a Latin letter to the physician and biologist Joachim Camerarius the Younger when they met in Vienna in 1577.⁹ And Greville, whom George Puttenham describes in *The Art of English Poesy* (1589), for instance, as one of a 'crew of courtly makers, noblemen and gentlemen of her Majesty's own servants, who have written excellently well', is a very different figure from Bruno's constantly questioning 'Sig. Folco Grivello'.¹⁰ Nonetheless, characterisations such as Puttenham's often tend to be outweighed by those accounts that emphasise philosophical engagement and self-examination. This apparently caused Bruno to represent him as curious, eager for new knowledge of complex phenomena and keen to stimulate debate, but also led others to characterise him as not only intellectually but also morally discriminating. Adjectives to describe Greville interestingly recur between earlier and subsequent readers, although the emphasis placed on one adjective particularly – 'worthy' – shifts from Greville's personal qualities to the complexity of his writing. While in 1826 Hazlitt had written of the 'worthy knots' of Greville's writing, in 1599 his friend and protégé Samuel Daniel dedicated *Musophilus*, his 'General Defence of Learning', and a dialogue between Musophilus and Philocosmus', 'To the right *Worthy* and Iudicious Fauourer of Vertue, Master Fulke Greuill' (my emphasis), promising in the dedicatory sonnet to 'present thee, onely modelled / In this poor frame, the forme of mine owne heart', an artful expression of sincerity and a compliment to the exaltation that we see in Greville's own poetry of simplicity and humility ('onely modelled / In this poor frame') as an important principle, even if simplicity was not consistently his own poetic practice.¹¹

In 1968 Thom Gunn too wrote that Greville makes '[d]eprivation and despair . . . his peculiar province, even as early as this, by the intensity of his apprehension of them'.¹² In the *Dedication*, Greville brings that intensity to the writing of poetry, and to the argument that poetry should achieve certain didactic aims that the reader may have to work to understand. The *Dedication* proposes tenacious yet sensitive reading, and a willingness to work hard to understand, usually framed by those readers as valuable for the eventual intellectual and even moral benefits. The 'intensity of apprehension' Gunn observes has its late Elizabethan roots in Daniel's characterisation of Greville as 'right Worthy and Iudicious', as an individual carefully sifting and able to evaluate the poetry of others due to the value of his own, a 'Fauourer of Vertue' because of his own virtue. Granted, it is not unusual for a dedication to pay a compliment, but Daniel's emphasis on the *quality* of Greville's attentiveness is striking.

Whether or not Greville personally cultivated difficulty as part of his 'intensity of apprehension' is a complicated question. Like the rhetorical 'gift' proudly claimed by the schoolmaster Holofernes in Shakespeare's *Love's Labour's Lost* (*c.* 1595), Greville's densely articulated poetry and plays are 'full of forms, figures, shapes, ideas, apprehensions, motions, revolutions'.[13] A similar judgement could be made of many of Greville's late Elizabethan contemporaries, of course, but in the case of his two plays especially, *Alaham* and *Mustapha*, paradoxes, the subtly varied repetition of cognates, classical allusions, scientific (especially cosmological and nautical) terms, words from language families unfamiliar even to his humanistically educated readers, such as Ottoman Turkish, as well as intricately knotted philosophical and theological arguments abound. Gavin Alexander has argued that Greville was 'a man preoccupied with his posthumous influence',[14] and whether or not his hope was that such influence would inspire others to write difficult poetry, the reception of his writing as difficult from the seventeenth century onwards has constituted a substantial part of his posthumous reputation.

In his 1978 essay 'On Difficulty'[15] George Steiner defined poetry as a form 'knit of words compacted with every conceivable mode of operative force'.[16] Steiner's textile metaphor evokes some of the more tightly packed moments in Greville's compositions and aligns with similar images used by earlier readers, especially Romantic readers, to describe the grammatical, syntactical and conceptual densities of Greville's dramatic writing. Steiner considers difficulty as a literary and philosophical mode that can be subdivided into four fundamental categories: 'contingent', or elements of the text that need '[t]o be looked up'; 'modal', in which the 'idiom and orders of apprehension' in the text 'are no longer natural to us', given that 'we cannot coerce our own sensibility into the relevant frame of perception'; 'tactical', through which the author 'must literally create new words and syntactic modes', and '[i]f the reader would follow the poet into the *terra incognita* of revelation, he must learn the language'; and finally 'ontological difficulties', which 'confront us with blank questions about the nature of human speech, about the status of significance'.[17] Greville's writing at times falls within all four of Steiner's categories. We need to look up many allusions and words fully to understand their meaning and resonance within his writing, such as references to contemporary political frameworks (*Mustapha* in particular contains a number of terms taken from Ottoman power structures), and to the classical past. Greville does at times seem, if not to create his own language, as Lamb had claimed, then at least to make his reader carefully consider the status of words and how these reflect ideas, although for some of his readers his use of language did not always straightforwardly express the thinking that had driven it.

Readers of the *Dedication* encountered Greville's self-representation as a former courtier under a different monarch and a new dynasty, now retired from the ferment and competition of the political sphere. In the *Dedication*, as well as in the plays, Greville constantly stresses the congruence between lived experience and thought (practical, abstract *and* imaginative). For his argument, the abstract and the practical converge on the didactic. It is towards the end of the work that Greville discusses his writing in a more sustained way, and one of the earliest points he makes about his 'tragedies, with some treatises annexed' (D 90.1–2) – *Alaham*, *Mustapha* and the longer philosophical poems – is that, in writing them, he had scant interest in building 'the self-reputation of being an exact artisan in that poetical mystery', preferring instead to offer 'a perspective into vice, and the unprosperities of it' (D 90.8–10). Greville briskly rejects any claim to be a skilled ('artisan') poetic maker, but also that there is any kind of 'mystery' in his writing, insisting in this section of the *Dedication* at least that his commitment is to moral clarity, to a discernible 'perspective into vice': the optical metaphor suggests a wish to clarify rather than obfuscate a reader's sight and understanding.

In the *Dedication*, then, Greville suggests that fiction should ideally be morally instructive and political. For him the term 'political' functioned across its multiple humanistic senses: a work of fiction might be an instrumental *speculum principis*; it might advocate a philosophical imperative – scepticism, Stoicism – that lends itself to political positioning; it might counsel obliquely, even unscrupulously (thinking of that ambiguous contemporary label *politique*); and it might illuminate micro-polities (the academy, the household) in relation to the macro-political state. But Greville also acknowledges the difficulty of thinking through and communicating political ideas clearly, and the fear – and the potentially mortal stakes – of having one's writing misunderstood. He describes writing drama as a 'spreading ocean of images', but characterises his impulse towards political representation in the philosophical poems (he calls them 'treatises', explicitly signalling their didacticism) as a 'confusing mist'. Greville chooses this metaphor specifically to describe the treatise called in the *Dedication* 'The Declination of Monarchy', which was later, and more neutrally, known as 'A Treatise of Monarchy' (D 92). That he feared his political fictions might be misread is evidenced by his account of burning the third tragedy he wrote, another version of *Antony and Cleopatra*, which he worried in the *Dedication* was 'apt enough to be construed or strained to a personating of vices in the present governors or government' – most probably, that the story would be read as a *roman à clef* of Elizabeth and Essex (D 93).

In the *Dedication* Greville chooses and repeats a number of metaphors, or image clusters, to articulate the challenges of his own writing. He refers to his 'lack of a well-touched compass' on the 'ocean of images' again in the final section of the *Dedication*. He also uses scientific instruments to stand for his dramatic characterisation. He has exaggerated the figures in his plays, he suggests, 'finding all little instruments in discovery of great bodies to be seldome without errors' (D 133.13–14). As with another contemporary, John Donne, however, who also used scientific instruments as metaphors such as the 'stiff twin compasses' to denote the two lovers' 'souls' in 'A Valediction: Forbidding Mourning',[18] Greville's scientific interests – his strongest characteristic as represented in Bruno's 'Dialogo' – fed back into his poetry and prose. Samuel Johnson famously complained of the group including Donne, which he himself influentially termed the 'metaphysical poets', that in their verse, 'The most heterogeneous ideas are yoked by violence together; nature and art are ransacked for illustrations, comparisons, and allusions.'[19] Greville frequently uses new scientific discourse to inform his poetry, especially the language of technology and cartography. Greville is rarely grouped with the 'metaphysical poets', but Johnson's objections could as justifiably be levelled at his writing as at that of contemporaries such as Donne, especially the yoking together of 'heterogeneous ideas', which seems for so many of his readers to have prompted those accusations of difficulty.

Greville ends the *Dedication* by stating that he intends his tragedies for 'those only that are weather-beaten in the sea of this world, such as, having lost the sight of their gardens and groves, study to sail on a right course among rocks and quicksands' (D 134.25–8). In the *Dedication*, then, Greville sets out the theoretical – or 'abstract' (D 133.13), to use a word he frequently chooses – principles of how he thinks literature and drama should work. He suggests not only the difficulty of composition – the 'confusing mist' a poet has to penetrate to represent politics clearly – but also the difficulty of *interpretation*, of how often an author's *intentions* are misunderstood. As an example of clever men who fail to make themselves sufficiently clear, and again, expressly within the realm of politics, he invokes 'the fate of many metaphysical Phormios before me who had lost themselves in teaching kings and princes how to govern their people' (D 91.16–19). Phormio was the philosopher who advised Hannibal on war, as recounted by Cicero in *De oratore*, a foolish greybeard who presumed to lecture the ultimate military tactician.[20] The implication here is that the courtier/counsellor might *think* of himself as offering useful, clear advice, but the sovereign thought otherwise, or failed to grasp the point.

Central to the *Dedication*'s account of fictional purpose is the idea that those for whom Greville says he is writing – those 'that are weather-beaten in the sea of this world' and 'study to sail on a right course' – are shown as 'having lost the sight of their gardens and groves' (*D* 134.26–7). For Greville, the landscaped, soft pastoral *otium* of 'gardens and groves' maps on to the 'witty fictions' he has mentioned a few sentences beforehand: these are books 'in which the affections or imagination may perchance find exercise and entertainment, but the memory and judgement no enriching at all' (*D* 134.3–5). He calls these 'delicate images', bundling into his critique terms taken from rhetoric – excessive *copia* – and from the domestic sphere – where 'images' become houses stuffed with jumbled, proliferating polyglot meanings: 'I conceived those delicate images to be over-abundantly furnished in all languages already' (*D* 134.5–7). These 'delicate images' are sharply at odds with his own 'spreading ocean of images' (*D* 90.13): those may be large, sprawling and uncontrollable as the sea, but these are highly wrought, pretty, fashionable, too easy – not difficult, but over-familiar.

Uneasy, as we have seen, at the prospect of having his plays read as comments on contemporary statecraft, Greville cast writing about politics as especially difficult, and his interest in political theory and practice was undoubtedly viewed by several later readers, especially Charles Lamb, as one of the more challenging aspects of his work. In the *Specimens of English Dramatic Poets*, Lamb wrote that Greville's 'two Tragedies ... might with more propriety have been termed political treatises, than plays'.[21] We have already seen that Lamb characterised Greville's expression in the plays as being difficult to understand, the need for a 'study equivalent to the learning of a new language to understand [the characters'] meaning'.[22] But more readers have commented on the difficulty of his style, on the problems of locating meaning in such rebarbative, densely wrought poetry. Both forms of difficulty sit behind the characterisation of Greville's writing as 'cabalistical' by the character Charles Lamb as he appears in Hazlitt's essay 'On Persons One Would Wish to Have Seen'. By the early nineteenth century, 'cabalistical' certainly carried the sense of the complex knowledge enclosed in the Kabbalah, which seems significant in Hazlitt's discussion here; but the more recent political past had created the neologism of the 'cabal' to refer to the members of

Charles II's Restoration cabinet with whom the word's implication of a self-selected, scheming government élite originated, a term against which Hazlitt defines William Godwin: 'he is at the head of no cabal, he belongs to no party in the State'.[23]

In the *Dedication* Greville also casts himself as a man retired from politics, critical of 'the conspiracies of ambitious subalterns' (*D* 8.25). Concerns about political intention being misinterpreted have often historically led to cryptic writing needing to be deciphered, where the deliberate creation of political ambiguities causes difficulty of interpretation. If readers have subsequently focused on either political or hermeneutic difficulties in Greville's writing, it seems clear in the *Dedication* that the author himself saw the two as frequently intertwined. Alan Bray has written persuasively of how Greville's familiar letters, especially to Edward Coke, express a sense of danger about communications being misinterpreted, not least because 'friendship signified in a public sphere', the sphere in which as a courtier and political figure, as well as a cultural patron, Greville operated for much of his life.[24] The intention to write in what Hazlitt's Lamb calls a 'cabalistical' way may have stemmed at least in part from a choice to make explicit meaning obscure, encrypted, legible only to hopefully sympathetic readers. In the *Dedication* Greville articulates both his concerns about being misread, and the extreme actions he carried out to avoid such misinterpretation, principally setting fire to his play *Antony and Cleopatra*. Carefully wrought obscurity is one means of avoiding, or masking, possible danger: obscurity of style complicates the interpretation of political purpose.

In the *Dedication*, Greville characterises his talent as a 'creeping genius', halting and furtive when contrasted with the 'dexterity' of Sidney his 'noble friend', and 'the dashes of his pen' (*D* 134.22, 10–12). Such apparent self-deprecation is part of the *Dedication*'s extended tribute to a charismatic, well-connected, blazingly talented friend, of course, but it is also issues from the stance Greville cultivates in that work of retirement and weary familiarity with the world's ways which prompts self-representation as 'creeping' rather than 'noble' and dashing. The manuscript title 'Dedication' indicates one of the purposes Greville had in mind for that combination of elegy for a lost friend, political memoir and literary manifesto, to offer up his literary works to Sidney's memory,[25] and it was the tragedies *Alaham* and *Mustapha* that Greville wanted to 'dedicate'. He characterises these as plays of his 'youth', contrasted in the *Dedication* with the perspective from an older, disillusioned subject position:

'after I had once ventured upon this spreading ocean of images, my apprehensive youth, for lack of a well-touched compass, did easily wander beyond proportion' (*D* 90.15–16). Here, the idea of fiction-writing is figured as amorphous, ever-increasing and overwhelming, especially for younger authors: a 'spreading ocean of images' which takes the inexperienced poet out of his depth, unable to control the 'proportion' of the work, without a compass, let alone an adept, familiar, 'well-touched' one. Greville resorts often to such nautical and navigational metaphors to represent the act of writing, and these become a central aspect of how he figures both the difficulty of life and art, while also perhaps reflecting the interests in maritime travel he had demonstrated in the final decades of the sixteenth century.[26]

We have already seen that Greville includes '*Poesie*' as one of the 'Arts of Recreation' in 'A Treatie of Humane Learning' (111, p. 181). The 'Treatie' offers a wider examination and critique of the crabbed effects of academic learning on human thought and expression, whereby the institutions of learning, and especially of higher education, are witheringly described throughout as 'the *Schooles*' (e.g., 105, p. 180). This characterisation accords with a complex knot in Greville's representation of human thought across his writing: his own poetry may be difficult to understand, but he also criticises the way in which he and his contemporaries had been *taught* to understand. In the 'Treatie' the 'scope' of both '*Poesie* and *Musicke*' is figured as 'meerly contentation' (111, p. 181) – a somewhat bland 'making content' or 'making satisfied' – although for all of the reasons this chapter explores, not least its complex linguistic structures and densely philosophical arguments, such mere 'contentation' is not often offered by Greville's own poems. The 'Treatie' continues by arguing that the function of '*Poesie*' is to 'moue, but not remoue, or make impression / Really, either to enrich the Wit, / Or, which is lesse, to mend our states by it' (111, p. 181). 'Wit' was a fraught term for Greville: he sometimes associated it with trivial polish and sometimes with a serious capacity for thinking, and here he seems to intend the latter meaning, suggesting poetry's lightness in its inability to 'enrich' that mental faculty.[27] Here too '*Poesie*' is tainted by association with the *artes* of the pedagogical trivium taught by those detrimental '*Schooles*': '*Grammar*' (103, p. 179); '*Logike*' which with its 'Tyranny / Of subtile rules . . . Confounds of reall truth the harmony' (104, p. 180); and, particularly perniciously, the '*Siren*' that is '*Rhetorike* . . . with empty sounds misleading / Vs to false ends' (107, p. 180). Although '*Poesie*' is not so explicitly framed as the source of temptation in Homer's *Odyssey* that famously drove so many sailors to their deaths (a very different kind of nautical metaphor from those we see in the *Dedication*), by aligning it so unchallengingly with 'contentation' Greville undermines its capacity for that moral challenge and strenuous yet ultimately salutary opacity he described in the *Dedication*. Poetry here is the opposite of difficult: its only value to 'solid Iudgements' is 'as pleasing sauce to dainty food' (112, p. 182), fixed as a series of bright, trivial commodities – '[f]ine foyle for iewels, or enammels grace'.

The anti-ornamentation drive of these stanze on '*Poesie*', and the argument that its only value is 'to describe, or praise / Goodnesse, or God' (114, p. 182), is motivated by the speaker's theological concerns, and anticipates the conclusion of the 'Treatie' that 'Thus are true Learnings in the humble heart / A *Spirituall worke*' (148, p. 191). The 'pleasing sauce' and 'enammels grace' of poetry are not neutral, moreover, if they deceptively exalt something bad or base, as the final question of this stanza intimates: '*if the matter be in Nature vile, / How can it be made pretious by a stile?*' Here Greville anticipates two questions a far more avowedly straightforward poet George Herbert would pose at the start of 'Jordan (I)': 'Who sayes that fictions onely and false hair / Become a verse? Is there in truth no beautie?'[28] Greville takes a very different approach to Protestant poetics from the one Herbert would choose for *The Temple* (1633), but we can see an echo of Greville's 'pleasing sauce' and 'enammels' in Herbert's 'fictions' and 'false hair': both authors figure simplicity as truthful and art as deceptive in these poems, making a moral case for clarity. The central focus of the 'Treatie' is on original sin, the Fall and the Tree of Knowledge: learning, especially formally taught learning and its practitioners, are aligned with the diabolical temptation to know, rather than the pious acceptance of the limitations of human knowledge: '*These Arts, moulds, workes can but express the sinne, / Whence by mans follie, his fall did beginne*' (47, p. 165).

Some of Greville's earlier readers picked up on the metaphors he uses to characterise the difficulties of existence, and drew those into a discussion of the difficulty of understanding his writing. The plays, the *Dedication* concludes, are for those who 'study to sail on a right course among rocks and quicksands' (*D* 134.27–8). Several of those readers seem alert to his fondness for nautical metaphors, especially the idea that life is a treacherous voyage and that one only acquires wisdom through being buffetted by the waves. As the title of his epigram, printed in *The Scourge of Folly* (1610), suggests, John Davies was one of the earliest readers of Greville's plays to commit his opinion to print – 'To the immortall memory, and deserued honor of the Writer of the Tragedy of *Mustapha*, (as it is written, not Printed) by S^r: *Fulk Greuill*, Knight'. *Mustapha* was printed in quarto in 1609, but several manuscripts predate that publication, and through his place via his teaching work on the periphery of the Herbert–Sidney circle, Davies might have known of these earlier versions.[29] It is likely that Greville was writing the *Dedication* around the same time as the epigram was printed, and although no evidence found at the time of writing proves that Davies had access to any manuscript version, it is striking nonetheless that his poem opens with the kind of nautical metaphor we see throughout Greville's text:

> Swell prowdly *Numbers* on Words windy Seas
> To raise this Buskin-Poet to the *Skies*;
> And fix him there among the Pleyades,
> To light the *Muse* in gloomy *Tragedies* (1–4)

Davies then builds on the introduction to the tragic Muse we see in these lines to imply that her collaboration with Greville, 'this Buskin-Poet', challenges her to work harder than she has before, to surpass either her own understanding or that of her spectators (or perhaps both): 'Wherein the *Muse* beyond the Minde is forc'd / (In rarest *Raptures*) to *Arts* highest *Spheare*' (7–8). Davies's sonnet combines praise of Greville's exalted poetic skill and philosophical ambition: his achievement in pushing the Muse to '*Arts* highest *Spheare*' is consolidated by the following compliment to his versification: 'No *Line* but reaches to the *Firmanent* / Of highest *Sense*, from surest Ground of *Wit*' (9–10). But that verb 'forc'd' also implies that the Muse – and the reader – need to work to keep up with Greville, to make a strenuous effort to engage with his 'gloomy *Tragedies*'.[30]

In a later generation of poet-readers, Richard Flecknoe's sonnet 'On the Works of Fulk Grevil, Lord Brook' (1671) similarly combines praise with a suggestion of intellectual strain. If, as the first line of the poem makes clear, these 'Works' are '[f]ood, for *strong minds*!', the idea that they are not for every reader is also immediately introduced: 'of your lighter stuff / The *weaker* find in other *Books* enough' (1–2), and it is only 'great wits' (3) who feel the appropriate levels of 'reverence and admiration' (4). Flecknoe also suggests that as well as being an acquired taste, Greville's works are also for the mature literary palate: 'Novices, and those of meaner wit / Are not grown up' (5–6) enough to appreciate them. As we have already seen in Hazlitt and Daniel, Flecknoe also invokes Greville as extraordinarily 'worthy', and emphasises his excellence as Puttenham had: 'Thy works shall stand to posterity / As Relick of thy worth and Excellency' (7–8). The simile with which the sonnet ends stresses the solidity and monumentality of Greville's works: Flecknoe compares them to a different kind of 'Relick', a marble bust: 'Just as I've seen some *Statua's busto* stand, / The Relick of some Excellent Masters hand' (9–10). Flecknoe was writing four decades after Greville's death, unlike Davies, Daniel and Puttenham who were writing as his closer contemporaries; nonetheless, even though we know that Flecknoe's is a posthumous comment, the repetition of 'Relick' emphasises both that the object – the works – is sacred, but also that it is dead, belonging to a previous age. This is a 'Relick' that can perhaps only be properly appreciated by that age: '[w]hose worth only a *Michael Angelo* / Or a *Bernino* had the skill to know' (11–12). Michelangelo (1475–1564) died when Greville was only ten years old, while Gian Lorenzo Bernini (1598–1680) was a near-contemporary of Flecknoe's (*c.* 1600–1678). The sonnet's conclusion is that in these phases of recent cultural history, a certain kind of artist's worth can only be appreciated by another similarly skilled and high-minded artist. In expressing 'admiration' for Greville, Flecknoe situates himself among the other 'great wits' who recognise '*Master-strokes*' when they see them (3), as well as alongside the most revered sculptors of the sixteenth and seventeenth centuries: like Michelangelo and Bernini, he is able to recognise 'some Excellent Masters hand' (10) – another telling repetition. The poem's last thought is that Greville's works cannot be appreciated by '*Marble spoilers* and the common sort': these '[w]anted the knowledge, to admire them for't' (13–14). In Flecknoe's sonnet, discriminating insider 'knowledge' is necessary to appreciate Greville: 'those of meaner wit' and 'the common sort' are unable to do so.[31]

These bundles of ideas and figures, the product of a polymathic imagination that sometimes runs into its own 'confusing mist' and 'spreading ocean', bring us back to the English Romantic reception of Greville.[32] I have mentioned Robert Southey's view, published in his *Select Works of the British Poets from Chaucer to Jonson* (1831), in which he described Greville as 'one of the profoundest thinkers that ever clothed his thoughts in verse', and 'certainly the most difficult of all our poets'.[33] The two responses from Charles Lamb, one direct and one indirect, that we have mentioned offer a related but differently articulated view. Lamb's footnote on *Alaham* and *Mustapha* in his *Specimens of English Dramatic Poets* notes the interest in politics that Greville discusses in such detail in the *Dedication*, but casts this as a deadening flaw: 'These two Tragedies of Lord Brooke might with more propriety have been termed political treatises, than plays ... Whether we look into his plays, or his most passionate love-poems, we shall find all frozen and made rigid with intellect.' Here, in Lamb's view, the political didacticism so fundamental to Greville's sense of fiction's purpose *prevents* him from being an effective dramatist, turning him instead into 'nine parts Machiavel and Tacitus, for one part Sophocles or Seneca'. While Hazlitt's version of Lamb might like Greville's 'apocalyptical' and 'cabbalistical writing', Lamb's own emphasis in the *Specimens* is markedly different and less approving.

In Hazlitt's essay, on the other hand, Lamb's interest in 'Sir Thomas Browne and Fulke Greville, the friend of Sir Philip Sidney' is *based* on their hard-to-parse writing:

> The reason why I pitch upon these two authors is, that their writings are riddles, and they themselves the most mysterious of personages. They resemble the soothsayers of old, who dealt in dark hints and doubtful oracles; and I should like to ask them the meaning of what no mortal but themselves, I should suppose, can fathom.[34]

The words Lamb chooses bring us emphatically back to the question of difficulty: 'riddles', 'mysterious', 'dark hints', 'doubtful oracles', 'what no mortal but themselves ... can fathom'. And it is here that we come back to the example from Greville's tragedy *Alaham* with which this essay began, which Hazlitt's Lamb invokes to reinforce his opinion of Greville's fascinating mysteries of expression:

> As to Fulke Greville, he is like nothing but one of his own 'Prologues spoken by the ghost of an old king of Ormus,' a truly formidable and inviting personage: his style is apocalyptical, cabalistical, a knot worthy of such an apparition to untie; and for the unravelling a passage or two, I would stand the brunt of an encounter with so portentous a commentator![35]

We will end by 'unravelling a passage' from the *Alaham* Prologue, to identify some reasons why these readers may have considered Greville so deeply, idiosyncratically difficult. The 'old king of Ormus' – Hormuz on the Persian Gulf, in modern-day Iran – speaks as a ghost who has come up from the underworld, and his first priority is to describe the hell he has recently left. In opening with a ghost speech, Greville was following the convention made famous by plays such as Seneca's *Thyestes* (*c.* 60 CE): Seneca's play begins with a speech by *umbra Tantali* (the ghost of Tantalus), and Greville followed popular contemporaries such as Thomas Kyd in *The Spanish Tragedy* (1592) – in which the ghost of Andrea and the personification of Revenge begin the play – by giving his Prologue to a ghost. But geographical location and social status mark out an even earlier classical intertext for *Alaham*'s ghost Prologue, Aeschylus' Πέρσαι (*Persians*; 472 BCE), in which the Εἴδωλον Δαρείου (*Eidōlon Dareiou*, 'the Ghost of Darius') speaks to his wife Atossa and the Chorus of Persian elders in an extended scene of prophecy, political advice and despair over loss in war.[36]

Greville's evocation not only of the more familiar Latin Senecan tradition but also of an earlier Greek play situates *Alaham* within a long, complex dramatic tradition. Compared with Aeschylus' ghost of Darius, however, whose first words directly address Πέρσαι γεραιοί (*Persai geraioi*, 'the aged Persians') of the Chorus as companions from his youth,[37] the first lines spoken by Greville's Old King create a creeping sense of vagueness in indeterminacy, as he addresses a 'Monster' that is disturbingly never named:

> *Thou Monster horrible*! vnder whose vglie doome,
> Downe in Eternities perpetuall night,
> Mans temporall sinnes beare torments infinite . . . (Prologue 1–3)

The address – which is, of course, also our first impression of the play as readers – raises more questions than are answered: is this 'Monster' Satan, another diabolically efficient demon out of Hieronymus Bosch's visions of hell, or perhaps the three-headed dog Cerberus, guardian of the Greco-Roman underworld? The fact that the question is never resolved, and so the reader is never reassured by concrete knowledge and kept uncertain and anxious, is typical of the effects wrought by Greville's 'Prologue'. The puzzling quality of the opening lines is compounded by what the ghost goes on to discuss: his sequence of infernal paradoxes seems at times to anticipate Milton's in Book I of *Paradise Lost* (1667) – 'darkness visible', 'the Lake with liquid fire' and so on.[38] Greville works to prevent the reader from imagining this hell in concrete terms:

> A place there is vpon no centre placed,
> Deepe vnder depthes, as farre as is the skie
> Above the earth; darcke, infinitely spaced:
> *Pluto* the Kinge, the kingedome Miserie.
> The Chrystall may Gods gloriouse seate resemble;
> Horror it selfe theise horrors but dissemble. (Prologue 15–20)

Several elements in this passage suggest what we read in Bruno's representation of Greville's scientifically curious nature, as well as Davies's and Flecknoe's recognition of his poetry's hermeneutic challenges.

Greville's writing here falls into Steiner's taxonomy of difficulty too, especially its 'contingent', 'modal' and 'tactical' forms: there is much in these lines 'to look up', and even Greville's contemporary readers would have had to work to understand the articulation of modes of thought far distant in time even from the late sixteenth and early seventeenth centuries. In rhetorical terms, too, the sequence of paradoxes is deliberately obfuscatory, leaving all undefined. Both the syntax and the metrical pattern of the line 'A place there is vpon no centre placed' exemplifies 'tactical' difficulty, and anticipates, in its challenge visually to imagine the unimaginable, Milton's similarly amorphous account of Death in *Paradise Lost*: 'If shape it might be called that shape had none'.[39]

In theological terms, an even more 'confusing mist' – to revisit Greville's own metaphor from the *Dedication* – descends as we try to think through this depiction of hell. The invocation of Pluto by the 'old king of Ormus' is perhaps surprising in terms of the belief systems we might expect the play to represent, as he invokes Pluto – the Roman version of the Greek god Hades in the ancient Greek polytheistic pantheon – as the 'Kinge' of the place, while referring monotheistically in the same speech to 'Gods gloriouse seate'. Also blurring our perspective here is Greville's depiction of Pluto's realm both in abstract terms of suffering ('the kingedome Miserie') and in relation to the Ptolemaic cosmos: 'The Chrystall may Gods gloriouse seate resemble'. Demonstrating that interest in cosmology and planetary science which Bruno had also observed, Greville here refers to Ptolemy's seventh heaven, the *coelum crystallinum*, the crystal axis on which all of the other spheres revolve, as famously represented by Dante in Book 21 of the *Paradiso*.[40] By the time Greville was writing, the Ptolemaic cosmology had of course been overtaken by Copernican and Keplerian ideas of the universe, as Marlowe has his Mephistopheles acknowledge in the B-text of *Doctor Faustus*:

Faustus: But is there not coelum igneum et crystallinum?
Mephistopheles: No, Faustus, they be but fables.[41]

Greville's verse treatise 'Of Human Learning', especially, indicates how profoundly interested he was in such cosmological structures, 'fables' and otherwise: the fact that the *coelum crystallinum* is evoked here does not suggest an author outdated in his astronomical understanding, but deliberately adds to the blurred, inchoate outlines of an ineffable underworld described by a cloudy-brained character – 'old', as the stage direction tells us; weak (as he goes on to describe himself); confounded. Shapeless, infinite, classical, Christian, Ptolemaic: the underworld at the start of *Alaham*, to which so many characters are sent as the play progresses, is a complex proposition. The Prologue and its author expect the reader to work exceptionally hard.

We will end with a later nineteenth-century view on Fulke Greville, which takes a very different turn from the 'apocalyptical' and 'portentous' reading by Hazlitt, and Lamb's 'rigid and frozen with intellect'. Choosing 'obscure' rather than Southey's 'difficult' as his keyword, Algernon Charles Swinburne – who saw Greville and his contemporary George Chapman as 'of all English poets the two most genuinely obscure in style' – defined that quality as 'the natural product of turbid forces and confused ideas; of a feeble and clouded or of a vigorous but unfixed and chaotic intellect'. Swinburne's extended metaphor takes us back to Greville's own seafaring images in the *Dedication*, his gesture outwards to readers 'weather-beaten in the seas of this world': Swinburne represents himself as a nautically inclined risk-taking reader, as he thinks of the 'works' of these two poets as the 'most genuinely obscure' of all on which 'I have ever adventured to embark, in search of treasure hidden beneath the dark gulfs and crossing currents of their rocky and weedy waters, at some risk of my understanding being swept away by the groundswell'. For Swinburne, 'such a poet' as Greville is 'overcharged with overflowing thoughts . . . not sufficiently possessed by any one leading idea, or attracted towards any one central point, to see with decision the proper end and use with resolution the proper instruments of his design'.[42] As we have seen in the Prologue to *Alaham*, Greville's 'thoughts' can indeed be densely packed, closely argued, and can sometimes seem 'genuinely obscure in style'. But we could perhaps use the responses of Greville's readers and their consistent interest in the valuable challenges of his concerted difficulties, complexities and ambiguities to suggest that – rather than being 'overcharged with overflowing thoughts' – all of these qualities can be numbered among what Swinburne called the 'proper instruments of his design', and also what Lamb in Hazlitt's characterisation described as 'a knot worthy of such an apparition to untie', deliberately complicated for the edification of the reader.

Notes

I would like to thank the following friends and colleagues for constructive suggestions and questions that have informed and improved this essay:

Phil Shaw, Hannah Crawforth, Sonia Hernández-Santano, Felicity James, Mary Ann Lund, Zenón Luis-Martínez, Kathryn Murphy, Elizabeth Scott-Baumann and Jessica Wolfe.

1. Charles Lamb, in Hazlitt, 'On Persons One Would Wish to Have Seen', 33.
2. Lamb, *Specimens*, 1:264. For the text of *Alaham*, see Greville, *Poems and Dramas*, ed. Bullough, 2:138–213. Further references are given parenthetically in the text by line number and page.
3. For the *Dedication*, see Greville, *Prose Works*, ed. Gouws. References are cited parenthetically in the text by the abbreviation *D*, page and line numbers. For 'A Treatie of Humane Learning', see Greville, *Poems and Dramas*, 1:154–91. References are cited parenthetically in the text by stanza and page number.
4. Davies (of Hereford), *Scourge of Folly*, 154–5; Flecknoe, *Epigrams of all sorts*, 10–11.
5. Swinburne, *George Chapman*, 16. I thank Zenón Luis-Martínez for first bringing Swinburne's view of Greville to my attention, related to his own investigation of Chapman's poetry. See Luis-Martínez, 'George Chapman's "Habit of Poesie"', this volume, 261 n.14.
6. See Southey, *Select Works*, 912; see also Knight, 'Enriching the Judgement'.
7. Bruno, *Ash Wednesday Supper*, trans. Gatti, 54–5.
8. Bacon, *Advancement of Learning*, ed. Kiernan, 49.
9. See Hunger, *Charles de l'Escluse (Carolus Clusius)*, 69; Clusius's letter (numbered 'LII') can be found on pp. 340–1. See also the *Clusius Correspondence* database at <http://clusiuscorrespondence.huygens.knaw.nl/edition/entry/540/transcription> (accessed 29 July 2021).
10. See Puttenham, *Art of English Poesy*, ed. Whigham and Rebhorn, 149.
11. Daniel, *Musophilus*, 'To Fulke Greuill', 5–6, in *Poems and A Defence of Rhyme*, ed. Sprague, 67.
12. Gunn, 'Introduction', 23.
13. Shakespeare, *Love's Labour's Lost*, 4.2.61–3, in *Norton Shakespeare*, ed. Greenblatt, 766.
14. Alexander, 'Fulke Greville and the Afterlife', 205; see also Leo, Röder and Sierhuis, 'Introduction', 1–4.
15. First published as a journal article in 1978, Steiner's 'On Difficulty' was then included that same year in the collection *On Difficulty and Other Essays*, from which I am citing here.
16. Steiner, *On Difficulty*, 21.
17. For definitions of the four categories cited here, see Steiner, *On Difficulty*, 23, 33, 34 and 41 respectively.
18. Donne, 'A Valediction: Forbidding Mourning', 25–6, in *Complete Poems*, ed. Robins, 260.
19. Johnson, *Lives of the Poets*, ed. Lonsdale, 2:262.
20. Cicero, *De oratore*, II.18.75, ed. and trans. Sutton and Rackham, 1:254–5.

21. Lamb, *Specimens*, 1:264; see also Knight, 'Enriching the Judgement'.
22. Lamb, *Specimens*, 1:264.
23. Hazlitt, 'William Godwin', 32.
24. Bray, *The Friend*, 59.
25. Greville, *Dedication*, ed. Gouws, 'Introduction', xxi–xxiv (xxiii).
26. See, for example, Rebholz, *Life of Fulke Greville*, 70–3, 98–9 and 114–17; see also Rees, *Fulke Greville*, 26–44.
27. See also Knight, 'Not with the Ancient', 195–209.
28. Herbert, 'Jordan (I)', 1–2, in *English Poems*, ed. Wilcox, 200.
29. Finkelpearl, 'Davies, John'.
30. Davies (of Hereford), *Scourge of Folly*, 194–5.
31. Flecknoe, *Epigrams*, 10–11.
32. See Greville, *Dedication*, ed. Gouws, 'Introduction', xlv.
33. Southey, *Select Works*, 912, 515.
34. Hazlitt, 'On Persons One Would Wish to Have Seen', 33.
35. Ibid., 33.
36. Aeschylus, *Persians*, 681–842, in *Aeschylus*, ed. and trans. Smith, 1:164–83. I thank Lindsay Allen for discussion of this reference. On the reception of Aeschylus, see, among others, Arnold, 'Thomas Stanley's "Aeschylus"'; Bridges, Hall and Rhodes, eds, *Cultural Responses to the Persian Wars*; and Mund-Dopchie, *La Survie d'Eschyle à la Renaissance*.
37. Aeschylus, *Persians*, 683, in *Aeschylus*, ed. and trans. Smith, 1:164–5.
38. Milton, *Paradise Lost*, ed. Fowler, I.63, p. 64; and I.239, p. 74.
39. Milton, *Paradise Lost*, II.667, p. 144.
40. See Dante, *Paradiso*, XXI.25–27, ed. and trans. Sinclair, 302–3: 'Dentro al cristallo che 'l vocabol porta, / cerchiando il mondo, del suo caro duce / sotto cui giacque ogne malizia morta . . .' (Within the crystal which, circling about the world, bears the name of the world's famous chief under whom all wickedness lay dead). The 'caro duce' is a reference to Saturn.
41. Marlowe, *Doctor Faustus*, B-Text, 2.3.60–61, in *Doctor Faustus and Other Plays*, ed. Bevington and Rasmussen, 205.
42. Swinburne, *George Chapman*, 15–16.

Chapter 11

George Chapman's 'Habit of Poesie'
Zenón Luis-Martínez

firma quaedam facilitas, quae apud Graecos ἕξις nominatur.
Quintilian[1]

But to him that is more than a reader I write.
George Chapman[2]

The Settled Quality

George Chapman's epistle to Matthew Roydon which prefaces his second poetry collection, *Ouids Banquet of Sence* (1595), is often taken as the key exposition of the poet's reputed difficulty. The epistle's definition of '*Enargia*' as 'cleerenes of representation' and its controversial relation with a sought-for obscurity of expression have elicited scholarly debate.[3] But these ideas are seldom read in connection with another key though widely unscrutinised term in Chapman's poetics:

> I thought good to submit to your apt iudgment: acquainted long since with the true *habit of Poesie*, and now since your laboring wits endeuour heaven-high thoughts of nature, you have actual meanes to sound the philosophical conceits, that my new pen seriously courteth.[4]

Chapman had used the emphasised phrase in one of the end-glosses to the 'Hymnus in Cynthiam', the second poem of his debut collection, *The Shadow of Night* (1594), in an attempt to explain his use of a historical simile: 'And these like *Similes*, in my opinion drawne from the honourable deeds of our countrimen, clad in comely *habit of Poesie*, would become a Poeme as well as further-fetcht grounds' (44, gloss 19). In an Aristotelian scheme of causation, one could take 'habit' here to mean the poem's material cause – its fiction and its diction – clothing its formal cause, or sense. The habit, Chapman implies, *does* make the poem.

But the habit also makes the poet: Roydon's trained habit is the distinctive feature of poetry's efficient cause. His continued acquaintance with the material cause of poetry ensures his mastery over its formal cause: Roydon's 'laboring wits' provide him with 'meanes' to fathom the depth of Chapman's 'conceits', whose production by the poet is also the effect of habit. Through this communion of habit, the writer's laborious poesis and the reader's decoding skills share a common inclination to 'philosophical' enquiry. This explanation entails a more specialised Aristotelian sense. In the *Categories*, Aristotle subdivides ποιότης (*poiotēs*, quality) into διάθεσις (*diathesis*, disposition) and ἕξις (*hexis*, habit), the difference between them being the more lasting nature of the latter. Habits are settled dispositions of the human mind, mainly ἐπιστῆμαι (*epistēmai*, knowledges) and ἀρεταί (*aretai*, virtues).[5] Poetry is therefore a habit just as knowledge and learning are said to be habits in other texts by Chapman. In a later poem, *Euthymiae Raptus, or, The Teares of Peace* (1614), he writes:

> For Wisdome is nought else, then Learning fin'd,
> And with the vnderstanding Powre combin'd;
> That is, *a habite of both habits standing*;
> The Bloods vaine humours, euer countermaunding. (483–6, emphasis added)

These intellectual qualities are interrelated habits insofar as they ensue from conscientious processes of cultivation. And so is virtue, whose 'path long and steep' Chapman encountered in Hesiod's *Works and Days* on the occasion of his 1618 translation: 'But scaling once her [virtue's] height, the ioy is more, / Than all the peine she put you to before'.[6] The poet's gloss of these lines stresses the 'painefull passage' towards the attaining of 'the loue and *habite of knowledge, and vertue*': 'there is first necessarily required, a laborious and painefull conflict; fought through the knowledge, and hate of the miseries and beastlinesse of vice'.[7]

Habit thus settles in the human mind through a dialectics of labour and reward. The true poet and man of learning, personified in the heroic figure of Roydon, drifting between the pleasures of divine frenzy and the hardships of human effort, presides over the epistle prefacing *The Shadow of Night*:

> It is an exceeding rapture of delight in the deepe search of knowledge (none knoweth better than thy selfe sweet *Mathew*) that maketh men manfully indure th'extremes incident to that *Herculean* labour: Men must be shod by Mercurie, girt with Saturnes adamantine sword, take the shield of Pallas, the helme from Pluto, and have the eyes of Graea [*sic*] (as Hesiodus armes Perseus against Medusa) before they can cut of the viperous head of benumming ignorance, or subdue their monstrous affections to most beautiful iudgement. (19)

This mythographic clothing defines the poet's literary and social persona, which in Chapman's case included self-imposed alienation and an 'unfashionable habite of povertie':[8] 'We have example sacred enough that true Poesie's humility, poverty and contempt are *badges* of divinity, not vanity.'[9] But these traits, far from revealing the poet within, reinforce the elusive nature of his habit: 'Poesie is the flower of the Sunne and disdains to open to the eye of a candle.'[10]

As Michael Hetherington has observed, the pertinence of 'habit' (Greek *hexis*, Latin *habitus*) as a property connecting the theory and practice of the arts and as a quality of the artist resisted precise definition in early modern literary criticism. William Scott's *The Model of Poesie* (c. 1599) differentiated between *art*, or the systematic teaching of the rules for writing a poem; *ability*, or the natural talent that makes it possible; and the intermediate, less definite *habit* of the trained artist: 'in every art there must be a disposition and apt ability of nature before the habit or settled quality that reduceth the works thereof into being'.[11] Scott differentiated between the poet's 'active habit' and the reader's 'habitual understanding of poetry'.[12] Chapman's Roydon prefaces prefigure Scott's opinions, even if in his account the habits of learning and of poetry are rendered indistinguishable as qualities shared by poet and reader alike. Habit thus enlightens crucial aspects of Chapman's poetic agenda, binding together an array of creative, intellectual and interpretative qualities and practices along which the roles of poet, philosopher, translator and scholar overlap: these include literary learning, intellectual curiosity, attentiveness to style and subtle encoding/decoding skills. Dwelling primarily in the efficient cause (the poet), habit interpenetrates the causal scheme of the poetic process. It plays a primary part in 'reducing' matter (language, fiction) into form (sense) through the poet's act of 'courting' and the reader's act of 'sounding' poetry's 'philosophical conceits', thus enabling its final cause: the discovery of truth through the 'deepe search of knowledge'.

A quality that stimulates the creative process (poesis) and the interpretation of its product (allegoresis), habit finds expression through a practical poetics rather than in the form of systematic, formal art. Chapman's 'habit of Poesie' becomes a useful tool for unveiling aspects of his method and practice that his elusive poetic theory, scattered in epistles, prefaces and epilogues, often fails to clarify. What remains of the present chapter looks into Chapman's works of the 1590s, with occasional incursions into later texts, to argue that poetic habit, conceived from an authorial and readerly perspective, operates in the direction of *unwriting* two critical assumptions of/about his explicit poetics. The first assumption concerns the tensions between the defence of a laborious praxis and a declared predilection for ideas of divine inspiration, with specific consequences for a theory of the reader. It is the perspective of Chapman's early readers, as found in the laudatory sonnets prefacing *Ouids Banquet of Sence*, that first informs us of the tensions between the call for a passive, enraptured experience of his vatic poems and the exigency of an active, disciplined hermeneutic disposition. This scheme is reproduced in the paratexts of Chapman's first two Homer instalments: *The Seaven Bookes of the Iliades* and *Achilles Shield* (1598), particularly the laudatory poem to Thomas Hariot post-facing the latter. By gauging Hariot's scientific skills and Chapman's role as a translator against the Platonic ideal of Homer's philosophical wisdom and divinely inspired poesis, this poem domesticates the otherwise intangible Homeric model: while the 'habit of Poesie' endows the reader and translator with a surrogate form of access to the Homeric ideal, it conversely employs the interpreter's labour in the disciplining of a poetry of inspiration.[13]

The second assumption addresses Chapman's reputation as an obscure poet – which has dogged him from the days of his early readers to present-day criticism. His belief in the virtues of obscurity runs counter to the critical consideration of difficulty as the poet's own flaw.[14] Chapman approached difficulty as a means to achieving the facility of skill that Quintilian identified as *hexis*, or habit, and obscurity as the 'painefull passage' towards perspicuity. His persistent if not always successful endeavours towards intellectual clarity are manifest in the metapoetic quality of his figures and tropes (simile, metaphor, ekphrasis, mythography), often designed as didactic inventions about the nature and aims of poetry. Habit nurtures the poet's heuristic temperament and the reader's 'deepe searching' attitude, thus bridging the gap between a theory of poetic obscurity and a practice in which poetic method is revealed as a key layer of meaning of the poem's allegory. Ovid plays a key role in the metapoetic intent of Chapman's early work, particularly *Ouids Banquet of Sence* and the continuation of *Hero and Leander* (1598), adjoining an ironic underside to the idealisation of Homer professed in the early translations. In *Ouids Banquet of Sence*, Chapman constructs his fictional Ovid as a model of *furor poeticus* misguided by *furor amatorius*, whose sensuality hinders poets' and readers' aspirations to true 'sence'. Chapman's critique is built on mainly aesthetic grounds, often putting the intricacy of his 'philosophical conceits' at the service of unmasking the shortcomings of a rival model. Promoting self-referentiality, poetic habit invites the interpretation of the multilayered conceits of Chapman's poems as allegories of poetry's own methods and functions.

The Painful Passage: Labour into Rapture

The title page of *Ouids Banquet of Sence* contains two indices of Chapman's preoccupation with his readers. One is the device of the *baculus in aqua*, for whose associations with right and wrong interpretation I refer to former discussions.[15] The other is the epigraph adapting the opening of Persius's first satire, a diatribe against the corruption of post-Augustan Roman letters: *Quis leget haec? Nemo Hercule Nemo, / vel duo vel nemo*.[16] By aligning with Persius's belligerence and reputation for obscurity, Chapman reaffirms a commitment already expressed in the closing words of the first Roydon preface to *The Shadow of Night*: 'I rest as resolute as *Seneca*, satisfying my selfe if but a few, if one, or if none like it' (19). Chapman's quantification of his readers in terms of Senecan constancy – *si non tangent pauca, ne plura quidem*[17] – is coterminous with a qualitative discrimination between the inept and the able, the 'prophane multitude' characterised by a 'wilful pouertie of iudgements' and those 'serching spirits' with a 'light-bearing intellect' (49–50).

Besides, Chapman's *good* readers are often named. Attending to the works published in the 1590s, these readers can be classified into two groups. On one side, the triad of noblemen 'reported' by Roydon and led by Henry Percy, or 'deepe searching *Northumberland*', as well as Thomas Hariot, the scientific luminary of the Percy/Ralegh circle of speculative philosophers.[18] On the other, the more scholarly members of the Inns of Court who penned the five laudatory sonnets to *Ouids Banquet of Sence*: Richard Stapleton, presumptively the 'R. S. of the Inner Temple' who compiled the anthology *The Phoenix Nest* (1593);

'Tho[mas] Williams of the inner Temple'; and 'I[ohn] D[avies] of the Middle Temple'.[19] The first group supplies Chapman's two elaborate mirrors of true poetic habit – Roydon and Hariot. The second documents actual readers' responses to the first two poetry volumes.

Attending to the second group, while John Davies's two sonnets have received some attention for their sketch of Chapman's attitude to Ovid, the other three have been largely dismissed as mere exercises in hyperbolic praise.[20] Yet these sonnets, particularly Williams's, offer sophisticated accounts of the challenges of reading Chapman. Written in close imitation of its addressee's abstruse syntax and mythographic density, Williams's first sonnet portrays Chapman's *bad* readers:

> Issue of *Semele* that will imbrace
>   With fleshly arms the three-wingd wife [sic] of thunder:
>   Let her sad ruine, such proud thoughts abase
>   And view aloofe, this verse in silent wonder,
> If neerer your vnhallowed eyes wil pierse,
>   Then (with the Satyre) kisse this sacred fire,
>   To scorch your lips, that dearely taught thereby
>   Your onely soules fit obiects may aspire. ('Tho: Williams', 1–8, p. 51)

Williams bids these readers learn from the sad fate of the proud mother of Bacchus, burned up in her attempt to 'imbrace' her lover Jove – figurative for Chapman's verse – when the god appeared to her at close range and in all his splendour. Invoking Plutarch, Williams also transfers to Chapman's readers Prometheus's advice to the satyr who burned his lips in the attempt to kiss the stolen firebrand.[21] 'Taught' by the poet, these readers may learn to find the perspective necessary to 'aspire' (that is, inhale, absorb) the 'fit objects' contained in the 'sacred fire' of Chapman's Jovian/Promethean verse. By contrast, the sonnet's closing sixain apostrophises Chapman's able readers:

> But you high spirrits in thys cloud of gold
>   Inioy (like *Ioue*) this bright Saturnian Muse,
>   Your eyes can well the dazeling beames behold
>   This Pythian lightner freshly doth effuse
> To dant the basenes of that bastard traine
> Whose twise borne iudgments, formeles still remaine. ('Tho: Williams', 9–14)

Contrasting with Semele's story, this new allusion is to Jove's metamorphosis into the 'cloud of gold' that impregnated Danae. As she 'injoy[ed]' Jove, so readers are ravished by Chapman's 'Saturnian Muse' and Apollonian light, whose high poetic 'effus[ions]' rectify the 'formeles' senses caused by flawed interpretation, epitomised in the misshapenness that ensues from Bacchus's two unnatural births.

Williams's sonnet enfolds a paradox: while it portrays Chapman as a vatic poet, whose 'Pythian lightner' dazzles an enraptured audience as it puts off profane readers, its intricate referential web invites active, laborious allegoresis. The sonnet's conceits prove its author's first-hand acquaintance with Chapman's poetics. First, by contrasting Bacchus with Perseus, Williams addresses a crucial theme in Chapman's mythography: the heroic nature of 'true learning'. The arming of 'Perseus against Medusa' as an allegory of the moral and intellectual qualities of the man of learning nurtures an active idea of the reader significantly different from the one suggested by the ravished Danae.[22] Second, Williams's Prometheus, teaching the satyr/reader to value fire as an 'instrument of every craft for those who have learned to use it',[23] evokes the poet's pedagogical intent in *The Shadow of Night*:

> If then we frame mans figure by his mind,
> And that at first, his fashion was assignd,
> Erection in such God-like excellence
> For his soules sake, and her intelligence:
> She so degenerate, and growne deprest,
> Content to share affections with a beast,
> The shape wherewith he should be now indude,
> Must beare no signe of mans similitude.
> Therefore Promethean Poets with the coles
> Of their most genial, more-then-humane soules
> In liuing verse, created men like these,
> With shapes of Centaurs, Harpies, Lapithes,
> That they in prime of erudition,
> When almost sauage vulgar men were growne,
> Seeing them selues in those Pierean founts,
> Might mend their minds, asham'd of such accounts. ('Hymnus in Noctem', 123–38)

As Prometheus made man with heavenly fire, so poets create imaginary beings 'with the fire of their soules' (gloss, p. 22).[24] Chapman's marginal gloss to this passage does little justice to its 'high conceipt'. The argument has an ampler humanistic scope: humans were given an intellective soul, or mind, in the likeness of God, but they were also made to share their nature with a beastly body, in which their divine resemblance was lost. And so Promethean poets create negative mirrors of human imperfection to encourage anamnesis of their god-like essence.²⁵ In stressing a didactic aim, Chapman adheres to Giovanni Boccaccio's attribution, in the *Genealogiae deorum gentilium* (*Genealogy of the Pagan Gods*, c. 1360–74), of a double nature both to Prometheus and his creation: first, he created *naturalis homo*, whose soul is vegetative and sensitive only, sharing with the body a mortal, animal essence; but in his role as *doctus homo*, Prometheus also fashions a new *civilis homo* out of the first, endowing him with a rational soul that reforms his former nature.²⁶ Sharing the habit of learning and virtue of this second Prometheus, the poet's edifying function is committed to nourishing the fiery, rational soul against the body's tyranny. Just as those natural men civilised by learning, even bad readers can be reformed if guided by the poet's art.

Third, Williams's identification of reading with *seeing* recalls Chapman's preface to *Ouids Banquet of Sence*, where the painter's ability to transcend mere resemblance between artefact and sitter relies as much on his ability to 'lymn, giue luster, shadow, and heightening' as on the insightful viewer's 'iudiciall perspectiue' or capacity to perceive 'motion, spirit and life' in artistic representation (50). Williams's terms are those of Chapman's ekphrasis of Niobe's fountain in the volume's title poem, 'So cunningly to optick reason wrought', in which skilful artistry is at the service of the viewer's discerning the 'farre of', right perspective from the confusion of the 'neerely viewed' image ('Ouids Banquet', 3.6–9).²⁷ 'Iudiciall perspectiue' and 'optick reason' are thus features where the poet's pedagogical instruction (Prometheus) and the reader's own heroic propaedeutics (Perseus) are met. Chapman's closing remark in this preface needs to be read with caution: 'those that before-hand, haue a radiant, and light-bearing intellect, will say they can passe through Corynnas Garden without the helpe of a Lanterne' (50). 'Beforehand' iterates the long acquaintance with habit, art's laborious cultivation of a natural, inward light that is always to be preferred to any inauthentic shortcut aiding the human intellect. The poem, like the sunflower, will not open easily to the lantern's eye.

Williams's portrayal of Chapman's poetics of inspiration supplies a cliché with which the poet, despite his predilection for the theory, hardly felt comfortable in practice. Poetic frenzy features in the large paratextual body furnishing the translations of Homer's major poems (1598–1616). These paratexts comprise Chapman's greatest effort to explain the nature of poetic composition and interpretation, as well as the translator's mediating role. The *Seaven Bookes of the Iliads* and *Achilles Shield* came with a total of four prefaces – each volume contained a dedication to the Earl of Essex and an epistle to the reader – with the addition in the latter's case of the poem to Thomas Hariot.[28] In them Chapman represents Homeric poetry as the ultimate repository of 'true knowledge', a 'deduction' (i.e., derivation) of the immortal soul that emanates from, and returns to, a sort of Ficinian angelic mind:

> If the crowne of humanitie be the soule, and the soule an intellectuall beame of God, the essence of her substance being intellection or understanding the strength and eminence of her faculties, the differencing of men in excellencie must be directed onelie by their proportions of true knowledge. Homericall writing, then, being the native deduction, image, and true heire of true knowledge, must needs in desert inherit his father's dignitie.[29]

Chapman's Platonic Homer obtains his creativity from divine frenzy. This view is bluntly expressed in the comparison of Homer with Virgil: while Homer's poems are the result of 'a free furie, and absolute and full soule', Virgil's reveal 'a courtly, laborious and altogether imitatorie spirit' of his master.[30] The insistence on the conventional dichotomy of poetic body and soul – that is, fictional matter and allegorical sense – signals Virgil's poetry as a mere imitation of the Homeric body: 'Not a Simile hee hath but is Homer's, not an invention, person or disposition but is wholly or originally built upon Homericall foundations.'[31]

In voicing the unattainability of Homer's poetic soul for his imitators, Chapman implicitly acknowledges his own shortfall from the Homeric ideal. This in turn justifies the need for a compensatory poetics of translation. In his activity as Homer's translator Chapman thus found the perfect embodiment of the communion of writerly and readerly habit. Understood first as a laborious decoding process, translation further intends the custody of Homer's genuine sense, or soul, through a conscientious search for analogous poetic matter in the target language:

> [The] worth of a skilfull and worthy translator is to observe the sentences, figures and forms of speech proposed in his author, his true sence and height, and to adorn them with figures and forms of oration fitted to the original in the same tongue to which they are translated.[32]

Translation's dependence on the 'true habit of Poesie' invalidates scholarly 'word-for-word traductions'.[33] As argued in the 1611 paratexts to the full *Iliads*, the true translator or 'judiciall interpreter' of Homer must seek the 'ample transmigration' of the original's 'full soule' into 'Nature-loving Poesie'.[34] Homer's poetic soul must be searched in the 'materiall things themselves', which are the medium for this exercise in poetic metempsychosis.[35] Chapman's technical discussions of verse forms, of rhetorical figures, of the phonetic advantages of English over romance languages in rendering Homer's Greek, or of the comparisons between his lexical choices and those of his Latin predecessors, speak to the arduous search for apt poetic matter in the transference of Homer's soul from its original Greek into a new English body. By scaling the Platonic ladder from a poetics of labour towards one of rapture, Homeric translation shows its practitioner's 'painefull passage' to acquiring poetic habit.

In the context of these paratexts, the abovementioned verse epistle, 'To My Admired and Sovle-Loved Friend, Mayster of all essentiall and true knowledge, *M. Harriots*', contains Chapman's most important statement on habit. Hariot's scientific talent justifies his quasi-Homeric title as 'Mayster of all essential and true knowledge': consequently, he is Homer's, and Chapman's, ideal 'understander'.[36] Critics have stressed the significance of Hariot's 'perfect eye', a metaphor that singularises his reading skills in his work on the improvement of the telescope.[37] Jessica Wolfe rightly argues that this conceit equates the discerning reader with the scientist's employment of mechanical artefacts to 'rectify the "perviall"' appearance of texts.[38] But telescopes are not the only eyes alluded to in this poem. Beginning with the request that Hariot's wisdom judge Chapman's accomplishment, the poem praises Hariot's 'depth of soule' embodied in his 'cleare eyes', here the corporeal 'Spheres where *Reason* moues'. Chapman embraces a Plotinian/Ficinian conception of vision that entails the transformation of the physical act of seeing into an intellectual experience involving the mind's eye ('To *Harriots*', 1–5) – Plato's proverbial third eye in Ficino's commentary of the *Philebus*.[39] Hariot's rational powers thus contrast with Chapman's 'strange Muse', unable to avert the distractions of the body in the attempt 't'aspire / Instructiue light' from knowledge's 'whole Sphere of fire' (31, 33–4). Chapman's poesis seems steps below its own Promethean aspirations. His zealous yet limited verse resists even the telescope's clear-sightedness:

O had your perfect eye Organs to pierce
Into that Chaos whence this stifled verse
By violence breakes: where Gloweworme like doth shine
In nights of sorrow, this hid soul of mine:
And how her genuine forms struggle for birth,

Vnder the clawes of this fowle Panther earth;
Then under all those forms you should discerne
My loue to you, in my desire to learne. (41–8)

In its lack of 'Organs', Hariot's mechanical 'eye' becomes as limited an instrument as Chapman's own tortured verse. Making up for these imperfections, 'struggle' emerges, as Muriel Bradbrook noted, as 'the keyword of this passage'[40] – that is, the philosopher's endeavour but also the artist's labour, the path to an always-in-process attainment of habit. These lines describe the strenuous and rarely successful unveiling of the 'Gloweworme' clarity of the soul's 'genuine form' through the material farrago of the poet's 'stifled verse'.

By contrast, Hariot's 'True learning' is said to possess a 'body absolute' and an 'apparent sence' that triumph not only against Chapman's flawed art, but also against the 'ayrie termes' of the 'formall Clearkes', and the 'fowle conceits' of the 'braines / Of winde and vapor' of Chapman's much-criticised fellow poets (105–8). Chapman's privileging of Hariot's 'iudiciall kindnesse' over the dubious skills of pedantic scholars and sensual poets is justified by his 'true wisdom by learning wonne' (75). In the face of Hariot's immense knowledge, Chapman's commitment to poetry seems a questionable prospect:

For though I now consume in poesie,
Yet Homer being my roote I can not die.
But lest to vse all Poesie in the sight,
Of graue philosophie shew braines too light
To comprehend her depth of misterie,
I vow t'is onely strong necessitie
Gouernes my paines herein, which yet may vse
A mans whole life without the least abuse.
And though to rime and giue a verse smooth feet,
Vttering to vulgar pallattes passions sweet
Chaunce often in such weake capriccious spirits,
As in nought else haue tollerable merits,
Yet *where high Poesies natiue habite shines*,
From whose reflections flow eternall lines:
Philosophy retirde to darkest caues
She can discouer: and the proud worldes braues
Answere in any thing but impudence,
With circle of her general excellence. (125–42, emphasis added)

Against the crowd-pleasing abilities of the 'smooth' versifier, the 'natiue habite' of a poetry rooted in Homer neutralises its alleged inferiority to philosophy. 'Natiue' paints poetry's clothing as a natural, luminous disposition whose 'reflections' make philosophy's true mysteries shine in their full light. Operating a reversal of Plato's allegory of the cave, Chapman presents philosophy in darkness, and the access to true knowledge as the effect of poetry's overpowering of its sister art's feeble firelight.

Conversely, the philosopher Hariot's 'habit' – that is, his perfected 'skil' to sound the depth of poetry's high inventions – commends him, like Roydon in the former poems, as the primordial reader of Chapman's philosophical Englishing of Homer:

> For ample instance *Homer* more than serueth,
> And what is made a Courtly question now,
> His competent and partles iudge be you;
> If these vaine lines and his deserts arise
> To the high searches of your serious eyes
> As he is English . . . (144–9)

Homer's poetry, derived solely from his divine genius, enlightens Hariot's philosophical truths while it dignifies the strenuous though 'vaine lines' of Chapman's imperfect poetic art. Conversely, Homer's poetic soul is doubly custodied by true poetic habit: first, in the 'high searches' of Hariot's discerning mind, and second, in the translator's laborious transmigration of its original soul into new matter. Besides, and despite his rhetoric of self-debasement before Homer's genius and Hariot's learning, Chapman's mediation between true poet and perfect reader is an act of self-vindication as the ultimate bearer of 'Poesies natiue habite'. Whereas Chapman's Hariot mirrors the poet's self-image as the true philosophical interpreter of Homer, Chapman's (translation of) Homer permits the poet's appropriation of a natural genius and sublime poetry otherwise unavailable to him. Being the reward of labour, habit domesticates Homeric inspiration while it illuminates the interpreter's passage to its primordial *furor poeticus*.[41]

The Curious Frame: Didactic Aestheticism

The exploratory disposition that Chapman praises in Roydon and Hariot matches the author's profession of obscurity. Chapman's opaque style – what he himself called 'my farre-fetcht and, as it were, beyond-sea manner of writing'[42] – has been taken as a flaw from whose elucidation readers can be excused, or as an invitation to search for meaning in an intricate labyrinth of learned references.⁴³ However, Chapman's views on difficulty not as an end in itself but as a means to intelligibility invite considerations of the poem as a relatively autonomous vehicle towards the elucidation of its sense. Williams's second laudatory sonnet in *Ouids Banquet of Sence* again provides valuable clues to this conception. Depicting Chapman's poesis as dedicated farming, its first octave imagines obscurity as an enclosed field:

> Vngratefull Farmers of the Muses land
>   That (wanting thrift and iudgment to imploy it)
>   Let it manureles and vnfenced stand,
>   Till barbarous Cattell enter and destroy it:
> Now the true heyre is happily found out
>   Who (framing it t'inritch posterities)
>   Walles it with spright-fild darknes round about,
>   Grass, plants, and sowes; and makes it Paradise. ('Another', 1–8, p. 51)

Protecting the carefully planted garden inside, obscurity is a 'spright-fild' wall, that is, a spear- or arrow-shaped fence,⁴⁴ guarding its poetic truths. Obscurity dignifies poetic discourse by protecting its divine nature from unlearned readers.

Williams situates Chapman's poems within the scope of a theory of allegory popularised by Boccaccio. In Book XIV of the *Genealogy of the Pagan Gods*, Boccaccio argued that the poet's function is to protect (*tegere*) truth and distance it from listless eyes (*ab oculis torpentium auferre*). His concern is readers as much as poets, who, he observes, 'are sometimes obscure, but invariably explicable if approached by a sane mind'.⁴⁵ Williams's reading of Chapman equally insists on the difference between the 'barbarous Cattell' and the labouring reader whose intellectual reward is accession to truth's 'Paradise':

> To which without the *Parcaes* golden bow,
>   None can aspire but stick in errors hell;
>   A garland to engird a Monarchs brow,
>   Then take some paines to ioy so rich a Iewell
> Most prize is graspt in labors hardest hand,
> And idle soules can nothing rich command. ('Another', 9–14)

Poetic truth is a divine gift – the Virgilian golden bough permits escaping from the hell of ignorance.⁴⁶ Yet its reward is attained only through heroic 'paines' and 'labors'. Boccaccio's belief in the explicability of poetry equally relies on intellectual effort. His advice to those readers willing to 'unwind [poetry's] difficult involutions' (*enodare nexus ambiguos*) is again strenuous persistence: 'You must read, you must persevere, you must sit up nights, you must inquire, and exert the utmost power of your mind.'[47] In line with Boccaccio, Williams's reading of Chapman designs a space of shared labour between poets and readers. Boccaccio affirms that 'no one can believe that poets invidiously veil the truth with fiction, either to deprive the reader of the hidden sense, or to appear the more clever'.[48] Similarly, when Chapman praises the 'true habit of Poesie', this distinction does not aim to alienate readers but to gain them for his cause: the poet assures that he writes with a mind 'desirous other should be more worthily glorious', and 'no[t] professing sacred Poesie in any degree' ('To Royden', 50). The 'deeper misteries' of Chapman's poems, as John Davies calls them in the fifth laudatory sonnet, are, in Gerald Snare's words, 'secrets of aesthetic construction', whose accessibility requires less mystagogical initiation than communion of writerly and readerly habit.[49] Chapman's goal is an 'absolute poem' characterised by clarity of vision attained by difficult expression and strenuous decoding.

Scorn for oratorical transparency is stated in the second Roydon epistle: 'that Poesie should be a perviall as Oratorie, and plainness her special ornament, were the plaine way to barbarisme' (49). Yet Chapman's model is not entirely alien to that of the orator. Quintilian's conception of *hexis* as *facilitas*, or easy disposition to oratorical and writerly skill, prescribed a systematic programme of acquisition of doctrine and trained practice.[50] The difference between Quintilian and Chapman is the latter's belief in the necessity of a difficult medium. His key notion is *enargia*, or 'cleernes of representation', which calls for a 'high, and harty inuention', against the 'perspicuous delivery of a lowe inuention', and whose ideal of poetic ornament is 'fitnes of figure', in opposition to the 'affection of words, & indigested concets' of gratuitous obscurity, but also to the 'charms made of vnlerned characters' of a merely oratorical poetry (49).

Two models of clarity are thus contrasted, one undesirable and another attainable through labour; and simultaneously, two models of obscurity, one 'pedanticall and childish', and another seeking clarity through elaborate expression:

> where [obscurity] shrowdeth it selfe in the hart of its subiect, vtterd with fitness of figure, and expressiue Epethites, with that darknes will J still labour to be shadowed: rich minerals are digd out of the bowels of the earth, not found in the superficies of it. (49)

Difficulty and clarity are respectively instrument and end: 'that which being with a little endeauour searched, ads a kinde of maiestie to Poesie'. The 'skilfull Painters turne' is Chapman's master trope joining the penchant for difficulty and the enlightenment of poetic truth, thus presupposing a commitment to intelligibility on the poet's part. As Gordon Kendal puts it, 'however passionate Chapman was about obscurity, he wanted to be understood'.[51] *Enargia* highlights a dialectics between 'darknes' and 'cleereness'. Chapman's Plutarchan theory of language assumes the poet's commitment to accessibility: 'I . . . onlie consecrate my strange Poems to these serching spirits . . . endeauoring that material Oration, which you call *Schema*; varying in some rare fiction, from popular custome, euen for the pure sakes of ornament and vtilitie' (49).[52] The aesthetic nature of poetry's 'rare fiction' does not diminish its didactic usefulness. It is, then, in the 'fitnes' of these 'figures' and 'fiction[s]' that we must identify the 'passage' from obscurity to clarity. We should not see in Chapman's difficult conceits a sought-for impenetrability. Almost a century ago, A. S. Ferguson wrote that Chapman's 'images, however disparate, radiate from some central idea' carrying symbolic value.[53] This quality, Mario Praz agreed, assimilates his skills to those of an emblem writer.[54] And Phyllis Bartlett argued that 'wherever in Chapman's poetry a conceit strikes the reader at first glance as "indigest," it will, on further examination, be discovered rather to be *a method of approach* to the central subject'.[55] A perplexing conceit obliges readers to stop and go back, signalling a way simultaneously into the meaning of the poem and to its poetic method: the multilayered allegorical sense of these conceits includes a metapoetic level, which instils in audiences a habit of slow, meticulous reading in search not only of learned references but also of keys that might reveal their artistic mechanism.[56]

A first illustration of Chapman's didactic aestheticism relates two examples of avian metamorphosis in his texts to his consistent attack on that sort of poetic praxis which he regarded as inimical to *enargia*. In the epistle to *Ouids Banquet of Sence*, the 'perspicuous delivery of a low invention' is condemned by way of Ovidian allegory:

> charms made of vnlerned characters are not consecrate by the Muses which are diuine artists, but by *Euippes* daughters, that challenged them with mere nature, whose brests J doubt not had beene well worthy commendation, if their comparison had not turnd them into Pyes. (49)

Readers are referred to Pallas and the Muses' encounter with the nine magpies whose ability is to 'imitate any sound they please' in

Book V of the *Metamorphoses*. These are the daughters of Pierus, King of Emathia, and Evippe of Paeonia, who challenged the Muses to a singing contest with the boast that they could be vanquished *nec voce nec arte* ['neither in voice nor in skill'], and were transformed into magpies as punishment for their mocking protestations after their defeat. Ovid's tale closes with a comment on their 'hoarse garrulity and boundless passion for talk' (*raucaque garrulitas studiumque inmane loquendi*).[57]

The tale has a long allegorical tradition: Boccaccio compared the Pierides to those who, although they 'never knew any instruction, relying only on their wits, dare to put themselves before the learned' and 'to consider themselves poets, or to be judged poets by those that observe them'.[58] But Chapman's choice of the epithet 'Euippes daughters' is uncommon, even if 'Euippe' is the mother's name in his Ovidian source. Conversely, Cicero's *De natura deorum* identifies the Pierides as an alternative set of nine Muses, the daughters of Pierus and Antiope.[59] 'Euippe' might be intended to obscure the usual identification of these characters by their father's name. But Chapman may have also meant to fuse, through false etymology, 'Euipe' or 'Euippe' with Greek εὐεπής (*euepēs*), from εὐέπεια (*euepeia*; Latin, *verborum elegantia*), a notion that he could have found in Dionysus of Halicarnassus's discussion of euphony in his treatise *On Literary Composition*. Dionysus detects *euepeia* in the way in which well-sounding words can 'nestle together ... according to certain affinities and natural attractions of the letters'.[60] This possibility would reinforce Chapman's opposition between a poetic method committed to deep intellectual enquiry and a false oratorical poetry whose unworthy subjects fall short of their pretended verbal elegance.

The well-spoken Pierides recall Chapman's invention of a similar myth: the story of the maid Adolesche, as recounted by the nymph Teras during the wedding celebrations in the Fifth Sestyad of *Hero and Leander*.[61] In Teras's tale, Hymen, in female disguise, frequents a group of maids in the hope of winning Eucharis's love. Kidnapped by rovers and confined to a cave, the maids are freed by Hymen, who reveals his male identity and wins Eucharis. Yet he fears that her father may oppose their marriage. As he travels to Athens to negotiate this point, one of the girls, Adolesche, travels secretly too in order to ruin the lovers' plans with malicious slander, but gets lost on the way. Adolesche is 'a Nymph borne hie, / Made all of voice and fire'. The mischievous sensuality of her 'sharpe and tart' face matches her wit: 'All powers she had, euen her tongue, did so. / In spirit and quicknes she much ioy did take, / And lou'd her tongue, only for quicknes sake' (*Hero*, V.287–8, 291–3). Her name derives from Greek ἀδολεσχία (*adoleschia*), or garrulity. She reappears at the tale's end only to realise her failure, and, in Ovidian fashion, to face metamorphic punishment:

> To heare her deare tongue robd of such a ioy
> Made the well-spoken Nymph take such a toy,
> That downe she sunke: when lightning from aboue,
> Shrunk her leane body, and from mere free loue,
> Turnd her into the pied-plum'd *Psittachus*,
> That now the Parrat is surnam'd by vs,
> Who still with counterfeit confusion prates,
> Nought but newes common to the commonst mates. (V.417–24)

C. S. Lewis pointed to Adolesche's failed role as a 'the tale-bearer or *losengier* in an affair of courtly love'.[62] And D. J. Gordon hinted at similarities between Adolesche and the Pierides without noticing Chapman's previous use of the latter.[63] The 'well-spoken' Adolesche's metamorphosis into a '*pied*-plum'd' parrot directly puns on the 'pyes' and the trifling though well-sounding *euepeia*, expressing 'lowe inuention[s]' with misapplied quickness of tongue. Chapman's 'pied' (i.e., prating, imitative, showy, inconstant) birds allegorically condemn a practice of poetry that confounds its own 'natiue habite'.[64] As a practical instance of *enargia*, Chapman's Ovidian invention is also a metapoetic window to his artistic method, as it proves its aesthetic ideal by exposing the inferiority of a rival, misguided poetics.

Another cluster of examples links Chapman's much-loved conceits of visual perception to his attack on the Ovidian poetics of sensual love embodied in the early amatory elegies and the *Ars amatoria*.[65] Critical readings of 'Ouids Banquet of Sence' as a *trompe l'oeil* poem have aptly favoured this anti-Ovidian perspective. The abovementioned anamorphic quality of Niobe's fountain is often the crux of these interpretations. William Weaver has stressed the 'centrifugal' quality of Chapman's description of the setting of Ovid's infatuation with Corinna, progressing from the 'focal point' at the fountain to the 'soft enflowered banck' (9.1, p. 55).[66] Yet a previous focalising movement needs to be added to Weaver's reading, as Corinna is

> entic'd to a siluer spring,
> Enchasing a round Bowre; which with it sees,
> (As with a Diamant doth an ameld Ring.)
> Into which eye, most pitifully stood
> *Niobe*, shedding teares, that were her blood. (2.5–9)

Here Chapman proceeds centripetally: Corinna is pasted into the diamond-like spring, which the larger, ring-like bower enchases. The double eye-metaphor is explained in the marginalia: 'By *prosopopaeia*, he makes ye fountaine ye eye of the Arbor, as a Diamant seems to be the eye of a Ring: and therefore says, the Arbor sees with the Fountaine' (2 gloss, p. 53). Yet this gloss fails to explain that the primary function of the spring/eye in the poem is to be beheld rather than to see. In tune with a visual conception of *enargia*, Corinna and the fountain are miniaturised, 'lymn[d]' into a device that invites emblematic – that is, intellectual – contemplation rather than mere complicity with Ovid's lavish feast of the senses. The choice is between two competing voices: Ovid's and the narrator's – the latter further branching into a more specialised third, the glossarist's. Reading *with* Ovid and *through* his 'banquet of sence', Chapman contends, amounts to reading *without* the 'true habit of Poesie' and *against* true 'sence'.

Chapman insists on these forking paths, particularly as Ovid approaches his beloved through hearing and sight – the only legitimate Neoplatonic senses.[67] When Ovid hears Corinna's 'Sonnet' in stanza 12, he neglects to listen to its satiric, cautionary content, which attentive readers can easily discern. Rather, and inspired by its sound, Ovid embraces the 'furies' of his 'quick verse': 'And he the purifying rapture sings / Of his eares sence' (15.3–4). Similarly, the entranced contemplation of Corinna's naked body prevents him from noticing the three 'Iewels of deuise' attached to her heart-shaped hairdo (70.4–5). Stressing Chapman's avowed strategy of leaving their meaning open, John Huntington explains the jewels as emblems of the poem's professed obscurity.[68] And Martin Wheeler contends that they endorse a 'Neoplatonic aesthetic ideology' that tallies with a sympathetic attitude to Ovid's erotic aims.[69] However, the hairpins' devices escape Ovid's eye, and so does their meaning his intellect. They, and by extension the entire poem, remain obscure only if readers follow the path of Ovid, whose libidinous blindness also condemns his poetics: 'Now *Ouids* Muse as in her tropicke shinde, / And he (stroke dead) was mere heuen-borne become, / So his quick verse in equall height was shrinde' (57.5–7). Ovid's 'quick verse' – and 'quicknes' is also the vice that precipitates Adolesche's metamorphosis into the 'pied-plum'd *Psitacchus*' – is the effect of a misled Platonic frenzy. Conversely, the devices' miniaturising method – the same that presented the fountain as a jewel's eye – puts the poet's and glossarist's guidance at the service of the habited reader.

The first device, representing a 'Mans huge shaddow' growing at the sun's 'Eeuens [evening's] depart', concerns both the agent of poetic invention and its represented object: when found in the right poetic medium, figured forth here by the receding sunlight, the habit of the obscure poet becomes more prominent and the meaning of the obscure poem more apparent.[70] This is followed by two new devices:

> An other was an Eye in Saphire set,
> And close vpon it a fresh Lawrell spray,
> The skilfull Posie was, *Medio caret*,
> To show not eyes, but meanes must truth display.
> The third was an *Apollo* with his Teme
> About a Diall and a worlde in way,
> The motto was, *Teipsum et orbem*,
> Grauen in the Diall . . . (71.1–8)

These two impresas share a similar design: just as the second jewel presents the eye 'in Saphire set' as its centre, the gloss to the third clarifies that 'ye world is placed in the Dyall' – which again recalls the previous metaphor of the enchased fountain as the arbour's eye. The gloss grounds this disposition on the fact that 'The Sun hath as much time to compasse a Diall as the world', and declares that 'the conceite of the Empresse . . . hath a far higher intention' than it shows (71 gloss, p. 71). The dial is the *teipsum* in the motto, meaning a microcosmic human soul within which the entire world is contained. If Apollo's chariot stands for poetry, then its 'higher intention' points to a Ficinian allegory of the poet's soul, commanding a 'Teme' (i.e., team) of rational and sensual powers (Ficino's better and worse horses) in its attempt to unite nature's circuit (*circuitus naturae*, or 'the worlde') with the higher circuit of understanding (*circuitus intelligentiae*, or the 'Dyall').[71] Yet Ovid's sight and inspiration remain entirely blind to this alternative banquet of philosophical sense.[72]

In the central device, the laurel's closeness to the eye posits an obstacle to vision. Its 'skilfull Posie' demands the translation of *medio* as 'meanes' – 'To show not eyes, but *meanes* must truth display' – or, as in the marginal gloss, 'medium':[73]

> Sight is one of the three sences that hath his medium extrinsecally, which now (supposed wanting,) lets the sight by the close apposition of the Lawrell: the application whereof hath many constructions. (71 gloss, p. 71)

Moreover, 'let' means 'obstruct':[74] the laurel stands in the way of the eye, thus hindering, or altering, sight's natural 'medium', the Aristotelian transparent, which is here 'wanting'.[75] In accordance with Aristotelian theory, the 'close apposition' of a non-transparent obstacle – here the laurel – impairs vision by annulling the medium's transparency. Yet the laurel stands for poetry, thus advancing an alternative medium towards truth with an inner light of its own. As the Roydon epistle concludes, 'those that before-hand, haue a radiant, and light bearing intellect, will say they can passe through Corynnas garden without the helpe of a Lanterne' (50).[76] Denied to those seduced by Ovid's banquet, this inner light – 'Poesies natiue habit shining' – will enable readers to discover poetry's true forms projected behind the eye's surface. The organ of sight, but also the surface that displays the truths of the soul, the eye assists intricate allegorical routes from psychology to poetics. As we read in *Hero and Leander*:

> For as a glasse is an inanimate eie,
> And outward forms imbraceth inwardlie:
> So is the eie an animate glasse that shows
> In-formes without vs. (*Hero*, III.235–8)

Describing Hero's fears that her new 'deuirginate state' be apparent, this conceit is expanded to a cosmic dimension revealing an allegorical intent:

> And as Phoebus throwes
> His beames abroad, though he in clowdes be closed,
> Still glancing by them till he finde opposed,
> A loose and rorid vapour that is fit
> T'euent his searching beames, and vseth it
> To forme a tender twentie-coloured eie,
> Cast in a circle round about the skie:
> So when a firie soule, our bodies starre,
> (That euer is in motion circulare)
> Conceiues a forme; in seeking to display it
> Through all our cloudie parts, it doth conuey it
> Forth at the eye, as the most pregnant place,
> And that reflects it round the face. (III.238–50)

Comparing the iris to the rainbow, our souls to the sun, our mind's conceptions to the projected colours, and our bodies to the 'rorid' (i.e., dewy, thus semi-transparent) clouds that partly 'euent', or discharge, sunlight through it and partly fix it on their surface,[77]

Chapman completes a full allegory of the poetic process. The soul's 'in-Formes' are enlightened *through* and *in spite of* the clouding obscurity of the material poetic medium: as in the earlier poem, the poetic medium – emblematised by the laurel – both prevents and permits the display of true forms. But Ovid's failure to read Corinna's devices and his subsequent banquet of the senses ending in the prospect of writing 'The Art of loue' for the sake of 'Sweete touch' ('Ouids Banquet', 113.1–5), which is the least mediated and therefore the basest of all senses, exclude his praxis as reader and writer from the 'true habit of Poesie'. The medium, and not the senses, must display truth: the eye is nothing without the laurel's aid. For this reason, the poem's ending in a conceit alluding to the concealing tricks of the 'Painters Art', whereby Ovid is granted the ability to see more than is actually displayed, is meant to be read ironically: 'So in the compasse of this curious frame, / Ovid well knew there was so much intended, / With whose omission none must be offended' (117.7–8). Critics have noted Chapman's winking retort to Sidney's dismissal of 'allegorie's curious frame'.[78] 'Compass[ing]' Ovid's headstrong sensuality in the emblematic, visual logic of the poem, Chapman insists on the aesthetic as one necessary frame of its didactic, allegorical edifice.

Coda: Habit and Beyond

If Chapman ever borrowed, as this chapter suggests, from Ficino's interpretation of Plato's myth of the charioteer in *Phaedrus* to illustrate his poetics, one wonders the extent to which he could have imagined his philosophical Homer and his sensual Ovid as counterparts for the Ficinian better and worse horses. In Plato's and Ficino's portrait, both horses are necessarily yoked together, and the charioteer's task is necessarily a 'taxing and difficult' one.[79] Drawing on Chapman's title, one also wonders whether his laborious driving of the chariot was the process aimed at transforming Ovid's banquet of the five senses into a philosophical banquet of poetic meaning, or 'sence' – which poets such as himself and Ben Jonson called the 'soul' of language and poetry.[80] And one must at least wonder whether Chapman ever intended this pun in his title. Whether or not he intended any of these things, poetic habit emerges as the principle that balanced in his poetics and poesis the tensions between an unattainable Homeric model, in which writing stems from the divine frenzy of 'an absolute and full soule', and a less desirable model of 'sonnets and lascivious ballades' for which his fictional Ovid's 'quick verse' had served as illustration.

The inevitable tension between these two models is evinced by the fact that Chapman's more or less overt rejection of the latter involves the recognition of his own unworthiness with respect to the former. When visited by a vision of Homer at the beginning of *The Teares of Peace* (1609), an entranced Chapman concedes this limitation overtly: 'I view'd him at his brightest; though, alas, / With all acknowledgement, of what hee was / Beyond what I found *habited* in me' (69–71). However, even if the difference between Homer and Chapman is found in what characterises the latter's poetic habit, one could argue that it is ultimately in habit that Chapman found the true poet's distinction:

> Nor is there any such reality of wisdomes truth as in Poets fictions . . . nor Artist being so strictly confined to the lawes of learning, wisedom and truth as a Poet. For were not his fictions composed of the sinews and soules of all those, how could they defie fire, iron, and be combined with eternitie?[81]

Whatever it is that poets possess in excess of all other artists, Chapman also demanded that very quality from his readers. This justifies his demands on the 'Understander' (a word that he specifically used in reference to the reader of Homer), his insistence on the 'iudiciall' quality of his reader's discernment, and his conviction that 'to him that is *more than* a reader I write' (emphasis added). For all its rich polysemy and indeterminacy, Chapman's 'habit of Poesie' is best defined by the surplus inherent in that comparative.

Notes

I wish to thank Jonathan P. A. Sell, Sarah Knight and María Vera-Reyes for generously sharing with me their knowledge and readings of Renaissance literature during the writing of this chapter.

1. 'A certain settled facility, which the Greeks call *hexis* (habit)' (Quintilian, *Institutio oratoria*, X.1.1, ed. Butler, 4:2, my translation).
2. Chapman, *Seaven Bookes of the Iliades*, 'To the Reader', in *Chapman's Homer*, ed. Nicoll, 1:507.
3. Huntington, *Ambition, Rank and Poetry*, 90–2, has argued that this 'intentionally' misleading notion serves Chapman to discriminate between poetry audiences. Waddington, *The Mind's Empire*, 107,

stresses its potential to reflect poetry's quality as a perspective picture enabling readers to differentiate between right and wrong perceptions. For rhetoric-oriented readings, see Tuve, *Elizabethan and Metaphysical Imagery*, 32; and Snare, *Mystification*, 135–6. For its interpretation as the key concept in Chapman's construction of a polymathic, scholarly reader, see Wolfe, *Humanism, Machinery*, 161–202. For a recent reassessment, see Luis-Martínez, 'Friendlesse Verse'.
4. Chapman, *Poems*, ed. Bartlett, 50, emphasis added. All references to this volume are cited parenthetically in the text. Prose is cited by page number. Verse is cited by poem's abbreviated title (when necessary), part and/or stanza (when relevant), line and page (when necessary). Chapman's works from other volumes are cited in the notes.
5. Aristotle, *Categories*, VIII, 8b–9b, in *Categories. On Interpretation. Prior Analytics*, trans. Cook and Teddenick, 64–7.
6. Chapman, 'The Georgics', I.455–60, in *Minor Translations*, ed. Corballis, 35.
7. Ibid., I.49n, 63, my emphasis.
8. Chapman, *Seaven Bookes of the Iliades*, 'To the Earle of Essex', in *Chapman's Homer*, 1:505.
9. Chapman, *Iliads*, 'Preface to the Reader', in *Chapman's Homer*, 1:15.
10. Ibid.
11. Scott, *Model of Poesy*, ed. Alexander, 8; see Hetherington, 'Disciplining Creativity'.
12. Scott, *Model of Poesy*, 8.
13. My argument adapts Hulse's conclusion on Chapman's *Hero and Leander*: 'Chapman's great contribution . . . is nothing else than the domestication of inspiration. By seeing in it an impulse to formality, he moves the inspired poem back into the generic system of Renaissance verse' (*Metamorphic Verse*, 140). On Chapman's defence of a poetics of divine inspiration, see Bottrall, 'Defence of Difficulty', 642–4; Spivack, *George Chapman*, 30–7; MacLure, *George Chapman*, 32–5; and Waddington, *The Mind's Empire*, 7–10.
14. On Chapman's obscurity understood as a defect, see Swinburne, particularly as he compares his difficulty to Robert Browning's: 'The difference between the two is the difference between smoke and lightning; and it is far more difficult to pitch the tone of your thought in harmony with that of a foggy thinker, than with that of one whose thought is electric in its motion' (*George Chapman*, 18). See Knight, 'The Worthy Knots of Fulke Greville', this volume, 240, for more on Swinburne and poetic difficulty in relation to his views on Fulke Greville. On Chapman's view of difficulty as a theory of the reader, see Bottrall, 'Defence of Difficulty'. On obscurity and the social dimension of Chapman's poetic consciousness, see Huntington, *Ambition, Rank and Poetry*, passim.
15. Waddington, *The Mind's Empire*, 143–8; Wolfe, *Humanism, Machinery*, 165–6.

16. 'Who will read this? Nobody, by Hercules, nobody: either two or nobody', in Chapman, *Ouids Banquet of Sence*, title page; my translation. For Persius's original, see *Juvenal and Persius*, I.2–3, ed. Ramsay, 316.
17. 'If a few do not move him, neither will more' (Seneca, *De constantia*, XV.2–5, in *Moral Essays*, trans. Bashore, 1:92–3). In the words of Snare, Chapman's 'boast is about mastery and poetic accomplishment and poetic performance' (*Mystification*, 150).
18. '[H]ow ioyfully oftentimes you reported vnto me, that most ingenious *Darbie*, deepe searching *Northumberland*, and skil-imbracing *heire of Hunsdon*' (Chapman, 'To Mathew Roydon', in *Poems*, 19). These are Ferdinando Stanley, 5th Earl of Derby and Lord Strange, amateur poet and alchemist, and patron of letters; Henry Percy, 9th Earl of Northumberland; and George Carey, 2nd Earl of Hunsdon, briefly Lord Chamberlain of England between 1596 and 1597. On Northumberland and Hariot, see Kargon, *Atomism in England*, 1–42; see also Gatti, *Renaissance Drama of Knowledge*, 35–73.
19. Stapleton authored the translation 'The Amorous Contention of Phillis and Flora', which closed the first edition of *Ouids Banquet of Sence*. Thomas Williams is one of the two obscure bearers of that name in the Inner Temple's registers at the time (1576 and 1589); see Bartlett's note in Chapman, *Poems*, 430. John Davies had written a collection of epigrams and two brief sonnet sequences that could have influenced Chapman's own crown of sonnets in this volume; see Luis-Martínez, 'Friendlesse Verse', 572–3, 596.
20. On Davies's sonnets, see Moss, 'Second master of love', 457. For a recent brief commentary on the imagery of enclosure in Williams's second sonnet, see Stamatakis, 'Small parcelles', 106–7.
21. Plutarch, 'How to Profit from One's Enemy', II.2, in *Moralia*, trans. Babbitt, 2:6–9. For a different poetic treatment of this tale, see Edward Dyer's sonnet 'Prometheus, when first from heauen hie', in Sargent, *Life and Lyrics of Sir Edward Dyer*, 176. See also Sargent's notes on this sonnet's appearance in earlier manuscripts and printing in 1598 (202–4).
22. *ostenderetur quanto terrori esse hostibus sapientia iure debeat* (Conti, 'De Medusa', in *Mythologiae*, VII.11, pp. 751–2). Unless otherwise specified, translations of Conti are quoted from *Mythologiae*, ed. Mulryan and Brown. This quotation: 2:637. Neither Conti nor his sources say much about the allegorical meaning of these attributes. Chapman may have found inspiration in Boccaccio's 'De Perseo'; see *Genealogie*, ed. Romano, XII.25, 2:595–6.
23. Plutarch, 'How to Profit from One's Enemy', II.2, in *Moralia*, 2:8–9.
24. MacLure notes the 'pedestrian' quality of Chapman's paraphrase (*George Chapman*, 39). For the meanings of the Prometheus myth in Chapman's work, see Battenhouse, 'Chapman and the Nature of Man';

and Waddington, *The Mind's Empire*, 24–30. In the verse epistle to Prince Henry that opens *The Iliads* (1611), Chapman writes that poetry's 'Promethean facultie / Can create men and make even death to live' (*Iliads*, 'To the High Borne Prince', 137–8, in *Chapman's Homer*, 1:6).
25. As Battenhouse writes, 'like Prometheus, Chapman is ill at ease in the terrestrial order; but he believes, that a "Promethean" poet serves his fellowmen by making them likewise ill at ease' ('Chapman and the Nature of Man', 94).
26. *Circa quos secundus Prometheus insurgit, id est doctus homo, et eos tanquam lapideos suscipiens quasi de novo creet, docet et instruit, et demonstrationibus suis ex naturalibus hominibus civiles facit, moribus scientia et virtutibus insignes, adeo ut liquido pateat alios produxisse naturam, et alios reformasse doctrinam* (Around whom [i.e., natural men] rises the second Prometheus, that is, the learned man, and, holding them as if he created their stony nature anew, he teaches and instructs them, and with his arguments he makes civilised out of natural men, excellent by the virtues and habits of science, so much that it may be patent that nature produced one kind and doctrine reformed the other). Boccaccio, 'De Prometheo', in *Genealogie*, IV.44, 1:199; my translation.
27. Waddington, *The Mind's Empire*, 123–4.
28. Chapman, *Achilles Shield*, 'To My Admired and Sovle-Loved Friend, Mayster of all essential and true knowledge, M. Harriots', in *Poems*, ed. Bartlett, 381–4. References to this poem are cited parenthetically in the text by line number.
29. Chapman, *Seaven Bookes of the Iliades*, 'To the Earle of Essex', in *Chapman's Homer*, 1:505.
30. Chapman, *Achilles Shield*, 'To the Earle Marshall', in *Chapman's Homer*, 1:543–4.
31. Ibid.
32. Chapman, *Seaven Bookes of the Iliades*, 'To the Reader', in *Chapman's Homer*, 1:507.
33. On Chapman's poetics of translation, see Belle, 'Elizabethan Defences of Translation'.
34. Chapman, *Iliads*, 'To the Reader', 116–18, in *Chapman's Homer*, 1:9.
35. Chapman, *Iliads*, 'The Preface to the Reader', in *Chapman's Homer*, 1:17.
36. On another use of this word, see Chapman, *Achilles Shield*, 'To the Understander', in *Chapman's Homer*, 1:548.
37. See Bradbrook, *School of Night*, 145.
38. Wolfe, *Humanism, Machinery*, 174, and 174–6 for an extended commentary. For similar arguments, see Waddington, *The Mind's Empire*, 126–9.
39. For texts and traditions informing Ficino's argument on Plato's three eyes in his commentary to *Philebus*, see Allen, 'Marsilio Ficino on Plato's Pythagorean Eye'.

40. Bradbrook, *School of Night*, 144.
41. See note 13.
42. Chapman, *Achilles Shield*, 'To the Understander', in *Chapman's Homer*, 1:548.
43. Waddington, *The Mind's Empire*, is an example of the latter, even if it remains the best comprehensive reading of Chapman's poetry.
44. See the meanings of 'spright', n.1 and of 'sprit', n.1, †2, and of 'file', v3, †2 in *OED* online, 2nd edn: <https://www.oed.com/view/Entry/187708>, <https://www.oed.com/view/Entry/187805>, and <https://www.oed.com/view/Entry/70163>.
45. *obscuros esse, sed extricabiles semper, si sanus ad eos accesserit intellectus* (Boccaccio, 'Damnanda non est obscuritas poetarum', in *Genealogie*, XIV.12, 2:715; English translation from *Boccaccio on Poetry*, ed. Osgood, 60).
46. Ironically, the association of the golden bough with the Parcae rather than the Sybil seems to be Williams's error.
47. *legendum est, insistendum vigilandumque, atque interrogandum, et omni modo premende cerebri vires!* (Boccaccio, *Genealogie*, XIV.12, 2:717; English translation: *Boccaccio on Poetry*, ed. Osgood, 62). On similar views on difficulty and reading, see Knight, 'The Worthy Knots of Fulke Greville', this volume, 239.
48. *Nec sit quis existimet a poetis veritates fictionibus invidia conditas, aut ut velint omnino absconditorum sensum negare lectoribus, aut ut artificiosiores appareant* (Boccaccio, *Genealogie*, XIV.12, 2:715–16; English translation: *Boccaccio on Poetry*, ed. Osgood, 60).
49. Snare, *Mystification*, 137. The phrase 'deeper misteries' closes John Davies's first laudatory sonnet in *Ouids Banquet of Sence*: 'I. D. of the Middle Temple', 14, in *Poems*, 52.
50. See opening epigraph and note 1 to this chapter. Quintilian propounds a systematic programme of reading and writing as a means towards the acquisition of such habits. On Quintilian and habit, see Murphy, 'Roman Writing Instruction'.
51. Kendal, 'Introduction', 35.
52. Schoell, *Études sur l'humanisme*, 224. See also Snare, *Mystification*, 136.
53. Ferguson, 'Review of Schoell, *Études sur l'humanisme*', 150.
54. Praz, *Studies in Seventeenth-century Imagery*, 218–19. See also Ribner, 'The Compasse of This Curious Frame', 235.
55. Chapman, *Poems*, ed. Bartlett: 'Introduction', 11; my emphasis.
56. As Murrin argues of the allegorist's obscurity, it 'did not permanently divide his audience into two parts, but left a small door open through which some of the multitude could join the ranks of the elite' (*Veil of Allegory*, 39).
57. Ovid, *Metamorphoses*, trans. Miller, V.678, 1:284–5.
58. *Sunt non nulli tam inepte audacie, ut, cum nullam noverint disciplinam, suo tamen innitentes ingenio, audeant se disciplinatis preferre . . . sese*

audent extimare poetas, aut a circumspicientibus arbitrari (Boccaccio, *Genealogie*, XI.2, 2:542–3; my translation). After Chapman in England, George Sandys argues that 'The Pye is the hieroglyphic on vnreasonable loquacity: deciphering those illiterate Poetasters (By the Satyre called the Pye-poets) who boast their owne composures, and detract from the glory of the learned' (Sandys, *Ovid's Metamorphoses*, 199).

59. Cicero, *De natura deorum*, III.21, trans. Rackham, 338–9. 'Pierides' is, however, a common epithet for the Muses themselves. While Conti states that Pierus the Macedonian named his nine daughters after the Muses (*Mythologiae*, 'De Musibus', VII.15, p. 773; trans. Mulryan and Brown, 2:655), Boccaccio argues that the Muses took the name from the nine daughters of Pierus after their defeat and metamorphosis into magpies (*Genealogie*, XI.2, 2:539). Like Chapman, Marlowe differentiates between the nine Muses and the nine daughters of Pierus in Zenocrate's praise of Tamburlaine's voice: 'His talke much sweeter than the Muses song, / They sung for honor gainst *Pierides*' (*Tamburlaine* I, 3.3.50–51, in *Complete Works, Vol. 1*, ed. Bowers, 109).
60. Dionysius of Halicarnassus, *On Literary Composition*, XXIII, 240–1.
61. On Chapman's originality and the sources of the tale, see Bush, *Mythology*, 216–17; and Gordon, *Renaissance Imagination*, 106–8.
62. Lewis, 'Hero and Leander', 245.
63. Gordon, *Renaissance Imagination*, 298–9 n.24.
64. See the different senses in 'pied, adj.1 and n.', in *OED* Online: <https://www.oed.com/view/Entry/143564>, and '†pie, v.2: To repeat like a magpie' <https://www.oed.com/view/Entry/143543>. Also suggesting inconstancy and showiness, see Chapman's 'pyed show' ('Hymnus in Cynthiam', 374). On Sidney, poetry and the chatter of pies, see Sell, 'Philip Sidney's Sublime Self-Authorship', this volume, 183.
65. Waddington (*The Mind's Empire*, 13–51) and Wolfe (*Humanism*, 161–202) argue that visual conceits such as perspective paintings and optic artefacts are recurrent mediators between Chapman's readers and poems. In the particular case of 'Ouids Banquet of Sence', my argument generally aligns with those who understand the poem as a critique of Ovidian sensualism; see Kermode, 'The Banquet of Sense'; Gless, 'Chapman's Ironic Ovid'; and, more recently, Weaver, 'The Banquet of the Common Sense'. For an alternative look at Chapman's Ovid, see Moss, 'Second master of love'; and Gorman, 'Atomies of Love', this volume, 84–8.
66. Weaver, 'The Banquet of the Common Sense', 773.
67. '[I]t is the intellect, seeing and hearing by which we alone are able to enjoy beauty ... What need is there for smell? What need is of taste, or touch? These senses perceive odors, flavors, heat, cold, softness and hardness, and similar things. None of these is human beauty ... [A]n appetite which follows the other senses is not called love, but lust or madness' (Ficino, *Commentary on Plato's Symposium*, I.4, p. 41).

68. Huntington, *Ambition, Rank and Poetry*, 142–3.
69. Wheeler, 'The obiect', 335–6.
70. I subscribe here to the readings in Wheeler, 'The obiect', 336, and Huntington, *Ambition, Rank and Poetry*, 142.
71. For Ficino's views on Plato's myth of the charioteer in *Phaedrus*, VII, see Ficino, *Commentaries on Plato: Volume I: Phaedrus*, 66–70. Although I agree with Wheeler in considering Ficino an inspiration for Chapman, my interpretation of this emblem differs from his: 'in the creative synthesis of the chariot horses of Apollo, poetry becomes a philanthropic instrument of the complementarily balanced passion and reason' ('The obiect', 336).
72. For a perceptive account of misinterpretation in relation to Chapman's poem, see Gorman, 'Atomies of Love', this volume, 88.
73. Wheeler errs in the translation: 'It has no middle point' ('The obiect', 336), while Hudston translates it correctly (Chapman, *Plays and Poems*, 411, n. 71.39).
74. 'let, v.2: archaic. 1a. transitive. To hinder, prevent, obstruct, stand in the way of', *OED* Online: <https://www.oed.com/view/Entry/107497>.
75. On Aristotle's notion of the medium, see Johansen, *Aristotle on the Sense Organs*, 116–47. In Chapman, the 'meanes' controls the poem's organisation, beginning with the three senses that have an extrinsic medium (hearing, smell, sight), and proceeding to those whose medium manifests itself intrinsically (taste and touch).
76. In comparing the eye to a lantern, Aristotle 'retains the Empedoclean doctrine that the exercise of the capacity for sight involves fire in the eye's interior, understood as the fiery substance illuminating the internal medium' (Kalderon, *Form Without Matter*, 144).
77. '†rorid, adj.: Dewy; of the nature of dew'; '†event, v.1: 1. transitive. To discharge or expel (something) through an outlet', *OED* Online: <https://www.oed.com/view/Entry/65289>. *OED* registers Chapman's examples.
78. On Chapman's allusion to Sidney's sonnet 28 in *Astrophil and Stella*, see Myers, 'This Curious Frame'; and Wheeler, 'The obiect', 343. On Sidney's sonnet and allegory, see Sell, 'Philip Sidney's Sublime Self-Authorship', this volume, 170.
79. In Ficino's translation of Plato, *dura et difficilis necessario sit aurigatio nostra* (*Commentaries: Volume I*, 'Mythical Hymn', 9).
80. '[I]f the Bodie (being the letter, or historie) seems fictiue, and beyond Possibilitie to bring into Act: the sence then and the Allegorie (which is the soul) is to be sought' (Chapman, *Odyssey* [1616], 'To the Earle of Somerset', in *Chapman's Homer*, 2:5). See also: 'In all speech, words and sense are as the body and the soul. The sense is as the life and soul of language, without which all the words are dead', lines 1335–7). On matter and form, body and soul distinctions in Chapman's poetics, see Waddington, *The Mind's Empire*, 10–16. See also Sumillera, 'Bloody Poetics', this volume, 109.
81. Chapman, *Iliads*, 'The Preface to the Reader', in *Chapman's Homer*, 1:14.

Afterword
Clark Hulse

> Theory is nothing else but the attempt to escape practice . . . no one can reach a position outside practice.
>
> Stephen Knapp and Walter Benn Michaels[1]

> The highest thing would be so to grasp things so that everything factual was already theory.
>
> Erwin Panofsky[2]

Early modern literary theory and criticism, especially as it appeared in England, has lived in paradox. This is striking since English literature of this period has been one of the primary sites for the development of postmodern literary theory for decades. And it is all the more striking since the early modern period – if it has any valid claim to call itself the 'Renaissance' – has itself been described as an age of theory, not only in literature but in the visual arts as well.

Some reasons for this were hinted at by Rosalie Colie in the passage that supplies the subtitle to this volume:

> In one generation . . . Aristotle's *Poetics*, together with Horace's long-known *ars poetica*, the epistle to the Pisos, had established a Renaissance genre . . . I shall refer from time to time to some of the many *artes poeticae* written in the period, since from them we can recover the ideas consciously held, governing the written criticism and theory of the Renaissance. From 'real' literature as opposed to criticism and theory, of course, we recover what is far more important, the unwritten poetics by which writers worked and which they themselves created.[3]

As Colie makes clear, there was an explosion of theoretical and critical writing about literature in the sixteenth century, mostly inspired by Aristotle and Horace, a proliferation that she says created its own genre, just as contemporary theoretical and critical writings about literature are distinct from novels, poetry, drama, creative non-fiction, graphic novels and so forth. And as Colie makes equally clear, the fit between that new genre and the poetry of the time (for it was mostly poetry that it addressed) was at best imperfect, just as it is now. This mismatch is described not just as a difference in genre, but a difference, it would seem, between the 'real' and, by implication, the 'unreal', between the 'unwritten' and, by implication, the 'written', between 'work' and 'creation' on one hand and, by implication – what? – the dilettantish and derivative?

Colie's sly paragraph blows open many of the questions that the criticism and theory of early modern literature have laboured to answer. First, are criticism and theory one thing, or two? Are Aristotle's *Poetics* and Horace and the many such writings in their wake indeed all *artes poeticae* or are they themselves diverse kinds with diverse motives and forms? Are they indeed distinct from the creative work of poetry, or reflections of that work, or shapers of it, that is, are they either descriptive or prescriptive or simply something that floats off on its own? Above all, what are an 'unwritten' poetics and 'unwritten' arts? – are they a dimension of practice, as Knapp and Michaels would seem to have it, or are they, as Panofsky suggests, things within the 'real' work of literature that aspire to or gesture towards an abstract statement *about* the individual work and literature in general?

Sorting out the terms is itself a work of historical intricacy. Colie calls the early modern offspring of the *Poetics* and *Ars poetica* 'the written criticism and theory of the Renaissance' as if they were one thing, but the three forms (*ars poetica*, criticism, theory) need to be pulled apart before they can be put back together. It was with Kant that the Aristotelian form of writing became *aesthetics*, or the philosophical theory of the arts. Kant of course placed this in the category of 'judgement', as opposed to 'pure reason', but still a thing distinct from Horatian-style criticism.

This leaves the phrase 'criticism and theory' in need of unbundling. Baxter Hathaway worked part-way through the muddle half a century ago by differentiating *poetics*, or the theory of literary works, from criticism proper, or the judgement of their worth, while noting that 'the term 'criticism' has, however, taken over the place of the term 'poetics' with somewhat broader implications. In either its theoretical or its practical aspects it is the philosophical ordering of literary perceptions.'[4] Gavin Alexander has recently reasserted the distinction between criticism and theory, arguing that 'if poetics is the theory and the poetry is the practice, criticism is the judgment of this practice by the measure of that theory'.[5] Both leave the art of making poesy to fend for itself, with theoretical discussions floating up into the ethereality of abstraction, discussions of practice sinking into the mud of how-to manuals (like composition textbooks), and criticism wandering a middle earth, analysing and explaining practice while gesturing towards the higher condition of theory. Hathaway and Alexander both recognise that the discourses of poetics and criticism are generally distinct from literary artworks themselves, though Alexander adds that 'where works of imaginative literature hint at or explore how they might be judged . . . they are simultaneously acts of criticism'.[6]

Colie is empirically correct, though, in seeing that Horace and Aristotle were persistently bundled together in the sixteenth century, *especially* in the English writings about poetic art. Likewise, discussions of how to write imaginative literature are mingled persistently with theories about its intellectual and social utility and judgements about contemporary writers. So we must ask the question, how distinct are these categories even now? Are theory, criticism and the arts of making distinct from one another and from *poesis* itself? If we start at the antipode of 'pure' theory, we can note how, as Derrida suggested in his essay 'White Mythology' and Charles Mills explored in *Blackness Visible*, the supposed neutrality ('whiteness') of Kantian discourse has persistently occluded an ideologically tinctured metaphoric substrate.[7] One can thereby answer Colie's dilemmas by suggesting that the entanglement of aesthetic theory, critical judgement and the arts of making in Renaissance writings – though they separate later into non-literary discourses – subjects them in their historical context to the same sort of analysis as early modern literature proper. She is right in calling them a genre, and, one must insist, it was a *literary* genre.

To this end, Margaret Ferguson took this analytic step in her early book, *Trials of Desire: Renaissance Defenses of Poetry* (1983), arguing that works such as Sir Philip Sidney's *Defense of Poesy* and Guillaume DuBellay's *Défense et illustration de la langue française* are not just arguments *for* poetry, but are indeed defending literature *against* the perception that it poses emotional and social threats.[8] I suggested a while ago that Tudor 'aesthetic' writing persistently used metaphors of the body that expressed prevalent social anxieties about gender,[9] while in this volume Rocio Sumillera probes how critical treatises frequently constitute the poem 'as a living body that is run through by flows of blood that keep it alive'. Thus, the early modern genre of the *ars poetica* – a mixed and figurative genre of its own – swerves towards the canonical genres of epic, lyric, pastoral and so forth, though it does not submerge into any of them. Rather, it becomes an over-and-under-voice within the system of genres.

The *ars poetica* is of course only one of the written genres underpinning the practice of early modern literature. The training of the poet began with his earliest education (I say 'his' since the education of women poets was less structured and more varied). We might think of these preliminary studies as the ur-arts to the poetic art itself. Vitally important are the arts of rhetoric and logic and, persistently in the background, theology. Each of these points of critical access has a long and distinguished history in modern literary study, and they provide the deep roots for the essays in this volume. Logic, especially with regard to the Ramistic revolution, has been prevalent as an avenue for the exploration of early modern literature since Walter Ong's *Ramus, Method, and the Decay of Dialogue* (1958), an approach exemplified here by Emma Annette Wilson's essay.[10] Theology has been explored in a strong strand of work epitomised by Barbara Lewalski's *Protestant Poetics and the Seventeenth-Century Religious Lyric* (1979).[11] Among the essays in this volume, advancing this line of inquiry in radically different ways, on the theological concept of grace are the contributions by Joan Curbet Soler and María Jesús Pérez-Jáuregui.

Paramount among these ur-arts is rhetoric. Important work, inspired initially by Rosemond Tuve's *Elizabethan and Metaphysical Imagery* (1947), has demonstrated the foundational role of rhetoric for the making (and understanding) of early modern poetry, and critics from Richard Lanham and Brian Vickers to Gavin Alexander and Lynn Enterline have expanded on her insights.[12] Over time, however, this analysis has led to the question of what differentiates poetry from its rhetorical parent. Renaissance humanists did not always make the distinction between the two that Aristotle did, and even when they did, they often aligned poetry with rhetorical aims, as when Sidney argued in his *Defense of Poesy* that poetry had the goal of creating a virtuous man. But a number of recent critics, including Harry Berger, Jr. and Marc Fumaroli, have shown how poetics begins to turn itself against the ends of rhetoric, such that Rachel Eisendrath sums it up by saying that as poetry turned the mind towards contemplation and self-reflection (something Sidney himself recognised and celebrated), 'an independent poetics seemed to be emerging, and with it a critical perspective on rhetoric'.[13] Indeed, in this volume, the essays by David Amelang and Sonia Hernández-Santano exemplify how rhetoric itself can be used to subvert the intentions of rhetoric to poetic purposes. Early modern writers, including Sidney and Shakespeare, exploit rhetorical figures to show states of extreme passion where eloquence breaks down into ineloquence. But if rhetoric can nurture poetics, both can, if mishandled, turn against the poet. The fate of the writer who ties himself too severely to rhetoric or follows too closely the core poetic principle of imitation is exemplified by Thomas Lodge, as examined here by Cinta Zunino-Garrido. Better to let these ur-arts and the *artes poeticae* themselves float above, below and around poetry.

What then are the 'unwritten arts'? In his introduction, Zenón Luis-Martínez has identified three. The first follows Colie's invocation of the arts implicit in the works themselves, 'by which writers worked and which they themselves created', as opposed to those set down by an Aristotle or Horace or Castelvetro or Scaliger, and which might guide a reader, but have less impact on the act of creation. Cassandra Gorman proposes in her essay that erotic metaphors in sixteenth-century poetry carried an implied poetics that directly contrasted with their overt moral intent, while Jonathan Sell, in his subtle analysis of Sidney's *Astrophil and Stella* and *The Defence of Poetry*, suggests a circular cross-definition through which the sonnets simultaneously complement and contest the formally written poetics.

Second are 'the unformulated critical assumptions outside official theory', which may be thought of as what was in the air at a particular time and place and scene of writing, whether the Elizabethan stage or the Inns of Court or the courts themselves of monarchs, earls and countesses. This form of unwriting depends upon a communicative interaction between writer and reader. In their essays on the notorious difficulty of Greville and Chapman, Sarah Knight and Luis-Martínez delineate the ways in which the poet, by seeming to obstruct communication with his reader, actually forces the reader into a deeper inquiry and higher understanding.

Third is 'the blank surface that is left unmarked by writing and that admits – palimpsest-like – unexplained, marginalised or novel meanings'. This is the subtlest, and the most persistent. It is the next thought that the writer leaves unwritten, the self-reflection of the staircase, the hovering, not fully formulated internal poetics. It is this meaning, especially, that may more likely contest rather than complement the formally written poetics, to write against them, unravel and unwrite them. Instead of constructing the poetry or construing it, the *artes poeticae* are themselves deconstructed by it.

Of all the forms of the 'unwritten', this one above all occurs at the margins or intersections of the poetic text. This critical point of attack occurs repeatedly in these essays, and is invoked by Alexander and Eisendrath as well as Luis-Martínez and his colleagues. We may indeed say that the approach from marginality and intersection is the current scholarly consensus for investigating early modern poetics (and, it is worth noting, a persistent aspect of the aesthetics of many postmodern writers). By circling back to Colie and moving forward, current research is undoing the mistaken emphases derived from prescriptive readings of the *artes poeticae*. As Luis-Martínez summarises the matter:

> Even if Robortello's ordered outline featuring definition, effect, end, subject matter and means and Scaliger's procedure through the Aristotelian four-cause scheme inspired Puttenham and Scott, English poetic treatises, in the words of Michael Hetherington, 'persistently undo their claims to systematic completeness, reinscribing theory and practice alike in a more personal and contingent world of work, memory, and habit'.

The challenge of the unwritten is that it works against the systems of the written, indeed, works against the drive towards systematicity itself that is the motive for writing either rhetoric or logic or poetics or, especially, theology. It simultaneously aspires towards theory while opposing the systematicity that theory requires.

The struggle between systematicity and granularity, between top-down and bottom-up, between centre-out and margin-in, has thus characterised the long history of the study of the early modern *ars poetica*. At stake is how we read poems, and how we think they are made. But also at stake is the shape of literary history itself. Here, a comparative look at recent thinking about Renaissance art history is useful. The field remains persistently Italo-centric, with occasional challenges from the adherents of Dutch or German art and only a gradual opening towards the art of Spain and its New World colonies. Systematic treatises are far more dominant in contemporary Italian theory and criticism, and critical judgements are overshadowed by those of Giorgio Vasari, the great sixteenth-century biographer of artists. From Vasari too comes the relentlessly teleological scheme of art history, rising to its climax of excellence with Leonardo, Michelangelo, Raphael and Titian, so well paralleled by the scheme of Renaissance humanist excellence surrounding Dante, Petrarch and Boccaccio or, for that matter, Sidney, Spenser and Shakespeare (or, if you prefer, Spenser, Shakespeare and Milton). Simply discarding the term 'Renaissance' will not undo the teleological burden, since the alternative terms 'early modern' or 'pre-modern' have their own teleology, not looking backward towards what these cultural makers thought they knew of the past, but instead looking forward towards what they could not know of the future.

These strong schemata, often resisted or subverted by scholars but never fully dislodged, give rise to the question posed by Rebecca Zorach: 'Does Renaissance Theory mean anything more than "theories about the Renaissance", on the one hand, or "art theory in the Renaissance" on the other?'[14] Or, as we might reappropriate that to literature, is an account of early modern English *artes poeticae* a description of theories and practices of a collection of writers, or does it have something larger to tell us about systems of writing and culture generally?

Some years ago I suggested that the latter is as inescapable as it is desirable:

> Each gesture, each act of linkage between the arts, or between artistic theory and practice, is also a gesture from within toward cultural totality. Hence each local and individual union of artistic products, social, and conceptual modes . . . has hidden somewhere within it a dream of cultural synthesis that is paradigmatic for the totalizing impulses within Renaissance culture generally.[15]

More recently, the art historian Robert Williams has echoed and greatly expanded this idea in response to Zorach's question. Williams argues that as each work of art explores a new possibility, it is absorbed into a wider set of possibilities that in turn map why the surrounding society thinks that art matters. This bears some resemblance to what Colie meant by 'the resources of kind': each genre is a set of possibilities on which the maker (poet or visual artist) can draw. Those possibilities come from perceptions of the world as well as perceptions about how the materials of art (whether words or images) can be made to fit together. Each act of making, in turn, alters the set of possibilities, and thereby alters the possibilities about what art or poetry might be. It is an implicit theoretical statement, an implicit definition of creative acts as forms of knowledge.[16] And it is by examining this circularity between theory and practice, between the act of making and the reflection on making, that allows us to define the achievements of the Renaissance or early modern culture 'in such a way as to define its distinctive historical importance and thus its distinctive interest'.[17]

Whatever the continuity between Italian Renaissance art and English early modern poetry, this line of inquiry shows up their discontinuities as well. Notably, the circularities between theory and practice mark off one of the major differences between the creative renaissances in Italy and England. Italian writers and visual artists could readily assert their position as heirs and successors to the classics, with their accompanying Aristotelian and Horatian critical and theoretical tradition. But for all their skill at the theories of *imitatio*, English writers were faced at the most material level with incommensurate measures between English and either Greek, Latin or romance vernaculars. The issue comes to a head in the debate between Thomas Campion and Samuel Daniel over the use of rhyme, leading Daniel to reject outright the notion of the Italian humanist movement as a disruptive cultural phenomenon, as, that is, the moment of an epistemic break with the past:

> All our understandings are not to be built by the square of Greece and Italie. We are the children of nature as well as they . . . Nor can it be but a touch of arrogant ignorance, to hold this or that nation Barbarous, these or those times grosse, considering how this manifold creature man, wheresoeuer hee stand in the world, hath always some disposition of worth, intertaines the order of societie, affects that which is most in vse, and is eminent in some one thing or other, that fits his humour and the times.[18]

This resistance based on local practice to the entire ideological framework of 'Renaissance' (and equally, for that matter, to the ideology of modernity) leads Daniel instead to an alternative construction of his own cultural moment, and an alternative poetics, based on a general theory of culture arguably much closer to our own.

A similar dynamic played out in the mid-twentieth-century scholarship on Renaissance or early modern literary criticism and theory. Much of it followed the teleological scheme that the sixteenth-century drive towards systematic theory in the wake of the rediscovery of Aristotle was a key part of an epochal movement towards the scientific rationality of modernism. Bernard Weinberg, in his deeply learned, necessary and scarcely readable study of 1961, and Baxter Hathaway, in *The Age of Criticism* (1962) and *Marvels and Commonplaces* (1968), both writing about Italian criticism, alike focused on the Aristotelian treatises to give their accounts a decidedly teleological bias. O. B. Hardison did the same for the English in *English Literary Criticism: The Renaissance* (1963). The lonely countervoice was J. W. H. Atkins back in 1947, arguing that the 'disorderly' nature of early modern English criticism and theory arose from its impulse to establish the grounds of a native literature.[19]

The essays here and in other recent collections wisely focus on spaces, places, margins, ur-writings, counter-writings and unwritings, that is, all the factors that drive or enact the circulation between theory and practice. An important element in future work will be the further exploration of keywords, a tactic already well advanced here and explored in the Introduction. Keywords such as 'grace', 'love', 'cause', 'imitation', 'art', 'habit' or 'blood' gesture towards the systematicity of theory while remaining an open set, stubbornly never-quite systematic. David Summers' *Michelangelo and the Language of Art* (1981) provides an exhaustive and erudite model from the field of art history, while Roland Greene's *Five Words: Critical Semantics in the Age of Shakespeare and Cervantes* (2013) is splendidly incisive.[20] Another avenue into early modern criticism-before-theory lies in what Bernard Weinberg called 'criticism by epithet', by which he meant the investigation of the descriptive vocabulary that inhabits the margins of early modern editions and commentaries on classical texts, and then is reapplied to vernacular texts, as when Francis Meres in the *Palladis Thamia* used the Ovidian epithets of honey and sugar for Shakespeare's sonnets.[21]

I can best conclude by reinvoking Robert Williams's challenge: to pursue the complex relationship of theory and practice in order to define what makes early modern literature so distinctive and so very interesting. As much of its overt ideology become more distant and alien to us, its ur-, under- and un-writings paradoxically become more resonant. That is what criticism should do: enrich today's reader, and help us to understand how poems were – and are – written.

Notes

1. Knapp and Michaels, 'Against Theory', 742.
2. Panofsky, *Dürer's Kunsttheorie* (Berlin, 1915), cited by Podro, *Critical Historians of Art*, 178.
3. Colie, *Resources of Kind*, 4.
4. Hathaway, *Marvels and Commonplaces*, 3.
5. Alexander, Gilby and Marr, 'Introduction: Placing Early Modern Criticism', 17. This introduction includes a learned and useful account of the history of the term 'criticism' from the classical to early modern period.
6. Ibid.
7. Derrida, 'White Mythology'; and Mills, *Blackness Visible*, esp. 73–4 in his chapter 'Dark Ontologies: Blacks, Jews, and White Supremacy'.
8. Ferguson, *Trials of Desire*. For a recent counter-argument, see Bates, *On Not Defending Poetry*.
9. Hulse, 'Tudor Aesthetics'.
10. Ong, *Ramus, Method*.
11. Lewalski, *Protestant Poetics*.

12. Tuve, *Elizabethan and Metaphysical Imagery*; Lanham, *Handlist of Rhetorical Terms*; Vickers, *Classical Rhetoric in English Poetry*; Adamson, Alexander and Ettenhuber, eds, *Renaissance Figures of Speech*; Enterline, *Rhetoric of the Body*.
13. Eisendrath, 'Poetry at the Limits of Rhetoric', 56.
14. Zorach, 'Renaissance Theory: A Selective Introduction', 3.
15. Hulse, *Rule of Art*, 19.
16. Williams, 'Italian Renaissance Art and Systematicity'.
17. Ibid., 160.
18. Daniel, *Defence of Rhyme*, in *Poems and A Defence of Rhyme*, ed. Sprague, 139–40.
19. Atkins, *English Literary Criticism: The Renascence*, 343–4.
20. See Summers, *Michelangelo and the Language of Art*; more recently, Mac Carthy, *Grace of the Italian Renaissance*; also Greene, *Five Words*.
21. Weinberg, *History of Literary Criticism*, 1:198; see also Baxandall, *Painting and Experience*, 118–51; and Hulse, *Metamorphic Verse*, 96–7.

Bibliography

Primary Sources

Manuscript

Berkeley, Berkeley Castle, Select Books 85.
Dublin, Marsh's Library, MS Z3.5.21.
London, British Library, MS Harley 7553.
London, The National Art Library, V&A Museum, MS Dyce 44.

Print and Digital

Aeschylus. Edited and translated by Hubert Weir Smyth. 2 vols. Cambridge, MA: Harvard University Press, 1922.
Agricola, Rudolph. *De inventione dialectica libri tres*. Paris, 1554. 1st edn, 1485.
Airay, Christopher. *Fasciculus praeceptorum logicorum*. Oxford, 1628.
Alexander, William. 'Anacrisis: or, A Censure of some Poets Ancient and Modern'. In *The Works of William Drummond of Hawthornden ... Now Published from the Author's Original Copies*. Edinburgh: James Watson, 1711. 159–62.
Aristotle. *The 'Art' of Rhetoric*. Translated by John Henry Freese. Cambridge, MA: Harvard University Press, 1926.
Aristotle. *The Categories. On Interpretation. Prior Analytics*. Translated by Harold P. Cook and Paul Teddenick. Cambridge, MA: Harvard University Press, 1912.
Aristotle. *De anima (On the Soul)*. Translated by Hugh Lawson-Tancred. London: Penguin, 1986.
Aristotle. *Metaphysics. A New Translation*. Translated by Joe Sachs. Santa Fe: NM: Green Lion Press, 1999.
Ascham, Roger. *The Scholemaster*. London, 1570.
Ashfield, Andrew, and Peter de Bolla, eds. *The Sublime: A Reader in British Eighteenth-Century Aesthetic Theory*. Cambridge: Cambridge University Press, 1996.
Bacon, Francis. *The Advancement of Learning*. Edited by Michael Kiernan. Oxford: Oxford University Press, 2000.

Bacon, Francis. *Of the Wisdom of the Ancients*. In *The Works of Francis Bacon*, vol. 13. Edited by James Spedding, Robert Leslie Ellis and Douglas Denon Heath. Boston, MA: Houghton Mifflin, 1860. 67–172.
Barnes, Barnabe. *A Divine Centurie of Spirituall Sonnets*. London, 1595.
Barnes, Barnabe. *Parthenophil and Parthenophe*. Edited by Victor A. Doyno. Carbondale, IL: Southern Illinois University Press, 1971.
B[enson], J[ohn]. 'To the Right Honourable Thomas Lord *Windsore*'. In Ben Jonson, *Q. Horatius Flaccus: His Art of Poetry. Englished by Ben: Jonson. With Other Workes of the Author, Never Printed Before*. London, 1640.
Beurhaus, Frederick. *P. Rami Dialecticae libri duo: et his e regione comparati Philippi Melanth. Dialecticae libri quatuor*. Frankfurt am Main, 1586.
Bible and Holy Scriptures Conteyned in the Olde and Newe Testament. Geneva, 1560.
Blount, Thomas. *The Academie of Eloquence Containing a Compleat English Rhetorique*. London, 1654.
Boccaccio, Giovanni. *Boccaccio on Poetry*. Edited and translated by Charles Osgood. New York: The Liberal Arts Press, 1956.
Boccaccio, Giovanni. *Genealogie deorum gentilium libri*. Edited by Vincenzo Romano. 2 vols. Bari: Laterza, 1951.
Braden, Gordon, ed. *Sixteenth-Century Poetry: An Annotated Anthology*. Oxford: Blackwell, 2005.
Browne, Thomas. *Religio Medici, Letter to a Friend and Christian Morals*. Edited by William Greenhill. Peru, IL: Sherwood Sugden and Company, 1990.
Bruno, Giordano. *The Ash Wednesday Supper*. Edited and translated by Hilary Gatti. Toronto: University of Toronto Press, 2018.
Calvin, Jean. *Institutes of the Christian Religion*. Edited and translated by Henry Beveridge. 3 vols. Edinburgh: The Calvin Translation Society, 1895.
Cartari, Vincenzo. *Imagini degli dei degli antichi*. Venice, 1556.
Castiglione, Baldesare. *The Courtyer of Count Baldessar Castilio diuided into foure bookes*. Translated by Thomas Hoby. London, 1561.
Chambers, E. K., ed. *The Oxford Book of Sixteenth Century Verse*. Oxford: Clarendon Press, 1961.
Chapman, George. *Homer: The Iliad, The Odyssey and The Lesser Homerica*. Edited by Allardyce Nicoll. 2 vols. London: Routledge and Kegan Paul, 1957.
Chapman, George. *Minor Translations: A Critical Edition of His Renderings of Musaeus, Hesiod and Juvenal*. Edited by Richard Corballis. Salzburg: Institut für Anglistik und Amerikanistik, 1984.
Chapman, George. *Ouids Banquet of Sence, A Coronet for His Mistresse Philosophie, and His Amorous Zodiacke*. London, 1595.
Chapman, George. *Plays and Poems*. Edited by Jonathan Hudston. Harmondsworth: Penguin, 1989.

Chapman, George. *The Poems of George Chapman*. Edited by Phyllis Brooks Bartlett. New York: Modern Language Association of America, 1941.
Charron, Pierre. *Of Wisdome Three Bookes*. Translated by Samson Lennard. London, 1608 (?).
Cicero, Marcus Tullius. *Brutus. Orator*. Translated by G. L. Hendrickson and H. M. Hubbell. Cambridge, MA: Harvard University Press, 1971.
Cicero, Marcus Tullius. *De natura deorum*. Translated by H. Rackham. Cambridge, MA: Harvard University Press, 1967.
Cicero, Marcus Tullius. *De oratore*. Translated by E. W. Sutton and M. Rackham. 2 vols. Cambridge: MA: Harvard University Press, 1967.
Clusius Correspondence Database. <https://clusiuscorrespondence.huygens.knaw.nl/edition/entry/540/transcription>.
Constable, Henry. *The Complete Poems of Henry Constable: A Critical Edition*. Edited by María Jesús Pérez-Jáuregui. Toronto: Pontifical Institute of Mediaeval Studies, forthcoming.
Constable, Henry. *Diana. The praises of his Mistres, in certaine sweete Sonnets*. London, 1592.
Conti, Natale. *Mythologiae, sive explicationum fabularum, Libri decem*. Frankfurt, 1581. 1st edn, 1568.
Conti, Natale. *Mythologiae*. Edited and translated by John Mulryan and Steven Brown. Tempe, AZ: Arizona Center for Medieval and Early Modern Studies, 2006.
Crooke, Helkiah. *Mikrokosmographia A Description of the Body of Man*. [London], 1615.
Da Fonseca, Pedro. *Institutionum dialecticarum libri octo*. Tournan: Claude Michael, 1597.
Daniel, Samuel. *Poems and a Defence of Rhyme*. Edited by Arthur Colby Sprague. Cambridge, MA: Harvard University Press, 1930.
Dante Alighieri. *Paradiso*. Edited and translated by John Sinclair. New York: Oxford University Press, 1939.
Davies, John. *The Original, Nature, and Immortality of the Soul A Poem: With an Introduction Concerning Humane Knowledge*. London, 1697.
Davies, John. *The Poems of Sir John Davies*. Edited by Robert Krueger. Oxford: Oxford University Press, 1975.
Davies, John (of Hereford). *The Scourge of Folly*. London, 1610.
Davies, John (of Hereford). *Wittes Pilgrimage (by Poeticall Essais), Through a World of Amorous Sonnets, Soule-Passions, and Other Passages, Divine, Philosophicall, Moral, Poeticall, and Politicall*. London, 1605.
Day, Angel. *The English Secretarie*. London, 1592.
De Vries, Gerard. *Logica compendiosa*. Utrecht, 1684.
Dionysius of Halicarnassus, *On Literary Composition*. Edited and translated by W. Rhys Roberts. London: Macmillan, 1910.
Donne, John. *The Complete Poems of John Donne*. Edited by Robin Robbins. Harlow: Pearson, 2010.

Donne, John. *Devotions upon Emergent Occasions*. Edited by Anthony Raspa. Montreal: McGill-Queen's University Press, 1975.
Dowland, John. *The Third and Last Booke of Songs or Aires*. London, 1603.
Drayton, Michael. *The Works of Michael Drayton*. Edited by J. William Hebel. 5 vols. London: Shakespeare Head Press, 1961.
Dryden, John. 'Dedication of the *Aeneis*'. In *The Works of John Dryden. Volume VI: Poems: The Works of Virgil in English, 1697*. Edited by William Frost and Vinton Adams Dearing. Berkeley, CA: University of California Press, 1987. 267–341.
Dryden, John. 'A Defence of *An Essay on Dramatic Poesy*, Being an Answer to the Preface of the Great Favourite, or the Duke of Lerma'. In *The Works of John Dryden. Vol. IX, Plays: The Indian Emperor; Secret Love; Sir Martin Mar-all*. Edited by H. T. Swedenberg. Berkeley, CA: University of California Press, 1966. 3–22.
Dryden, John. 'A Parallel, of Poetry and Painting'. In *Prose 1691–1698: De arte graphica and Shorter Works*. Edited by A. E. Wallace Maurer and George Robert Guffey. Berkeley, CA: University of California Press, 1989. 38–77.
Dryden, John. 'Preface to Fables Ancient and Modern'. In *The Works of John Dryden, Volume VII: Poems, 1697–1700*. Edited by Vinton A. Dearing. Berkeley, CA: University of California Press, 2000. 24–47.
Dryden, John. 'The Preface to the Play [*Troilus and Cressida*]'. In *The Works of John Dryden, Volume XIII: Plays: All for Love, Oedipus, Troilus and Cressida*. Edited by Maximillian E. Novak, George R. Guffey and Alan Roper. Berkeley, CA: University of California Press, 1984. 225–48.
Du Bartas, Guillaume Salluste. *Du Bartas his Divine Weekes And Workes*. Trans. Josuah Sylvester. London: Robert Young, 1633.
Du Bellay, Joachim. 'The Defence and Illustration of the French Language'. In *Poetry & Language in 16th-Century France: Du Bellay, Ronsard, Sébillet*. Edited and translated by Laura Willett. Toronto: Centre for Reformation and Renaissance Studies, 2004. 37–96.
Du Moulin, Pierre. *Elementa logica*. Leiden, 1603.
Du Trieu, Philippe. *Manductio ad logicum*. Oxford, 1678.
Eck, Johann. *Elementarius dialectice*. Augsburg, 1518.
Featley, Daniel, *Ancilla pietatis: Or, the Hand-Maid to Private Devotion*. London, 1626.
Fenner, Dudley. *The Artes of Logike and Rethorike*. Middleburg, 1584.
Ficino, Marsilio. *Commentaries on Plato: Volume I. Phraedrus and Ion*. Edited and translated by Michael J. B. Allen. Cambridge, MA: Harvard University Press, 2008.
Ficino, Marsilio. *Commentary on Plato's Symposium: On Love*. Translated by Sears Jayne. Woodstock, CO: Spring, 1985.
Flecknoe, Richard. *Epigrams of all sorts*. London, 1671.
Fletcher, Giles. *The English Works of Giles Fletcher the Elder*. Edited by Lloyd E. Berry. Madison, WI: University of Wisconsin Press, 1964.

Fletcher, Phineas. *The Purple Island, or, The Isle of Man*. Edited by Johnathan H. Pope. Leiden: Brill, 2017.
Fraunce, Abraham. *'The Shepherds' Logic' and Other Dialectical Writings*. Edited by Zenón Luis-Martínez. Cambridge: Modern Humanities Research Association, 2016.
Gascoigne, George. *The Posies of George Gascoigne, Esquire. Corrected, perfected and augmented by the Authour*. London, 1575.
Gibbons, Stella. *Cold Comfort Farm*. London: Longmans, Green, 1933.
Greville, Fulke. *Poems and Dramas*. Edited by Geoffrey Bullough. 2 vols. Edinburgh: Oliver and Boyd, 1938.
Greville, Fulke. *The Prose Works of Fulke Greville, Lord Brooke*. Edited by John Gouws. Oxford: Clarendon Press, 1986.
Gyraldus, Lilius Gregorius. *Opera omnia*. Leiden, 1696.
Heereboord, Adrian. *Ermhneia logica*. Cambridge, 1657.
Herbert, George. *The English Poems of George Herbert*. Edited by Helen Wilcox. Cambridge: Cambridge University Press, 2007.
Hermogenes. *On Types of Style*. Edited by Cecil W. Wooten. Chapel Hill, NC: University of North Carolina Press, 1987.
Hesiod. *Theogony, Works and Days, Testimonia*. Edited and translated by Glenn W. Most. Cambridge, MA: Harvard University Press, 2006.
Hill, Thomas. *The Contemplation of Mankind*. London, 1571.
Hobbes, Thomas. 'The Answer of Mr. Hobbes to Sr. Will. D'Avenant's Preface before *Gondibert*'. In William D'Avenant, *Sir William Davenant's Gondibert*. Edited by David F. Gladish. Oxford: Clarendon Press, 1971. 45–55.
Hobbes, Thomas. *Leviathan*. Edited by J. C. A. Gaskin. Oxford: Oxford University Press, 1996.
Hookes, Nicholas. *Amanda, A Sacrifice to an Unknown Goddesse, or a Free-Will Offering of a Loving Heart to a Sweet-Heart*. London, 1653.
Huarte de San Juan, Juan. *Richard Carew's The Examination of Men's Wits (1594)*. Edited by Rocío G. Sumillera. London: Modern Humanities Research Association, 2014.
Humphrey, Laurence. *Interpretatio linguarum* [*The translation of languages*] (1559). In *English Renaissance Translation Theory*. Edited by Neil Rhodes, Gordon Kendal and Louise Wilson. London: Modern Humanities Research Association, 2013. 263–94.
Hutchinson, Lucy. *The Works of Lucy Hutchinson, Vol. 1: The Translation of Lucretius*. Edited by Reid Barbour, David Norbrook and Maria Zerbino. Oxford: Oxford University Press, 2012.
Isocrates. *Isocrates Volume II: On the Peace. Areopagiticus. Against the Sophists. Antidosis. Panathenaicus*. Translated by George Norlin. London: Heinemann, 1929.
James VI. *The Essayes of a Prentise, in the Divine Art of Poesie*. Edinburgh, 1585.
Johnson, Samuel. *A Dictionary of the English Language*. Dublin, 1768.

Johnson, Samuel. 'The Life of Pope'. In *The Works of Alexander Pope. With notes by Dr. Warburton*. Philadelphia, PA: Willis P. Hazard, 1859. 9–74.

Johnson, Samuel. *The Lives of the Poets*. Edited by Roger Lonsdale. Oxford: Oxford University Press, 2006.

Jonson, Ben. *Discoveries* (1641). Edited by Lorna Hutson. In *The Cambridge Edition of the Works of Ben Jonson Online*. <https://universitypublishingonline.org/cambridge/benjonson/> Accessed 5 September 2022.

Jonson, Ben, *The English Grammar* (1641). Edited by Derek Britton. In *The Cambridge Edition of the Works of Ben Jonson Online*. <https://universitypublishingonline.org/cambridge/benjonson/> Accessed 5 September 2022.

Jonson, Ben. *Q. Horatius Flaccus: His Art of Poetry. Englished by Ben: Jonson. With Other Workes of the Author, Never Printed Before*. London, 1640.

Juvenal and Persius. Translated by G. G. Ramsay. London: William Heinemann, 1928.

Keckermann, Bartholomaeus. *Systema Logicae*. Hanover, 1602. 1st edn, 1600.

Lamb, Charles. *Specimens of English Dramatic Poets*. London: Edward Moxon, 1849. 1st edn, 1808.

Lanyer, Aemilia. *The Poems of Aemilia Lanyer: Salve Deus Rex Judaeorum*. Edited by Susanne Woods. Oxford: Oxford University Press, 1993.

Lodge, Thomas. *The Divel Coniured*. London, 1596.

Lodge, Thomas. *A Fig for Momus: Containing Pleasant Varietie, included in Satyres, Eclogues, and Epistles*. London, 1595.

Lodge, Thomas. *The Life and Death of William Long Beard*. London, 1593.

Lodge, Thomas. *Phillis: Honoured with Pastoral Sonnets, Elegies and Amorous Delight Where-unto is Annexed, The Tragicall Complaynt of Estred*. London, 1593.

Lodge, Thomas. *A Reply to Stephen Gosson's Schoole of Abuse in Defence of Poetry, Musick, and Stage Plays*. London, 1579.

Lodge, Thomas. *Scillaes Metamorphosis, Enterlaced with the unfortunate love of Glaucus*. London, 1589.

Lodge, Thomas. *Wits Misery, and The Worlds Madnesse: Discouering the Deuils Incarnat of this Age*. London, 1596.

Lomazzo, Giovanni Paolo. *A Tracte Containing the Artes of Curious Painting, Carvinge and Building*. Translated by Richard Haydocke. London, 1598. 1st edn, 1584.

Longinus. *On the Sublime*. Edited and translated by James A. Arieti and John M. Crossett. New York: Edwin Mellen Press, 1985.

Longinus, Cassius. *On Sublimity*. Translated by D. A. Russell. In *Ancient Literary Criticism: The Principal Texts in New Translations*. Edited by D. A. Russell and M. Winterbottom. Oxford: Oxford University Press, 1972. 460–503.

Lucian of Samosata. *Lucian in Eight Volumes*. Trans. A. M. Harmon. Cambridge, MA: Harvard University Press, 1921.

Lucretius, Titus Carus. *On The Nature of Things*. Translated by William Ellery Leonard. London: E. P. Dutton, 1916.

MacIlmaine, Roland. *The Logike of the Moste Excellent Philosopher P. Ramus Martyr*. London, 1574.

Marlowe, Christopher. *The Complete Works of Christopher Marlowe, Vol. 1: Dido, Queene of Carthage; Tamburlaine; The Jew of Malta; The Massacre at Paris*. Edited by Fredson Bowers. Cambridge: Cambridge University Press, 1973.

Marlowe, Christopher. *The Complete Works of Christopher Marlowe, Vol. 1: All Ovids Elegies, Lucans First Booke, Dido Queene of Carthage, Hero and Leander*. Edited by Roma Gill. Oxford: Oxford University Press, 1987.

Marlowe, Christopher. *Doctor Faustus and Other Plays*. Edited by David Bevington and Eric Rasmussen. Oxford: Oxford University Press.

Marston, John. *The Metamorphosis of Pigmalions Image and Certaine Satyres*. London, 1598.

Melanchthon, Philipp. *Dialecticae Philippi Melanchthonis libri tres*. Lyons, 1535.

Milton, John. *Complete Shorter Poems. With Original Spelling and Punctuation*. Edited by Stella P. Revard. Oxford: Wiley-Blackwell, 2009.

Milton, John. *Paradise Lost*. Edited by Alastair Fowler. Harlow: Longman, 2014. 1st edn, 1998.

Nashe, Thomas. *The Works of Thomas Nashe*. Edited by Ronald B. McKerrow. 5 vols. Oxford: Oxford University Press, 1958. 1st edn, 1904–08.

O'Brien, Denis. *Empedocles' Cosmic Cycle: A Reconstruction from the Fragments and the Secondary Sources*. Cambridge: Cambridge University Press, 1969.

Ovid [Publius Ovidius Nassus]. *Heroides. Amores*. Translated by Grant Showerman, revised by G. P. Goold. Cambridge, MA: Harvard University Press, 1914.

Ovid [Publius Ovidius Nassus]. *Metamorphoses*. Translated by Frank Justus Miller. 2 vols. Cambridge, MA: Harvard University Press, 1951.

Peacham, Henry. *The Garden of Eloquence*. London, 1593.

Peletier, Jacques. 'Art poétique'. In *Traités de poétique et de rhétorique de la Renaissance*. Edited by Francis Goyet. Paris: Librairie Générale Française, 1990. 235–344.

Percy, William. *Sonnets to the Fairest Coelia*. London, 1594.

Philostratus the Elder. *Imagines*. Translated by Arthur Fairbanks. London: William Heinemann, 1931.

Pimadauye, Pierre de la. *The French Academie, wherin is discoursed the institution of maners, and whatsoeuer els concerneth the good and happie life of all estates and callings*. Translated by T. B. London, 1586.

Piscator, Johannes. *In P. Rami dialecticam animadversiones.* London, 1581. 1st edn, 1580.

Plato. *Euthyphro; Apology; Crito; Phaedo; Phaedrus.* Translated by Harold North Fowler. Cambridge, MA: Harvard University Press, 1977.

Plutarch. *The Lives of the Noble Grecians and Romans, Vol. II.* Translated by John Dryden, edited by Arthur Hugh Clough. New York: Modern Library, 1992.

Plutarch, *Moralia.* Translated by Frank Cole Babbitt. 15 vols. Cambridge, MA: Harvard University Press, 1917.

Pope, Alexander. *The Poems of Alexander Pope.* Edited by John Butt. London: Methuen, 1963.

Pope, Alexander. 'Preface to the Iliad'. In *The Twickenham Edition of the Poems of Alexander Pope, VII: The Iliad of Homer, Books I–IX.* Edited by Maynard Mack. London: Methuen, 1967. 5–25.

Puttenham, George. *The Art of English Poesy.* Edited by Frank Whigham and Wayne E. Rebhorn. Ithaca, NY: Cornell University Press, 2007.

Quintilian [Marcus Fabius Quintilianus]. *Institutio oratoria.* Edited and translated by H. E. Butler. 4 vols. Cambridge, MA: Harvard University Press, 1921.

Ramus, Petrus. *Bucolica, praelectionibus exposita.* Paris, 1555.

Ramus, Petrus. *Dialecticae libri duo.* Cambridge, 1592. 1st edn, 1556.

Ramus, Petrus. *Partitiones dialectiae.* Paris, 1543.

Richardson, Alexander. *The Logicians School-Master: Or, A Comment vpon Ramus Logicke.* London, 1629.

Sackville, Thomas. *The Last Part of Mirour for Magistrates.* London, 1578.

Sandys, George. *Ovid's Metamorphoses: Englished, Mythologiz'd and Represented in Figures.* Oxford, 1632.

Scaliger, Julius Caesar. *Poetices libri septem.* Lyons, 1561.

Scaliger, Julius Caesar. *Select Translations from Scaliger's Poetics.* Edited and translated by Frederick Morgan Padelford. New York: H. Holt, 1905.

Scheibler, Christoph. *Opus logicum.* Geneva, 1651.

Scott, William. *The Model of Poesy.* Edited by Gavin Alexander. Cambridge: Cambridge University Press, 2013.

Seneca, Lucius Annaeus. *Moral Essays.* Translated by John W. Bashore. 2 vols. London: William Heinemann, 1928.

Shakespeare, William. *The Norton Shakespeare. Based on the Oxford Edition.* Edited by Stephen Greenblatt, with Walter Cohen, Jean E. Howard and Katharine Eisaman Maus. New York: Norton, 1997.

Shakespeare, William. *The Poems. Venus and Adonis, The Rape of Lucrece, The Phoenix and the Turtle, The Passionate Pilgrim, A Lover's Complaint.* Edited by John Roe. Cambridge: Cambridge University Press, 2006. 1st edn, 1992.

Shakespeare, William. *The Rape of Lucrece.* London, 1594.

Shakespeare, William. *Sonnets.* Edited by Katherine Duncan-Jones. London: Thomas Nelson, 1997.

Shakespeare, William. *Venus and Adonis*. London, 1593.
Sidney, Philip. *An Apology for Poetry*. Edited by Geoffrey Shepherd. Manchester: Manchester University Press, 1973.
Sidney, Philip. *Miscellaneous Prose of Sir Philip Sidney*. Edited by Katherine Duncan-Jones and Mark van Dorsten. Oxford: Oxford University Press, 1979.
Sidney, Philip. *The Poems of Sir Philip Sidney*. Edited by William A. Ringler. Oxford: Clarendon Press, 1962.
Southey, Robert. *Select Works*. London: Longmans, 1831.
Spenser, Edmund. *The Faerie Queene*. Edited by A. C. Hamilton, with Hiroshi Yakamata, Toshiyuki Suzuki and Shohachi Fukuda. Abingdon: Routledge, 2013. 1st edn, 2001.
Spenser, Edmund. *The Poetical Works of Edmund Spenser*. Edited by J. C Smith and E. de Selincourt. London: Oxford University Press, 1912.
Spenser, Edmund. *The Yale Edition of the Shorter Poems of Edmund Spenser*. Edited by William A. Oram, Einar Bjorvand, Ronald Bond, Thomas H. Cain, Alexander Dunlop and Richard Schell. New Haven, CT: Yale University Press, 1989.
Stanyhurst, Richard. *Thee First Foure Bookes of Virgil his Aeneis Translated intoo English Heroical Verse*. Leiden, 1582.
Tacitus, Publius Cornelius. *Agricola. Germania. Dialogue on Oratory*. Translated by M. Hutton and W. Peterson. Cambridge, MA: Harvard University Press, 1914.
Tottel's Miscellany: Songs and Sonnets of Henry Howard, Earl of Surrey, Sir Thomas Wyatt and Others. Edited by Amanda Holton and Tom MacFaul. Harmondsworth: Penguin, 2011.
Vega, Lope de. *Los locos de Valencia*. Edited by Hélène Tropé. Madrid: Castalia, 2003.
Vives, Juan Luis. *Selected Works of J. L. Vives, Volume XI: De ratione dicendi*. Edited and translated by David Walker. Leiden: Brill, 2018.
Watson, Thomas. ἙΚΑΤΟΜΠΑΘΙΑ *[Hekatompathia], or Passionate Centurie of Love*. London, 1582.
Webbe, William. *A Discourse of English Poetry (1586)*. Edited by Sonia Hernández-Santano. Cambridge: Modern Humanities Research Association, 2016.
Wilde, Oscar. *Complete Works*. Vol. 4. Edited by Robert Baldwin Ross. Boston, MA: The Wyman-Fogg Company, 1921.
Wilson, Thomas. *The Art of Rhetoric (1560)*. Edited by Peter E. Medine. University Park, PA: Pennsylvania State University Press, 1994.
Wilson, Thomas. *The Rule of Reason, Conteinyng the Arte of Logique*. London, 1551.
Wright, Thomas. *The Passions of the Minde in Generall*. London, 1604. 1st edn, 1601.
Wyatt, Thomas. *The Complete Poems*. Edited by R. A. Rebholz. Harmondsworth: Penguin, 1978.

Secondary Sources

Adams, J. N. 'Anatomical Terminology in Latin Epic'. *Bulletin of the Institute of Classical Studies* 27 (1980): 50–62.
Adamson, Sylvia, Gavin Alexander and Katrin Ettenhuber, eds. *Renaissance Figures of Speech*. Cambridge: Cambridge University Press, 2007.
Akrigg, G. P. V. *Shakespeare and the Earl of Southampton*. London: Hamish Hamilton, 1968.
Alexander, Gavin. 'Fulke Greville and the Afterlife'. *Huntington Library Quarterly* 62 (1999): 203–31.
Alexander, Gavin. 'Introduction'. In William Scott, *The Model of Poesy*. Edited by Gavin Alexander. Cambridge: Cambridge University Press, 2013. i–lxxxiv.
Alexander, Gavin. 'Sidney's Interruptions'. *Studies in Philology* 98 (2001): 184–204.
Alexander, Gavin, Emma Gilby and Alexander Marr. 'Introduction: Placing Early Modern Criticism'. In *The Places of Early Modern Criticism*. Edited by Gavin Alexander, Emma Gilby and Alexander Marr. Oxford: Oxford University Press. 1–21.
Alexander, Gavin, Emma Gilby and Alexander Marr, eds. *The Places of Early Modern Criticism*. Oxford: Oxford University Press, 2021.
Allen, Michael B. 'Marsilio Ficino on Plato's Pythagorean Eye'. *Modern Language Notes* 97 (1982): 171–82.
Amelang, David J. '"A broken voice": Iconic Distress in Shakespeare's Tragedies'. *Anglia. Journal of English Philology/Zeitschrift für Englische Philologie* 137 (2019): 33–52.
Anderson, Judith H. *Words that Matter: Linguistic Perception in Renaissance English*. Stanford, CA: Stanford University Press, 1996.
Arnold, Margaret. 'Thomas Stanley's "Aeschylus": Renaissance Practical Criticism of Greek Tragedy'. *Illinois Classical Studies* 9 (1984): 229–49.
Atkins, J. W. H. *English Literary Criticism: The Medieval Phase*. Cambridge: Cambridge University Press, 1934.
Atkins, J. W. H. *English Literary Criticism: The Renascence*. London: Methuen, 1947.
Atkins, J. W. H. *English Literary Criticism: 17th and 18th Centuries*. London: Methuen, 1950.
Auerbach, Erich. *Literary Language and Its Public in the Late Latin Antiquity and in the Middle Ages*. Translated by Ralph Manheim. Princeton, NJ: Princeton University Press, 1965.
Auger, Peter. 'A Model of Creation? Scott, Sidney and Du Bartas'. *Sidney Journal* 33.1 (2015): 69–90.
Auger, Peter. 'William Scott's Translation from Du Bartas' *Sepmaine*'. *English Literary Renaissance* 47 (2017): 21–72.
Austin, J. L. *How to Do Things with Words: The William James Lectures Delivered at Harvard University in 1955*. Oxford: Clarendon Press, 1962.

Balizet, Ariane M. *Blood and Home in Early Modern Drama: Domestic Identity on the Renaissance Stage*. Abingdon: Routledge, 2014.
Barchiesi, Alessandro, and Philip Hardie. 'The Ovidian Career Model: Ovid, Gallus, Apuleius, Boccaccio'. In *Classical Literary Careers and their Reception*. Edited by Philip R. Hardie and Helen Moore. Cambridge: Cambridge University Press, 2010. 59–88.
Bates, Catherine. *On Not Defending Poetry: Defence and Indefensibility in Sidney's 'Defence of Poesy'*. Oxford: Oxford University Press, 2017.
Battenhouse, Roy. 'Chapman and the Nature of Man'. *English Literary History* 12 (1945): 87–107.
Baumbach, Sibylle. *Shakespeare and the Art of Physiognomy*. Penrith: Humanities-Ebooks LLP, 2008.
Baxandall, Michael. *Painting and Experience in Fifteenth Century Italy*. Oxford: Oxford University Press, 1972.
Belle, Marie-Alice. 'Elizabethan Defences of Translation, from Rhetoric to Poetics: Harington's and Chapman's "Brief Apologies"'. In *Elizabethan Translation and Literary Culture*. Edited by Gabriela Schmidt. Berlin: De Gruyter, 2013. 43–79.
Bennet, Tony, Lawrence Grossberg and Meaghan Morris, eds. *New Keywords: A Revised Vocabulary for Culture and Society*. Oxford: Blackwell, 2005.
Benson, Pamela J. 'The Stigma of Italy Undone: Aemilia Lanyer's Canonization of Mary Sidney'. In *Strong Voices, Weak History: Early Women Writers and Canons in England, France and Italy*. Edited by Pamela J. Benson and Victoria Kirkham. Ann Arbor, MI: University of Michigan Press, 2008. 146–75.
Bildhauer, Bettina. *Medieval Blood*. Cardiff: University of Wales Press, 2006.
Blank, Philip E. *Lyric Forms in the Sonnet Sequences of Barnabe Barnes*. The Hague: Mouton, 1974.
Boitani, Piero. *The Tragic and the Sublime in Medieval Literature*. Cambridge: Cambridge University Press, 1989.
Booth, Stephen. 'Shakespeare's Language and the Language of Shakespeare's Time'. *Shakespeare Survey* 50 (1997): 1–18.
Bottrall, Margaret, 'George Chapman's Defence of Difficulty'. *The Criterion* 16 (1937): 638–54.
Bradbrook, M. C. *The School of Night: A Study in the Literary Relationships of Sir Walter Raleigh*. Cambridge: Cambridge University Press, 1936.
Bradburne, James M., ed. *Blood: Art, Politics, and Pathology*. Munich: Prestel, 2001.
Braden, Gordon, ed. *Sixteenth-Century Poetry: An Annotated Anthology*. Oxford: Blackwell, 2005.
Brady, Andrea. 'The Physics of Melting in Early Modern Love Poetry'. *Ceræ: An Australasian Journal of Medieval and Early Modern Studies* 1 (2014): 22–52.

Brain, Peter. *Galen on Bloodletting: A Study of the Origins, Development, and Validity of His Opinions*. Cambridge: Cambridge University Press, 1986.
Braudy, Leo. *The Frenzy of Renown: Fame and its History*. Oxford: Oxford University Press, 1986.
Bray, Alan. *The Friend*. Chicago: University of Chicago Press, 2003.
Bridges, Emma, Edith Hall and P. J. Rhodes, eds. *Cultural Responses to the Persian Wars*. Oxford: Oxford University Press, 2007.
Brljak Vladimir, and Micha Lazarus, eds. '*Artes poeticae*': Formations and Transformations, 1500–1650. Special issue of *The Classical Receptions Journal* 13.1 (2021).
Brown, Georgia. *Redefining Elizabethan Literature*. Cambridge: Cambridge University Press, 2004.
Bush, Douglas. *Mythology & the Renaissance Tradition in English Poetry*. New York: Norton, 1963. 1st edn, 1932.
Buxton, John. *Sir Philip Sidney and the English Renaissance*. Basingstoke: Macmillan, 1987. 1st edn, 1954.
Byatt, A. S. 'Feeling Thought: Donne and the Embodied Mind'. In *The Cambridge Companion to Donne*. Edited by A. Guibbory. Cambridge: Cambridge University Press, 2006. 247–57.
Chang, Leah L. *Into Print: The Production of Female Authorship in Early Modern France*. Newark, DE: University of Delaware Press, 2009.
Charney, Maurice. 'Shakespeare's Unpoetic Poetry'. *Studies in English Literature, 1500–1900* 13 (1973): 199–207.
Cheney, Patrick. *English Authorship and the Early Modern Sublime: Fictions of Transport in Spenser, Marlowe, Jonson and Shakespeare*. Cambridge: Cambridge University Press, 2018.
Cheney, Patrick. '"The Forms of Things Unknown": English Authorship and the Early Modern Sublime'. In *Medieval and Early Modern Authorship*. Edited by Guillemette Bolens and Lukas Erne. Tübingen: Narr, 2011. 137–60.
Cheney, Patrick. 'Literary Careers'. In *The Oxford History of Classical Reception in English Literature. Volume 2: 1558–1660*. Edited by Patrick Cheney and Philip Hardie. Oxford: Oxford University Press, 2005. 172–86.
Cheney, Patrick. *Marlowe's Republican Authorship: Lucan, Liberty and the Sublime*. Basingstoke: Palgrave Macmillan, 2009.
Cheney, Patrick. *Reading Sixteenth-Century Poetry*. Oxford: Wiley-Blackwell, 2011.
Cheney, Patrick. *Shakespeare's Literary Authorship*. Cambridge: Cambridge University Press, 2008.
Cheney, Patrick. *Spenser's Famous Flight: A Renaissance Idea of a Literary Career*. Toronto: University of Toronto Press, 1993.
Clarke, Danielle. '"Signifying, but not sounding": Gender and Paratext in the Complaint Genre'. In *Renaissance Paratexts*. Edited by Helen Smith and Louise Wilson. Cambridge: Cambridge University Press, 2011. 133–50.

Clewett, Richard M., Jr. 'James VI of Scotland and His Literary Circle'. *Aevum* 47 (1973): 441–54.
Cockcroft, Robert. *Rhetorical Affect in Early Modern Writing: Renaissance Passions Reconsidered.* Basingstoke: Palgrave Macmillan, 2003.
Colie, Rosalie. *The Resources of Kind: Genre-Theory in the Renaissance.* Berkeley, CA: University of California Press, 1973.
Conrad, Peter. *The Everyman History of English Literature.* London: J. M. Dent, 1985.
Costelloe, Peter, ed. *The Sublime: From Antiquity to the Present.* Cambridge: Cambridge University Press, 2012.
Cox, John D. 'Barnes, Barnabe (bap. 1571, d. 1609), poet and playwright'. *Oxford Dictionary of National Biography* (2004). <https://doi.org/10.1093/ref:odnb/1467> Accessed 3 June 2020.
Craik, Katherine A. *Reading Sensations in Early Modern England.* Basingstoke: Palgrave Macmillan, 2007.
Crane, R. S. 'On Writing the History of Criticism in England, 1650–1800'. In *The Idea of the Humanities: And Other Essays Critical and Historical.* 2 vols. Chicago: University of Chicago Press, 1967. 2:157–75.
Crow, Martha Foote. *Elizabethan Sonnet Cycles. Phillis. Licia.* Chicago: A. C. McClurg, 1896.
Cummings, Brian, and Freya Sierhuis. *Passions and Subjectivity in Early Modern Culture.* Farnham: Ashgate, 2013.
Cunningham, Andrew. *The Anatomical Renaissance: The Resurrection of the Anatomical Projects of the Ancients.* Aldershot: Scolar Press, 1997.
Curtius, Ernst Robert. *European Literature and the Latin Middle Ages.* Translated by Willard R. Trask. London: Routledge and Kegan Paul, 1953.
Davis, Joel B. *The Countesse of Pembrokes Arcadia and the Invention of English Literature.* New York: Palgrave Macmillan, 2011.
Derrida, Jacques. 'White Mythology: Metaphor in the Text of Philosophy'. *New Literary History* 6 (1974): 5–74.
De Witt Thorpe, Clarence. *The Aesthetic Theory of Thomas Hobbes, with Special Reference to His Contribution to the Psychological Approach in English Literary Criticism.* Ann Arbor, MI: University of Michigan Press, 1940.
Dodds, Madeleine H. 'Barnabe Barnes'. *Archaeologia Aeliana* 24 (1946): 1–59.
Dowlin, Cornell March. 'Sir William Davenant's *Gondibert*, Its Preface, and Hobbes's *Answer*; A Study in English Neo-classicism'. PhD dissertation, Philadelphia, 1934.
Dubrow, Heather. *The Challenges of Orpheus: Lyric Poetry and Early Modern England.* Baltimore, MD: Johns Hopkins University Press, 2008.
Dubrow, Heather. '"Dressing old words new"? Re-Evaluating the "Delian Structure"'. In *A Companion to Shakespeare Sonnets.* Edited by Michael Schoenfeldt. Malden, MA: Blackwell, 2008. 90–103.

Dumouchel, Paul. 'Hobbes on Literary Rules and Conventions'. In *Rules and Conventions: Literature, Philosophy, and Social Theory*. Edited by Mette Hjort. Baltimore, MD: Johns Hopkins University Press, 1992. 95–114.
Duncan-Jones, Katherine. *Sir Philip Sidney, Courtier-Poet*. New Haven, CT: Yale University Press, 1991.
Dundas, Judith. *Sidney and Junius on Poetry and Painting. From the Margins to the Center*. Newark, DE: University of Delaware Press, 2007.
Dures, Alan. *English Catholicism 1558–1642*. Cambridge: Cambridge University Press, 1983.
Earl, Anthony. 'Late Elizabethan Devotional Poetry and Calvinism: A Re-evaluation of Barnabe Barnes'. *Renaissance Studies* 11 (1997): 223–40.
Eck, Caroline van, Stijn Bussels and Maarten Delbeke. 'Introduction'. In *Translations of the Sublime. The Early Modern Reception and Dissemination of Longinus' 'Peri Hupsous' in Rhetoric, the Visual Arts, Architecture and the Theatre*. Edited by Caroline Van Eck, Stijn Bussels and Maarten Delbeke. Leiden: Brill, 2012. 1–10.
Eck, Caroline van, Stijn Bussels and Maarten Delbeke, eds. *Translations of the Sublime. The Early Modern Reception and Dissemination of Longinus' 'Peri Hupsous' in Rhetoric, the Visual Arts, Architecture and the Theatre*. Leiden: Brill, 2012.
Eisendrath, Rachel. 'Poetry at the Limits of Rhetoric'. In *Elizabethan Narrative Poems: The State of Play*. Edited by Lynn Enterline. London: Bloomsbury, 2019. 45–68.
Enterline, Lynn. 'Introduction: On Schoolmen's Cunning Notes'. In *Elizabethan Narrative Poems: The State of Play*. Edited by Lynn Enterline. London: Bloomsbury, 2019. 1–17.
Enterline, Lynn. *The Rhetoric of the Body from Ovid to Shakespeare*. Cambridge: Cambridge University Press, 2000.
Enterline, Lynn. *Shakespeare's Schoolroom: Rhetoric, Discipline, and Emotion*. Philadelphia, PA: University of Pennsylvania Press, 2012.
Enterline, Lynn, ed. *Elizabethan Narrative Poems: The State of Play*. London: Bloomsbury, 2019.
Erickson, Robert A. *The Language of the Heart, 1600–1750*. Philadelphia, PA: University of Pennsylvania Press, 1997.
Evans, Malcolm. '"In love with curious words": Signification and Sexuality in English Petrarchism'. In *Jacobean Poetry and Prose: Rhetoric, Representation, and the Popular Imagination*. Edited by Clive Bloom. Basingstoke: Macmillan, 1988. 119–49.
Feingold, Mordechai. 'English Ramism: A Reinterpretation'. In *The Influence of Petrus Ramus*. Edited by Mordechai Feingold, Joseph S. Freedman and Wolfgang Rother. Basel: Schwabe, 2001. 127–76.
Feingold, Mordechai. 'The Humanities'. In *The History of the University of Oxford, Volume IV: Seventeenth-Century Oxford*. Edited by Nicholas Tyacke. Oxford: Oxford University Press, 1997. 211–358.

Ferguson, A. S. 'Review of Schoell, *Études sur l'Humanisme continental en Angleterre a la fin de la Renaissance*'. *Litteris* 4 (1927): 142–54.
Ferguson, Margaret W. *Trials of Desire: Renaissance Defenses of Poetry*. New Haven, CT: Yale University Press, 1983.
Ferry, Anne. *The 'Inward' Language: Sonnets of Wyatt, Sidney, Shakespeare, Donne*. Chicago: University of Chicago Press, 1983.
Finkelpearl, Philip J. 'Davies, John (1564/5–1618), Poet and Writing-master'. *Oxford Dictionary of National Biography*. <https://doi.org/10.1093/ref:odnb/7244> Accessed 29 July 2021.
Finn, Kavita Mudan. '"Of whom proud Rome hath boasted long": Intertextual Conversations and Popular History'. In *Conversational Exchanges in Early Modern England (1549–1640)*. Edited by Kristen Abbott Bennett. Newcastle upon Tyne: Cambridge Scholars Publishing, 2015. 70–100.
Fischer, Olga. 'Iconicity in Language and Literature: Language Innovation and Language Change'. *Neuphilologische Mitteilungen* 98 (1997): 63–87.
Fischer, Olga, and Max Nänny. 'Introduction: Iconicity as a Creative Force in Language Use'. In *Form Miming Meaning: Iconicity in Language and Literature*. Edited by Olga Fischer and Max Nänny. Amsterdam: John Benjamins, 1999. 15–36.
Fischer, Olga, and Max Nänny. 'Introduction: Iconicity and Nature'. *European Journal of English Studies* 5 (2001): 3–16.
Fleming, Juliet. 'Changed Opinions as to Flowers'. In *Renaissance Paratexts*. Edited by Helen Smith and Louise Wilson. Cambridge: Cambridge University Press, 2011. 48–64.
Frirtsch, Kelly, Clare O'Connor and A. K. Thompson, eds. *Keywords for Radicals: The Contested Vocabulary of Late-Capitalist Struggle*. Chico, CA: AK Press, 2016.
Fujimura, Thomas H. 'The Temper of John Dryden'. *Studies in Philology* 72.3 (1975): 348–66.
Furley, David J., and J. S. Wilkie. 'Introduction'. In *Galen: On Respiration and the Arteries*. Edited by David J. Furley and J. S. Wilkie. Princeton, NJ: Princeton University Press, 1984. 1–70.
García Hernán, David, and Miguel F. Gómez Vozmediano, eds. *La cultura de la sangre en el Siglo de Oro: entre literatura e historia*. Madrid: Sílex, D.L. 2016.
Gatti, Hillary. *The Renaissance Drama of Knowledge: Giordano Bruno in England*. London: Routledge, 1989.
Gless, Darryl J. 'Chapman's Ironic Ovid'. *English Literary Renaissance* 9 (1979): 21–41.
Goeglein, Tamara A. '"Wherein hath Ramus been so offensious?": Poetic Examples in the English Ramist Logic Manuals 1574–1672'. *Rhetorica* 14.1 (1996): 73–101.
Goldberg, Jonathan. *The Seeds of Things: Theorizing Sexuality and Materiality in Renaissance Representations*. New York: Fordham University Press, 2010.

Goldhill, Simon. 2007. 'What is Ekphrasis For?' *Classical Philology* 102 (2007): 1–19.
Gordon, D. J. *The Renaissance Imagination: Essays and Lectures*. Berkeley, CA: University of California Press, 1975.
Gorman, Cassandra. *The Atom in Seventeenth-Century Poetry*. Woodbridge: D. S. Brewer, 2021.
Grebe, Sabine. 'Why Did Ovid Associate his Exile with a Living Death?' *Classical World* 103 (2010): 491–509.
Green, John Ronald. 'The Martyrdom of Ramus in Marlowe's *The Massacre at Paris*'. *Papers on Language and Literature* 9 (1973): 365–79.
Greenblatt, Stephen. *Renaissance Self-Fashioning: From More to Shakespeare*. Chicago: University of Chicago Press, 1980.
Greene, Roland. *Five Words: Critical Semantics in the Age of Shakespeare and Cervantes*. Chicago: University of Chicago Press, 2013.
Greene, Roland. 'The Lyric'. In *The Cambridge History of Literary Criticism. Volume III: The Renaissance*. Edited by Glyn P. Norton. Cambridge: Cambridge University Press, 1999. 216–28.
Gunn, Thom. 'Introduction'. In *Selected Poems of Fulke Greville*. Edited with an introduction by Thom Gunn. Chicago: University of Chicago Press, 2009. 1st edn, 1969. 13–41.
Guy-Bray, Stephen. '*Rosamond's Complaint*: Daniel, Ovid, and the Purpose of Poetry'. *Renaissance Studies* 22 (2008): 338–50.
Habicht, Werner. '"My tongue-tied Muse": Inexpressibility in Shakespeare's Sonnets'. In *Shakespeare's Universe: Renaissance Ideas and Conventions. Essays in Honour of W.R. Elton*. Edited by John M. Mucciolo, Stephen J. Doloff and Edward A. Rauchut. Aldershot: Ashgate, 1996. 194–203.
Hadfield, Andrew. *Edmund Spenser: A Life*. Oxford: Oxford University Press, 2012.
Hager, Alan. 'The Exemplary Mirage: Fabrication of Sir Philip Sidney's Biographical Image and the Sidney Reader'. *English Literary History* 48 (1981): 1–16.
Haigh, Christopher. *English Reformations: Religion, Politics, and Society under the Tudors*. Oxford: Oxford University Press, 1993.
Halewood, William H. *The Poetry of Grace. Reformation Themes and Structures in English Seventeenth-century Poetry*. New Haven, CT: Yale University Press, 1970.
Hallett, Raphael. '"Reduced to order" and "Just for show"? Ramus, Print, and Visual Aesthetics'. In *The European Contexts of Ramism*. Edited by Sarah Knight and Emma Annette Wilson. Turnhout: Brepols, 2019. 187–215.
Halpern, Richard. *The Poetics of Primitive Accumulation: English Renaissance Culture and the Genealogy of Culture*. Ithaca, NY: Cornell University Press, 1991.
Harbage, Alfred. *Sir William Davenant. Poet Venturer, 1606–1668*. Philadelphia, PA: University of Pennsylvania Press, 1935.

Hardie, Philip. *Lucretian Receptions. History, The Sublime, Knowledge*. Cambridge: Cambridge University Press, 2009.

Hardie, Philip R., and Helen Moore. 'Introduction: Literary Careers – Classical Models and their Reception'. In *Classical Literary Careers and their Reception*. Edited by Philip R. Hardie and Helen Moore. Cambridge: Cambridge University Press, 2010. 1–16.

Hardie, Philip R., and Helen Moore, eds. *Classical Literary Careers and their Reception*. Cambridge: Cambridge University Press, 2010.

Hartmann, Anna-Maria. *English Mythography in its European Context, 1500–1650*. Oxford: Oxford University Press, 2018.

Hathaway, Baxter. *Marvels and Commonplaces: Renaissance Literary Criticism*. New York: Random House, 1968.

Hawhee, Debra. *Bodily Arts: Rhetoric and Athletics in Ancient Greece*. Austin, TX: University of Texas Press, 2004.

Hazlitt, William. 'On Persons One Would Wish to Have Seen', *New Monthly Magazine* 16 (1826): 32–41

Hazlitt, William. 'William Godwin'. In *The Spirit of the Age or Contemporary Portraits*. London: George Bell and Sons, 1825. 29–58.

Healy, Margaret, and Thomas Healy. 'Introduction'. In *Renaissance Transformations: The Making of English Writing, 1500–1650*. Edited by Margaret Healy and Thomas Healy. Edinburgh: Edinburgh University Press, 2009. 1–11.

Heath, Malcolm. 'Longinus and the Ancient Sublime'. In *The Sublime: From Antiquity to the Present*. Edited by Peter Costelloe. Cambridge: Cambridge University Press, 2012. 11–23.

Heninger, S. K., Jr. *Sidney and Spenser: The Poet as Maker*. University Park, PA: Pennsylvania University Press, 1989.

Heninger, S. K., Jr. *Touches of Sweet Harmony: Pythagorean Cosmology and Renaissance Poetics*. San Marino, CA: Huntingdon Library, 1974.

Herman, Peter C. *Squitter-wits and Muse-haters: Sidney, Spenser, Milton and Renaissance Antipoetic Sentiment*. Detroit, MI: Wayne State University Press, 1996.

Herrold, Megan. 'Compassionate Petrarchanism: The *Stabat Mater Dolorosa* Tradition in Aemilia Lanyer's *Salve Deus Rex Judaeorum*'. *Studies in Philology* 117 (2020): 365–96.

Hetherington, Michael. 'Disciplining Creativity: Habit, System, and the Logic of Late Sixteenth-Century Poetics'. *Parergon* 33.3 (2016): 43–66.

Hetherington, Michael. '"An instrument of reason": William Scott's Logical Poetics'. *The Review of English Studies* 67 (2015): 448–67.

Hetherington, Michael. '"Non per instituir altri"? Attitudes to Rule-Following in Sixteenth-Century Poetics'. *Classical Receptions Journal* 13 (2021): 9–30.

Hillman, David, and Carla Mazzio. 'Introduction: Individual Parts'. In *The Body in Parts. Fantasies of Corporeality in Early Modern Europe*.

Edited by David Hillman and Carla Mazzio. London: Routledge, 1997. xi–xxix.
Hobgood, Allison P. 'Feeling Fear in Macbeth'. In *Shakespearean Sensations: Experiencing Literature in Early Modern England*. Edited by Katharine Craik and Tanya Pollard. Cambridge: Cambridge University Press, 2013. 29–46.
Hock, Jessie. *The Erotics of Materialism: Lucretius and Early Modern Poetics*. Philadelphia, PA: University of Pennsylvania Press, 2021.
Holmes, J. 'Thomas Lodge's *Amours*: The Copy-Text for Imitations of Ronsard in *Phillis*'. *Notes and Queries* 53 (2006): 55–7.
Hotson, Howard. *The Reformation of Common Learning: Post-Ramist Method and the Reception of the New Philosophy, 1618–1670*. Oxford: Oxford University Press, 2020.
Houston, John Porter. *Shakespearean Sentences: A Study in Style and Syntax*. Baton Rouge, LA: Louisiana State University Press, 1988.
Hulse, Clark. *Metamorphic Verse: The Elizabethan Minor Epic*. Princeton, NJ: Princeton University Press, 1981.
Hulse, Clark. *The Rule of Art: Literature and Painting in the Renaissance*. Chicago: University of Chicago Press, 1990.
Hulse, Clark. 'Tudor Aesthetics'. In *The Cambridge Companion to English Literature 1500–1600*. Edited by Arthur F. Kinney. Cambridge: Cambridge University Press, 2000. 29–63.
Hunger, F. W. T. *Charles de l'Escluse (Carolus Clusius), Nederlandisch Kruidkundige 1526–1609*. 's-Gravenhage: Martinus Nijhoff, 1943.
Huntington, John. *Ambition, Rank, and Poetry in 1590s England*. Urbana, IL: University of Illinois Press, 2001.
Hyde, Thomas. *The Poetic Theology of Love: Cupid in Renaissance Literature*. Newark, DE: University of Delaware Press, 1986.
Jaeger, Stephen C., ed. *Magnificence and the Sublime in Medieval Aesthetics: Art, Architecture, Literature, Music*. New York: Palgrave Macmillan, 2010.
Jansen, Katherine. *The Making of the Magdalen: Preaching and Popular Devotion in the Later Middle Ages*. Princeton, NJ: Princeton University Press, 2001.
Jay, Martin. *Cultural Semantics: Keywords of Our Time*. Amherst, MA: University of Massachusetts Press, 1998.
Johansen, T. K. *Aristotle on the Sense Organs*. Cambridge: Cambridge University Press, 1997.
Josipovici, Gabriel. *The World and the Book: A Study of Modern Fiction*. London: Macmillan, 1971.
Kalderon, Mark Eli. *Form Without Matter: Empedocles and Aristotle on Colour Perception*. Oxford: Oxford University Press, 2015.
Kargon, Robert Hugh. *Atomism in England from Hariot to Newton*. Oxford: Oxford University Press, 1966.
Kastner, L. E. 'Lodge as an Imitator of the Italian Poets'. *Modern Language Review* 2 (1907): 155–61.

Keach, William. *Elizabethan Erotic Narratives: Irony and Pathos in the Ovidian Poetry of Shakespeare, Marlowe and Their Contemporaries*. New Brunswick, NJ: Rutgers University Press, 1977.
Kendal, Gordon. 'Introduction'. In George Chapman, *Homer's Odyssey*. Edited by Gordon Kendal. Cambridge: Modern Humanities Research Association, 2016. 1–36.
Kermode, Frank. 'The Banquet of Sense'. In *Shakespeare, Spenser, Donne: Renaissance Essays*. New York: Viking Press, 1971. 84–115.
Kermode, Frank. *Shakespeare's Language*. Harmondsworth: Penguin, 2000.
Kerrigan, John. 'Introduction'. In *William Shakespeare, The Sonnets and A Lover's Complaint*. Edited by John Kerrigan. Harmondsworth: Penguin, 1986. 7–63.
Kesson, Andy. *John Lyly and Early Modern Authorship*. Manchester: Manchester University Press, 2014.
Kingsley-Smith, Jane. *Cupid in Early Modern Literature and Culture*. Cambridge: Cambridge University Press, 2016.
Kinney, Arthur F. *Humanist Poetics: Thought, Rhetoric, and Fiction in Sixteenth-Century England*. Amherst, MA: University of Massachusetts Press, 1986.
Knapp, Steven, and Walter Benn Michaels. 'Against Theory'. *Critical Inquiry* 8 (1982): 723–42.
Knight, Sarah. 'Enriching the Judgement: Fulke Greville and Didactic Drama'. *Parergon* 33.3 (2016): 145–60.
Knight, Sarah. 'Flat Dichotomists and Learned Men: Ramism in Elizabethan Drama and Satire'. In *Ramus, Pedagogy, and the Liberal Arts*. Edited by Steven J. Reid and Emma Annette Wilson. Farnham: Ashgate, 2011. 47–68
Knight, Sarah. '"Not with the Ancient, nor yet with the Modern": Greville, Education and Tragedy'. In *Fulke Greville and the Culture of the English Renaissance*. Edited by Russ Leo, Katrin Röder and Freya Sierhuis. Oxford: Oxford University Press, 2018. 195–209.
Knight, Sarah, and Emma Annette Wilson, eds. *The European Contexts of Ramism*. Turnhout: Brepols, 2019.
Koller, Kathrine. 'Abraham Fraunce and Edmund Spenser'. *English Literary History* 7 (1940): 108–20.
Lally, Steven. 'Introduction'. In *The Aeneid of Thomas Phaer and Thomas Twyne: A Critical Edition Introducing Renaissance Metrical Typography*. Edited by Stephen Lally. New York: Garland, 1987. xi–lxii.
Lanham, Richard A. *A Handlist of Rhetorical Terms: A Guide for Students of English Literature*. Berkeley, CA: University of California Press, 1968.
Lee, Sidney, ed. *Elizabethan Sonnets*. 2 vols. Westminster: Archibald Constable, 1904.
Lehtonen, Kelly. '*Peri Hypsous* in Translation: The Sublime in Sixteenth-Century Epic Theory'. *Philological Quarterly* 95 (2016): 449–65.
Leo, Russ, Katrin Röder and Freya Sierhuis. 'Introduction. The Resources of Obscurity: Reappraising the Work of Fulke Greville'. In *Fulke Greville*

and the Culture of the English Renaissance. Edited by Russ Leo, Katrin Röder and Freya Sierhuis. Oxford: Oxford University Press, 2018. 1–25.
Leo, Russ, Katrin Röder and Freya Sierhuis, eds. *Fulke Greville and the Culture of the English Renaissance*. Oxford: Oxford University Press, 2018.
Lerner, Laurence. 'Ovid and the Elizabethans'. In *Ovid Renewed: Ovidian Influences on Literature and Art from the Middle Ages to the Twentieth Century*. Edited by Charles Martindale. Cambridge: Cambridge University Press, 1988. 121–35.
Lewalski, Barbara K. *Donne's Anniversaries and the Poetry of Praise: The Creation of a Symbolic Mode*. Princeton, NJ: Princeton University Press, 1973.
Lewalski, Barbara K. *Protestant Poetics and the Seventeenth-century Religious Lyric*. Princeton, NJ: Princeton University Press, 1979.
Lewis, C. S. 'Hero and Leander'. In *Elizabethan Poetry: Modern Essays in Criticism*. Edited by Paul J. Alpers. Oxford: Oxford University Press, 1967. 235–50.
Linke, Uli. *Blood and Nation: The European Aesthetics of Race*. Philadelphia, PA: University of Pennsylvania Press, 1999.
Lipking, Lawrence. *The Life of the Poet: Beginning and Ending Poetic Careers*. Chicago: University of Chicago Press, 1981.
Lowrance, Bryan. 'Sidney's Strangers: Language, Materiality, and Authenticity in *Astrophil and Stella*'. Unpublished thesis submitted to the Department of English, Cornell University, April 2006.
Luis-Martínez, Zenón. '"Friendlesse verse": The Poetics of Chapman's "A Coronet for His Mistresse Philosophie" (1595)'. *Studies in Philology* 118 (2021): 565–604.
Luis-Martínez, Zenón. 'Ramist Dialectic, Poetic Examples, and the Uses of Pastoral in Abraham Fraunce's *The Shepherds' Logic*'. *Parergon* 33.3 (2016): 69–95.
Luis-Martínez, Zenón. 'Shakespeare's Wicked Pronoun: *A Lover's Discourse* and Love Stories'. *Atlantis* 22.1 (2000): 133–62.
Luis-Martínez, Zenón, and Sonia Hernández-Santano. 'Poetry, the Arts of Discourse, and the Discourse of the Arts'. *Parergon* 33.3 (2016): 1–14.
Lyall, Roderick J. 'Stella's Other Astrophel: Henry Constable's Diana and the Politics of Elizabethan Courtiership'. In *Gloriana's Rule: Literature, Religion and Power in the Age of Elizabeth*. Edited by Rui Carvalho Homem and Fátima Vieira. Porto: Editora da Universidade do Porto, 2006. 187–205.
MacBride, Kari Boyd. 'Remembering Orpheus in the Poems of Aemilia Lanyer'. *Studies in English Literature, 1500–1900* 38 (1988): 87–108.
Mac Carthy, Ita. 'Grace'. In *Renaissance Keywords*. Edited by Ita Mac Carthy. Cambridge: MHRA/Legenda, 2013. 63–78.
Mac Carthy, Ita. *The Grace of the Italian Renaissance*. Princeton, NJ: Princeton University Press, 2020.

Mac Carthy, Ita, ed. *Renaissance Keywords*. Cambridge: MHRA/Legenda, 2013.
Mack, Michael. *Sidney's Poetics: Imitating Creation*. Washington, DC: Catholic University of America Press, 2005.
Mack, Peter. *Renaissance Argument: Valla and Agricola in the Traditions of Rhetoric and Dialectic*. Leiden: Brill, 1993.
Mack, Peter. 'Rudolph Agricola's Reading of Literature'. *Journal of the Warburg and Courtauld Institutes* 48 (1985): 23–41.
Mack, Peter. 'Vives's *De ratione dicendi*: Structure, Innovations, Problems'. *Rhetorica* 23 (2005): 65–92.
MacLure, Millar. *George Chapman: A Critical Study*. Toronto: University of Toronto Press, 1966.
MacNeil, Anne. 'Weeping at the Water's Edge'. *Early Music* 27 (2007): 406–17.
Manley, Frank, 'Introduction'. In *John Donne: The Anniversaries*. Edited by Frank Manley. Baltimore, MD: Johns Hopkins University Press, 1963. 1–61.
Marotti, Arthur. 'Love is Not Love: Elizabethan Sonnet Sequences and the Social Order'. *English Literary History* 49 (1982): 396–428.
Marotti, Arthur F. *Manuscript, Print, and the English Renaissance Lyric*. Ithaca, NY: Cornell University Press, 1995.
Marr, Alexander, Raphaële Garrod, Jose Ramon Marcaida and Richard J. Oosterhoff. *Logodaedalus: Word Histories of Ingenuity in Early Modern Europe*. Pittsburgh, PA: University of Pittsburgh Press, 2019.
Martin, Éva Madeleine. 'The "Prehistory" of the Sublime in Early Modern France'. In *The Sublime: From Antiquity to the Present*. Edited by Peter Costelloe. Cambridge: Cambridge University Press, 2012. 77–101.
Maslen, R. W. 'Introduction'. In Sir Philip Sidney, *An Apology for Poetry (or The Defence of Poesy)*. Manchester: Manchester University Press, 2002. 1–78.
Matz, Robert. *Heroic Diversions: Sidney's Apology for Poetry*. Cambridge: Cambridge University Press, 2000.
May, Steven W. 'Marlowe, Spenser, Sidney and – Abraham Fraunce?'. *Review of English Studies* 62 (2011): 30–63.
Mazzio, Carla. 'Sins of the Tongue'. *Modern Language Studies* 28.3/4 (1998): 93–124.
McCabe, Colin, and Holly Janacek, eds. *Keywords for Today: A 21st Century Vocabulary*. Oxford: Oxford University Press, 2018.
McLean, Hugh. 'Fulke Greville and the Poetic of the Plain Style'. *Studies in Philology* 61 (1970): 657–70.
Meerhoff, Kees. 'Petrus Ramus and the Vernacular'. In *Ramus, Pedagogy, and the Liberal Arts: Ramism in Britain and the Wider World*. Edited by Steven J. Reid and Emma Annette Wilson. Farnham: Ashgate, 2011. 133–52.
Merchant, Eleanor Kathleen. '"Doctissimus pater pastorum": Laurence Humphrey and Reformed Humanist Education in Mid-Tudor England'.

Unpublished PhD dissertation, Queen Mary, University of London, 2013.

Miles, Geoffrey, ed. *Classical Mythology in English Literature: A Critical Anthology*. London: Routledge, 1999.

Miller, Jacqueline T. 'The Passions Signified: Imitation and the Construction of Emotions in Sidney and Wroth'. *Criticism* 43 (2001): 407–21.

Miller, Jacqueline T. '"What words may say": The Limits of Language in *Astrophil and Stella*'. In *Sir Philip Sidney and the Interpretation of Renaissance Culture: The Poet in His Time and Ours*. Edited by Gary F. Waller and Michael D. Moore. Totowa, NJ: Barnes and Noble, 1984. 95–109.

Mills, Charles W. *Blackness Visible: Essays on Philosophy and Race*. Ithaca, NY: Cornell University Press, 1998.

Moss, Daniel. '"The second master of love": George Chapman and the Shadow of Ovid'. *Modern Philology* 111 (2014): 457–84.

Mulroy, David. 'Introduction'. In *The Complete Poetry of Catullus*. Edited by David Mulroy. Madison, WI: University of Wisconsin Press, 2002. ix–xliv.

Mund-Dopchie, Monique. *La Survie d'Eschyle à la Renaissance*. Leuven: Peeters, 1984.

Murphy, James J. 'Roman Writing Instruction as Described by Quintilian'. In *A Short History of Writing Instruction*. Edited by James J. Murphy. New York: Routledge, 2012. 36–76.

Murrin, Michael. *The Veil of Allegory: Some Notes Toward a Theory of Allegorical Rhetoric in the English Renaissance*. Chicago: University of Chicago Press, 1969.

Myers, James Phares, Jr. 'This Curious Frame: *Ovids Banquet of Sence*'. *Studies in Philology* 65 (1968): 192–206.

Navarrete, Ignacio. *Orphans of Petrarch*. Berkeley, CA: University of California Press, 1994.

Neely, Carol Thomas. 'The Structure of English Renaissance Sonnet Sequences'. *English Literary History* 45 (1978): 359–89.

North, Marcy L. 'The Sonnets and Book History'. In *A Companion to Shakespeare's Sonnets*. Edited by Michael Schoenfeldt. Oxford: Blackwell, 2007. 204–21.

Norton, Glyn P. 'Introduction'. In *The Cambridge History of Literary Criticism. Volume III: The Renaissance*. Edited by Glyn P. Norton. Cambridge: Cambridge University Press, 1999. 1–22.

Norton, Glyn P., ed. *The Cambridge History of Literary Criticism. Volume III: The Renaissance*. Cambridge: Cambridge University Press, 1999.

Ong, Walter J. 'Latin Language Study as a Renaissance Puberty Rite'. *Studies in Philology* 56 (1959): 103–24.

Ong, Walter J. *Ramus, Method and the Decay of Dialogue: From the Art of Reason to the Art of Discourse*. Cambridge, MA: Harvard University Press, 1958.

Ong, Walter J. *Ramus and Talon Inventory, ca. 1510–1562 in their Original and in their Variously Altered Forms*. Cambridge, MA: Harvard University Press, 1958.
Oxford English Dictionary Online. 2nd ed. <https://www.oed.com/>
Papazian, Mary Arshagouni. 'The Augustinian Donne: How a "Second S. Augustine"'? In *John Donne and the Protestant Reformation: New Perspectives*. Edited by Mary Arshagouni Papazian. Detroit, MI: Wayne State University Press, 2003. 66–89.
Paradise, Burton. *Thomas Lodge: The History of an Elizabethan*. New Haven, CT: Yale University Press, 1931.
Park, Katharine. 'The Organic Soul'. In *The Cambridge History of Renaissance Philosophy*. Edited by Charles B. Schmitt et al. Cambridge: Cambridge University Press, 1988. 464–84.
Parker, Patricia. *Shakespearean Intersections: Language, Contexts, Critical Keywords*. Philadelphia, PA: University of Pennsylvania Press, 2018.
Parker, Tom W. N. *Proportional Form in the Sonnets of the Sidney Circle: Loving in Truth*. Oxford: Oxford University Press, 1998.
Paster, Gail Kern. *The Body Embarrassed: Drama and the Disciplines of Shame in Early Modern England*. Ithaca, NY: Cornell University Press, 1993.
Patterson, Annabel M. *Hermogenes and the Renaissance: Seven Ideas of Style*. Princeton, NJ: Princeton University Press, 1970.
Pérez-Jáuregui, María Jesús. 'A Queen in a "Purple Robe": Henry Constable's Poetic Tribute to Mary, Queen of Scots'. *Studies in Philology* 113 (2016): 577–94.
Platt, Peter G. *Reason Diminished: Shakespeare and the Marvellous*. Lincoln, NE: University of Nebraska Press, 1998.
Plett, Heinrich F. *Rhetoric and Renaissance Culture*. Berlin: De Gruyter, 2004.
Podro, Michael. *The Critical Historians of Art*. New Haven, CT: Yale University Press, 1982.
Poel, Marc van der. 'Ramus and Agricola'. In *The European Contexts of Ramism*. Edited by Sarah Knight and Emma Annette Wilson. Turnhout: Brepols, 2019. 67–108.
Porter, James I. 'The Sublime'. In *A Companion to Ancient Aesthetics*. Edited by Pierre Destrée and Penelope Murray. Hoboken, NJ: John Wiley and Sons, 2015. 393–405.
Porter, James I. *The Sublime in Antiquity*. Cambridge: Cambridge University Press, 2016.
Praz, Mario. *Studies in Seventeenth-Century Imagery*. Rome: Edizione di Storia e Letteratura, 1964.
Prescott, Anne Lake. 'Divine Poetry as a Career Move: The Complexities and Consolations of Following David'. In *European Literary Careers: The Author from Antiquity to the Renaissance*. Edited by Patrick G. Cheney and Frederick Alfred De Armas. Toronto: University of Toronto Press, 2002. 206–30.

Pritchard, Arnold. *Catholic Loyalism in Elizabethan England*. London: Routledge, 1979.
Pulleyn, Simon. 'Homer's Religion: Philological Perspectives from Indo-European and Semitic'. In *Epic Interactions: Perspectives on Homer, Virgil, and the Epic Tradition*. Edited by Michael J. Clarke, Bruno G. F. Currie and R. O. A. M. Lyne. Oxford: Oxford University Press, 2006. 47–74.
Purcell, William Michael. *Ars Poetriae: Rhetorical and Grammatical Invention at the Margin of Literacy*. Columbia, SC: University of South Carolina Press, 1996.
Rebholz, Ronald A. *The Life of Fulke Greville, First Lord Brooke*. Oxford: Clarendon Press, 1971.
Rees, Joan. *Fulke Greville: A Critical Biography*. London: Routledge and Kegan Paul, 1971.
Refini, Eugenio. 'Longinus and Poetic Imagination in Late Renaissance Literary Theory'. In *Translations of the Sublime. The Early Modern Reception and Dissemination of Longinus' 'Peri Hupsous' in Rhetoric, the Visual Arts, Architecture and the Theatre*. Edited by Caroline van Eck, Stijn Bussels and Maarten Delbeke. Leiden: Brill, 2012. 33–53.
Reisner, Noam. 'The Paradox of Mimesis in Sidney's *Defence of Poesie* and Marlowe's *Doctor Faustus*'. *Cambridge Quarterly* 39 (2010): 331–49.
Reiter, Barret. 'William Perkins: The Imagination in Calvinist Theology and "Inner Iconoclasm" after Frances Yates'. *Intellectual History Review* (2021): <https://doi.org/10.1080/17496977.2021.1981695>.
Rhodes, Neil. 'Introduction'. In *English Renaissance Translation Theory*. Edited by Neil Rhodes, Gordon Kendal and Louise Wilson. London: Modern Humanities Research Association, 2013. 1–67.
Rhodes, Neil. *Shakespeare and the Origins of English*. Oxford: Oxford University Press, 2004.
Ribner, Rhoda M. '"The compasse of this curious frame": Chapman's *Ovids Banquet of Sence* and the Emblematic Tradition'. *Studies in the Renaissance* 17 (1970): 223–58.
Richards, Jennifer. 'Gabriel Harvey, James VI, and the Politics of Reading Early Modern Poetry'. *Huntington Library Quarterly* 71 (2008): 303–21.
Riley, Henry Thomas. *Dictionary of Latin Quotations, Proverbs, Maxims, and Mottos, Classical and Mediæval*. London: Bell and Daldy, 1866.
Ringler, William A. 'An Early Reference to Longinus'. *Modern Language Notes* 53 (1938): 23–4.
Roche, Thomas P., Jr. *Petrarch and the English Sonnet Sequences*. New York: AMS Press, 1989.
Rodríguez Peregrina, José Manuel. 'Algunas consideraciones en torno al *De ratione dicendi* de Luis Vives'. *Humanistica Lovaniensia* 45 (1996): 348–71.
Rodríguez Peregrina, José Manuel. 'Introducción'. In Juan Luis Vives, *Del arte de hablar*. Granada: Editorial Universidad de Granada, 2000. xi–cxxvii.

Ryrie, Alec. *Being Protestant in Reformation Britain*. Oxford: Oxford University Press, 2015.
Sacks, Peter. 'Where Words Prevail Not: Grief, Revenge, and Language in Kyd and Shakespeare'. *English Literary History* 49 (1982): 576–81.
Sanchez, Melissa E. *Erotic Subjects: The Sexuality of Politics in Early Modern English Literature*. Oxford: Oxford University Press, 2012.
Sansonetti, Laetitia. 'Out-Oviding Ovid in Shakespeare's *Venus and Adonis*'. In *The Circulation of Knowledge in Early Modern English Literature*. Edited by Sophie Chiari. Abingdon: Routledge, 2015. 175–88.
Sargent, Ralph M. *The Life and Lyrics of Sir Edward Dyer: At the Court of Elizabeth*. Oxford: Oxford University Press, 1935.
Sawday, Jonathan. *The Body Emblazoned: Dissection and the Human Body in Renaissance Culture*. London: Routledge, 1995.
Schmitt, Charles B. *John Case and Aristotelianism in Renaissance England*. Montreal: McGill-Queen's University Press, 1983.
Schoell, Franck L. *Études sur l'humanisme continental en Angleterre á la fin de la Renaissance*. Paris: Honoré Champion, 1926.
Schoenfeldt, Michael. *Bodies and Selves in Early Modern England*. Cambridge: Cambridge University Press, 1999.
Schoenfeldt, Michael. 'Eloquent Blood and Deliberative Bodies: The Physiology of Metaphysical Poetry'. In *Renaissance Transformations: The Making of English Writing 1500–1650*. Edited by Margaret Healy and Thomas Healy. Edinburgh: Edinburgh University Press, 2009. 145–60.
Scholar, Richard. 'The New Philologists'. In *Renaissance Keywords*. Edited by Ita Mac Carthy. Cambridge: MHRA/Legenda, 2013. 1–10.
Scott, J. G. 'Parallels to Three Elizabethan Sonnets'. *Modern Language Review* 21 (1926): 190–2.
Scott, J. G. *Les sonnets élisabéthains: les sources et l'apport personnel*. Paris: Honoré Champion, 1929.
Sell, Jonathan P. A. 'Terminal Aposiopesis and Sublime Communication: Shakespeare's Sonnet 126 and Keats' "To Autumn"'. In *The Ethics of Literary Communication: Genuineness, Directness, Indirectness*. Edited by Roger D. Sell and Inna Lindgren. Amsterdam: John Benjamins, 2013. 167–88.
Serjeantson, Deirdre. 'The Book of Psalms and the Early Modern Sonnet'. *Renaissance Studies* 29 (2015): 632–49.
Sgarbi, Marco. *The Aristotelian Tradition and the Rise of British Empiricism: Logic and Epistemology in the British Isles (1570–1689)*. Dordrecht: Springer, 2012.
Shagan, Ethan. 'Introduction: English Catholic History in Context'. In *Catholics and the 'Protestant Nation': Religious Politics and Identity in Early Modern England*. Edited by Ethan Shagan. Manchester: Manchester University Press, 2005. 1–21.
Sharratt, Peter. 'Ramus 2000'. *Rhetorica* 18 (2000): 399–455.
Shell, Alison. *Catholicism, Controversy, and the English Literary Imagination, 1558–1660*. Cambridge: Cambridge University Press, 1999.

Shuger, Debora K. *Sacred Rhetoric: The Christian Grand Style in the English Renaissance*. Princeton, NJ: Princeton University Press, 1988.
Smith, Bruce R. *The Acoustic World of Early Modern England*. Chicago: University of Chicago Press, 1999.
Smith, Helen, and Louise Wilson. *Renaissance Paratexts*. Cambridge: Cambridge University Press, 2011.
Snare, Gerald. *The Mystification of George Chapman*. Durham, NC: Duke University Press, 1989.
Sobecki, Sebastian. *Unwritten Verities: The Making of England's Vernacular Legal Culture, 1463–1569*. Notre Dame, IN: University of Notre Dame Press, 2015.
Spiller, Elizabeth. *Science, Reading, and Renaissance Literature: The Art of Making Knowledge, 1580–1670*. Cambridge: Cambridge University Press, 2004.
Spiller, Michael R. G. *The Development of the Sonnet. An Introduction*. London: Routledge, 1992.
Spivack, Charlotte. *George Chapman*. New York: Twayne, 1967.
Stamatakis, Chris. '"The restful place": Criticism in Early Tudor Poetry'. In *The Places of Early Modern Criticism*. Edited by Gavin Alexander, Emma Gilby and Alexander Marr. Oxford: Oxford University Press, 2021. 22–37.
Stamatakis, Chris. '"Small parcelles": Unsequenced Sonnets in the Sixteenth Century'. In *The Early Modern English Sonnet: Ever in Motion*. Ed. Rémi Vuillemin, Laetitia Sansonetti and Enrica Zanin. Manchester: Manchester University Press, 2020. 95–113.
Steiner, George. *On Difficulty and Other Essays*. Oxford: Oxford University Press, 1978.
Stillman, Robert E. *Philip Sidney and the Poetics of Renaissance Cosmopolitanism*. Aldershot: Ashgate, 2008.
Strier, Richard. *The Unrepentant Renaissance. From Petrarch to Shakespeare to Milton*. Chicago: University of Chicago Press, 2011.
Stump, Donald P. 'The Two Deaths of Mary Stuart: Historical Allegory in Spenser's Book of Justice'. *Spenser Studies* 17 (2003): 81–103.
Sumillera, Rocío G. 'From Inspiration to Imagination: The Physiology of Poetry in Early Modernity'. *Parergon* 33.3 (2016): 17–42.
Sumillera, Rocío G. *Invention: The Language of English Renaissance Poetics*. Cambridge: MHRA/Legenda, 2019.
Summers, David. *Michelangelo and the Language of Art*. Princeton, NJ: Princeton University Press, 1981.
Sutherland, Nicola M. *Henry IV of France and the Politics of Religion: 1572–1596*. Bristol: Elm Bank, 2002.
Swinburne, Algernon Charles. *George Chapman: A Critical Essay*. London: Chatto and Windus, 1875.
Till, Dietmar. 'The Sublime and the Bible: Longinus, Protestant Dogmatics, and the "Sublime Style"'. In *Translations of the Sublime. The Early Modern Reception and Dissemination of Longinus' 'Peri Hupsous' in*

Rhetoric, the Visual Arts, Architecture and the Theatre. Edited by Caroline van Eck, Stijn Bussels and Maarten Delbeke. Leiden: Brill, 2012. 55–64.

Trilling, Lionel. *Sincerity and Authenticity*. Oxford. Oxford University Press, 1974.

Tuve, Rosemond. *Elizabethan and Metaphysical Imagery: Renaissance Poetic and Twentieth-Century Critics*. Chicago: University of Chicago Press, 1947.

Tuve, Rosemond. 'Imagery and Logic: Ramus and Metaphysical Poetics'. *Journal of the History of Ideas* 3 (1942): 365–400.

Vickers, Brian. *Classical Rhetoric in English Poetry*. London: Macmillan, 1970.

Vickers, Brian, ed. *English Renaissance Literary Criticism*. Oxford: Clarendon Press, 1999.

Vuillemin, Rémi. 'Barnabe Barnes's Sonnet Sequences: Moral Conversion and Prodigal Authorship'. In *The Early Modern English Sonnet. Ever in Motion*. Edited by Rémi Vuillemin, Laetitia Sansonetti and Enrica Zanin. Manchester: Manchester University Press, 2020. 128–40.

Vuillemin, Rémi, Laetitia Sansonetti and Enrica Zanin, eds. *The Early Modern English Sonnet: Ever in Motion*. Manchester: Manchester University Press, 2020.

Waddington, Raymond B. *The Mind's Empire: Myth and Form in George Chapman's Narrative Poems*. Baltimore, MD: Johns Hopkins University Press, 1974.

Waddington, Raymond B. 'Visual Rhetoric: Chapman and the Extended Poem'. *English Literary Renaissance* 13 (1983): 36–57.

Walker, Alice. 'Italian Sources of Lyrics of Thomas Lodge'. *Modern Language Review* 22 (1927): 75–9.

Weaver, William P. 'The Banquet of the Common Sense: George Chapman's Anti-Epyllion'. *Studies in Philology* 111 (2014): 757–85.

Weaver, William P. *Untutored Lines. The Making of the English Epyllion*. Edinburgh: Edinburgh University Press, 2012.

Webb, Ruth. *Ekphrasis, Imagination and Pleasure in Ancient Rhetorical Theory and Practice*. Farnham: Ashgate, 2009.

Webster, John. '"The methode of a poete": An Inquiry into Tudor Conceptions of Poetic Sequence'. *English Literary Renaissance* 11 (1981): 22–43.

Weinberg, Bernard. *A History of Literary Criticism in the Italian Renaissance*. 2 vols. Chicago: University of Chicago Press, 1961.

Weinberg, Bernard. 'Translations and Commentaries of Longinus, "On the Sublime", to 1600: A Bibliography'. *Modern Philology* 47 (1950): 145–51.

Weiner, Andrew D. *Sir Philip Sidney and the Poetics of Protestantism*. Minneapolis, MN: University of Minnesota Press, 1979.

Westin, Monica. 'Aristotle's Rhetorical *Energeia*: An Extended Note'. *Advances in the History of Rhetoric* 20 (2017): 252–61.

Wheeler, Martin. '"The obiect whereto all his actions tend': George Chapman's *Ouids Banquet of Sence* and the Thrill of the Chase'. *Modern Language Review* 101 (2006): 325–46.
White, Harold Ogden. *Plagiarism and Imitation during the English Renaissance: A Study in Critical Distinctions*. Cambridge, MA: Harvard University Press, 1935.
Whitworth, Charles Walters. 'The Literary Career of Thomas Lodge, 1579–1596: Studies of the Plays, Prose Fiction and Verse'. Unpublished PhD dissertation, University of Birmingham, 1978.
Wickes, George. 'Henry Constable, Poet and Courtier, 1562–1613'. *Biographical Studies* 2 (1954): 272–300.
Wickes, George. 'Henry Constable's Spiritual Sonnets'. *Month* 18 (1957): 30–40.
Williams, Raymond. *Keywords: A Vocabulary of Culture and Society*. Oxford: Oxford University Press, 2015. 1st edn, 1976.
Williams, Robert. 'Italian Renaissance Art and the Systematicity of Representation'. In *Renaissance Theory*. Edited by James Elkins and Robert Williams. New York: Routledge, 2008. 159–84.
Wilson, Emma Annette. 'The International Nature of Britannic Ramism'. In *The European Contexts of Ramism*. Edited by Sarah Knight and Emma Annette Wilson. Turnhout: Brepols, 2019. 109–31.
Wilson, Emma Annette. 'Marvell and Education'. In *The Oxford Handbook of Marvell*. Edited by Martin Dzelzainis and Edward Holberton. Oxford: Oxford University Press, 2019. 26–42.
Wimsatt, James. 'St. Bernard, the Canticle of Canticles, and Mystical Poetry'. In *An Introduction to the Medieval Mystics*. Edited by Paul E. Szarmach. New York: State University of New York Press, 1984. 77–96.
Winston, Jessica. 'From Discontent to Disdain: Thomas Lodge's *Scillaes Metamorphosis* and the Inns of Court'. In *Elizabethan Narrative Poems: The State of Play*. Edited by Lynn Enterline. London: Bloomsbury, 2019. 143–66.
Wolfe, Jessica. *Humanism, Machinery and Renaissance Literature*. Cambridge: Cambridge University Press, 2004.
Zorach, Rebecca. *Blood, Milk, Ink, Gold: Abundance and Excess in the French Renaissance*. Chicago: University of Chicago Press, 2005.
Zorach, Rebecca. 'Renaissance Theory: A Selective Introduction'. In *Renaissance Theory*. Edited by James Elkins and Robert Williams. New York: Routledge, 2008. 3–36.

Index

actio, 140, 147, 150, 153
Agricola, Rudolph, 48, 50, 58, 59, 65, 72n
  De Inventione dialecticae, 51–3, 67–8
Alexander, Gavin, 6, 126, 243, 287–8, 290–1, 294n
Alexander, William, 'Anacrisis: or, A Censure of some Poets Ancient and Modern', 101, 165
allegory, 74–7, 186n, 262, 277–8, 283n
Amelang, David J., 289
Anne of Denmark [Queen], 9
antanaclasis, 195, 200–1
anthropomorphism, 180–1
aposiopesis, 125–6, 132
Aristotle
  The 'Art' of Rhetoric, 167, 177
  The Categories, 259
  cause, theory of, 4, 57–62, 258–9, 291
  energeia, 177–8, 182, 189n
  English Aristotelianism, 72n
  heart, 109
  Metaphysics, 177
  Nichomachean Ethics, 177
  Physics, 177
  Poetics, 286–7
  poetry and rhetoric, 289
  transparent, 277, 285n

artes poeticae, 1–5, 7, 9–10, 211, 286–92
Ascham, Roger, 149
  The Scholemaster, 143
Atkins, J. W. H., 293
atoms, 74–92
atomies of love, 74–99
atomised Cupids, 80–92
atomism, 75, 85
auctoritas, 42–3
Augustine, 167, 206, 208, 211
authenticity, 9, 165–90, 228

Bacon, Francis, 78, 84, 93
  The Advancement of Learning, 241
  Of the Wisdom of the Ancients, 74–6
Barclay, John, *Argenis*, 101
Barnes, Barnabe, 191–215
  A Divine Centurie of Spirituall Sonnets, 192, 199, 201, 205–8
  Parthenophil and Parthenophe, 191–5, 225
Bartlett, Phyllis, 272
Bates, Catherine, *On Not Defending Poetry*, 11
Baumbach, Sibylle, 141, 157
Benson, Pamela J., 46n
Berger, Harry, Jr, 289
Berkeley Castle, 200, 212n

Beurhaus, Friedrich, 55–7
birds, 198–201, 213n, 272
Blank, Philip E., 212n
blood, 16, 158
   and digestion, 112
   and the epic and heroic poem, 101–20
   as style indicator, 106
bloodlessness, 112–13
Blount, Thomas, *The Academie of Eloquence Containing a Compleat English Rhetorique*, 111–12
Boccaccio, Giovanni, 81, 83, 273, 282n, 284n
   Genealogy of the Pagan Gods, 77, 265, 270–1
body, 104–8, 150–5
   and discussions of style, 104–8
   and eloquence, 142–58
Boileau, Nicolas, 183
Booth, Stephen, 130–2, 134
Bradbrook, M. C., 268
Braden, Gordon, 96n
Bray, Alan, 247
Browne, Sir Thomas, 157
Browning, Robert, 280n
Bruno, Giordano, *La Cena de le Ceneri*, 240–2
Busby, John, 229

Calvin, Jean, 31–2
Camerarius, Joachim, the Younger, 241–2
Campion, Thomas, 293
   poetic career, 20, 193–211, 213n
caritas, 194–5
Cartari, Vincenzo, 77
Castelvetro, Lodovico, 179, 183
Castiglione, Baldesare, 5
   Il Cortegiano, 38–9

Catholicism
   and Constable, 191–211, 211n, 213n
   and grace, 33
   and Petrarchism, 28
Catullus, Gaius Valerius, 213n
cause, 4, 16–17, 50–5, 57–71, 258–9, 291
   accountability, 67–8
   and Aristotle, 4, 57–62, 258–9, 291
   efficient, 55, 58–61, 65–7, 70, 174
   final, 66, 68, 69
   formal, 69
   material, 65, 69, 259
   obedient, 61–2
   physical, 77–80
   'workyng', 58–9
Chapman, George, 258–85
   Achilles Shield, 112, 189n, 261, 265–6
   allegory in, 262–78
   Euthymiae Raptus, or, The Teares of Peace, 259
   and Greville, 240, 255
   Hero and Leander, 262, 273–4, 277–8, 280n
   and Homer, 114, 179, 189n
   'Hymnus in Cynthiam', 258
   The Iliads of Homer Prince of Poets, 109
   'To My Admired and Sovle-Loved Friend, Mayster of all essentiall and true knowledge, M. Harriots', 267–8
   and obscurity, 261–2, 271, 280n, 283n, 290
   Ouids Banquet of Sence, 79, 84–8, 95n, 96–7n, 186n, 258, 261–5, 270, 272–7, 284n
   The Seaven Bookes of the Iliades, 261, 265–6

Chapman, George (*cont.*)
  The Shadow of Night, 258–60, 262, 264
  and Sidney, 188–9n
  The Teares of Peace, 279
  The Whole Works of Homer, 168
Charles II, 247
Charney, Maurice, 134
Charron, Pierre, *La Sagesse (Of Wisdome)*, 102
Cheney, Patrick, 168–9, 198, 206, 213n
Cicero, Marcus Tullius, 52, 150–1, 154, 176, 178
  De natura deorum, 273, 284n
  Orator, 107
Clarke, Danielle, 229–30
Clusius, Carolus, 241–2
Cockcroft, Robert, 67
Coke, Edward, 247
Colie, Rosalie, 2, 11, 286–8, 290–2
Constable, Henry, 185n, 191–215
  Diana, The praises of his Mistre, in certaine sweete Sonnets, 191, 195–7
  Spiritual Sonnets, 191–2
Constable, Robert, 211n
Conti, Natale, 77, 81–4, 90, 93, 95n, 284n
  Mythologiae, 78–9
Corpus Christi College, Cambridge, 67
courtesy books, 38–9
Crane, R. S., 10–11
criticism, 6, 286–94, 294n
Crooke, Helkiah, *Mikrokosmographia*, 109–10
Crow, Martha Foote, 217, 218
Cumberland, Countess of, 41–3
Cummings, Brian, 141
Cupid, 68–9, 74–99

Curbet Soler, Joan, 289
curious frame, 269–78

Daniel, Samuel, 132, 223, 229, 293
  The Complaint of Rosamond, 218, 237n
  Defence of Rhyme, 219
  Delia, 218, 229
  Musophilus, 242
Dante Alighieri, 167
  Paradiso, 254, 257n
D'Avenant, William, *Gondibert: An Heroic Poem*, 110, 112
Davies, John, 263, 271, 281n
  'To the immortall memory, and deserued honor of Writing of the Tragedy of *Mustapha* by Sr: Fulk Greuill, Knight', 239–40
  Nosce teipsum, 109, 119n
  Orchestra, or A Poeme of Dauncing, 233
Davies, John (of Hereford)
  The Scourge of Folly, 249–50
  Wittes Pilgrimage, 228
Davis, Joel B., 218
Day, Angel, 127–8
  The English Secretarie, 123–7, 136n
democracy, 188n
Demosthenes, 107, 108, 113, 178
Dennis, John, *The Advancement and Reformation of Modern Poetry*, 171–2
Derrida, Jacques, 'White Mythology,' 288
desire, 32, 79, 87–90
Despréaux, Nicolas Boileau, translation of *Peri hupsous*, 167
Devereaux, Penelope, 169
Devereux, Robert, Earl of Essex, 191, 266
didactic aestheticism, 269–78

difficulty in poetry, 31, 45, 96n, 238–55
Dionysus of Halicarnassus, *On Literary Composition*, 273
divine fury, 207–8
divine gift, 203, 207–8, 210–11, 270–1
donna angelicata, 194–7
Donne, John, 201, 245
  Devotions upon Emergent Occasions, 110
  Holy Sonnets, 203, 206
  'A Valediction: Forbidding Mourning', 245
Drayton, Michael, 172, 223, 228, 235n, 237n
  Englands Heroicall Epistles, 127–8
  Idea, 90, 92–3, 97–8n
  Ideas Mirrour, 218, 219
Dryden, John, 104, 113–16
  'Dedication of the *Aeneis*', 113–15
  Fables Ancient and Modern, 115
  preface to *Troilus and Cressida*, 113
  translation of Plutarch, 113
Du Bartas, Guillaume Salluste, 190n, 199, 207
  La Sepmaine, ou Création du monde, 179–80
  'L'Uranie', 213n
Du Bellay, Joachim
  Défense et illustration de la langue française, 112, 288
Dubrow, Heather, 13, 237n
Duncan-Jones, Katherine, 229, 236n

Earl, Anthony, 200, 204–5, 214n
ecphonesis, 123–5, 127–8, 133
ecstatic self, 178–83
educational practice, 142–50, 160n, 240, 248–9

efficacia, 177
efficient cause, 55, 58–61, 65–7, 70, 174
  voluntary, 60–1
Eisendrath, Rachel, 289–91
ekstasis, 171
elements, theory of the, 78–9
Elizabeth I, 40
eloquence, 139–63, 160n
  ineloquence, 121–38
Emerson, Ralph Waldo, 171, 186–7n
emotions, 150–1
Empedocles, 78–9, 95n, 285n
enargeia, 7–8, 140, 150, 151, 177, 189n, 258, 271–3
energeia, 7–8, 91, 176–8, 182, 189n
energetic instrumentality, 183–5
Enterline, Lynn, *The Rhetoric of the Body*, 139–40
Epicureanism, 75, 81
Epistolary Style, 111–12
epizeuxis, 123–5, 127–8, 130
epyllion, 13, 139–63
Erasmus, 148
erotic poetry, 19, 93
  Constable, 205–6
  epyllion, 16, 125
  love, 77
  Marlowe, 89
  metaphors, 290
  Ovid, 86–7, 275
  Spenser, 213n
euepeia, 273–4
Euippe, 272–3
euphony, 273
euphues, 143
exile, 211, 213n

Featley, Daniel, 35
Feingold, Mordechai, 72n
Fenner, Dudley, 54

Ferguson, Margaret W., *Trials of Desire: Renaissance Defenses of Poetry*, 288
Ferry, Anne, 213n
Ficino, Marsilio, 97n, 267, 284n, 285n
figura, 105–6, 140–1, 156
Finn, Kavita Mudan, 229
Fischer, Olga, 136n
Fitzgerald, Elizabeth, Countess of Lincoln, 127–8
Flecknoe, Richard, 'On the Works of Fulke Grevil, Lord Brook', 240, 250–1
Fleming, Juliet, 229–30
Fletcher, Giles, 228
  Licia, or Poemes of Love, 97n, 218, 225, 232–3, 236n
Fletcher, Phineas, *The Purple Island*, 110–11, 119n
flogging, 143–4, 154
France, 167, 209–10, 211n
Fraunce, Abraham, 54
  Lawyers' Logike, 48–9
  The Shepherds' Logic, 3
Freige, Johann Thomas, 48
French poets, 113–14, 213n, 216–17, 219–20
Fumaroli, Marc, 289
Furies, Three, 194
furor amatorius, 262
furor poeticus, 174–6, 179, 262, 269

Galen, 106, 109–12, 141–3, 152, 155
Gascoigne, George
  A Hundreth Sundrie Flowers, 1
  Posies, 1
Giacomini, Lorenzo, *Discorso del furor poetico*, 167
Gide, André, 171
Gilby, Emma, 6, 294n

Giraldi, Grigorio, *Historia de deis gentium*, 77
Gless, Darryl J., 96–7n
glosses, 56–9
Godwin, William, 247
Goeglein, Tamara A., 63
Gordon, D. J., 274
Gorman, Cassandra, 290
grace, 16, 27–46, 191–215, 289
  amiable, 37–8
  in Barnes, 191–215
  in Constable, 191–215
  courtly, 37–40
  as divine inspiration, 204, 207
  in exile, 209–10
  in Greville, 249
  in Lanyer, 40–3
  physical, 37–8
  and poetic career, 191–211
  and poetic worth, 43–4
  in the religious sonnets, 199–206
  in the secular sonnets, 192–7
  in Sidney, 30–3
  in Spenser, 37–40
Graces, Three, 27–8, 44, 194
Gray's Inn, 144
Greene, Graham, 61
Greene, Roland, 6, 13
  Five Words: Critical Semantics in the Age of Shakespeare and Cervantes, 15, 294
Greville, Fulke, 29–30, 44, 238–57, 290
  Alaham, 238, 241, 243, 252–5
  Antony and Cleopatra, 244–5, 247
  cabalistical style of, 246–7, 252
  Caelica, 33–7
  as cultural critic, 33–7
  The Dedication to Sir Philip Sidney, 165, 239, 242, 244–50, 255
  Mustapha, 243, 249–50

'A Treatie of Humane Learning',
    239–41, 248–9, 254–5
Gunn, Thom, 242

Habicht, Werner, 223
habit, 5–6, 16–17, 258–85,
    283n, 291
'habit of Poesie', 258–62
Halewood, William H., 202, 214n
Hall, John, 168
Halpern, Richard, 144
Hardison, O. B,, *English Literary Criticism: The Renaissance*, 293
Hariot, Thomas, 261, 262, 266–9
Harrington, John, *Orlando Furioso*, 235n
Harvey, Gabriel, 211n
Harvey, William, 110–11
Hathaway, Baxter, 287–8
    The Age of Criticism, 293
    Marvels and Commonplaces, 293
Hazlitt, William, 238, 242, 252, 255
    'On Persons One Would Wish to Have Seen', 246–7
hearing sense in nonsense, 130–4
heart, 109–10, 214n
Hegel, Georg Wilhelm Friedrich, *Phenomenology of Spirit*, 170
Heninger, S. K., 180, 189n, 190n
    Sidney and Spenser: The Poet as Maker, 11
Herbert, George, 249
Herbert, William, 165
Hermogenes, *On Types of Style*, 107
Hernández-Santano, Sonia, 289
Hesiod, 78
    Theogony, 94n
    Works and Days, 259

Hetherington, Michael, 4, 260, 291
Hill, Thomas, *The Contemplation of Mankinde*, 157
Hillman, David, 152
Hobbes, Thomas, 110–13, 170
    'The answer of Mr. Hobbes to Sr. Will. D'Avenant's preface before *Gondibert*', 110, 119n
    Leviathan, 186n
Hoby, Thomas, 38
Holiday, Barton, 101–2
Homer
    actuality, 177
    and Chapman, 261, 265–9, 278–9
    and Dryden, 114
    and Humphrey, 111
    Iliad, 114, 189n
    Odyssey, 109
    sublimity in, 167
    translators of, 108–10, 114–15
    and Virgil, 114–16, 179
Hookes, Nicholas, 83–4
    Amanda, a Sacrifice to an Unknown Goddess, 80–1, 90–1
Horace (Quintus Horatius Flaccus), 173, 183, 286–7, 293
    Ars poetica, 101–2
Houston, John Porter, 122–3, 138n
Howard, Henry, Earl of Surrey, 'The Geraldine', 127
Huarte de San Juan, Juan, *The Examination of Men's Wits*, 106
Hulse, Clark, 12, 13, 139, 141–2, 150, 159n, 280n
humanism, 148–9, 156–7, 217, 293
humours, 106, 141, 155
Humphrey, Laurence, *Interpretatio linguarum*, 111
Huntington, John, 275, 279n
Hyde, Thomas, 77–9

iconicity, 121–2, 133, 135, 136n
iconophilia, 35–6
imitatio, 218, 221–34, 235n, 293
imitation
  Crane, 10
  in the epyllion, 144
  Humphrey, 111
  La Primadauye, 39
  Lodge, 161n, 216–37, 290
  Scaliger, 102
  Scott, 5
  Sidney, 176, 179–80
  Virgil, 266
  Williams, 263
ineloquence, 121–38
Inns of Court, 144, 262–3, 281n, 290
Isocrates, 103
  Antidosis, 107–8
Italian poets, 3–4, 28, 216–17, 219–20, 292–3

James VI/I, 167
  The Essayes of a Prentise, in the Divine Art of Poesie, 1, 6–8
  'A Treatise of the airt of Scotis Poesie', 1
  'Twelf Sonnets of Inuocations to the Goddis', 7
John [King], 41–2
Johnson, Samuel, 116, 245
Jonson, Ben, 104, 174–5, 278
  The English Grammar, 103
  Timber: Or, Discoveries Made Upon Men and Matter, 104–5, 156–7
  translation of Horace, 101–2

Kant, Immanuel, 287, 288
Kastner, L. E., 219
Keach, William, 153
Keckermann, Bartholomaeus, 59
Kendal, Gordon, 272

Kermode, Frank, 96n, 138n
Kerrigan, John, 229
keywords, 14–16, 294
Kingsley-Smith, Jane, 89, 92, 94n, 97n
Kinney, Arthur F., 217–18
Knapp, Stephen, 286, 287
Knight, Sarah, 290
Kyd, Thomas, *The Spanish Tragedy*, 252–3

La Primadauye, Pierre de, *French Academie*, 39
Lady-Saints, 192–7
Lamb, Charles, 238, 243–4, 255
  Specimens of English Dramatic Poets, 238, 246, 251–2
Lanbaine, Gerald, 168
Landino, Cristoforo, 167
Lanyer, Aemilia, 29–30, 40–3, 46n
  Salve Deus Rex Judaeorum, 8–9, 41–4
Lee, Sidney, 216–18
Lehtonen, Kelly, 176, 188n
Leonard, William Ellery, 94n
Lerner, Laurence, 84
Lewalski, Barbara K., 201
  Protestant Poetics and the Seventeenth-Century Religious Lyric, 289
Lewis, C. S., 274
liber corporum, 102, 157
Lipking, Lawrence, 212n
literary promotion, 40–3
literature of tears, 213n
loci, 51–4
Lodge, Thomas, 151–2, 216–37, 290
  An Alarum against Usurers, 217–18
  Amorous Delights, 216
  The Complaint of Rosamond, 229
  The Complaint of Elstred, 216–18, 228–33

The Divel Coniured, 221
Elegies, 216
A Fig for Momus, 217, 220, 222, 235n
Phillis: Honoured with Pastoral Sonnets, 161n, 216–37
A Reply to Stephen Gosson's Schoole of Abuse in Defence of Poetry, Musick, and Stage Plays, 219, 220
Rosalynde, 218, 219–20
Scillaes Metamorphosis, 13, 144–59, 223
Truth's Complaint over England, 218
William Longbeard, 221
Wits Misery, 220
logic, 47–73
  as *ars artium*, 47
  and Beurhaus, 55–7
  early reforms of, 51–4
  efficient cause in, 52–70
  in Marlowe, 67–9
  and Melanchthon, 53–7
  and Ramus, 54–7
  in Sidney, 65–7
  in Spenser, 63–5
  and Wilson, 57–62
Longinus, Cassius, 102, 171–2, 175–85, 188n, 189n
  Peri hupsous, 167–8, 171, 175, 178, 183, 188n
Lope de Vega, Félix, *Los locos de Valencia* (*Madness in Valencia*), 135–6
Lucian of Samosata, 3
Lucretius, Titus Carus, 81, 86, 94n, 167
  De rerum natura, 75–6, 85, 93
Luis-Martínez, Zenón, 48, 87, 96n, 140, 228, 236n, 290–1
Lutheranism, 35, 41
Lyly, John, 184

Mac Carthy, Ita, *Renaissance Keywords*, 15–16
MacBride, Kari Boyd, 46n
MacIlmaine, Roland, 54
Mack, Peter, 52, 67
Manley, Frank, 202
Mann, Thomas, 171
Marlowe, Christopher, 50, 67–71, 284n
  Doctor Faustus, 254
  Hero and Leander, 82–3, 88–9
  The Massacre at Paris, 67
  translation of Ovid, 125–6
Marotti, Arthur, 213n
Marr, Alexander, 6, 294n
Marston, John, *Metamorphosis of Pygmalion's Image*, 125–6
Marvell, Andrew, 47
Mary, Queen of Scots, 40, 215n
Mary Magdalene, 203–4, 214n
materialism, 75, 79, 86
Matilda de Brionne, 41–2
Matthew, Tobie, Bishop of Durham, 200
Mazzio, Carla, 152, 157
Melanchthon, Philipp, 48, 50, 65
  Dialecticae Philippi Melanchthonis libri tres, 53–7
'mental imprint', 184
mentis character, 151, 156–9
Meres, Francis, *Palladis Thamia*, 294
metamorphosis, 159n, 180–1
metaphor, 13–14
  blood, 110–12
  Cupid, 76–7, 81
  erotic, 290
  in Greville, 244–5, 249–50, 254–5
  heart, 214n
  horses, 175
  veins as rivers, 110–11, 119n

metaphysical poets, 245
Michaels, Walter Benn, 286, 287
microcosmos, 113
Miles, Geoffrey, 96n
Miller, Jacqueline T., 151, 161n
Mills, Charles W., *Blackness Visible*, 288
Milton, John, 59
  Paradise Lost, 253–4
misinterpretation, 74–99
Moffet, Thomas, *Nobilis, or a View of a Life and Death of a Sidney*, 165
Muret, Marc-Antoine, 167
Murrin, Michael, 283n
Muses, 216–37, 250, 272–3, 284n
mythography, 77–80
mythology, 74–6

Nänny, Max, 136n
narratio, 173
Nashe, Thomas, 30, 211n
Neoplatonism, 11, 31, 78, 79, 84, 86–7, 97n, 167, 275
new humoralism, 141
new learning, 74–5
Nietsche, Friedrich, 171, 186–7n
North, Marcy L., 200
Norton, Glyn P., 12
number three, 213–14n
numerology, 212n

obscurity, 261–2, 271, 280n, 283n
Ong, Walter J., 154
  Ramus, Method, and the Decay of Dialogue, 72n, 289
oratory, 54, 103–4, 140, 150, 154
Ovid (Publius Ovidius Naso)
  allegory in, 272–3
  Amores, 67–8, 125–6
  Ars amatoria, 213, 274
  and Chapman, 96–7n, 97n, 262–3, 274–9, 284n

criticism, 294
Cupid, 84–8
Epistulae ex Ponto, 210
epyllion, 13–14
exile of, 198–9, 209–11, 213n
imagery in, 141–2
Metamorphoses, 139, 273
mutilated tongues in, 151–2, 156–7
and rhetoric, 140
and sublimity, 167, 174
Tristia, 210

Panofsky, Erwin, 286, 287
Papazian, Mary Arshagouni, 203
Paradise, Burton, 219, 221
parenthesis, 126, 132–3
Parker, Patricia, 15, 212n
Patrizi, Francesco, *Poetica*, 167
Peacham, Henry, 127–8
  The Garden of Eloquence, 123–7, 136n
pedagogy, 47–8, 144, 148–9
Peletier, Jacques, *Art poétique*, 111
Percy, Henry, 262
Percy, William, *Coelia*, 225
Pérez-Jaúregui, María Jesús, 289
'perfect man', 148
Petrarchism
  and Catholicism, 28
  donna angelicata, 194–7
  and love, 34, 77, 96n, 145–7, 152–3, 169–70, 201
  and lyric sequences, 216
  and metrical variety and range, 212n
  pattern, 213n
  and Sidney, 30–1
  sonnets, 183, 192, 224–5
Phaer, Thomas, 108–9, 118n
phantasia, 176
Philippo-Ramism, 55–7
Philostratus the Elder, 95n

Pierrepont, Grace, 196, 212n
plagiarism, 216–17, 219–22
planetary science, 254–5
Plato
  Chapman and, 84, 86, 266–8, 278
  Phaedrus, 107, 174, 285n
  and rhetoric, 148–9
  Sidney and, 178, 183
  sublimity in, 167, 173, 175
ploce, 123–5, 128, 130
Plutarch, 176, 263, 272
  Life of Demosthenes, 113
poetic career, 20, 193–211, 213n
poetic practice, 1–19, 33, 122, 140, 150, 167, 242, 246, 260, 274, 286–94
poetic rapture, 168, 172–5, 178–9, 207, 250, 260–4, 267, 275
poetic theory, 2–20, 65, 122, 166–7, 183, 232, 260, 261, 286–94
poetic worth, 27–46
poetics of action, 47–73
politics, 245–7, 251–2
Pope, Alexander, 182
  'Preface to the *Iliad*', 115
Porter, James I., 167
Praz, Mario, 272
Prescott, Anne Lake, 198
printing, 229–30
Proctor, Thomas, 'A Proper Sonnet, how Time Consumeth All Things', 129
Prometheus, 263–5, 281–2n
pronuntiatio, 143
prosody, 103, 121–2, 127–8, 153–4
Protestantism
  and Barnes, 192, 201, 206–7, 210–11, 213n, 214n
  English, 33, 35, 94n
  and Lanyer, 41–2

  and Ramus, 71–2n
  and Sidney, 31–3, 165–6, 169, 175, 188n
Psalms, 204–5, 214n
Ptolemy, 254
Puttenham, George, 15, 127–8, 151, 170, 177, 188n, 250, 291
  The Art of English Poesy, 3–5, 13, 102–4, 123–7, 221, 235n, 242

Quintilian (Marcus Fabius Quintilianus), 150–1, 176, 258, 261–2, 271, 283n
  Institutio oratoria, 107, 140

Rainolds, John, 168
Raleigh, Walter, 165, 184
Ramus, Petrus, 15, 47–59, 62–7, 71–2n, 72n, 103, 289
  Bucolica, praelectionibus exposita, 48–9
  Dialecticae libri duo, 55–7
  Dialecticae partitiones, 54–5
rhetoric, 121–38, 139–63, 160n, 289–90
  Barnes, 193, 197
  of the body, 103–4
  Chapman and, 267, 269
  Dryden and, 113
  of grace, 29
  Greville and, 239–46, 254
  Isocrates and, 107–8
  Lodge and, 221
  Melanchthon and, 53–4
  pretence, 236n
  Ramus and, 54, 72n
  sacred, 207–8
  Sidney and, 176–7
  Wilson and, 58
Rhodes, Neil, 111, 156
Richardson, Alexander, *The Logicians School-Master*, 103

Robortello, Francesco, 167, 291
  In librum Aristoteli de arte poetica explicationes, 3–4
Romantic poets, 70
Ronsard, Pierre, 216–17
Roydon, Matthew, 172, 188–9n, 258–60, 262, 271, 277

Sackville, Thomas, *The Mirror of Magistrates*, 128
St Bartholemew's Day Massacre, 71–2n
St Bernard, 214n
St Catherine of Alexandria, 200–1
St Colette, 205
St Margaret, 204
Sandys, George, 284n
Sawday, Jonathan, 102
Scaliger, Julius Caesar, 167, 177, 291
  Poetices libri septem, 4, 102, 168
Schmitt, Charles B., *John Case and Aristotelianism*, 72n
Schoenfeldt, Michael, 141
science, 240–1, 245, 253–4
  elements, theory of the, 78–9
  planetary, 254–5
Scott, William, 9–10, 179, 291
  The Model of Poesy, 3–4, 5–6, 165, 180, 260
'The Seafarer', 128
self-affirming and self-denying poetics, 205–9
self-alienation, 170
self-authorship, 165–90
self-canonisation, 40–3
self-denying, 210–11
self-image, 178–9
self-justification, 40–3
Sell, Jonathan P. A., 219, 290
Seneca, Lucius Annaeus, 174, 262
  Thyestes, 252–3
Serjeantson, Deirdre, 206, 214n

Seton, John, *Dialecticae*, 67
Sgarbi, Marco, *Aristotelian Tradition*, 72n
Shakespeare, William, 121–2, 130–4, 140, 172, 294
  As You Like It, 90
  Hamlet, 121–2, 138n
  King Lear, 123–4
  Othello, 124–5
  The Rape of Lucrece, 144–59, 160n
  Richard III, 131–2
  Sonnets, 236n
  Venus and Adonis, 144–59
  The Winter's Tale, 131–2
Shuger, Debora K., 207
Sidney, Mary, Countess of Pembroke, 43, 46n, 125
Sidney, Philip, 29, 44, 50, 96n, 97n, 126, 132, 154, 223, 278
  Astrophil and Stella, 30–3, 65–7, 79, 89–92, 129–30, 133, 165–90, 218–19, 223, 228, 232–3, 290
  Certaine Sonnets, 213n
  The Defence of Poesy, 4, 11, 75–6, 90–1, 165–90, 219, 288–90
  Euphues: The Anatomy of Wit, 184
  grace, 30–3
  The Old Arcadia, 228
  the sublime in, 165–85
Sierhuis, Freya, 141
Snare, Gerald, 95n, 96n, 271
Socrates, 107
sola fide, 71–2n
sola gratia, 33, 192, 210
sonnet sequences (or sonnet cycles), 216–18, 237n
  Barnes and, 191–211
  Constable and, 191–211
  Davies and, 281n

Drayton and, 92
Fletcher and, 232–3
and grace, 28
Hookes and, 80
Lodge and, 218–19, 223, 229
Sidney and, 65–6, 89–90, 165, 170, 179, 182
Southampton, Earl of, 144
Southey, Robert, 240, 255
Select Works of the British Poets from Chaucer to Jonson, 251
Southwell, Robert, 213n
Spanish dramatists, 135–6
speculum principis, 244
Spenser, Edmund, 29–30, 44, 50, 206–7, 220
Amoretti, 63–5, 82–3
and courtly grace, 37–40
The Faerie Queene, 27–8, 37–40, 44, 133–4
Fowre Hymnes, 213n
Muiopotmos, 11
The Shepheardes Calender, 180, 220
sprezzatura, 4–5, 9
Stamatakis, Chris, 3
Stanyhurst, Richard, 108–9
Stapleton, Richard, 281n
The Phoenix Nest, 262–3
Steiner, George, 254
'On Difficulty', 243
Stoicism, 3, 5, 148–9
Stuart, Lady Arbella, 198
style, 100–63
sublime, the, 165–90, 188n
Sumillera, Rocio G., 156, 184, 288
Summers, David, *Michelangelo and the Language of Art*, 294
'Supple Muse', 216–37
Swinburne, Algernon Charles, 240, 255
Sylvester, Josuah, 180

Tacitus, Publius Cornelius, *Dialogus de oratoribus*, 107
Talbot, Mary, Countess of Shrewsbury, 196–7, 212n, 234
Tasso, Torquato
Discorsi del poema eroico, 167
Gerusalemme liberata, 167
Tate, Nahum, 119n
tears, 153–4
Temple, William, 63, 66
Thucydides, 176
Tottel's Miscellany, 75, 128
transcendence, 27–46
translatio, 79, 90, 266–7
Trilling, Lionel, *Sincerity and Authenticity*, 170–1, 186–7n
trivium, 48, 50
Tuve, Rosemond, 170
Elizabethan and Metaphysical Imagery, 289
Twyne, Thomas, 118n

unwritten arts, 1–25, 29, 49–51, 287, 290–1

van der Poel, Marc, 52
vates, 172–3, 178
Vautrollier, Thomas, 1
Virgil (Publius Vergilius Maro)
The Aeneid, 108–9
and Agricola, 52
and career models, 206, 211
and Constable, 198, 210
and divine gift, 270
Eclogues, 48–9
Georgics, 55, 75–6
and Homer, 114–16, 179, 266
and Ovid, 213n
and sublimity, 167
translators of, 108–10, 114–15, 118n

Virgin Mary, 192, 196, 200–1, 208
Vives, Juan Luis, 104, 113
  De causis corriptarum atrium, 105
  De disciplinis, 105
  De ratione dicendi, 105–7, 156
vocabula artis, 7–8, 14–17
Vuillemin, Remi, 213n

Waddington, Raymond B., 96–7n, 279–80n, 284n
Watson, Thomas, 178
  Hekatompathia, 228
Weaver, William, 140, 148, 160n, 274–5
Webbe, William, *A Discourse of English Poetry*, 76
Weinberg, Bernard, 3, 293, 294
Wheeler, Martin, 97n, 275
White, Harold Ogden, 220
Whitworth, Charles Walters, 217, 219
Wilde, Oscar, 184–5, 186–7n
  The Decay of Lying, 170–1

Williams, Raymond, *Keywords: A Vocabulary of Culture and Society*, 14–15
Williams, Robert, 292, 294
Williams, Thomas, 263–6, 270–1, 281n
Wilson, Emma Annette, 289
Wilson, Thomas, 12–13, 50, 58–9, 64–6, 70
  The Art of Rhetoric, 158, 176–7
  The Rule of Reason, 59–62
Windet, John, 192
winged poet, 198, 208
wings, 199–201
Winston, Jessica, 144
Wolfe, Jessica, 267, 284n
Wright, Thomas, 149
  The Passions of the Minde in Generall, 143, 150–5
Wyatt, Thomas, 129–30

Zorach, Rebecca, 292
Zunino-Garrido, Cinta, 161n, 290

www.ingramcontent.com/pod-product-compliance
Lightning Source LLC
Chambersburg PA
CBHW050201240426
4367ICB000I3B/2203

EU representative:
Easy Access System Europe
Mustamäe tee 50, 10621 Tallinn, Estonia
Gpsr.requests@easproject.com